OPERATION
YAO
MING

OPERATION
YAO
MING

The Chinese Sports Empire,
American Big Business, and the
Making of an NBA Superstar

BROOK LARMER

GOTHAM BOOKS

GOTHAM BOOKS
Published by Penguin Group (USA) Inc.
375 Hudson Street, New York, New York 10014, U.S.A.
Penguin Group (Canada), 90 Eglinton Avenue East, Suite 700, Toronto Ontario, M4P 2Y3, Canada (a
division of Pearson Penguin Canada Inc.); Penguin Books Ltd., 80 Strand, London WC2R 0RL, England;
Penguin Ireland, 25 St. Stephen's Green, Dublin 2, Ireland (a division of Penguin Books Ltd.);
Penguin Group (Australia), 250 Camberwell Road, Camberwell, Victoria 3124, Australia (a division of
Pearson Australia Group Pty. Ltd.); Penguin Books India Pvt. Ltd., 11 Community Centre, Panchsheel
Park, New Delhi - 110 017, India; Penguin Books (NZ), cnr Airborne and Rosedale Roads, Albany,
Auckland 1310, New Zealand (a division of Pearson New Zealand Ltd.); Penguin Books (South Africa)
(Pty.) Ltd., 24 Sturdee Avenue, Rosebank, Johannesburg 2196, South Africa

Penguin Books Ltd., Registered Offices: 80 Strand, London WC2R 0RL, England

Published by Gotham Books, a division of Penguin Group (USA) Inc.

First printing, November 2005
10   9   8   7   6   5   4   3   2   1

Gotham Books and the skyscraper logo are trademarks of Penguin Group (USA) Inc.

Library of Congress Cataloging-in-Publication Data

Larmer, Brook.
Operation Yao Ming : inside China's great leap to the NBA / by Brook Larmer.
p. cm.
ISBN 1-59240-078-7 (hardcover : alk. paper)
1. Yao, Ming, 1980–   2. Basketball players—China—Biography.   I. Title.
GV884.Y36L37 2005
796.323'092—dc22   2004019364

Printed in the United States of America
Set in Sabon
Designed by Leonard Telesca

For Hannah

Contents

Preface   xi

PART I: East

  1. Birth of a Giant   3
  2. Red Guard Rising   18
  3. Mao's Fallen Star   33
  4. Childhood Denied   48
  5. Cogs in the Machine   66
  6. The Experiment   84

PART II: East Meets West

  7. NBA Dreams   107
  8. The New Evangelists   125
  9. Strangers in a Strange Land   141
 10. The Gathering Storm   153
 11. Mavericks and Mandarins   165
 12. Hoop Diplomacy   179
 13. The Battle for Yao Ming   194

PART III: West

14. Soldier Gone AWOL   217
15. Houston, We Have a Problem   228
16. Summer of Discontent   244
17. In Da Club   262
18. American Idol   280
19. Generation Next   295
20. The Flag-Bearer   309
    End Notes   325
    Acknowledgments   333
    Index   336

"Don't forget, the whole Chinese race is depending on you."
—Wang Shuo, *Please Don't Call Me Human*

Preface

At the dawn of a new era in China, two young boys piqued the interest of Communist Party officials for their singular gift: They were tall, almost freakishly so. The first boy, whose feats would one day be erased from the record books for his perceived betrayal of the nation, resided near the ancient Temple of Heaven in China's center of Communist power, Beijing. His name was Wang Zhizhi. The younger child, who would become the most recognized—and, some would say, most exploited—Chinese citizen in the world, was just a toddler living in Shanghai, a city at the heart of the country's imminent capitalist revival. His name was Yao Ming.

The men in faded Mao suits made pilgrimages to the cramped apartments where each of the boys' families lived in the early 1980s, bearing the only gifts to be found in a land still reeling from the ravages of the Cultural Revolution: a few pieces of fruit, a clutch of food-ration coupons, and some wrinkled yuan notes. Over pots of bitter tea, the visitors solemnly informed the parents that their sons belonged to the nation, their special gifts destined to bring glory to the motherland. The officials proceeded to poke and prod the boys, testing their reflexes and hand–eye coordination. Then, in an act that symbolized China's yearning to once again stand tall among nations, they pulled out their measuring tapes. After carefully recording the boys' heights, the men stretched the narrow strips of cloth across their delicate hands, making measurements that, backed by decades of scientific experimentation (and, later, the use of X-rays), enabled them to predict future growth with uncanny accuracy.

The Communist officials had expected something extraordinary; indeed, they had long been waiting for the appearance of two boys such as these. But the test results still astonished them. Both boys, the officials predicted, would grow to be more than seven feet tall—an almost mythical height that would make them not only a head taller than virtually the entire Chinese population, but among the tallest men in the world. There was one more vital detail: The youngsters were genetically predisposed to have a talent for tossing a ball through a little hoop. The news spread quickly through the sports commissions in Shanghai and Beijing, rising through the bureaucracy toward the man most obsessed with raising China's stature in the world, Deng Xiaoping. The paramount leader himself stood just 4'11", an embarrassing fact that was guarded like a state secret.

What nobody could have predicted then was that the lives of Yao Ming and Wang Zhizhi would trace the arc of China's inexorable rise and its fitful emergence into the world. As the boys, like their country, grew into behemoths, they would be pushed and pulled by forces far beyond their families' control. Sports in China, after all, were not just a game; they were a projection of national ambition on the international stage—an ambition that Beijing had turned into an obsession with cultivating world-class athletes. The boys' parents did not wish such a fate on their only children, but they understood the demands of the state all too well. All four of them were former basketball players themselves, forcibly recruited into the sports system because of their extraordinary height—and then, in retirement, paired off in the expectation that they would produce a new generation of giants.

Rebellion against the impositions of the Chinese state would come later. But from the moment the men in Mao suits first pulled out their measuring tapes, both families braced themselves for the day when their sons would be taken away to train in China's state-run sports machine, whose unforgiving factories were designed to churn out Olympic champions. Over the next decade, a small army of coaches, scientists, minders, and ideological tutors would be enlisted to indoctrinate Yao and Wang in the rigid certainties of "basketball with Chinese characteristics," a world in which there would be no questioning of authority, no glorification of individual achievement, and little freedom to think for oneself.

Their mission was simple: to bring honor to the largest nation on earth, a country that, after centuries of insecurity, was only beginning to recapture the confidence that had led it to call itself Zhongguo, "the Middle Kingdom."

Halfway around the earth, in glass-enclosed executive suites across the United States, the titans of global capitalism were beginning to turn their gaze on the mysterious land across the sea. The romance of finding untold riches in the Middle Kingdom had tantalized the Western imagination ever since Marco Polo returned from his travels seven centuries earlier with awestruck accounts of a civilization more advanced than Europe.

"Big-nosed barbarians," as the Chinese called western interlopers, had pried open the insular empire at various times in its history, plying locals with cotton, opium, or religion while loading up on silk, tea, or cheap labor. But China had gone into hibernation after Mao Zedong's communist revolution. Only the Great Helmsman's death in 1976 would allow the country to reawaken to the West, shaking off three decades of economic torpor as it sought to leap from third world to first world in a single bound. Western businessmen salivated at the prospect of cracking what many considered the last great untapped market on earth: 1.3 billion people, one-fifth of the world's population, five times the number of Americans—all of them, it was imagined, eager to fulfill the mantra that defined Deng Xiaoping's new era: "To get rich is glorious."

Few Westerners were more entranced by the hypnotic allure of China than the leaders of the global sports industry. The universal language of sports has long been able to reach across the barriers of race, culture, dialect, and nation. But now, fueled by the forces of globalization—satellite television, the computer revolution, transnational capitalism, the demise of Communism—sports were morphing into a multitrillion-dollar industry, what historian Walter LaFeber would call the most globalized business in the world after drug trafficking. For any industry with truly global pretensions, China was the final frontier.

Leading the incursion into China were two burgeoning sports empires that were fashioning themselves as the arbiters of hip American youth culture: Nike Inc. and the National Basketball Association. During his first trip to Beijing in July 1980, two months before Yao Ming was born, Nike founder Phil Knight told friends he longed not simply to manufacture shoes on the mainland but to shod every Chinese foot in the company's signature swoosh. Five years later, NBA commissioner David Stern would invite the Chinese national team for a tour of America—even arranging a friendly scrimmage with Michael Jordan and the Chicago Bulls—in hopes that high-flying NBA games would soon be beamed into every Chinese household.

But nothing in the encounter between East and West would be easy. Though China would soon boast double-digit growth rates—and the highest level of foreign direct investment in the world—the country was still caught halfway between strait-jacketed socialism and a rambunctious frontier capitalism. The first thing foreigners learned was that closing a deal in China meant making the right connections, or *guanxi,* in the byzantine bureaucracy. But Chinese officials, for all their eagerness to attract investment, were wary of surrendering control to foreigners rushing in to claim a piece of the motherland. Introductory smiles would often melt into mutual incomprehension, with the foreigners emerging dazed by their efforts to decipher the intricate rituals and hierarchies that defined business in China.

As China boomed, taking on the sheen of a modern society, it was easy for Westerners to believe that the slogan "socialism with Chinese characteristics" was merely a euphemism for a word that Beijing's leaders couldn't quite say out loud: capitalism. But China was still deeply socialist, and no place more so than the sports system. So entrenched was the idea that sports should ennoble rather than entertain the masses that the NBA initially had trouble giving away its programming for free. Even when the state-run television monopoly, CCTV, recognized NBA basketball's appeal among China's youth, it still saw no reason to pay for the broadcast rights. Nike would also hit roadblocks. The company finally began making shoes in China, but it took five years before the state-owned factories could produce a white shoe that wasn't a dull, dishwater gray. Chinese consumers were hard to manufacture, too, for as much as the locals grew to love the emblems of American culture, their purchasing power was limited—and cheap knockoffs abounded. By the mid-1990s, Nike and the NBA had become two of the most lucrative brands in the world—and among the most recognized in China. But neither enterprise had made any real money in the Middle Kingdom.

To attract the Chinese masses, the foreigners needed inside help. Not just the right *guanxi* and a consumer boom, but a charismatic local hero who could do for businesses in China what the leading global icon, Michael Jordan, had done in the rest of the world. The proposition was more complicated than it sounded, not least because the very idea of individual heroes was still considered taboo in the People's Republic. Over the previous half century, the Chinese had been taught to venerate essentially only one hero: Chairman Mao. But the Western prospectors rushed in anyway, undeterred in their search for a Chinese icon who could stride across the international stage and play in the NBA.

Then, in the late 1990s, a tantalizing rumor surfaced about two teenage giants hidden deep inside the Chinese sports system. Both boys stood more than seven feet tall, and although rail-thin, they were remarkably well-trained in the fundamentals of basketball. Were these boys the heroes-in-the-making the foreigners had been seeking, the future NBA players who could act as a bridge into China for the most powerful companies in the world? And, if so, would the Chinese state, caught between its fear of losing control and its desire for international prestige, ever be willing to relinquish its carefully cultivated athletes?

Yao and Wang already carried on their bony shoulders the expectations of their emergent motherland. The burden was about to get even heavier.

A cloud of cigarette smoke hung over the basketball court, stubbornly resisting the gusts of wintry air blowing through the unheated gymnasium. It was December 1999, and few places on earth could have felt further removed from the glitzy world of the NBA than the home court of the People's Liberation Army team, a dimly lit arena in the coastal Chinese city of Ningbo. The temperature inside the gym hovered a few degrees above freezing. Blank-faced players—some still in parkas—moved mechanically through their pregame drills, while ruddy-cheeked fans stomped their feet in unison to the beat of a traditional gong and drum. The numbing cold didn't seem to bother anybody. After all, everybody lucky enough to be inside the gym that night was about to witness something special: the long-awaited showdown between China's biggest stars, two gifted giants whose emerging talents augured the ascendance of their homeland—and the coming collision of East and West.

Out on the hardwood court that night, Yao Ming and Wang Zhizhi already seemed like natural foils, two players as inextricably linked as lightning and thunder. Wang was lightning. A twenty-two-year-old PLA soldier who had sparked the Chinese army team to four consecutive national championships, he flashed across the court with dancing, unpredictable moves, combining a deadly outside shot with knifing drives to the hoop. Now at his full height of 7'1", Wang—whose surname means "king" in Mandarin—had established himself as the undisputed ruler of Chinese basketball.

Yao, on the other hand, was thunder. Three years younger than Wang, the lumbering nineteen-year-old center for the Shanghai Sharks already measured an astonishing 7'4"—and he told the scientists who monitored his development that he could still feel himself growing. Sure of hand but slow of foot, Yao still lagged a few beats behind Wang. But as the elapsed time between flash and boom grew shorter, the giants' rivalry intensified, and few observers could help but to frame it as a battle of two Chinas: soldier vs. civilian, Beijing vs. Shanghai, the past vs. the future. By the time the two went head-to-head that night, Yao had

Wang by three inches and thirty pounds. But the boyish-looking army soldier still possessed a sweeter shot, a quicker step, and an absolute belief in himself that bordered on arrogance.

I was sitting in the crowd that night in Ningbo. As a correspondent for *Newsweek*, I had come to chase down the rumors about the pair of Chinese giants. The on-court battle was riveting, but what truly captivated me was the cloak-and-dagger drama developing behind the scenes. The transpacific struggle to bring the first Chinese players to the NBA had just begun. And though it was too early to tell where the story would lead, the narrative already seemed emblematic of the far bigger encounter between China and the world. What tugged at me that night, in fact, was the promise of a journey that captured the story of the century—China's inexorable rise—along with its equally important corollary: America's quest to understand, or at least to profit from, the emerging superpower. If I needed any further proof that the plot would thicken, I only had to look at the people sitting next to me in the stands that night: an NBA agent, a Nike rep, an Asian Internet tycoon, and a top Chinese basketball official. All four of them, for four very different reasons, fixed their eyes hungrily on the two giants out on the floor.

Like the "Ping-Pong diplomacy" that led to the thaw in U.S.–China relations thirty years before, the drama surrounding Yao and Wang was already moving far beyond sports to the realms of business, politics, culture, and superpower relations. These two athletes, rising stars in the fastest-growing sport in the world, would soon be touted as the prisms through which hundreds of millions of Chinese would encounter America, as well as the lenses through which curious Americans would get a glimpse into the Middle Kingdom. The two worlds were so far apart, however, that the encounter was bound to bring as much disappointment as delight—not just for the Chinese officials who developed the two giants and then agonized over their fates, but also for the Western businessmen driven to turn them into international icons.

With all of the forces in motion, it was easy to forget that, at the center of the story, were two young athletes nursing the most innocent of hoop dreams. Yao and Wang—rivals, teammates, and, at one time, nearly friends—just wanted the chance to play basketball against the best in the world. Soon their paths would diverge, turning one into a reluctant superstar, the other into a rebel unwelcome in his homeland. But on that night, in that cold gym, as they battled back and forth across the hardwood, neither of them could have imagined just how difficult their journeys would be.

PART I

EAST

1

Birth of a Giant

The faint whispers of a genetic conspiracy coursed through the corridors of Shanghai No. 6 Hospital on the evening of September 12, 1980. It was shortly after 7:00 P.M., and a patient in the maternity ward—a woman who must have been instantly recognized by hospital staff when she checked in earlier—had just endured an excruciating labor to give birth to a baby boy. An abnormally large baby boy.

The doctors and nurses on duty that day should have anticipated something out of the ordinary. The boy's parents, after all, were retired basketball stars whose marriage the year before had made them the tallest couple in China. The mother, Fang Fengdi, an austere beauty with a pinched smile and threadbare clothes, measured 6'2"—more than half a foot taller than the average Shanghai man. The father, Yao Zhiyuan, was a 6'10" giant whose body pitched forward in the kind of deferential stoop that comes from a lifetime of perpetually ducking under door frames and listening to people of more normal dimensions. So imposing was their size that ever since childhood, the two had been known simply as Da Yao and Da Fang—Big Yao and Big Fang.

Still, the medical staff at No. 6 Hospital must have been astonished. In all their years tending to a population that was, by Western standards, congenitally small, they surely had never seen a newborn quite like this: the enormous legs, the broad, squarish cranium, the hands and feet so fully formed they seemed to belong to a three-year-old. The official measurements gave their wonder some mathematical certitude: At more than 11.2 pounds and twenty-three inches long, the infant was nearly double the size of the average Chinese newborn. The name his parents gave him, taken from a Chinese character that unifies the sun and moon, was Ming, meaning "bright."

3

News of Yao Ming's birth was quickly relayed across town to the top leaders of the Shanghai Sports Commission. Perched in their fortresslike headquarters next to People's Square—a prime location that reflected their privileged position in the Communist hierarchy—the bureaucrats in their Mao suits greeted the news with satisfaction, if not surprise. It was these men and women, after all, who had been trying to cultivate a new generation of athletes who could embody the rising power of China. The boy in the maternity ward was the culmination of their plan.

The experiment had no special code name, but in Shanghai basketball circles it might as well have been known as "Operation Yao Ming." The wheels had been set in motion more than a quarter of a century earlier, when Chairman Mao Zedong exhorted his followers to funnel the nation's most genetically gifted youngsters into the emerging Communist sports machine, modeled after the Soviet system. Two generations of Yao Ming's forebears had been singled out by authorities for their hulking physiques, and his mother and father were both drafted into the sports system against their will. "We had been looking forward to the arrival of Yao Ming for three generations," says Wang Chongguang, a retired Shanghai coach who first heard of Yao's grandfather in the 1950s, played with Yao's father in the 1970s, and would coach the boy himself in the 1990s. "That's why I thought his name should be changed to Yao Panpan."

Long-awaited Yao.

It may have been a protracted wait, but the birth of the Shanghai behemoth—like the delivery in Beijing, three years earlier, of another oversize boy named Wang Zhizhi—could not have come at a more auspicious time. In September 1980, China was preparing for its reemergence in international athletic competition after more than two decades of isolation, and sports officials were under increasing pressure to produce world-class athletes who could bring home the gold for China. The baby Yao offered a tantalizing glimpse into the future. He was a genetic marvel, encoded with the DNA of two basketball players, who could be molded from childhood into an athletic superstar. Giddy with the sense of possibility, some officials wanted to start helping the family immediately with food and finances. Others even began pushing for an exception to the country's strictly enforced one-child policy, which had begun to be implemented a year earlier. If China truly wanted to compete internationally, they asked, why shouldn't the nation's tallest couple be allowed to breed an entire team of champions?

One Communist leader didn't share in the delight. This man, one of the most powerful sports officials in Shanghai, had bitter memories of the torment inflicted on him by Yao Ming's mother when she was a youthful revolutionary. How could such a proud leader forget the beatings, the public humiliation, the years of backbreaking labor—all of which he blamed on the group of Red Guards to which Da Fang belonged? It had taken the man nearly a decade to battle his way back to the top. He was in no mood to start bending the rules to help Da Fang.

For him, revenge sounded far sweeter.

The marketing wizards at the NBA like to talk about China as basketball's "final frontier." But the Middle Kingdom's fascination with hoops began long before Michael Jordan and the Chicago Bulls made their debut on Chinese television in the late 1980s. Perhaps China didn't invent the game of basketball, as some Chinese historians claim, pointing to the ancient pastime known as *shouju,* a form of Han dynasty handball. But basketball did, in fact, land in China nearly at the same time it arrived in Chicago, and only a few years after an eccentric Canadian named Dr. James Naismith invented the game in 1891.

When Doc Naismith hung two peach baskets from a ten-foot-high balcony encircling a gymnasium in Springfield, Massachusetts, the thirty-year-old physical-education instructor was simply devising a way to keep a group of unruly boys occupied during the long New England winter. But the game would one day circumnavigate the globe for one simple reason: Naismith made his invention at the international training school of the Young Men's Christian Association, a place that groomed young missionaries for postings abroad to promote a vision of "muscular Christianity," in which the development of the body, mind, and spirit were considered inseparable.

One of the YMCA's fastest-growing missions at that time happened to be China, then a land of four hundred million that was opening up to Western religions. Over the next few years after Naismith's invention, dozens of missionaries would set off for the mysterious Middle Kingdom, their rucksacks packed with Bibles and "The 13 Rules of Basketball." A century later, global visionaries at Nike and Reebok would look at China's massive population and dream about all the soles to be sold. But at the end of the nineteenth century, the YMCA saw China as the world's biggest market for souls to be saved. And in their eyes, salvation would come through God and sports, although not necessarily in that order.

Basketball arrived in China in the waning years of the final imperial dynasty, the Qing, just as the conniving Empress Dowager, Ci Xi, was maneuvering madly to hold on to her shrinking empire. Depending on whose account one believes, the game was first introduced in either 1895 or 1898 in the city of Tianjin. The reformist intelligentsia embraced the Christian missionaries and their Western sports as part of a campaign to transform the corrupt and weakened empire into a strong and modern nation. As China expert and University of Iowa journalism professor Judy Polumbaum has noted, the nascent popularity of basketball helped get rid of what reformers considered the most humiliating symbols of emasculated feudalism: the long gowns, fingernails, and ponytails that formed part of the imperial court's traditional dress. The first young men who flocked to the YMCA's basketball courts tucked their robes up under their sashes and wound their long, braided queues into buns on top of their heads. Max J. Exner, the YMCA's first physical-education director in China (and a participant in Naismith's first game in 1891), reported: "Wherever athletes go, the queue falls into disfavor because of the hindrance it presents."

With her bound feet and imperial finery, the empress dowager couldn't have been much of a sports fan. Deeply suspicious of both modernity and the missionaries, she at one point felt compelled to support a two-year uprising against foreigners that resulted in the massacre of two hundred Christian missionaries and several thousand Chinese Christians. The turmoil caused by the so-called Boxer Rebellion hastened the demise of the Qing dynasty and paved the way for a republican government led by Sun Yat-sen in 1911, a period that saw an influx of Western ideas from Marxism and marketing to democracy and the man-to-man defense. The YMCA helped usher in the new era by organizing the country's first national games, athletic competitions that, like the recently inaugurated Olympic Games, were seen as vital expressions of nationalism and modernity. In 1907, the staff at YMCA headquarters in Tianjin tried to motivate Chinese athletes and educators by issuing a challenge. "When will China be able to send a winning athlete to the Olympic contests?" they asked. "When will China be able to invite all the world to come to Peking for an International Olympic contest?" The answers would come a century later.

The YMCA's emphasis on athletics as a way of fostering self-reliance, moral rectitude, and national pride resonated in a society wary of more dogmatic evangelical appeals. By 1920, the organization had more foreign missionaries in China than anywhere else in the world, and it operated athletic centers in all of the country's major cities. Basketball became a mainstay among urban youth, and migrants and missionaries soon carried the game to the vast rural interior. In 1935, the sport was officially declared a national pastime. An American traveler named M. V. Ambros marveled at the proliferation of courts in China during the 1930s, even the most primitive of which seemed to draw clusters of workers and peasants vying for a game. "You can just feel what the game means to them," he wrote in a letter to Naismith. "It will be a real pleasure for you to travel through the Orient to see how much basketball is played. It cannot be described or pictured; it cannot be told; it must be seen."

Naismith never made it to China, but his life and legacy would be linked to a man regarded today as the godfather of Chinese basketball. Mou Zuoyun is well over ninety years old now. He lives with his wife in an apartment compound just off of Stadium Road, a boulevard that, radiating out from the east gate of the Temple of Heaven, has served as the epicenter of China's centralized sports system for half a century. Mou is a bit hard of hearing and he tires easily these days, but he still wears the dapper tweed outfits he sported before the 1949 Communist Revolution—and his voice resonates in clear, unaccented English as he recounts the tale of how China went from the YMCA to the NBA.

As a boy in the 1920s, Mou and his friends in his hometown of Tianjin used to gather almost every day after school at the YMCA, where they tested their skills in bowling and basketball. Sports had become a national concern by then, and China's participation in regional sports competitions helped a new generation see through localist concerns and cheer for the Chinese team—the ultimate symbol of a nation that was modern and unified. A decade later, the country was racked by turmoil, and many American missionaries returned to the United States to escape the intensifying civil strife between the nationalists and the communists. But the YMCA remained an oasis of athletic bliss. Even during the war with Japan in the 1930s, when the organization turned its attention to poverty alleviation and famine relief, there were still YMCA basketball tournaments—and Mou, a 5'11" forward, guided his team to repeated victories.

Mou was a twenty-three-year-old university student when he was selected to play in the 1936 Olympic Games in Berlin. Basketball was making its Olympic debut, and so, in a sense, was China. Four years earlier, the Chinese government had sent a token delegation to the 1932 Games in Los Angeles as a ploy to stop the Japanese puppet state of Manchuria from sending a team under the Chinese flag. (The lone athlete to compete, a twenty-two-year-old sprinter named Liu Changchun, failed to qualify for the finals, but he was hailed as a hero back home for rejecting Japanese pressure and competing as "a descendant of the Yellow Emperor.") In June 1936, Mou formed part of China's first full contingent of 140 athletes as they steamed out of Shanghai on a twenty-five-day ocean voyage to Venice, where they would catch the train to Berlin. "We were hit by typhoons all the way," Mou recalls. "We all got seasick. We couldn't sleep, exercise, or hold our food down. It was miserable."

By the time they reached Berlin, the Chinese athletes were sapped of their strength, but they donned their crisp Western suits and dark ties and marched solemnly off the train through a gauntlet of Nazi salutes. The Chinese delegation was one of the few that did not salute Adolf Hitler with a *Sieg Heil* as it paraded past his reviewing stand in Berlin's Olympic stadium. Mou and his compatriates simply took off their hats and placed them over their hearts. For the young basketball player, another person in the stands was far more significant than the Führer: Doc Naismith, then seventy-five, was there to witness the official coronation of the game he had invented forty-five years earlier.

At the basketball grounds, Mou found himself thunderstruck by the American team, which boasted two centers taller than 6'8". The International Basketball Federation (FIBA) had tried to level the playing field by holding the tournament on outdoor courts made of dirt, limiting each team to seven players a game, and banning all players over 6'2". The American team successfully repealed the last rule and went on to win the gold medal in a rain-soaked mud bath over Canada. Final score: 19–8. The Chinese team didn't fare too badly, winning four games and losing four. With Naismith in the stands, Mou even had a chance to show off his quick dribbling and long-distance artillery in China's upset victory over France. But neither the basketball team, nor any other Chinese athlete, made it to the medal podium. A German cartoon reflective of the times ridiculed China's failure to win a single medal, showing Chinese athletes searching for medals next to a large goose egg. The failure stung even more deeply because the Japanese team returned from Berlin with eighteen medals.

Returning to China, Mou felt driven to prove that China could compete with the world. He finished up his degree, started teaching physical education at prestigious Tsinghua University, and married the daughter of China's nationalist sports czar, Ma Yuehan. (Through his father-in-law, who also served as the head of China's Olympic Committee, Mou traces his hoop history back to the end of the Qing dynasty.) For years, Mou coached the Tsinghua University team. But by the late 1940s, the best hoops in China had shifted to the factories as the nation's top capitalist enterprises, led by a Shanghai shoe company called Huili Rubber, began to hire ringers to help boost their prestige—and sales—in semi-professional leagues. Just as Nike would try to latch on to Yao Ming and Wang Zhizhi a half-century later, Huili lured away the country's best players, including a tenacious guard named Wang Yong-fang, paying them good salaries and outfitting them in Huili shoes and uniforms. At halftime during games, a plane dropped coupons for free shoes on the crowds. Shoe sales boomed.

For his part, Mou saw basketball more as a path to enlightenment than a road to riches. Like Naismith himself, who had died a poor man in 1939, Mou wanted little more than to master all aspects of the game. His father-in-law, who had studied in the 1920s at the YMCA International Training School (by then renamed Springfield College), worked his connections to get Mou a scholarship to study at the birthplace of basketball. Naismith was long dead by the time Mou landed in America in 1946, but the thirty-three-year-old Chinese graduate student soaked up instruction from the finest basketball strategists in the land, including former Stanford University coach John Bunn and the University of Kentucky legend (and U.S. Olympic coach) Adolph Rupp. "I was very lucky to have the best teachers," he says. "They gave me ideas to last a lifetime."

In Mou's tidy apartment, there is a small room off the front hall that is filled with trophies and medals, mementos from his early career and from the more prominent role he would play after the Communist Revolution. Mou doesn't seem overly proud of the awards. With a gnarled hand, the old man guides a visitor past the memorabilia to a small bookcase near his desk, pointing to a collection of weathered hardback books, their spines cracked from years of use. "My bibles," he says, smiling wistfully. "I hauled them back in a trunk from America."

The books are in English. There is Rupp's *Championship Basketball for Player, Coach, and Fan,* Bunn's *Basketball Methods,* and a dozen other titles—all published before 1949. The information they contain may be slightly outdated, designed for an era when players were slow, white, and under six feet tall. But the trove of books is Mou's most treasured possession, for it represents the repository of knowledge that he gleaned, so long ago, in America—knowledge that he has hoarded for more than half a century, almost as if there had been no revolution at all.

When Mao seized power in 1949, China did not have much to show for its vaunted five thousand years of history. Poor, backward, and feudal, the Middle Kingdom seemed more like a failed Third World state than the most glorious civilization in the world. China had invented gunpowder but then misplaced the recipe. It had devised the compass but somehow lost its naval superiority. It had originated many of the martial arts and a game the Chinese claim to be the precursor to soccer. But in the international competition where the strength of nations is judged most severely—the Olympic Games—the most populous country in the world had never won a single medal in any sport. The final embarrassment had come at the 1948 Olympics in London, when a team of thirty-three Chinese athletes again came away empty-handed—and had to pay their own way on the long trip home.

Under Mao, sports would play a much more vital role. At an early age, the charismatic Communist firebrand had viewed sports as an essential tool for national rebirth and ideological indoctrination. In his first published essay, a 1917 article entitled "A Study of Physical Culture," Mao—then just twenty-four—focused on how sports could bolster both the body and the body politic. "Our nation is wanting in strength," he wrote. "This is an extremely disturbing phenomenon. The development of our physical strength is an internal matter, a cause. If our bodies are not strong, we will be afraid as soon as we see enemy soldiers, and how then can we attain our goals and make ourselves respected?"

Building an athletic juggernaut was one way to reestablish China's historical greatness after decades of humiliation at the hands of foreign powers. Physical fitness and sporting prowess, Mao reasoned, could help restore the nation's self-confidence and command respect around the world. It didn't matter that China's most popular sports, such as basketball and table tennis, were foreign imports introduced by Christian missionaries. Or that China's first National Games, in 1910 and 1914, had been organized by the YMCA. If the "foreign devils" could use sports to help extend the reach of Christianity, why couldn't Mao use them to spread the gospel of Communism and nationalism?

Mao's first experiment with the power of sports came at the height of the revolutionary struggle against the Nationalists in the mid-1930s. The Long March, as the Communists' six-thousand-mile epic retreat from southern China is known, decimated Mao's troops, reducing the estimated one hundred thousand soldiers who began the journey to just ten thousand. At one point during the yearlong trek, Mao's deputy Zhu De lifted his exhausted soldiers' spirits by organizing a game of basketball, using an animal hide stuffed with grass as the ball. The ploy worked so well that when the Red Army (later known as the People's Liberation Army, or PLA) fomented rebellions in towns along their route, Zhu and his men would often pilfer balls to bring back to their bases. When the ragged Communist forces finally settled into the caves around the impoverished, north-central Chinese town of Yan'an, hoops made of bamboo baskets were erected in and around the rocky out-croppings.

And so the Communists claimed the imported American sport as their own—not simply as an idle diversion, but as an instrument of ed-ucation and diplomacy. Basketball, after all, was an egalitarian sport that rewarded Communist values such as teamwork and selfless sacri-fice. Unlike other team sports, such as soccer, where certain positions get all the goals and the glory, basketball offers scoring opportunities to every player, as long as the team shares the ball and works together to create the best shot.

As Mao and his band of Communist rebels licked their wounds and gathered strength in the hills above Yan'an, they also came to see bas-ketball as a useful tool in the battle for the hearts and minds of a fright-ened population. One of Mao's top deputies, He Long, a pipe-smoking former athlete who would become the first minister of sport after the revolution, forged a basketball team out of a group of athletic young soldiers and dispatched them across the mountainous region to put on clinics and exhibition games. The "Fighting Army Team," or *Zhandou,* as Marshal He's squad was known, sometimes infiltrated enemy zones to play underground games with sympathetic villagers, even engaging in firefights with Nationalist troops on their way in and out. Thus began the Chinese Communist Party's use of athletics as propaganda—and the army's dominance of Chinese sport.

So effective was Mao's first foray into sports as politics that he con-tinued his athletic mission after the founding of his People's Republic. Even today, nearly every gymnasium or athletic field around China carries Mao's famous slogan in bright red Chinese characters: PRO-MOTE PHYSICAL CULTURE AND SPORTS AND BUILD UP THE PEOPLE'S HEALTH. In the early days of the People's Republic, Mao pushed physical fitness as a way to enhance the strength and productivity of the socialist workers. Sports were also meant to inspire the collective spirit needed to fuel a resurgent nationalism. One of the most popular early pieces of propaganda was a 1957 film entitled *Female Basketball Player No. 5.* It told the story of how a game defiled by Nationalist-era corrup-tion and individualism was transformed by a group of hardworking players and coaches dedicated to the Communist ideals of sportsman-ship and collective honor.

Perhaps no single act symbolized Mao's politicization of sports more than his first famous dip in the Yangtze River in June 1956. Hiking his black swimsuit up over his ample belly, Mao plunged into the waters near Wuhan with his entourage of guards and sycophants and drifted downriver for two hours before emerging triumphantly. The moment, eulogized in one of Mao's ubiquitous poems, was a piece of ingenious political theater that showed off his fitness for leadership at a time when his revolution seemed to be losing steam.

The swim also served as potent propaganda. A healthy worker made a healthy revolution, Mao declared, and daily exercise—carried out in schools, factories, farms, and public offices—became another way to carry out the revolution. The ripple effects of Mao's mantra can still be seen in China today, where public squares are filled each morning with elderly people practicing the graceful motions of tai chi. In Beijing, during all but the coldest months, residents brave the city's fetid channels for their daily swim, their white bathing caps bobbing up and down in the algae-covered water.

The Great Helmsman's deeper ambition, however, was to develop world-class athletes worthy of representing the fledgling People's Republic. A population of several hundred million tai chi practitioners was fine, but a nation—even a Communist one—is measured not by its ordinary citizens but by its extraordinary ones. The Soviet planners who poured into the Middle Kingdom after the 1949 revolution helped Mao build everything his new society needed, including a vast network of sports schools to develop elite athletes and to exemplify China's superiority over the capitalist West.

By the mid-1950s, a sports system based on the militaristic Soviet model began to take shape. For every event from diving and gymnastics to table tennis and basketball, the nation's most genetically gifted athletes were selected at a young age; put through an arduous, year-round training regimen; supplied with good food, nutrition, and medicine (no small thing is this still-impoverished nation); and inspired to sacrifice their bodies for the glory of the motherland. For the first time in Chinese history, sports became a truly national project, pulling in hundreds of thousands of recruits from China's massive pool of poor peasants, workers, and—most revolutionary of all—women, who barely two generations before could barely walk because of their bound feet.

The West would not catch a glimpse of China's athletic harvest for three decades, because the Middle Kingdom was, once again, heading into hibernation. By the mid-1950s, Mao's campaign to purify China of foreign influences had shut down most capitalist enterprises and sent Western investors packing; later, he would even boot his Soviet bene-factors back to Moscow for being insufficiently revolutionary. Throughout this period, Mao's Communist government engaged in a global battle for recognition with the defeated Nationalists in Taiwan, a struggle that continues today. In the darkest days of the Cold War, nearly every international body, including the United Nations, regarded the Nationalists in Taiwan as the legitimate government of China, shut-ting off the Communist mainland from the world. The International Olympic Federation, however, remained on the fence for years, and Mao saw that sports could be an important bargaining chip in his quest for international legitimacy.

Mou Zuoyun tried to help forestall China's slide into isolation. He had made the journey back from America soon before the Communist Revolution, and, having hidden away his American books, the former Olympian was soon named the head basketball coach for the national team. In 1952, Mou led a hastily assembled delegation of forty athletes to the Summer Olympics in Helsinki. As Taiwan withdrew its team in protest, Mou and his compatriots boarded a propeller plane that took three days flying across the vast Russian wilderness to Helsinki. By the time they arrived, the games had already begun. Only one Chinese ath-lete averted disqualification—a female swimmer who lost badly in a pre-liminary heat—but Mou left the Olympics feeling triumphant. "We felt that we had won because we had competed and Taiwan had not," he says. "At that time, some people around the world did not want us in the games. So our very appearance in Helsinki was in itself a victory."

Four years later, their luck wouldn't hold. During an inspection tour of the Olympic venue in Melbourne two weeks before the 1956 games were to begin, Mou noticed that special villas were being constructed for a Taiwanese delegation. After arguing in vain with Olympic officials, Mou telexed the bad news to his bosses in Beijing. The Chinese Olympic delegation team never set sail for Australia, boycotting the games to protest Taiwan's presence. Three years later, Beijing angrily pulled out of the Olympic movement altogether. It would be more than two decades before a team from mainland China would see Olympic com-petition again.

Despite the Olympic blackout, the massive Chinese sports system continued to churn out athletes. In only one sport, however, did they make headlines. By a fluke of history, China turned itself into a world power in a game that, to American minds, was more associated with the linoleum-lined basements of suburbia: table tennis, better known as

Ping-Pong. The International Table Tennis Federation was one of the only governing bodies in sports to switch its post-1949 allegiance to the Communist leaders in Beijing. As a result, the grateful Chinese leaders transformed Ping-Pong—then just a casual pastime played on the southern coast—into a national sport. They turned thousands of the country's most agile young athletes into human backboards.

Rarely has a country achieved such dominance in a single sport over such a long period as China has in table tennis. With their unusual grips—until recently, all Chinese players held their paddles like a pair of chopsticks—they have won more than half of all world titles, including a sweep of the men's and women's world championships in 2005. When a player named Rong Guotuan began this amazing run by winning the 1959 world championship—the first world title ever for a Chinese athlete—it was cause for national celebration. Fireworks exploded in Tiananmen Square; squads of bicyclists raced down the streets proudly waving red Chinese flags. Rong's victory was offered to the Chinese people and to the world as evidence of the superiority of the Communist system—a symbolic victory that Mao would call "a spiritual nuclear weapon."

Still, this was only Ping-Pong. The game required lightning-fast reflexes and extraordinary agility, but it was hardly the kind of sport to command fear and respect around the world. Even in the Chinese bureaucracy, the sport was classified almost apologetically as one of the "small balls." The top leaders in Beijing knew that real respect would come only when China could compete with the Western powers in the "big balls": soccer, volleyball, and basketball. In an offhand remark that quickly assumed the weight of a political imperative, Premier Zhou Enlai, second only to Chairman Mao in influence, vowed that China would one day excel not just in "small balls" but in "big balls," too. Marshal He Long, the beloved Long March veteran who became Mao's first minister of sport, threw down the gauntlet even more melodramatically. "If we don't reach the highest level in the three big balls," he said, "I will never shut my eyes—even after death."

To most Chinese officials, this goal seemed like a pipe dream. There were too many cultural and physiological barriers, they maintained, for Chinese athletes to compete with their Soviet and American counterparts in sports like basketball, which required physical superiority. Bai Jinshen, a basketball sage who delivered commentary for China Central Television, explained the problem to *Sports Illustrated*'s Alexander Wolff: "Ancient Chinese sports were always performances, always art. Sports were for health and exercise, not competition. So it's been a tradition for us to be better at performance sports, like diving and gymnastics and shooting, than competitive sports. Or, if the sport must be competitive, let it be table tennis and volleyball, where there's a net. Dividing the competitors is better, so there's no body contact."

The cultural aversion to body contact reflected a deeper sense of physiological inferiority. Solemnly invoking the questionable science of morphology, the study of body type, Chinese scientists would explain that the small, compact torso of the average Chinese is suited to technical sports like gymnastics or table tennis, not to those requiring strength or height. Several foreign coaches who have worked in China say the belief in the physiological inferiority of Chinese vis-à-vis blacks and whites created psychological barriers that even today hold Chinese athletes back. In the 1950s, the situation was particularly bleak in size-dominated sports such as swimming, volleyball, and basketball. How, for example, could China's female hoopsters hope to compete with the 6'6" behemoths of Eastern Europe when the starting center on the Chinese national women's team stood barely 5'6"?

The era of the Chinese giants, however, was fast approaching. The problem, scientists now say, was not so much one of genetic inferiority as decades of deprivation and malnourishment—and the lack of a program that brought together the biggest, most talented youngsters in the country. In the mid-1950s, Mou Zuoyun, by this time the official in charge of "big ball" sports, made a decree that would help change that situation. "I made a rule that all girls who showed the potential to grow taller than 1.80 meters [5'11"], and all boys who showed the potential to grow taller than two meters [nearly 6'7"], should be recruited to play basketball," he says. Armed with scientific manuals that showed how to predict a child's height, coaches and scouts fanned out across the land to cull the tallest youths in the country for the national athletic cause.

The new strategy soon began to bear fruit. By the late 1950s and early 1960s, even as the devastating famine caused by Mao's Great Leap Forward persisted, an army of tall athletes began appearing in the sports schools to train in basketball and volleyball. Many of these recruits were found in China's most forbidding climes, such as Heilongjiang, a northeastern province wedged between North Korea and Siberia, which would later gain renown for sending, at one time, eight young women over six feet tall to the national volleyball team.

In Beijing, two towering basketball recruits captured the most attention. One was Wang Weijun, a 6'5" teenage boy with broad shoulders and a flattop haircut. The other was a 6'2" girl from rural Shanxi Province named Ren Huanzhen. Ren's father was an itinerant railway-construction worker, a robust 6'5" man who could carry so much soil that the weight of his baskets often broke his wooden shoulder pole. Ren was skinny, by contrast, but by age twelve, she had already sprouted past most of the adults in her rural town. When a railway station manager discovered her at a train depot in the late 1950s, he promptly recruited her to play for the local railway unit basketball team. Ren was just thirteen and largely unschooled. But less than two years later, the national railroad team brought her to Beijing, where she would continue her climb up the sports pyramid.

Ren and Wang would both become fixtures for the Beijing teams in the 1960s and 1970s. Their height helped change the dimensions of the Chinese game, but it was their eventual marriage that yielded the biggest contribution. The couple's only son, born in 1977, would become a basketball prodigy with skills so sublime that rival Chinese forces—and eventually American ones, too—would wrestle over the right to call the youngster their own. The boy's name was Wang Zhizhi.

The tallest of that era's Chinese giants would rise from a small village in the swampy wetlands west of Shanghai. The residents of Zhengze, whose low-slung houses line a series of narrow canals, are not known for their height. Like most southern Chinese, they are generally squat people whose lack of stature is exacerbated by lives of backbreaking labor in the nearby rice paddies and sweet potato fields. Even today, many of the town's older women are bent like crooked sticks, their faces low to the ground as they trudge through the streets.

But there was one family in Zhengze that towered over the rest. The Yao family had produced a continuous line of giants, each generation taller than the next. Yao Xueming, who would never live to see his famous grandson play basketball, stood 6'8"—and looked even taller next to his wife, who barely reached five feet. Toiling in the fields was too difficult for someone his size, and the rumor of factory jobs lured him to Shanghai. The couple moved to the sprawling port city shortly before Mao's troops swept in victoriously in 1949. Yao Zhiyuan, Yao Ming's father, was born two years later, a true child of the revolution.

The Gold Star Pen Factory, where Yao Ming's grandfather landed a job, had a basketball court, like many factories in Shanghai at the time. Yao Xueming had never played before, but as Shanghai coaches tell the story, the workers organized boisterous pickup games after their shifts ended, and they often recruited the awkward giant to play. Then in his late twenties, Yao Xueming would plant himself underneath the opponents' basket, swatting at their shots with propeller-blade arms. His shooting form was ugly, his movements clumsy and lead-footed. But every time he blocked a shot—or, just as frequently, every time a little ball handler dribbled circles around him—the workers would hoot and holler with satisfaction.

One day in 1956, a veteran basketball coach named Tian Fuhai caught a glimpse of Yao Xueming on the streets of Shanghai. The workers of the Gold Star Pen Factory had joined a street parade to celebrate the government takeover of dozens of capitalist enterprises, and Yao Xueming was pounding on the drums, punctuating the militaristic chanting of Communist slogans. He stood head and shoulders above the crowd, and Coach Tian figured the man must have been perched on a soapbox. Moving closer, though, he saw a pair of gigantic feet planted firmly on the ground. Tian tapped the giant on the back.

"Excuse me, comrade, how old are you?" Tian asked, craning his neck upward.

Yao Xueming turned around. "I'm thirty-three," he said.

Tian had arrived too late. Nobody could learn to play basketball effectively at his age, much less a giant whose physical coordination requires more time to develop. Still, Tian pressed on.

"Do you have any children?"

"Yes, four," Yao responded.

"Any of them as tall as you?"

"Well, not yet," he said. "My eldest son is only six."

Tian reported his discovery to the newly formed Shanghai Sports Commission, and the local officials kept an eye on the eldest son, Yao Zhiyuan. Long before the soft-spoken child reached his full height of 6'9", the coaches, inevitably, came calling. They sent Da Yao to train in a specialized sports school in Shanghai's Xuhui District—the very place where, a quarter of a century later, his own son would start his career. Da Yao had no interest in playing basketball and no recognizable aptitude for the game aside from his prodigious height. Moreover, he didn't want to move away from home. But the state commanded him to start training, and even if he hadn't been an obliging eldest son with a deep aversion to conflict, that was all that mattered.

"I was tall, so I had to learn how to play basketball," Da Yao recalled years later, smiling ruefully. "I had no choice."

2

Red Guard Rising

The marble archway at No. 651 Nanjing Road loomed ahead of her—enormous and forbidding, even to a girl who was more than six feet tall. Fang Fengdi, then just fifteen, pedaled toward the entrance of Shanghai's elite sports-training center that first day on a bicycle that was, almost inevitably, several sizes too small. Nobody in Da Fang's family had expected her to grow so tall. Her parents were both relatively short, like most native Shanghainese, and her three siblings would only grow to modest heights. But over the previous year, Da Fang had sprouted like bamboo after the spring rains, making her a head taller than most of the boys—and teachers—in her school.

It was 1965, and Da Fang had arrived at the place that would become her home for the next five years—a place that would witness her transformation from frivolous young girl to national basketball star to something even more pivotal to Chinese history. But at the time, the entrance to No. 651 Nanjing Road may have seemed all the more forbidding to Da Fang for one simple reason: She didn't want to be there. "I was just a young girl who loved to sing and dance," she recalls. "I always thought I'd be an entertainer, but I didn't like basketball at all." Da Fang's unexpected growth spurt, however, had caught the attention of a local coach in Shanghai's Jing'an District, and soon sports officials paid a visit to her family's small apartment.

The officials explained to her parents that Da Fang had been selected for athletic training at Shanghai's premier sports institute. As one of the tallest girls in Shanghai, if not *the* tallest, Da Fang had the potential to bring glory to the city, and perhaps to the nation, through her efforts on the basketball court. The officials' unspoken message was also clear: Because the sports system would now become her "iron rice bowl," taking care of her food, shelter, and employment for the rest of her life, she wouldn't have to follow her mother into the cramped assembly lines of the local garment factory. There would be a price, of course. From that moment on, the apple-cheeked girl would have to give up her childhood dreams. Behind the gate at No. 651 Nanjing Road, life as she knew it was about to come to an abrupt halt.

Before 1949, when foreigners ruled Shanghai and the city's main thoroughfare was known as Bubbling Well Road, No. 651 was the site of an elegant social club that catered to pampered expatriates, the ultimate symbol of the city that opium built. More than a century earlier, a Chinese empire weakened by domestic instability and the widespread addiction to a plentiful supply of British opium had tried to halt the trade in the "barbarian poison," only to find itself drawn into a war it could not win. China's defeat in the Opium Wars led the emperor to hand over much of Shanghai and four other treaty ports, plus Hong Kong, to Britain and other Western powers. More humiliations followed as China lost control over more territory—the Russians in the northeast, the Japanese in Taiwan—and over key elements of its trade and foreign policies. China became "the sick man of Asia." A central aim of every Chinese leader since that shameful period has been the recovery of national sovereignty and pride, to restore the Middle Kingdom to its rightful position as the center of the civilized world.

No place more acutely symbolized the national trauma than Shanghai, a sleepy town on the mudflats that foreigners had transformed into the most decadent and dynamic city in the Orient. "The barbarians from across the sea," as the Chinese referred to these interlopers, built a bustling metropolis at the mouth of the Yangtze River that was seething with sex and crime—and rooted in an apartheid economy that kept many Chinese in virtual serfdom. The foreigners erected grand neoclassical structures along the Huangpu River to serve as banks and corporate headquarters. They designed colonial mansions along the graceful tree-lined streets of the French-ruled Concession. And on Bubbling Well Road, they encouraged the proliferation of establishments that could satisfy their every need: brothels, gambling dens, movie theaters, department stores, and—on the site that would later be known as No. 651—a luxurious private oasis known simply as the Country Club.

The well-heeled foreigners arriving through the front gate of the Country Club in their rickshaws or DeSotos would alight on the circular driveway. Sweeping past the turbaned Indian porters, they ascended the curving staircase to a second-floor terrace overlooking the manicured gardens and tennis courts below. Sitting around the massive oak bar in their linens and silks, the Western colonialists—French, British, American—surveyed their peaceful domain with glasses of brandy and champagne, far removed from the misery and chaos of the China that teemed outside the gates. The only hints that these foreigners inhabited the Middle Kingdom came from the white-gloved Chinese waiters delivering drinks and the coolies in straw hats pruning the rose-bushes below.

One of the most astonishing examples of the foreigners' obliviousness to the reality of China came in the Country Club ballroom in November 1948, when the British consul-general to Shanghai, Robert Urquhart, made a famously shortsighted speech on the eve of the Communist Revolution. "We are under no immediate threat," he told the British Residents' Association that night. "Most of the fears which have been conjured up are founded on rumor and pure imagination . . . We are not going to up and leave our community home at the first signs of an approaching storm. Does anyone suggest that if there is a change of government here, the new one will be so unreasonable that they will make civilized life and normal trading impossible?"

Within a year, Mao's peasant army swept into Shanghai, and the complacent foreigners who had whiled away their leisure hours at the Country Club fled. China's puritanical new rulers, appalled by the capitalist excesses that had turned Shanghai into the "Whore of Asia," seized all of the city's clubs as part of their strategy to suffocate the former center of "bourgeois influence." In 1953, the club at No. 651 Nanjing Road—now, even the street names were changed—was transformed into the city's main training center for elite athletes. Shanghai's new leaders ordered the lush gardens ripped up to install a running track and a soccer field. A grove of trees was chopped down to make way for four basketball courts. The mahogany gazebo was destroyed, the pond drained, and three tanks of fish hauled off to the city aquarium.

By the time Da Fang arrived in 1965, the pleasure palace had long since taken on the air of a military camp. The graceful old clubhouse remained, yes, but dour Communist officials rather than foreign colonialists now patrolled the second-floor terrace, monitoring the hordes of young athletes training below. The Country Club was under new management, and it had a far more long-winded name: the Shanghai Sports and Athletic Competitions Direction Section. More than two hundred of the city's most promising recruits lived in the compound, training in everything from swimming and gymastics to soccer and volleyball. From the moment Da Fang arrived, she, too, would abide by the principle of the *san jinzhong*, the "three togethers," by which Chinese athletes live, eat, and train together nearly every day of the year.

Life in the sports factories, in fact, wasn't so different from life in the garment factories, where Da Fang's mother toiled. Both occupations provided workers with (or, depending on one's perspective, condemned them to) lifetime employment within the same *danwei,* or work unit. The best athletes usually lived five or six to a room, but they received a steadier diet of milk and meat than the rest of the population, a significant perk in a land where food was still severely rationed. But like the factory job, athletic training was physically punishing, poorly compensated, and subject to the *danwei's* dictatorial rule. For most Chinese citizens, Communist power manifested itself most palpably through the *danwei's* minipotentates. They made, or at least enforced, nearly all of the key decisions in people's lives: where to live, where to work, what to eat, whom to marry, and—most insidiously—what to think.

Da Fang's generation, born in the flush of the revolution, was the first to be fully indoctrinated from childhood in the rigid certainties of Mao Zedong Thought. By the mid-1960s, the ideological training at No. 651 Nanjing Road had become almost as intense and monotonous as the athletic training itself, for elite athletes were considered a revolutionary vanguard that might one day represent China in international competitions. Like most of the other athletes (except for rural recruits), Da Fang returned home one day a week, leaving Saturday afternoon and returning on Sunday evening in time for an obligatory session called, without a trace of irony, "Democratic Life Meeting." For all the Communist diatribes against religion, the evening ritual had a distinctly ecumenical feel, more High Mass than town hall. Party leaders delivered sermons extolling the Great Helmsman, exhorting the faithful to show ever more revolutionary spirit. Then the athletes engaged in a self-flagellating round of confession and repentance. (The process, amazingly, remains virtually the same for China's top athletes today. Their six-day-a-week training is sprinkled with ideological study meetings—only these days, instead of praising Mao, the party ideologues try to explain how former president Jiang Zemin's abstruse theory of "the Three Represents" can help make them better ballplayers.)

In Da Fang's day, the high priest presiding over many of the Democratic Life Meetings at No. 651 was a handsome but imperious party cadre named Zhu Yong. A member of the Communist underground before the revolution, Zhu (pronounced "ju") was first rewarded for his courage and commitment with a job as a union leader for Shanghai's Changning District. In 1959 he became a top Communist official at the sports institute. Zhu was technically the official in charge of women's basketball, even though he didn't know the rule book nearly as well as Mao's *Little Red Book*. His real authority, however, came from his position as deputy Communist Party secretary, which gave him the power to make sweeping political commands—and to shape the minds of the young athletes.

Several times a week, Zhu Yong summoned the basketball players to the institute's first-floor lecture hall for "political thought" meetings. They were a captive audience, and the self-important commissar—silently scorned for his ignorance on the basketball court—seemed to relish the opportunity to show his wisdom and lay down the law. He droned on about mind-numbing Communist theories on the dictatorship of the proletariat and the ownership of the means of production. He chastised players for sacrificing too little for the revolution, for succumbing to the evils of individualism, and for engaging in secret romantic relationships.

Young and impressionable, Da Fang was putty in the hands of the propagandists who extolled her workers' background and imbued her with the desire to carry on the class struggle. Molding her basketball game proved more difficult. Arriving at the asphalt courts in her shorts and tennis shoes, the teenager seemed more suited at first to chatting with friends than putting in long hours of grueling practice. Da Fang was the tallest female player in Shanghai, but "she was terrible at first," says one of her early coaches. "She ran very slowly, she couldn't catch the ball, and she got so tired she could only run up and down the court a couple times before she had to stop." While the other players raced through their drills with military precision, Da Fang was taken aside to learn the fundamentals: dribbling, shooting, passing, rebounding, and—most importantly—developing a revolutionary spirit.

By the time Da Fang arrived, sports training in China focused on squeezing as much *jingshen*—or spirit—out of players as possible. The clinical Soviet advisors who had helped build the sports system were long gone, casualties of Mao's acrimonious rejection of Soviet premier Nikita Khrushchev as an ideological "revisionist." Into the breach stepped a sporting savior from Japan, Hirofumi Daimatsu. Famous for having led Japan's female volleyball team to three world championships, in which they overcame the goliaths of Europe and America with an almost superhuman display of zeal and determination, Daimatsu was called upon by China's leaders in 1964 to bring his fanatical training methods to all of China's athletic teams.

The six hours of daily practice at the institute—an amount already considered excessive in the West—suddenly expanded to eight, even ten, hours a day. All year round, the hoopsters trained on outdoor courts that were bitterly cold in winter and blisteringly hot in summer. If players had ten minutes free in the evening, they were pushed—indeed, they pushed themselves—to go back outside to work on their shot. Some players became too exhausted to eat, others cried tears of pain throughout practice. Still others vomited at the sight of a basketball court. Coaches routinely beat their players and forced them to play while sick or injured. Lin Meizheng, an agile forward on the Shanghai women's team, suffered for years from a painful kidney infection, but she never missed a practice. "It sounds strange now, but at the time, we always felt that showing spirit was the top priority," she says. "You may not be able to improve your technique, but you can always improve your spirit." Still, the training was too intense. "It was fascism," says Lin. "People need to have time to rest and recuperate. We're human beings, not machines."

Most of the young players began viewing themselves as nothing more than revolutionary robots. Lu Bin was a high-scoring 5'11" forward who joined Da Fang on both the Shanghai and national teams. Like her younger teammate, she played most of her career in pain, her ulcers and high blood pressure getting worse with each grueling year. "If we got hurt or sick, we didn't dare talk about it," says Lu, now in her mid-fifties, sitting in a coffee shop just down the road from the site of the old training grounds on Nanjing Road. "Sometimes we'd even ask for more hours of practice because we worried that we weren't being revolutionary enough." Lu pauses for a minute, searching for a way to explain the blind devotion of a young athlete in Mao's China. "We were so naive," she says. "There was a lot of pressure on us. It wasn't fear, exactly. It was that we all had the passion to be good revolutionaries."

Da Fang was developing that spirit, too, and it began to show on court. After more than a year of training, the sixteen-year-old was still an awkward player, her motor skills struggling to catch up with her sprouting body. But she fought more aggressively for rebounds, and she sometimes hurled her now 6'2" body to the ground in pursuit of loose balls. Da Fang's former coaches and teammates say her stiffening resolve had to do with a growing conviction in the purity of her "red" roots as the daughter of a long line of poor workers. Infused with Maoist propaganda from her study sessions, Da Fang wanted to do everything she could to expand the power and purity of the workers' revolution. For the time being, playing basketball was her only way to carry out the revolution. But that, like everything else, would soon change.

*   *   *

The girl with the red armband pushed the prisoner through the frenzied crowd into a familiar space in the old clubhouse at No. 651 Nanjing Road—a graceful Concession-era ballroom that had been transformed into an indoor basketball court and now, in early 1967, was being used as a "people's tribunal" for the dispensation of cruelty and mob justice.

"Enemy of the people!" screamed the young athletes, pushing and punching the man as he stumbled past. "Spy! Traitor! Counterrevolutionary!"

The prisoner's head was crudely shaved. His hands were tied behind his back. And his dark eyes, which had once flashed with a sense of smug self-satisfaction, now seemed so filled with fear that several of the young athletes in attendance had a hard time believing it was Zhu Yong. Could this hunched figure really be the powerful Communist Party secretary who, just months before, had ruled over the sports institute with an iron fist?

The crowd went silent as Zhu reached center court. Along with the others, the girl ordered him to kneel on the hard, cold asphalt, while another young militant pressed down on his head until his chin dug into his chest. The middle-aged party leader, who had courted danger in the Communist underground before many of these athletes were born, made no attempt to resist. He had been locked up in solitary confinement for nearly six months, long enough to know that there was no escape from the ritualistic torture and humiliation of these revolutionary "struggle sessions." All he could hope for was to survive.

The session began, like all the others, with the singing of "The East Is Red," an anthem to the wisdom and leadership of Chairman Mao. A few months earlier, it would have been Zhu standing proudly in front of his athletes, leading them in the revolutionary hymn. But on that day, he was bent over on the ground, and his former pupils—now his captors—were belting out the lyrics with their arms held high, most of them clutching a copy of Mao's *Little Red Book*. The song, once a source of comfort for him, now took on an aura of menace. When the triumphant finale faded—"He works for the people's happiness; he is the people's savior!"—the court fell silent again.

"Enemy of the people, confess your crimes!"

The voices came from all around him, and one of the most vociferous of them all was the girl's voice, one that he had heard many times before—thin and high, but laced with a chilling hardness. It was the voice of Fang Fengdi.

Da Fang was barely seventeen, but on the basketball court that day, she seemed transformed. Her sweet demeanor had been replaced by an air of self-righteousness and zealous asceticism. Her lively banter was gone, supplanted by a fervent recitation of Mao's famous sayings memorized from the *Little Red Book*. Her hair had been cut very short in a display of revolutionary ardor. (Long or wavy hair was considered a vain imitation of Western fashion and sexuality.) Her usual sports garb had been replaced by a baggy Mao suit and black cloth shoes, the same genderless uniform now worn by nearly everybody in the country, male or female, young or old. The only splash of color was the red armband on her sleeve bearing three characters that were enough to strike fear in millions of Chinese: *Hongweibing*. Red Guard.

Da Fang had enlisted as one of Mao's "little revolutionary generals," the shock troops who would carry out the most extreme acts of the Great Proletarian Cultural Revolution. The decade-long cataclysm, which Mao launched in 1966 as a way to purify the Communist Revolution and purge his enemies, produced cruelty and oppression on a horrific scale. Thousands of intellectuals, former capitalists, and people with ties to the West were beaten to death in the wave of Maoist hysteria. Millions more were humiliated, tortured, and imprisoned, while tens of millions were forcibly displaced to the countryside for "reeducation" through hard labor. The period left an indelible imprint on the lives of most Chinese families, and the mere mention of the Cultural Revolution today conjures up memories that most would rather forget, from the otherwise normal people who committed unspeakable acts of cruelty to the innocent victims who suffered at their hands.

Like many Chinese, Da Fang is loath to talk about her role during that tumultuous period. "The Cultural Revolution really didn't affect me very much," she says while sitting in her son's house in Houston, looking out at the fountains bubbling in the man-made lake outside. "We had to stop our basketball training and focus on other things for a while. But I came from a workers' family, so it didn't have much impact on us." In a narrow sense, that is true. Her poor family belonged to one of the so-called "five red categories" (workers, soldiers, poor peasants, martyrs, and Communist cadres), so Da Fang was automatically considered a privileged member of the revolutionary vanguard. As such, she was spared the cruelty and persecution that the "five black categories" (landlords, rightists, capitalist roaders, counterrevolutionaries, and rich peasants) faced at the hands of the Red Guards. But according to her friends and former teammates, the Cultural Revolution was a major watershed for Da Fang. The explosive events would shape her life and personality—and the future of her only son.

Few of the athletes and leaders living at No. 651 Nanjing Road can forget Da Fang's transformation from bubbly basketball novice to belligerent Red Guard. "I don't know if I should tell you this or not," one of Da Fang's former teammates says, her voice falling to a whisper. "Perhaps it was because of her 'red' background, but Da Fang seemed especially eager to improve herself as a revolutionary. Some of us wanted to join the Red Guards to avoid trouble, because anybody who wasn't with them was considered an enemy. But Da Fang was a true believer." The former player paused and leaned forward. "And true believers, you know, were capable of anything."

The madness had begun in earnest in August 1966, when an aging Mao appeared in Beijing's Tiananmen Square before a gathering of more than a million worshipful Red Guards. Born of "pure" families and weaned on Mao Zedong Thought, these teenagers longed for nothing more than to carry out their leader's commands. And now, Mao desperately needed them to reinvigorate the revolution. The Cultural Revolution was actually the culmination of a bitter power struggle between Mao and a more moderate faction headed by, among others, national Communist Party secretary Deng Xiaoping. But that's not how the Great Helmsman sold it to the masses. Standing in front of the gate to the Forbidden City, underneath a massive portrait of himself, Mao exhorted the nation's youth to redeem the Communist Revolution by smashing the "four olds": old culture, old customs, old habits, and old ways of thinking. Only the Red Guards could purify Chinese society, he told them, because "your eyes are bright and clear as snow."

It was hard to resist the allure of being one of Mao's chosen people. Blindly following the Great Helmsman's dictates, Red Guards were soon rampaging through the streets of Shanghai, turning the former bastion of capitalist excess into the vanguard of the Cultural Revolution. The militant youngsters shut down schools and universities, ransacked the homes of capitalists and intellectuals, and demolished ancient temples and monuments, even beating up the Buddhist monks at the Jing'an Temple down the road from the sporting grounds. The Red Guards eliminated anything with a trace of decadent Western influence, from women's cosmetics and French bakeries to classical music and traffic lights. Street names were changed—the road in front of the former British consulate, for instance, became Anti-Imperialist Street—though a new regulation making the revolutionary color, red, mean "go" and green mean "stop" was mercifully scrapped after a test run resulted in a spate of accidents.

Competitive sports, another insidious legacy of Western colonialism, were similarly consigned to the trash heap. All athletic training stopped, competitions were called off, and an entire generation of athletes was lost. When officials had forcibly recruited Da Fang less than two years earlier, they soothed the young girl by saying that sports were a noble way to advance the revolution. Now, in the kind of psychological whiplash that Chinese have learned to endure in the past half century, they told her that sports were a dangerous manifestation of bourgeois self-centeredness. Nobody dared to question the logic of such a reversal. In the miasma of mass psychosis, blatant contradictions were blatantly ignored. Somehow, it seemed only natural that Chairman Mao, who had built a sports system for the purpose of winning international championships, would attack the country's best coaches and athletes— the very products of his system—for their obsession with medals. Their counterrevolutionary crime even had a shiny new name: *jinmao zhuyi*, which, roughly translated, means "trophyism."

Under the direction of Mao's third wife, a former B-movie actress from Shanghai who led a radical cabal later vilified as the Gang of Four, the Red Guards laid waste to the sports system. They plowed under athletic fields, shut down the national sports commission, and imprisoned its chairman, Marshal He Long. The famously mustachioed Long March veteran, who had formed the first Red Army basketball team in the mountains of Yan'an in the 1930s, would die on the floor of his prison cell in 1969. The Red Guards also hounded and harassed some of the country's most beloved athletic champions. Rong Guotuan, the table-tennis sensation who set off wild celebrations in 1959, escaped the continual beatings and humiliation by hanging himself in his prison cell.

"Everything was turned upside down," says the former Shanghai forward Lin Meizheng, whose career was cut short by the Cultural Revolution. Years later, Lin's husband would coach Da Fang on the newly resurrected Shanghai team, and her son, Frank Sha, would become one of Yao Ming's close friends and business associates. But at that time, Lin could only watch her younger colleague rise in the ranks of the Red Guards even as her own family was brought low. The rebels ransacked Lin's family home and persecuted her father. His crime? He was an engineer (thus considered a bourgeois intellectual) who had once, before the revolution, been given a few shares in his company (making him a capitalist roader, too). "Things happened that you just couldn't imagine," says Lin. "There was no law, no government, no human rights.

Black was white, and white was black. The old order fell and suddenly the youngsters were in charge."

The first sign of danger at No. 651 Nanjing Road came in the form of threatening graffiti. "Counter-revolutionary academic authority!" screamed one message scribbled on the wall of Zhu Yong's office in late 1966. Another note scrawled on the desk of his older colleague, veteran basketball coach Wang Yongfang, was less cryptic: "Rotten wood, get out!"

Under normal circumstances, Zhu might have tracked down the vandals and punished them severely. But these were hardly normal times, and he didn't want to confront the group of radical rebels—known as *zaofanpai* (literally: "turn-upside-down group")—that was likely responsible. Loyal to Mao's conniving third wife, Jiang Qing, the *zaofanpai* had already taken over the Shanghai sports commission and were threatening to usurp its building near People's Square. (The imposing nine-story structure had originally served as the YMCA's China headquarters, but during the Cultural Revolution, it would house a secret revolutionary court complete with interrogation rooms and torture chambers. Nien Chang, author of *Life and Death in Shanghai*, believes her daughter was tortured to death there.) Now the writing was on the wall for Zhu as well. His power was eroding so fast he didn't dare to wash off the graffiti.

Nearly all of Da Fang's older teammates—both veterans and rising stars—were trundled off to the factories soon after the Cultural Revolution began. Their participation in tournaments, the Red Guards contended, proved that they had a bad case of "trophyism" that could only be cured through backbreaking labor. Thus it was that the city's best basketball players spent the next decade hauling bricks at the Shanghai Fireproof Materials Factory or toiling on the assembly line at the Dragon Machine Factory. Most of them never played basketball again. "It was a terrible shame," says Xu Weili, a standout player in the 1950s and 1960s who escaped the worst persecution in part because she had retired—and joined the Communist Party—just a year earlier, in 1965. "These players should've been taking over the team, but their generation disappeared entirely."

Getting banished to the labor camps was, in some ways, easier than staying behind at No. 651 Nanjing Road, where a reign of terror descended. In a putsch known as "January Storm," a group of radical rebels seized control of the Shanghai government, including the twenty-one organizations ruled by the city sports committee. The *zaofanpai* who controlled the sports institute at No. 651 Nanjing Road—a group that included Da Fang—imprisoned Zhu and some three dozen other top coaches and administrators in makeshift jails on the second floor. The Red Guards called the cells the "cowshed," after Mao's reference to class enemies as "cow's demons." At night, the young captors took turns harassing and haranguing their former bosses to keep them from sleeping. During the day, they forced the haggard leaders to read Mao's works or write "self-criticisms" confessing to crimes ranging from having relatives living abroad to not showing enough enthusiasm while singing the final chorus of "The Three Rules of Discipline and Eight Points of Attention."

"It was a test of human will," says Wang Yongfang, the vice-chairman of the sports-training center, who spent three months in solitary confinement in a cell next to Zhu's. "If you dozed off for a second, the Red Guards would come and hit you or yell at you."

The old leaders may have been living in terror, but for many Red Guards, the sense of power and freedom was exhilarating. Suddenly, there were no more grueling practices, no more slave-driving coaches, no more condescending leaders—just a cocksure community of young believers overseeing the creation of a new world, like the little dictators in *Lord of the Flies*. Mao decreed that Red Guards could ride public transport free of charge and receive free food, a policy that led tens of thousands of Red Guards to travel all over the country in a bizarre Chinese version of the "freedom rides." But No. 651 Nanjing Road had more than its share of drama, as Da Fang and her fellow Red Guards spent their days running political meetings, putting their former taskmasters on trial, or writing *dazibao* (large-character posters) denouncing whichever enemy Mao had singled out in that morning's *People's Daily*. Often, they would take to the streets, banging on drums and gongs in what seemed more like a festive parade than a sinister political campaign. "Sometimes, well past midnight, we received word of a new declaration from Chairman Mao," recalls Lu Bin. "We would commandeer fishmongers' carts and ride around the city all night pasting *dazibao* and shouting 'Long Live Chairman Mao!' "

For all the excitement, it was sometimes easy to forget the deadly serious tasks that the young Red Guards had been given by their Chairman. Nearly every day at the sports institute, Red Guards hauled out one of the deposed leaders for a "struggle session," a ritualized show trial that involved denunciation, interrogation, and—in the most serious cases—beatings and torture. With mob justice replacing judge and jury, these sessions resembled inquests more than trials—and many former leaders couldn't bear the suffering and humiliation. In September 1966, the first full month of the Cultural Revolution, there were more than seven hundred suicides recorded in Shanghai alone—along with some 350 deaths by beatings, torture, and other forms of abuse. One of Wang's fellow prisoners tried to commit suicide by swallowing shards of glass. The modest coach of the Shanghai men's basketball team, Shang Congyue, escaped the looming possibility of interrogation and torture by leaping to his death from his family's fourth-story apartment window. The Red Guards didn't seem fazed by the crumpled corpse on Nanjing Road. The suicide, they said, only confirmed Shang's guilt. His crime: Twenty years earlier, as a teenager, he had played briefly for a basketball team controlled by the Nationalist army.

Da Fang was one of the Red Guards whom the old leaders in the "cowshed" feared most. She was just a teenager, but in the Cultural Revolution, her youth and innocence were badges of authority. They made her revolutionary spirit more pure, her conviction more steadfast, her actions more extreme. Da Fang hadn't yet played a meaningful minute of basketball. But as an acolyte of the so-called "Strong Wind Rebels" who took over the institute, the seventeen-year-old became one of the leaders of the basketball section, where she lorded over her former bosses with a haughty attitude that one described as *hujiahuwei*—"bullying people by flaunting one's powerful connections."

Da Fang's group of Red Guards had one primary task: to investigate, punish, and reeducate the "bad elements" among their former coaches and leaders. The youngsters' prosecutorial methods were hardly scientific—and the crimes could consist of nothing more than having a relative who operated a "capitalist" fruit stand in the 1940s—but they painstakingly divided up the work. While other teammates investigated the leaders' backgrounds, Da Fang helped mete out the punishment. According to several former players and coaches who lived in the compound during these years, Da Fang was one of the most zealous disciplinarians at No. 651, leading many of the struggle sessions herself. "She treated people badly," says one former coach, who remembers watching her cut off another woman's braided hair as one of the gentler forms of punishment. "The Cultural Revolution gave her a sense of pride, arrogance," says another coach who witnessed the events there. "She became very active and very willing to publicly denounce the former leaders." Even thirty years later, the former coach still searches for some kind of explanation, just as many other Chinese are still looking for an explanation of what madness gripped their nation's youth. "She was just a child. What did she know, right?"

*   *   *

The gaunt prisoner hunched before Da Fang at center court that day wouldn't crack easily. Zhu Yong had been the main target of the institute's Red Guards from the outset. For all their invective against the evils of competition, the young revolutionaries were guilty of "trophyism" themselves—and Zhu was the biggest trophy available at No. 651 Nanjing Road. The Communist Party secretary had been the highest political authority at the sports-training center, a man who, with just a word, could ruin an athlete's career or reward him with a coveted party membership. Now he was considered an enemy of the state, a "revisionist" who represented the old, corrupted orthodoxy.

Even worse, there were rumors about his past. Everybody knew that Zhu had worked for the Communist underground before 1949, gathering intelligence and preparing the way for the revolution. But Lu Bin, who led the Red Guards' investigation, found that he had used his job at the candy counter at the Forever Peace Department Store as a cover for his party activities. Wasn't that a capitalist enterprise? And how did he gain the confidence of Nationalists to gather his intelligence? For Red Guards who had become expert at turning slivers of innuendo into sledgehammers of evidence, this was damning enough. "I didn't really understand what was happening," says Lu. "I just recorded the truth, wrote down what other people told me, and put it in my report. Then I handed it over to Da Fang and her group. The rest was out of my hands."

Zhu was treated far more harshly than the rest. Locked up in solitary confinement for six months, he survived on meager morsels of food and the barest hint of news from his wife and children. On one occasion, Zhu's teenage daughter arrived with a cake for her father, but the Red Guards upbraided her for being the daughter of a criminal and refused to deliver it. Most of the other leaders endured public humiliation, but Zhu was beaten and tortured as well. During his interrogations, the Red Guards tied his arms behind his back and pulled them upward into an excruciating position known as the "airplane." They then made their accusations, beating him with clubs when he denied his guilt.

There's no evidence that Da Fang participated in Zhu's physical abuse, but she often led the struggle sessions against him—and many former athletes remember her voice rising above the rest of the frenzied Red Guards. During one such session, in an apparent attempt to turn the old leaders against each other, Da Fang commanded Zhu to engage in hand-to-hand combat with his former second-in-command, the old coach Wang Yongfang. "Show us that you're willing to overthrow the old order," she reportedly said. The two former leaders refused to hit each other, and Da Fang exploded in rage.

That day, out on the basketball court, it was happening all over again. For months, Zhu had denied the charges against him, but now, weakened and exhausted, he was starting to break. Zhu's captors, including Da Fang, recited the list of accusations against him—his supposed espionage, his contacts with the KMT, his deviation from the true path of Maoist thought—and the mob of athletes repeated each denunciation in full-throated unison. The chorus of voices grew in intensity as somebody pulled Zhu's arms up behind his back.

This time, the old party leader cracked. "Yes, yes," he said. "I confess."

A few weeks later, in the spring of 1967, Zhu was shipped out, along with two hundred other sports officials, to the Chongming Cadre Reeducation School, a reform-through-labor camp on an island in the mouth of the Yangtze River near Shanghai. He would spend the next five years doing hard labor on the farms. The revolutionaries running the camp were again tougher on Zhu than on most of the others: They deprived him of food, prevented him from seeing family even when his son was critically ill, and assigned him the most strenuous and meaningless of jobs. Wang Yongfang was sent to the same reeducation camp, but he only saw Zhu a couple of times, when their work units passed near each other. The last time he saw him there, in late autumn 1968, the former leader was standing knee-deep in an icy stream, pulling rotten grass out of the water and piling it in heavy loads on the bank. His hands were cracked and bleeding from frostbite, and his eyes had gone dead.

3

Mao's Fallen Star

Chairman Mao didn't need his "little revolutionary generals" for long. By late 1968, the worst violence was over, and Mao—having used the turmoil to consolidate power—called in the real army to help establish order and seize control of the organs of state. Once the radical new leadership was installed, the idealistic Red Guards were demobilized. Within weeks, millions of Mao's political foot soldiers were shipped off to the countryside—many to a barren wilderness in Manchuria known as "the Great Northern Wasteland"—to temper their revolutionary zeal with years of hard labor. Confronted with the harsh reality of the revolution they had romanticized, many of these young radicals would end up as embittered as Zhu Yong. And some would never make it home again.

Da Fang, however, would have a different fate.

Ever on the cutting edge of social change, Shanghai was now one of the first places in China to emerge from the chaos, and Da Fang was, once again, at the forefront of this transformation. The revival of basketball—the sport she had been taught to vilify as a bourgeois Western import—saved her from going to a labor camp. Under the new slogan "Friendship First, Competition Second," sports were now meant to restore the lost sense of communal feeling inside China and to rebuild diplomatic relations outside—first with many of China's former socialist allies and then, eventually, with its biggest enemy, the United States. Training sessions resumed tentatively in Shanghai at the end of 1969, only now the purity of a player's revolutionary politics was considered more important than the purity of his or her jump shot. Beijing didn't want Chinese teams to be humiliated in friendly international matches, but "trophyism" was still considered a crime—and many of the nation's best athletes were still toiling away at factories and collective farms, as they would for years to come.

The gaping hole in the Chinese sports system gave young players a rare opportunity to shine. Da Fang, then nineteen, wasn't the only beneficiary. The dearth of veterans also hastened the rise of Yao Zhiyuan, the 6'10" center who had joined the Shanghai men's team after escaping the brunt of the Cultural Revolution as a worker at the Shanghai No. 8 Machinery Factory, and Ren Huanzhen, a rail-thin 6'2" center from Beijing. In the finals of the first national competition in five years, in 1970, Ren and her Beijing team powered to a convincing victory over Da Fang and the Shanghai team. Nobody paid too much attention to the outcome of the game, but a curious precedent was established. Three decades later, Ren's only son, Wang Zhizhi, would battle it out with Da Fang's only son, Yao Ming, in a rivalry that would alter the face of Chinese basketball—and presage two very different leaps across the ocean.

As a player, Da Fang would far outshine Ren, just as her son would eventually eclipse Wang Zhizhi. Whereas Ren spent most of her career on the Beijing city squad, only joining the national team for a short stint in the early 1970s, Da Fang's star kept rising. She would soon become one of the standout centers of her generation, one of the best in all of Asia. Her success derived in part from her physical gifts: she and Ren were both 6'2", but Da Fang was more solidly built, and she had begun to develop a soft shooting touch to go along with her tenacious under-the-basket play. She also got a boost from her revolutionary politics. The former Red Guard was still a loyal Maoist, and the leadership in Beijing sensed she would be a perfect role model for the nation.

If it were not for her obedience to the Maoist leadership, her former teammates say, Da Fang would never have been selected year after year as national-team captain—and, in 1974, as a national sports representative at the ceremony celebrating the twenty-fifth anniversary of the Communist Revolution in Beijing's Great Hall of the People. During the latter years of the Cultural Revolution, from 1971 to 1976, Da Fang moved from the basketball court to the highest echelons of political power. The comely team captain often greeted arriving foreign delegations at the airport, meeting presidents and dignitaries and mingling with members of the Chinese Politburo, including Deng Xiaoping and Zhou Enlai. Around her teammates, though, Da Fang rarely smiled, not even when the team was mobbed by adoring fans on the street or when the players gossiped in one another's rooms after practice. "Da Fang was very closed," says Luo Xuelian, the national team's effervescent point guard, who—unlike Da Fang—had a real thirst for the game. (When army soldiers used basketballs for target practice during the Cultural Revolution, Luo recovered one leather ball from the firing squad and hid it in her room until, years later, she was allowed to play again.) "After practice, Da Fang would just sit in her room knitting sweaters. If you needed to talk to her, you had to go to her room. She'd rarely come out." The aloofness only added to Da Fang's aura of authority.

Basketball teams in those "Friendship First" days served mostly as traveling entertainers, a sort of Harlem Globetrotters with a Communist twist. The main purpose of sports in the early 1970s was to make friends and to bring people together—not to battle for championship medals. For a few weeks each year, the players showed their solidarity with the proletariat by helping them harvest their crops or work on the assembly line. Afterward, the basketball players would put on a clinic on the local mud-packed courts, drawing thousands of enthusiastic spectators. "The people welcomed us as though we were the PLA coming to liberate them," says the point guard Luo. "They'd be pounding drums, chanting slogans, cheering our every move. We were surprised because we felt this was just our job: to serve the people."

The masses, though, were hardly looking for another object lesson in the virtues of the Communist system. Instead, they were reveling in the opportunity, so rare during the Cultural Revolution, to express unfettered excitement in public and to witness a fresh, unpredictable form of entertainment. "There was no other entertainment in those days except the 'model works,'" says former Shanghai forward Lu Bin, referring to the canon of propagandistic songs, operas, and ballets that were the only works allowed during the Cultural Revolution. "People liked basketball because, unlike the operas, every play was different and the outcome was always in doubt."

Sex was a factor, too. In a repressed society where everybody wore the same dull outfit—a shapeless Mao suit and flat black-cloth shoes—who could resist the allure of long-legged athletes running around in bright red jerseys, white sneakers, and tight shorts? "The rest of society was a boring panorama of gray and green," says Xu Jicheng, a former army player who is now a Xinhua News Agency journalist and China's premier basketball commentator. "Just seeing a different kind of uniform was exciting." Da Fang and her teammates were considered glamorous. It wasn't just their looks—though Da Fang was well known for her high cheekbones and long legs—but their access to things far beyond the reach of the typical Chinese worker: good food, foreign travel, even high fashion. In 1974, when the team made its debut in the Asian Games in Tehran, the women for the first time in a decade wore leg-baring dresses instead of pants, and one-inch heels instead of their usual flat shoes. Several newspapers displayed titillating photos of the Chinese players—showing only their legs from the knee down.

Sportsmanship served even better as an instrument of international diplomacy. In the early 1970s, mainland China was still an outcast from the Olympic Games and most world championships. But after years of self-imposed isolation, Beijing was now keen on opening up to the outside world. Mao's desperate attempts to show that China could stand up on its own had been unmitigated disasters. The Great Leap Forward had resulted in a massive famine that killed tens of millions, and the Cultural Revolution's mass hysteria was pushing the country in the same direction. A 1969 military standoff between Chinese and Soviet troops along the Sino-Soviet border showed how vulnerable China could be facing a major crisis alone. Mao decided that the nation's survival might best be served by joining the international order rather than trying to overthrow it. What China needed now was powerful friends, and the easiest, least threatening way to appeal to the world was through the universal language of sports.

"Ping-Pong diplomacy" helped thaw the icy hostility that had built up between Beijing and Washington ever since the Communist takeover in 1949. In April 1971, Mao invited the U.S. table tennis team—including several guys with shaggy locks and multicolored bell-bottoms—to tour mainland China. The impromptu visit paved the way for President Richard Nixon's historic trip to Beijing in February 1972, the first step in normalizing relations between the two nations. Two months later, after Beijing had been reinstated, with America's blessing, into the United Nations, a group of mainland Chinese table-tennis players charmed a packed house in the U.N. General Assembly with a dazzling demonstration of dinks and smashes.

"Basketball diplomacy" never had quite so dramatic an impact, but it was also vital to China's reemergence. Hoops was a more universal sport than Ping-Pong, enabling Beijing to expand its goodwill tours. Both the men's and women's teams toured extensively through Asia, Africa, and Europe. (Before Da Fang would move to Houston in 2002 to manage her son's NBA career, she had already traveled with the national team for friendly matches in places like Cuba, Albania, Italy, and France.) So eager was Beijing to build diplomatic ties that it sometimes ordered the traveling Chinese teams to lose games on purpose. "The intrusion of politics made us angry," says Zhang Weiping, a high-scoring forward on the men's national team. "The Chinese embassy talked to our coach and told him that we needed to give the locals some face. So we had to find creative ways to throw the game."

Chinese athletes learned quickly that such good deeds were worth more than good plays. When the national team played "friendlies" abroad, Da Fang and her teammates often befuddled their hosts by apologizing profusely after committing fouls or insisting on helping opposing players who had fallen down. (Before going abroad, the Chinese players also received instructions on how to eat noodles without making their customary slurping noises, which might offend their hosts.) Back in China, local spectators had become so indoctrinated in the "Friendship First" mentality that they often watched games in virtual silence, unmoved by the dazzling individual moves and cheering only displays of teamwork or sportsmanship.

Nagging health problems forced Da Fang to miss several overseas trips, including a 1975 tour of the United States. Her lower back ached, and she appeared in a permanent state of exhaustion. The grueling practices took a lot out of Da Fang; she could exert herself hard one day, but for the next couple of days, she would barely have the energy to move. "When Da Fang was hurting, she would lie down like a kitten," recalls one of her former teammates. "But when she was healthy, she played like a tiger."

As her career wound down, Da Fang would have one final chance to roar. The death of Chairman Mao in September 1976, at age eighty-three, plunged the country into grief and confusion. Da Fang and her teammates wept for the only leader they had ever known, the man who was their prophet and guide. A month later came the shocking arrest of Mao's wife and the rest of the Gang of Four. "We asked ourselves, 'How will China survive?'" says Da Fang's teammate Luo. "We were just so confused about the future. But that only made us pour all of our energy into training."

The team soldiered on, traveling to Hong Kong in November for the Asian Championships, determined to win for their turmoil-ridden country. This wasn't about friendship anymore; it was about national pride. The heavy favorites were the South Koreans, who had won four consecutive Asian Championships, including a victory over China in the 1974 finals in Tehran. During pregame warm-ups, the Chinese team was so jittery that two players accidentally slammed into each other and fell to the floor. Luo, the floor leader, tried to calm the team down. But the first half was a disaster. Taking advantage of their inside strength, the Koreans powered over Da Fang to establish a twelve-point lead.

In the second half, however, Da Fang came alive. Mustering all of her energy, China's veteran center fought for every rebound and made a succession of short turnarounds from the left side of the key. The packed crowd at Hong Kong's Queen Elizabeth Stadium cheered madly for the Chinese team—especially as Da Fang and her young teammate Song Xiaobo pulled them to within striking distance. With the score tied and three minutes remaining, South Korea's star center fouled out of the game and Da Fang drained a free throw to give China its first lead. The second Korean tower fouled out a minute later, leaving Da Fang with shorter defenders who couldn't contain her. When the final buzzer sounded, China had won, 71–68, and Da Fang had turned in the best performance of her career, scoring more than twenty points.

Nobody had expected the Chinese team to pull off the upset. So surprised were the hosts that when the players climbed the podium to accept the championship trophy, there was no Chinese anthem played in their honor—and no Chinese flag prepared to be raised. More disappointments awaited at home. As the players flew to Beijing, passing around the enormous trophy, they imagined the crowds that would surely be awaiting their triumphant return. But nobody came to the airport to greet them. Five years later, they might have been hailed as national heroes, perhaps even have had their images plastered onto postage stamps. But in the anarchy that gripped China in late 1976, news of their victory had not even made it to Beijing.

An airport security guard asked them what the trophy was for. "Well, congratulations," he said. And that was all.

"We felt emotionally lost," says Luo. "We had fought so hard for China and nobody even came to greet us. But for all of us on the team, we still remember that game as the highlight of our lives."

When Chinese athletes reach the end of their playing days, they don't use the normal word for "retire," *tuixiu*. Rather, they use the word *tuiyi*, meaning "to be released from military service or general servitude." Even that formulation falls short of expressing their role in Chinese society, however, because Chinese athletes are never truly released from their obligations to the motherland. Until recently, most athletes were automatically absorbed into the sports system, where, as coaches or administrators, they passed on their knowledge to the next generation of young recruits. And if they happened to be extraordinarily tall or talented, they were expected to pass along something even more fundamental: their genes.

By 1978, Da Fang was ready to hang up her sneakers and call it quits. Though just twenty-eight, she was hobbled by gimpy knees and chronic back pain—the dubious rewards of a decade of punishing training. Younger players had already replaced her on the national team, and now, after a couple of injury-plagued years on the Shanghai team, Da Fang wanted out. Still, an athlete can't simply walk away from the game in China. That decision, like her forced recruitment into the game, rested with higher authorities. When Shanghai sports officials finally did let Da Fang retire, they suggested that she should go out and breed a champion. The tone may have been jocular, but in China, the process of preparing the way for the next generation of athletes had become deadly serious.

But whom could Da Fang marry? From the time she had begun training at age fifteen, she had never kissed a boy, much less dated one. Like most Chinese athletes at the time, she had spent her entire adult life focusing on two things: sports and revolution. Even if there were time or inclination, dating was strictly forbidden in the sports system. The "Ten Rules for Athletes" published in the *People's Daily* newspaper made it clear that elite athletes were duty bound to "refrain from falling in love" and to "postpone marriage" so they could focus all of their energies on winning for the motherland. Male athletes were forbidden from getting married until they were thirty, female athletes until they were twenty-eight. If a player got pregnant, she would be forced to have an abortion or kicked off the team. Though enforcement has relaxed considerably in recent years, these rules still exist today. In early 2004, four table-tennis players were expelled from the national team for letting their romantic relations with teammates affect their performances.

If one of the responsibilities of a Chinese coach was to "guard against love as if standing guard against a flood," as the writer Zhao Yu put it, another was to help arrange suitable matches among their most genetically gifted athletes upon retirement. Arranged marriages were still common in China in the late 1970s, and the sports system strictly adhered to the nationwide regulation that all marriages must be approved by work-unit leaders. (That regulation, in fact, was only dropped in 2004.) "We had to do a lot of work as matchmakers," says Wang Yongfang, the former sports-institute leader who coached Da Fang early in her career and, after a long stint of hard labor in the countryside, was rehabilitated as the leader of the Shanghai women's team. "These girls spent far more time with the coaches and team leaders than with their own parents. Who else was there to make sure everything was okay?"

Finding mates for towering female basketball players, however, wasn't easy, both because they weren't allowed to get married until age twenty-eight—much later than the average Chinese woman—and because they were far taller than most Chinese men. Luckily, there were often a few male basketball and volleyball players available. "I'd contact the men's coach and he would speak directly to his player," says Wang, now almost ninety years old, fondly recalling the marriages he facilitated. "If there was no interest, the players could refuse. But they usually went along with our suggestions." For athletes who have been conditioned their entire lives to obey their coaches' words, such marital advice could often sound like a commandment.

Even today, the practice of matchmaking persists. A few years ago, for instance, sports authorities tried to find a mate for the tallest women's player in Chinese history, Zheng Haixia, a 6'8", 300-pound center on the army and national teams who, in the mid-1990s, played two years in the WNBA. A towering peasant woman known more for her basso profundo and meat-cleaver hands than any trace of femininity, Zheng didn't have much hope of attracting a man on her own. But officials found a 6'10" peasant playing on the Hunan provincial basketball team who obligingly came to Beijing to carry out their wishes. The two giants became a couple, and authorities began to imagine the offspring that such a union could bring. After a year together, however, the boyfriend bolted—and Zheng, now an official on the army team, never married.

However kindly the officials' efforts at matchmaking might seem, they often carried the darker overtones of eugenics—a concept that China's Communist Party leaders have explored since the founding of the People's Republic. By the late 1970s, as their impoverished, over-populated nation struggled to emerge from a time of scarcity and suffering, the leaders openly embraced this idea of manipulating the gene pool to improve the hereditary qualities of a population. In 1979, for instance, when Beijing imposed the most comprehensive birth-control program the world had ever seen—later known simply as the "one-child policy"—its most vigorous explanation came in a document called "Several Rules about the Implementation of Eugenics Planning." Even as late as 1993, Beijing would unveil a draft law on "Eugenics and Health" that sought to "upgrade the quality of the population" by requiring abortion, sterilization, or the deferral of marriage for those most likely to give birth to children with major congenital defects. The draft law provoked outrage in the West for its evocation of Nazi-style eugenics, and Beijing quietly renamed it "The Natal and Health Care Law"— but the substance remained the same.

The goal was the same in the sporting world. Anything that could hasten China's rise as a great nation, after all, was considered reasonable, even desirable. Tall players tend to breed even taller children, especially if the children are well-nourished, so the sports authorities began carrying out a grand genetic experiment that has spanned nearly three generations. Since the 1950s, the sports system has brought together the nation's tallest people into a controlled environment, provided them with nourishment and training, fostered their intermarriage and procreation, and culled their tallest and most talented offspring to become basketball players themselves.

Naturally, this would be Da Fang's fate as well. Before she even started to look for a husband on her own, Shanghai officials had already chosen a partner for her: Yao Zhiyuan, the 6'10" center on the Shanghai men's team. Yao, an active player who was two years her junior, was an agreeable man whose ready smile and love of a good quip contrasted sharply with Da Fang's grim demeanor. The two players were already familiar with each other. For several years, they had eaten in the same cafeteria, lived in the same dormitory, and practiced on adjoining courts at the Shanghai training facility. But they were both quite shy, so they had rarely exchanged more than pleasantries. "We didn't know each other very well," Da Fang says, "but we did see each other a lot on the practice court."

Nevertheless, Shanghai sports officials thought this kind of "courtship" made them a perfect fit: They were both introverted centers born into working-class families and nurtured by the state-run sports system. And, of course, they were the tallest basketball players in Shanghai—probably the tallest people in the city, period. What could be better for the future of Chinese basketball than their marriage? "We were always telling Da Yao and Da Fang, 'You both are so tall, you should get together, you'll understand each other,' " recalls Sha Feng'ao, who was Da Fang's former head coach on the Shanghai team and married a basketball player himself. "We'd joke with them and say, 'Just imagine how tall your children would be.' "

What began as teasing quickly became an official endorsement. And it was up to a portly team leader named Liu Shiyu to make it a matrimonial reality. "Fat Liu," as he was known, took each player aside and persuaded them that they could "make do" with the other—and that they had the official stamp of approval, according to several coaches active at the time. Given such high-level interest, how could Da Fang and Da Yao refuse?

The simple civil union of Da Fang and Da Yao was not bogged down by unnecessary frills or sentimentality. Aside from their families, the only people in attendance were teammates, coaches, and sports leaders. Romance might be the driving force for weddings in the West, but in China, marriage—especially marriage between the two tallest people in the city sports system—was about one thing: procreation. The sports community didn't have to wait long for the first offspring of what the press was calling "the first couple of Asia." Barely a year later, in September 1980, Yao Ming was born, and word flew around town. In the small apartment where Da Fang and Da Yao lived—surrounded by other athletes and coaches—everyone gathered to see the miracle child.

Long-awaited Yao.

The arrival of Yao Ming gave Shanghai authorities a glimpse of the future, and for many of them, one child hardly seemed enough. Operation Yao Ming seemed to demand more—a desire expressed not by Da Yao and Da Fang as much as by a group of patriotic coaches and officials who wanted to circumvent the country's one-child policy to allow the couple to produce a few more basketball prodigies, perhaps an entire team.

China's one-child policy, which had gone into effect the year before Yao was born, was designed to slow the nation's unbridled population growth and help lift its living standards—both of which it did dramatically. But the birth-control program became (and still remains) one of the most despised policies of the post-Mao era, especially in urban centers, where its rules and enforcement were most stringent. The local work units that controlled everything from food coupons to apartment allocation now had the power to invade the most private realm of people's behavior: their sex lives. If families caught violating the one-child policy couldn't pay a stiff fine, the women were sometimes forced to be sterilized or, more often, undergo abortions, at times perilously late in the pregnancy. (Baby girls were the main casualties of the birth-control plan, as the traditional preference for boys led some Chinese families to cull females either through infanticide or, more recently, through the use of ultrasound. As a result, there are now around 119 boys born for every 100 girls in China.) For most couples around the country, the one-child policy meant getting contraceptives from the same family-planning officials who kept careful track of women's menstrual cycles.

The snooping grannies of the neighborhood committee—the street-level spies who were the Communist state's last line of defense—pursued their roles so zealously in the early days that they sometimes went so far as to report any sounds in the night that might constitute unauthorized sex.

Not long after Yao was born, a group of well-respected basketball coaches trooped to the Shanghai sports commission on Nanjing Road to persuade their leaders to suspend the one-child policy in the special case of Da Fang and Da Yao—and to give the poor family financial assistance to help raise their growing giant. One of the petitioners that day was Da Fang's former coach, Sha Feng'ao, who lived one floor above Yao's parents in the sports-compound dormitory with his wife and twin sons. The one-child policy made an exception in the case of twins, making Sha one of the few people in Shanghai to have two sons. But the coach wanted Da Fang and Da Yao to have that good fortune, too, so China could have more prospective basketball giants. (After Yao Ming was born, Sha's boys, then four years old, took turns carrying the infant Yao Ming around in the hallways—a bond that would endure into adulthood, when the elder twin, later known as Frank, went to work for Nike.) On several occasions, Sha Feng'ao asked his towering neighbors if they would consider having more children for the good of the nation. "They just laughed," Sha recalls. "I think they didn't want to break any rules. Besides, they didn't have the money to raise a large family."

The approval for further procreation—and the money needed to raise another child—resided with the sports-commission leaders. "I told [the leaders] that the couple's children would be very tall and that would be very useful for the country," says Sha, who was only one of many coaches making the same argument. "If they wanted this to happen, they would have to authorize the suspension of the one-child policy and give the couple financial support."

"Ah yes, that's a very good idea," replied one official.

Weeks and months passed, however, and there was no word from the sports commission. The coaches were perplexed. Why would the leaders show such enthusiasm for an idea and then fail to act? Some friends of Yao's family thought they knew the answer. The former Communist Party secretary at the sports-training center—the man Da Fang had hurt and humiliated years ago—had reassumed political prominence within the sports system, and rumor had it he was nursing a grudge.

*   *   *

If Chinese history has always resembled a roller-coaster ride, the last half-century has been one of the most breathtaking loops of all, with successive waves of people propelled to the top and then hurled down in a death-defying plunge, only to be lifted back up again. Nearly every Chinese citizen who has lived through this period has some dramatic tale of having his or her life turned upside down for better or worse. But few have risen so high or fallen so far as Da Fang and her old antagonist at the sports institute, Zhu Yong. They just happened to be on opposite ends of the track.

Near the end of her playing career, Da Fang had experienced a rare crystalline moment at the top of the precipice just before the vertiginous fall. It was August 1, 1977, the day that marked the fiftieth anniversary of the founding of the People's Liberation Army, and Da Fang had been appointed to serve as a delegate representing sports at the formal commemorative ceremony in Beijing's Great Hall of the People. As national-team captain, she had become accustomed to rubbing shoulders with the nation's secretive Communist rulers. But on this occasion, the daughter of humble factory workers stood with China's new leaders, including Deng Xiaoping, the former Communist Party secretary who, after three stints in political exile, had been restored to the Politburo just two weeks before the PLA's 50th-anniversary celebration.

For a population brutalized and exhausted by the Cultural Revolution, the new faces on the rostrum served as reassuring signs that the anarchy was over, that Mao's disastrous ten-year detour had finally come to an end. For Da Fang, it was a sign that her world was crumbling. Her political lodestars were now either dead (Mao) or destroyed (the Gang of Four), and the brightest light in the Chinese firmament was the little man whom they had tried and failed to extinguish. The Red Guards had carried out a smear campaign that helped bring Deng down in disgrace for his advocacy of economic modernization, the worst of revisionist evils. The anticapitalist attack would be long forgotten by the time Da Fang was helping negotiate multimillion-dollar endorsement contracts for her son, but for true Communist believers at the time, Deng was the anti-Mao, a maddening pragmatist bent on diluting their faith.

Deng was not the only one who had risen from the ashes. Zhu Yong had also been rehabilitated after five years of hard labor in the reeducation camps. After a short time running a sports school, the former party cadre was given the top job at Shanghai's main sports-training center. Then, not long after Da Fang's final appearance as a revolutionary role model in 1977, he was catapulted into the job of deputy director at the Shanghai sports commission. The huge promotion reflected a widespread practice by which those who suffered most during the Cultural Revolution received the greatest reward afterward. Zhu's new perch would give him the power to influence the lives of thousands of people in the Shanghai sports system—and, in some cases, to settle old scores.

The political reversal was so sudden that many traumatized athletes refused to believe it could be true. Zhu sent emissaries to the factories to coax persecuted players to come back to help build the tattered sports system, but many were too disoriented by the Cultural Revolution to return. "We'd been told that it was good to be a worker," says Xu Weili, a former player who spent seven years laboring in a ship-building factory. "Why would we want to get involved with sports again?" Huang Xiafei, Xu's former teammate, feared that the overtures were just a ploy—or part of a temporary revolt that wouldn't last. "When they first came to us, we thought it was another power struggle," says Huang. "We were still very sensitive to political shocks, so we figured it was safer to stay in the factory." Huang wouldn't emerge for another three years.

It was the former Red Guards, however, who had the most to fear. "The revenge was fierce," says Lu Bin. "The leaders had long memories, and now that they were in power again, they wanted to 'clear accounts.'" Lu took advantage of the turmoil after Mao's death to escape to Beijing, where she was safe from the worst repercussions. Nevertheless, she bumped into Zhu Yong a couple of years later when she was watching a game in Shanghai with other retired players. The old leader shook hands warmly with each of the players. But when he reached Lu, he turned away without even looking at her.

"Why are you leaders so arrogant?" Lu responded angrily. "It was not my decision to denounce you back then. It was an order from above!"

Nevertheless, Zhu blamed his suffering on a small group of Red Guards that included Da Fang, and she would pay the price. In a system based on status and seniority, former national stars like Da Fang are often given top coaching jobs or mid-level administrative posts. Her predecessor on the national team, Liu Yumin, eventually rose to become the top official in charge of all basketball in China. When Da Fang retired in 1978, she moved naturally into the position of assistant coach for the Shanghai junior women's team, an ideal training ground for a former star who might one day vie for a top coaching job or leadership role.

But when the leaders persecuted during the Cultural Revolution gained a full grip on power, Da Fang's coaching days were over. The Communist Party secretary who controlled job allocation in the sports system—once again, Zhu Yong—had her transferred to what one former teammate described as "the worst job in the sports system": doing menial work at a compound for retired athletes. For a time, the former national hero found herself stocking bathrooms with soap for the equivalent of a few dollars a week. Later, she would be transferred to a clerical job at the Shanghai Sports Science Research Institute. But she would never work as a coach again, and she lacked the basic education and political connections to find other employment. Her husband, too, failed to land a job as a coach, and ended up working his entire career in the Shanghai port. Together, the couple made less than eighty yuan per month—about fifty dollars at the time—barely more than half the average salary of an urban Chinese household and hardly enough to raise a rapidly growing child.

The tables had turned so completely that, like many former Red Guards Da Fang herself became the subject of an internal investigation. Her new employers at the research institute dispatched investigators to interview the former leaders whom she had allegedly persecuted at the old Nanjing Road sporting grounds. The results of this investigation would inevitably land in her *dang'an*—the secret dossier that the government kept (and still keeps) on all Chinese citizens from childhood to death, recording their school grades, work history, disciplinary records, along with notes from teachers, bosses, and informants about their personal habits and political views. Not all of the former leaders Da Fang helped imprison and punish at No. 651 Nanjing Road testified against her. "What was the use?" says one of these leaders, recalling the investigation. "That was all in the past. I had come out okay, and I didn't want the cycles of revenge to continue."

Zhu Yong, apparently, didn't feel the same way. His office at the sports commission not only refused to act on any requests to help Da Fang financially, whether it was to raise Yao Ming or to facilitate the procreation of more siblings. Several of Da Fang's friends and former teammates say Zhu also saw to it that the sports system housed the tallest family in Shanghai in a makeshift apartment without a kitchen or bathroom. Cut off from political power, stuck in menial jobs, Da Fang and her husband languished in relative poverty for most of the next two decades. As she struggled to raise her only son, the former Red Guard would ride her bicycle to the same workplace day after day, unable to escape the shadow of her role in the Cultural Revolution.

4

Childhood Denied

It is one of the delicious ironies of history that the fate of China's tallest athletes would rest in the hands of one of history's shortest rulers. Deng Xiaoping was so small that he might have made Napoleon lose his complex. Former U.S. Secretary of State Henry Kissinger once called Deng "that nasty little man," but many Chinese referred to him affectionately as "Xiao Pingzi," or "Little Bottle," a play on his name that alluded both to his size and to his ability to float back to the top of Chinese politics after being tossed into the depths of oblivion.

In a nation struggling once again to stand tall in the world, however, the paramount leader's exact height was a closely guarded state secret. Most historians say he stood barely 4'11", probably even less in later years. (Napoleon was 5'6".) Deng was so self-conscious about his height that he tried to avoid being photographed standing beside Western leaders, lest the image of such a blatant disparity diminish China's international stature. When such pictures were unavoidable, as during his first trip to the United States in 1979, the Chinese media shot his meetings with President Jimmy Carter from a forty-five-degree angle to make Deng look almost statuesque. (Deng's obsession with China's image vis-à-vis the rest of the world even led the government to institute strict height requirements at some top universities where future diplomats are trained. Such regulations, many of which are still in effect today, have prompted hundreds of average-size students to undergo leg-lengthening operations—an excruciating procedure in which both legs are broken and stretched in a medieval-looking brace that forces new bone tissue to grow.)

Back home in the Chinese leadership compound, aides stuffed cushions into Deng's chair so he could see his visitors eye to eye, even if the extra lift sometimes made his feet dangle off the floor. Despite his short stature, few dared to laugh at the rough-hewn revolutionary from rural Sichuan, for he had a remarkable will to change the course of history.

When the little man in a gray tunic rose to power in 1978, rebounding after years of persecution, he had little interest in creating a Mao-like cult of personality. Deng's concerns were far more pragmatic. Whether driven by his own size or not—a question best left to psychoanalysts—Deng was consumed with returning the Middle Kingdom to its former heights as a global superpower. To do that, he needed to foster more than the détente of "Ping-Pong diplomacy;" he needed to end the ideological isolation Mao had created. But what was the swiftest way to open up a nation that was still on its knees, barely emerging from the wreckage of the Cultural Revolution? An economic renaissance would take time. Even with boisterous growth rates, it would be decades before China could contend with the international powers economically, militarily, diplomatically.

The one high-profile arena in which China could hope to compete as equals with the rest of the world—and break down the old walls of fear and isolation—was sports. For more than two decades, Beijing had been shunned by the International Olympic Committee and banned from world championships in nearly every sport. Deng's diplomatic démarche changed all that. One by one, the international sports federations welcomed Beijing back. In 1979, the same year Beijing and Washington normalized relations, mainland China managed to elbow Taiwan aside and rejoin the Olympic movement. (The rehabilitation was nudged along by the 1936 Olympian Mou Zuoyun, who would later be named an honorary member of the IOC.) Taiwan, which had previously been recognized as China's only representative at the Olympics, was relegated to a nebulous new status as "Chinese Taipei," the awkward moniker under which it still competes today. Grateful for the new recognition, Beijing sent a token delegation of twenty-eight athletes the next year to the Winter Games in Lake Placid but then joined the American-led boycott of the 1980 Summer Games in Moscow.

Deng's ambition was to build an athletic powerhouse that commanded awe and admiration abroad and deep feelings of national pride at home. The era of Mao's "Friendship First" made way for Deng's glory-seeking "Gold-Medal Strategy." Winning medals, an act so vilified just a few years before that it sent many athletes to their deaths, was all that counted now. Somehow, just as in his radical economic reforms, Deng made the 180-degree turn sound like a natural outgrowth of

Mao's policies. "To win friends we must first of all win gold medals," read a 1980 editorial in a state-run sports newspaper, encapsulating the new thinking in Beijing. "If we merely take part in competitions and are incapable of obtaining brilliant results, then the dignity of our country and our people will be adversely affected."

The only way to win more gold medals, Deng decided, was to revamp the rusty old sports machine that had fallen into disrepair during the Cultural Revolution. Beijing still paid lip service to Mao's ideal of fitness for the masses. But the country was too poor and too vast—and in too much of a hurry—to build the kind of mass-participation programs that existed in the West. Public recreation was almost nonexistent: In the mid-1980s, the government estimated there was only one gymnasium for every 3.5 million people—and most facilities, both then and now, were off-limits to common folk. Meanwhile, the State Commission for Sport funneled nearly all of its resources to the elite few who could add to the luster of the People's Republic. In a land where the average annual income hovered around four hundred dollars and bicycles still outnumbered cars 137 to 1, the government lavished $500 million during the 1980s on top-level sports, building impressive stadium complexes in Beijing and Shanghai, an Olympic training center in southwestern Yunnan Province, and even a state-of-the-art regatta course outside of Shanghai.

The new strategy targeted disciplines that offered a high density of Olympic gold, even if that meant learning the sport from scratch. Suddenly, young athletes began training in sports foreign to many Chinese, such as swimming, weight lifting, shooting, even rowing and kayaking. Many lower-level basketball recruits morphed into team handball players, while thousands of gymnasts were obliged to become divers (or, later, free-style skiers). In 1980, Beijing even reinstated competitive boxing, a sport that had long been banned for being too barbaric. The reason for the reversal was a knockout: Boxing offered forty-eight Olympic medals.

China's competitive advantage came from two sources: a massive pool of more than three hundred million youngsters under eighteen—and the power to compel them to train, even against their will. Exploiting these conditions, Deng and his aging deputies moved rapidly to expand the network of sports factories. By the mid-1980s, there were more than thirty-two hundred sports schools across China, training nearly half a million youths. The biggest influx of youngsters arrived from the deepest interior, tough kids who were valued for their extraordinary ability to *chi ku,* to "eat bitterness"—the kind of stoic perseverance that Chinese revere as the most noble way to achieve success.

One of the most impressive countryside recruits in the 1990s was a shepherd's son born in a hut on the grasslands of Inner Mongolia. An ethnic Mongolian—part of a minority long shunned by the Han majority—Mengke Bateer was six feet tall by age nine. He had no hope of leaving the impoverished plains until the local mayor showed up at his elementary school one day and, mistaking the towering kid for the teacher, complimented him on his well-behaved class. Once the confusion was cleared up, Bateer was quickly recruited to play basketball in the provincial sports school. The hulking Mongolian, who would grow to 6'11" and eventually join Yao Ming and Wang Zhizhi for a few seasons in the NBA, spoke only a few words of Mandarin when he arrived. But for a boy who grew up in utter destitution, two of them were among the most important: *chi fan,* or "eat food."

For rural kids like Bateer, the sports schools were a passport out of poverty, a guarantee of a roof over their heads and food in their bellies. In a culture of scarcity that placed food at the center of the social contract—even today, a common form of greeting is "have you eaten yet?"—food was used as an important tool to drive athletes harder. Coaches rewarded good play with coupons for extra food, punishing bad behavior by taking them away. Even Yao Ming's parents, who lived in relative comfort compared to Bateer's family on the Mongolian grasslands, would consider food a major factor in relinquishing their son to the sports system. At the highest levels of sport, meanwhile, athletic success became a ticket to previously unimaginable riches, after Deng and his deputies initiated a star system that would have been anathema in Maoist China. In the run-up to the 1984 Summer Olympics in Los Angeles, it was an open secret that Beijing—emulating some capitalist countries in the West—promised to pay athletes around $3,500 per gold medal.

The elitist perks were considered a small price to pay for an incalculable boost to the nation's pride and international prestige. When the women's volleyball team won the 1981 World Championships, China's first ever in a team sport, hundreds of thousands of ecstatic Beijing residents descended on Tiananmen Square in the largest outpouring of spontaneous emotion up to that point in the history of the People's Republic. The victory gave the Chinese a jolt of pride in their country's sudden rise in the world, along with a smug pleasure in beating foreigners at their own game—payback, they felt, for decades of subjugation at the hands of foreign powers. At one point, crowds of unruly Chinese fans gathered outside the embassies of Japan and the United States, their two vanquished rivals in the World Championships, and started crowing nationalist slogans at the frightened diplomats inside.

When the volleyball champions returned home, they were turned into poster girls for national progress. Just a decade earlier, athletic champions had been hounded or imprisoned; a few years before, Da Fang and the victorious women's basketball team had been virtually ignored when they returned from the 1976 Asian Championships. Now, the government issued a series of commemorative stamps emblazoned with the players' images, and an official poem canonized them as engines of Deng's "four modernizations."

The one global event that could truly help restore China's *mianzi,* or face, was the Olympic Games. The country's return to the Olympic fold after thirty-two years in the wilderness would come, fittingly, in Los Angeles—the very city where, fifty-two years earlier, China had made its first-ever Olympic appearance. In 1932, the Nationalist government had sent a lone sprinter; in 1984, the proud Communist leaders would send a delegation of 224 athletes to symbolize the reemergence of the People's Republic, a nation of 1.2 billion people. So eager was Beijing to come out of isolation and prove its newfound strength that it rejected a Soviet-led "hundred-nation boycott" that threatened to ruin the Games. Peter Ueberroth, who organized the 1984 Olympics, remembers his profound relief when, in the middle of the night, he received a phone call from Beijing informing him that China would be breaking with the Soviets and coming to Los Angeles. "China really saved the Olympics," Ueberroth says. "Once Beijing said no to Moscow, only six countries ended up supporting the boycott."

Nevertheless, on the eve of China's coming-out party, national pride wasn't the only sentiment coursing through the Middle Kingdom. Fear of humiliation—the flip side of the face—was equally powerful. China seemed to teeter perpetually between a ferocious, can-do optimism and an age-old inferiority complex. In 1984, as the Chinese athletes traveled to the heart of the decadent West, the worry wasn't simply that mainland China had not participated in the Summer Games in more than three decades or that the country had yet to win an Olympic medal of any color. Security was a concern, too. Two years earlier, a nineteen-year-old female tennis player named Hu Na had defected during a tournament in nearby Santa Cruz, provoking a humiliating row between Beijing and Washington—and making Hu the most famous Chinese athlete in the world. This time, except for a few anxious hours when a busload of Chinese athletes got lost on the L.A. freeways, everybody was kept under tight control. The extra contingent of Chinese security personnel made sure of that.

Nothing, then, could have gratified the insecure nation more than the final tally in Los Angeles: fifteen gold medals (thirty-two overall), zero defections, and a cuddly reception from the rest of the world. When the Chinese delegation of 224 athletes entered the L.A. Coliseum during the opening ceremonies, the largely American crowd erupted into a spontaneous and spine-tingling standing ovation. China surely got a medals boost from the absence of the Soviet bloc countries. But once a pistol-shooter named Xu Haifeng won China's first Olympic event on the first day of the Games, all that mattered—and glittered—was gold. China's lithe young divers ended the sixty-year reign of the North Americans. Chinese fencers, weightlifters, and high jumpers parried, heaved, and leaped for gold. And when the beloved women's volleyball team won the gold-medal game over the U.S. team—a contest whose live broadcast brought offices and factories to a halt all over China—fireworks erupted over Beijing. After nearly three decades in darkness, the Middle Kingdom had finally emerged to give the world a glimpse of its awesome potential.

The celebratory fireworks of Olympic glory were a lifetime away for Wang Weijun. For the fifty-eight-year-old basketball coach, who was sitting next to a court behind Beijing's Workers' Stadium on a cold, blustery day in the winter of 2003, the only spot of color came from the shower of golden sycamore leaves twirling down around him. Hands shoved deep into his parka, Wang impassively watched a group of youngsters running up and down the court. The coach had once been a standout on the Beijing men's team, a lumbering 6'5" left-hander whose shot blocking and mid-range shooting were appreciated by a generation of fans. Ever since his retirement in 1976, though, Wang had been stuck in his assigned job on the bottom rung of China's massive sports system. Sports propaganda has it that such a job is an honor, the first step in bringing athletic glory to the motherland, but at this level, it's often easier to feel like an inmate instead of a coach. Wang had spent nearly half his life at the Beijing Workers' Stadium Spare-Time Sports School. Ten thousand days with no parole.

The school hadn't changed much over the previous quarter-century. The basketball courts were made of hard-packed dirt, with all traces of the chalk lines long since rubbed out. The whitewashed wooden backboards were peeling badly, and the ragged nets clung forlornly to the rims by a few strands of thread. Coach Wang was not in much better shape. Lanky and square-shouldered, with the beginnings of a paunch, he wore dark sweatpants and white athletic shoes, his hair regimented into the same kind of crew cut he had during his playing days. The only time he moved on this day, though, was to take a swig from a jar of ocher-colored tea. Even when an errant ball careened in his direction, Wang let it roll past, his hands like lead stones in his pockets.

In the old days, with Deng's exhortations still ringing in his ears, Coach Wang lavished attention on the earnest youngsters who arrived for practice, pushing them hard in the vain hope that they would become stars on the national team. Only once did his dream come true, only once did a student absorb his knowledge of the subtle symmetries of the game and turn it into something sublime and glorious. But that dream was gone. Wang's wisdom and experience had meant something back then, but what did it matter now? The intricacies of basketball were lost on the group of youngsters out on the court that day. None of the boys, ranging in age from ten to fifteen, showed any glimmer of real talent, and they seemed more interested in mimicking the ball-hogging antics they'd seen on NBA videos than in learning the mechanics of a perfect pick-and-roll. So Wang just let them play.

The slate-gray Beijing sky had turned almost black by the time Wang trudged back across the street toward his office. Keeping his head down, he didn't bother to acknowledge the uniformed guards standing at attention in front of the stadium gate. Perhaps it was because the ruddy-cheeked soldiers reminded him too much of his only son, a young man who had spent more than a decade in the People's Liberation Army. The coach used to bring his boy to these same dirt courts years ago, training him with a group of older kids until darkness shrouded the basket. A sprouting left-hander with an uncanny shooting touch, Wang's son rose higher than any other basketball player in the school's history and, for a time, in Chinese history. The boy, Wang Zhizhi, was the one shining success who helped his father transcend a life of monotony and mediocrity.

It might have been easier if Coach Wang could have banished all thoughts of his son, just as the top leaders of Chinese basketball had tried to do. But that wasn't possible, not for a father whose own impoverished background had made his son's future seem so bright, and not here, on the same muddy path to his office where his son had first learned to dribble a basketball. Here, Wang Zhizhi was never far away, even though he had left long ago. For the previous eighteen months, the coach's son had been halfway around the world, locked in a struggle with the Chinese government that threatened to prevent him from ever returning home again. Hailed as a hero for years, his son had now been branded a traitor: kicked off the national team, vilified in the local press, expunged from the history books. His picture had once graced the entrance to the Chinese Basketball Association headquarters, but it had been removed, and his image was nowhere to be seen around the city. Even his name had become taboo. China officials didn't like to be reminded of the boy who had brought them the ultimate loss of face.

From the moment Wang Zhizhi was born on July 8, 1977, he seemed destined to fulfill the dream of both his father and his country. Like Yao Ming, who would arrive three years later, Wang had the genes to become a basketball star: his mother, the 6'2" Ren Huanzhen, had been the tallest player on the Beijing women's team and his father had been among the tallest on the Beijing men's team. The young family lived in a small apartment in the Beijing sports compound, and Wang grew up tagging along behind his father and mother, inevitably picking up the game of basketball along with some of their personality traits: a cowering, if begrudging, respect for authorities, a streak of stubborn self-reliance, and a sizable chip on the shoulder. When Coach Wang first brought his son to the sports school, the eight-year-old was the youngest and skinniest kid in class. But he was taller than most of the older boys, and he possessed a rare combination of agility, dexterity, and speed. The boy ran with such effortless grace that he earned a nickname: "Zhuifeng Xiaonian," "Young Wind-chaser." It wouldn't be long, however, before everyone just called him Big Zhi, or Da Zhi (pronounced "Dodger").

Like many coaches whose sons surpass them in talent, Wang Weijun was eager to turn Da Zhi into a star. His boy, however, seemed more interested in other kinds of stars at first. Fascinated by the constellations, which he could see only rarely through Beijing's industrial haze, he dreamed of becoming an astronomer. Da Zhi enjoyed playing basketball—it all seemed to come easily for him—but he despised the regimentation of training. "I used to throw tantrums," he says, recalling how much he resented being forced to go to weekend practices. "I put up a lot of resistance because practice was at the same time as the popular television show 'The Transformers.' All of my friends got to watch the show every Saturday, but I had to go to practice."

The sacrifice would pay off, however, and soon Da Zhi himself was stealing the show. His parents, desperate to give him the education that they never had, enrolled him in a middle school with a strong after-school basketball program, hauling him to the sports school only on weekends. By 1988, the lanky eleven-year-old, who already measured 6'3", was easily overwhelming the grade-school competition. He dominated a citywide elementary-school tournament called the Empower China Games, earning a spot on the competition's all-star team. Beijing officials had already heard the constant murmurs about Wang Weijun's son. But now they sensed he was truly special—the kind of prodigy who, given the right training and motivation, might become one of the best in the land. In the frenzied sports buildup that accompanied China's return to the Olympics, some officials even believed that Da Zhi could be the one to embody China's rise on the international stage.

On that winter day in 2003, however, only one place in China recognized the result of those great expectations: Wang Weijun's bare office. A single neon tube hanging from the ceiling illuminated the musty room, revealing deep cracks on the cement floor and a pair of athletic socks hanging over the railing of the metal bunk bed in the corner. The only splash of color came from the walls, which were covered with photos and posters. Da Zhi was everywhere. There he was behind a smudgy glass display case, a fourteen-year-old string bean in a red uniform, smiling as he held a trophy aloft. There he was above the coach's sagging desk, a twenty-three-year-old star—now at his full height of 7'1"— standing proudly in his Chinese uniform in a 2000 Olympic team photo. And there he was again in a framed copy of a 2001 *Newsweek* spread heralding his debut as the first Chinese player in the NBA. Looming large over a typical American subdivision, the twenty-four-year-old Da Zhi stood under a headline that asked, GREAT LEAP FORWARD?

It is, of course, only natural for proud parents to decorate their offices with pictures of their children. But Wang's display exuded a deep sense of melancholy, as if it were a traditional Chinese shrine to commemorate the dead. The stalwart coach didn't tend to indulge in sentimentality, but the pictures were an unapologetic tribute to his missing son—a reminder of the old days, the days before his boy went AWOL.

The vendors at the outdoor food market on Shanghai's Wukang Road knew the woman well. Nearly every evening at dusk, she would appear before them—a tall, elegant figure in worn clothes, quietly bargaining for day-old cuts of pork or surplus rations of rice. The shopkeepers could remember watching the rosy-cheeked former captain of the women's national basketball team during her playing days, a star known as much for her revolutionary purity as for her aggressive play. It was 1984 now, nearly a decade later, and Da Fang was scrounging for food to feed her family. Life was tough for everybody, but the vendors knew that, back home, Da Fang and her husband were struggling to raise a boy who was growing so fast they could hardly afford to feed him. Yao Ming was only four years old, but he was already well over four feet tall and a whopping sixty pounds—big enough, in China, to be charged adult prices on the bus and at the barber shop. Everybody called him "Xiao Juren"—"Little Giant."

Da Fang would ride her bicycle home through a city shrouded in darkness. Old sycamore trees formed a cathedral-like canopy over the streets of her neighborhood, blocking out the last glimmers of afternoon light. Shanghai, the once and future engine of China's economy, was still stuck in a deep depression, an economic torpor made all the more apparent by the frenzy of activity starting to transform the southern provinces of Guangdong and Fujian. Deng's reforms had not yet reached Shanghai, a lingering punishment for being a bastion of vice and materialism before the revolution. It was hard for anyone—least of all Da Fang—to imagine the magnitude of the economic boom that would one day be unleashed in the once-mighty city. At the time, the streets of the crumbling French Concession were filled with the stench of raw sewage and piles of uncollected melon rinds. There were few cars, just masses of bicycles and pedestrians, and no streetlights, only a dim yellow glow emanating from the houses set back from the street. When these stately colonial mansions had been built in the 1920s and '30s, they were designed for a single foreign family; now five or six extended Chinese families were crammed into the decrepit structures, one household per room, laundry billowing outside of every window like so many hostages signaling their surrender.

The high walls of Shanghai's leadership compound stood just a block away from Yao Ming's childhood home on Kangping Road. Young soldiers guarded the gate, scolding passersby who dared to slow down for a longer-than-usual glance into the hidden precinct of the Communist Party leaders. A decade earlier, Da Fang might have had access to that rarefied world. But now, skulking home in the dark, she was just a shadow of her former self. Her family's apartment in the sports compound at No. 95 Kangping Road was better than the first place she and her husband had been assigned when they got married, but the conditions in Apartment 602 were still Spartan: The two small rooms had little furniture save for a table and two oversize beds. Like most Chinese apartments at the time, it had no kitchen, no toilet, no appliances—and, oddly, no door frames. "We removed the air vents above our doors," says Yao's father, Yao Zhiyuan "so we wouldn't bump our heads."

Feeding and clothing their growing son was a daily challenge. Da Yao got paid poorly at his job at the Shanghai port, and Da Fang—still doing clerical work at the sports-science library—received only around forty yuan a month, worth about seventeen dollars at the time, or barely half of what many of her colleagues made. Da Fang was so embarrassed by her paltry salary that she used to tell people she made sixty yuan, giving herself an imaginary 50 percent raise to save face. The couple could have used the extra money. Their boy was growing so fast that his trousers were always too short, his shoes too small. Da Fang and Da Yao were forced to wear the same faded clothes day after day, patching holes when the threads wore through.

With Yao eating nearly twice the amount of an average Chinese child, the family's supplies of milk, meat, and rice always seemed to be running out. Nearly everything in China was still sharply rationed in the early 1980s—food, cloth, soap, coal—and the ration coupons provided too little to feed the family of giants. Da Fang and Da Yao spent nearly their entire salary on food, and yet they often sat at the table watching their son gobble down his food while they themselves went hungry. When Da Fang's elderly father moved in with them after the death of her mother, the family's meager budget was stretched even further. Lu Bin remembers visiting her former Shanghai teammate one evening during this time. "It was a special occasion because Da Fang had bought this nice fish at the market," Lu recalls. "She gave the best middle part to Yao Ming, the head to her father, and the tail to her husband. There was nothing left for her."

Many years later, Da Fang would dutifully credit the government's policies for her son's stunning growth. "It's in his genes that he grew so tall," she said, "and because of China's one-child policy, he has had better nutrition than we had during our era." At the time, however, Da Fang was constantly anxious about where her son's next meal would come from—and how long the family could make ends meet. Yao Ming often felt weak and sick as a child, as though his growing body was constantly short of fuel. Da Fang was too proud to ask for help herself, but several of her friends pleaded with Shanghai officials on her behalf. "A lot of us went to the sports commission and told them Da Fang needed help giving proper nourishment to Yao Ming," says Lu. The officials all knew about Yao's case, she said, "but they never did anything." In other cities, the governments gave families with tall children extra rations of food and milk. A few years later, the Shanghai municipal government would even create a loophole in the one-child policy that allowed families to have more children—and financial assistance—if the father stood over 1.93 meters (6'4") and the mother measured more than 1.8 meters (5'11"). But in the mid-1980s, Zhu Yong was still on the scene, and "Operation Yao Ming" would be put on hold.

In the meantime, the family came to rely on the kindness of others. For stretches, Yao Ming stayed with his father's parents nearby, where he could get constant babysitting—and more food. One time, Da Yao struck up a conversation on a train with a man who worked in a Shanghai milk factory. When Da Yao mentioned that the family's milk-ration card only gave them about half of what they needed to fuel their growing boy, the milkman offered to help. For the next several years, he supplied the family with an extra ration card so Yao could get the calcium he needed to grow.

On September 12, 1984—Yao's fourth birthday—a reporter and photographer from the *Xinmin Evening Post,* a Shanghai newspaper, arrived at the family apartment to write a feature story about Yao. Da Fang and Da Yao were considered the tallest couple in China and the journalists wanted a glimpse at the long-awaited product of their union. Infused with an almost mythical sense of destiny, the article described the boy—whom they called "Xiao Pangzi," or "Little Fatty," a complimentary endearment in a land of scarcity—waking up grumpily from a nap and remaining disconsolate until his father handed him a basketball. "Dad, take me to play basketball!" the young Yao cried, and his father obliged. In the picture accompanying the piece, Da Yao is shown playing catch with the smiling four-year-old in the alleyway behind their apartment building.

The legend of Yao Ming would continue to grow along with his body. By age seven, he was already as tall as China's paramount leader—4'11"—towering over the other students at Gao'an Elementary School so much that his teachers said he looked like a "stork among the chickens." Everybody assumed he would become a basketball player, even though the ungainly boy, in a seeming refutation of the rhapsodic newspaper article, showed little interest in or aptitude for the game. One day, at an athletic event, his schoolmates voted to have him represent the class in a free-throw shooting contest. The boys and girls cheered as he walked to the line, but when Yao shot an air ball, his classmates went silent. His humiliation only deepened when the next boy, heaving the ball underhanded, sank the shot. "I lost a lot of face," Yao said, recalling his embarrassment.

Being abnormally tall was a double-edged sword. Yao enjoyed being treated like a grown-up—"I could ride my father's bike in the street and nobody bothered me," he recalls with obvious satisfaction—but his height also drew stares and pointed fingers and, occasionally, clenched fists. One day in primary school, the class troublemaker began punching Yao, testing himself against the biggest kid in school. Gentle and shy like his father, Yao just stood there, refusing to retaliate. Frustrated, the miscreant ran to Yao's parents and told them their son was a bully, and they believed him. "Because Yao Ming was so tall, we figured it had to be our son who had abused the other kid," recalled Da Fang. "We criticized him harshly after he came back home and asked him to apologize to that kid." When they found out the truth, Da Fang learned something about her son's character. "Everybody who knew Yao Ming would tell me the same thing: 'Your son is too pure and honest. People will take advantange of him when he grows up.'"

Da Fang dedicated herself to becoming her son's main protector, a role she would play with increasing ferocity as the years went by. But what power did one woman have against the call of the motherland? Yao Ming was already 5'7" at age eight, and his potential as a basketball player was literally too big for anyone to ignore. By 1988, Zhu Yong had retired from the sports commission—and two of Da Fang's old friends from No. 651 Nanjing Road began vying for the honor of having Yao Ming enroll in their respective sports schools. Lu Bin, her former teammate, was now a coach at the Luwan District Sports School. But she didn't stand much of a chance against Xu Weili, the top Communist Party official at the Xuhui District Spare-Time Sports School for children.

The gregarious 5'11" daughter of Shanghai's former urban-construction chief, Xu had known Da Fang ever since the gawky teenager arrived at the Nanjing Road sporting grounds two decades earlier. Though separated in age by twelve years, the two women shared both a position (center) and an ideology (far left of center). During the Cultural Revolution, Xu helped organize Maoist study meetings and guard the jail cells holding the sports leaders at No. 651 Nanjing Road before her "black" family background landed her in a Shanghai shipbuilding factory for seven years. Rehabilitated at the end of the Cultural Revolution, she was given her plum post at Xuhui, and like sports officials all over China, she was soon under pressure to turn it into a breeding ground for champions. So she set her eyes on Yao Ming.

It would not be easy to pry the boy away from his parents, who envisioned a very different life for their only son. But Xu visited the family's apartment frequently to discuss his future. The hunch-shouldered Communist Party secretary gently reminded the parents that their son's special talents—in this case, his prodigious height and his basketball genes—belonged to the nation. He could train part-time at first, Xu said, bicycling over to the Xuhui school after his regular morning classes were finished. Since both Da Fang and Da Yao worked all day, Xu would even send the coach over to the school to escort him to practice, a service she offered no other athlete.

Yao's parents eventually acquiesced, recognizing that it was their duty—even their destiny—to relinquish their only child to the sports machine. But Da Fang, the erstwhile Communist radical, still felt a shudder of regret. Years later, she would talk about the intense pressure they felt to let their son go. "We didn't choose this career for him," she says. "But we were basketball players. All of our old colleagues and coaches had their eyes on Yao Ming since he was young. He was projected to be so tall, and the sports school wanted him so much."

The secret rendezvous was set to take place one fall day in 1991 far from the Beijing sports compound where Wang Weijun lived with his family. Coach Wang and his wife, Ren Huanzhen, did not tell anybody where they were going, not even their fourteen-year-old son, Wang Zhizhi, whose future hinged on the outcome of the meeting. The family's neighbors—all coaches, colleagues, and former teammates from the Beijing team—wouldn't understand, and they certainly wouldn't approve. They might even try to stop the couple from moving ahead. Loyalty runs deep in China, and simply agreeing to talk to the man from the army could be construed as an act of betrayal.

That day, Coach Wang and his wife quietly rode their bicycles out the front gate of the sports compound and, passing the Temple of Heaven, set off across Beijing. The capital sprawled in every direction, wrapped in a thick gray haze that covered the trees with a fine layer of dust, making the sun, even at midday, little more than a pale orange disk in the sky. The broad sweeping boulevards leading to the center of Beijing are, by design, built on a monumental scale that is meant to make the masses (and, no less importantly, visiting foreign dignitaries) feel tiny and insignificant before the awesome power of the Chinese state. On this day, however, Wang and his wife had reason not to feel completely powerless. So few things had been under their control in their lives that the choice they were now being offered seemed like a light in the darkness, a flicker of freedom.

Then why did it seem like treachery, too?

For more than two decades, Wang and Ren had been loyal members of the Beijing team. The city basketball team was still Ren's official work unit; it controlled the couple's income, housing, and food—and now, it seemed, the future of their only son. A few years earlier, Beijing sports officials had registered the young prodigy on their so-called "emphasized list," making him, according to the rules of Chinese basketball, strictly off limits to any other team. Da Zhi, barely fourteen but already an incredible 6'9", was the best young prospect in the country, perhaps the best in Chinese history. Now, it seemed, he was locked in as Beijing's property for life.

The man who met with Wang and his wife that day wanted to pick that lock, and his organization alone had the power to do so. Though dressed in civilian clothes, he represented the strongest and most respected institution in China, the People's Liberation Army. He was a veteran coach with the PLA's legendary August 1 basketball team, named for the date when the Communist army was founded in 1927. The squad, a descendant of the original Red Army team formed in the mountains of Yan'an in the 1930s, won the national championship almost every year. For decades, the PLA had formed twenty full-time basketball teams around the country, from the No. 2 Missile Corps team to the Vanguard Police team, and Bayi—as the August 1 team was known in Mandarin—was the jewel in the crown, the pinnacle for any player in China. The squad was so dominant, in fact, that two-thirds of the Chinese national team came from its ranks. One privilege, above all, had given Bayi (pronounced bah-ee) its edge: It had carte blanche to recruit the best players around the nation, regardless of their prior commitments to local or provincial teams.

Ever since the 1949 revolution, the PLA had polished its reputation by excelling in nearly every form of sport and entertainment, from diving and gymnastics to ballet and Peking opera. But in 1991, the Cold War was ending, the Soviet Union was collapsing, and China was entering its second decade of economic reform. To prepare for this kinder, gentler era, the government was cutting the ranks of the PLA from four million to 2.5 million and dismantling most of its sports programs. Bayi's basketball team, which had, for the first time, lost three straight national championships, was one of the few that was spared—the last pillar of a crumbling sports empire.

The PLA's problem was that it no longer had a monopoly on talent. The provincial teams, once considered mere holding bins for Bayi to plunder freely, were starting to draw athletic talent away from the army. China's revved-up economy gave cities and provinces increasing financial clout and political power, and the Beijing team—taken over in 1989 by Beijing Steel, a state-owned conglomerate, in the first sign of the sport's commercialization—was emerging as one of Bayi's strongest competitors.

During the secret meeting in Beijing, the old army coach tried to sell Wang's parents on the benefits of Bayi basketball. The Beijing team, he pointed out, already had two established big men in Mengke Bateer and the veteran 7'1" center Shan Tao. Bayi was a superior team, but it lacked a dominating center—and Da Zhi could quickly fill that role. Being a starter on Bayi would then almost guarantee him a spot on the Chinese national team. Best of all, he would become a soldier in the most powerful and prestigious force in China, the PLA. As the meeting drew to a close, the army coach unveiled a scheme to set Da Zhi loose from the Beijing team. It sounded less like *Hoosiers* than *Mission: Impossible,* because it entailed risk and intrigue and certain controversy. Would his parents accept the plan? The choice, for the first time in their lives, was theirs.

The plot sounded alluring. Like many poor Chinese of their generation, Wang and Ren had been inculcated to admire the PLA. At that time, in 1991, two years after the army's massacre of protesters around Tiananmen Square, most Chinese still viewed the army as the great liberator of China and a vital stabilizing force in society. (Even today, propaganda posters along the most modern boulevards in Shanghai and Beijing rhapsodize about how "The Army and The People Are One Family.") Having a son join the military, not to mention the nation's premier basketball team, would bring honor to any Chinese family. "For a long time, it was everybody's highest aspiration to join the army," says Xu Jicheng, the television commentator and former army player. "It was a lifetime guarantee. Being a member of the army automatically gave you political and economic standing. Even after you left the army, the veteran's department would help you find a good job, a home, even a wife." Xia Song, a basketball entrepreneur with close ties to the army, puts it even more bluntly: "If you can represent the PLA and wear a Bayi uniform, you are an automatic hero."

Ren and Wang craved nothing more than respect. Ever since Ren had first arrived in Beijing from the backwater of rural Shanxi Province, many in the capital's sports community looked down on her and her family, ridiculing her lack of formal schooling and social graces. Ren's resentment of the Beijing authorities could be measured in the steady accumulation of indignities. By the time Da Zhi was twelve years old, for example, his 6'4" frame had outgrown the small cot in their apartment. One of the family's neighbors, former national-team star Zhang Weiping, had already received a longer bed from the Beijing sports commission. But when Wang's parents requested the same for their son, they were denied. "I know they felt slighted by that," says Zhang. Over the next two years, Da Zhi would have to sleep with his feet hanging farther and farther off the end of the bed.

Then there were the shoes. Da Zhi's feet grew so quickly that he constantly bust out of his canvas sneakers. One time, at age twelve, he was forced to sit on the sidelines for days, unable to play in games until he could find some new size-eleven shoes. Such a large size was (and continues to be) hard to find in China, and his family had neither the cash nor the access to acquire a new pair. The Beijing team didn't offer any help.

In desperation, Wang's mother turned to her old teammate Liu Yumin, with whom she had shared a peasant's hut during their forced stints of "reeducation through labor." Although their lives couldn't have turned out more differently—Liu became a top official, Wang's mother a lowly gatekeeper—their friendship endured. Madame Liu, as she was now known, said she would try to find a pair of shoes. When she appeared the next day with a sleek pair of size-eleven Tiger-brand shoes, Ren was overwhelmed by emotion. "I brought down the shoes and she just burst into tears," recalls Liu.

At the root of Ren's frustration was her menial job, to which she had been confined since retiring from the game fifteen years before. Most of her teammates on the city and national teams had become coaches, journalists, or even, like Liu, high-level bureaucrats. But Beijing officials assigned Ren to work at the gate of the city sports compound, where she sat in an unheated room checking identification papers and making visitors sign the guest log. It was a demeaning job, and the salary was abysmal. Officials attributed her low position to her lack of education, failing to appreciate the irony that Ren hadn't finished primary school precisely because she had been recruited into the sports system in her early teens. "Her job was the worst of all the retired basketball players," says one former colleague. "It wasn't fair the way they treated her. She was a member of the national team, a standout on the Beijing team. But she was too reticent to complain. It wasn't in her nature to go up to the leader and talk freely and say, 'Hey, why don't you give me a better job?'"

So Ren sat in her booth, suffering in silence.

But now, almost miraculously, she was being offered a chance to stand up for herself—and her family. It was a momentous decision. Letting Bayi take her son would surely provoke the wrath of the Beijing authorities, sinking any hopes she and her husband had of getting better jobs or salaries. It would also signal the end of their son's childhood, for the fourteen-year-old would suddenly become a full-time professional basketball player. Once Da Zhi left, they would only see him a few times a year, if that, for the rest of his career. Still, the Bayi coaches had offered a tantalizing vision of her son's future: He could become a prestigious PLA soldier, a player on the powerful Bayi team, and a member of the Chinese Olympic team.

Ren returned from the clandestine meeting nervous and excited. When she got home, she called on her friend Madame Liu, the one authority she could confide in about such a sensitive matter.

"Bayi's chasing after my son," Ren said.

"Really?" said Liu, taken by surprise.

"Yes, tell me what you think I should do."

"Well, what do you want to do?" Liu said.

"I want my boy to go to Bayi."

Madame Liu paused, unsure of how to respond. She was speaking to Ren as a friend, but as a top national official (the authority to whom the Beijing team reported) she was also duty bound to follow the rules. If Liu encouraged the Bayi plot, she would be in flagrant violation of the sports regulations. If she discouraged it, she could be hurting her friend and possibly harming the future of the boy she considered her godson.

"Don't worry," Madame Liu said, choosing her words carefully. "No matter which team Da Zhi ends up joining, he will be a star in the service of the motherland."

The reassuring words were apparently all Ren needed to set the plan in motion one evening in December 1991. The operation would have to happen at night, because if the Beijing authorities caught wind of the plan, they would surely do everything in their power to stop it. Ren and Wang knew that they would face punishment in any case, but they feared that if this opportunity were foiled, their son might never have another chance to join Bayi.

It was midnight when the unmarked army van eased to a stop across from the side gate of the Beijing sports compound, paralleling the canal that marked the southern edge of the Temple of Heaven. The vehicle's lights cut off, its engine idled. Wang Zhizhi slung a duffel bag over his shoulder, said good-bye to his parents, and strode quickly across the compound toward the gate. This was a rite of passage, and the boy tried to handle it like a man. Somewhere in the cluster of darkened buildings, Beijing's top sports officials were sound asleep, unaware that their prized basketball prospect was being stolen right out from under them. Outside the compound wall, a military man stepped out of the darkness and signaled for Da Zhi to get into the back of the vehicle.

In seconds, the van disappeared into the night.

5

Cogs in the Machine

The boys were mere shadows, darting through the darkness of a cold winter evening in Shanghai. The asphalt basketball court had all but disappeared in the gloom, and the temperature had dropped almost to freezing. But Li Zhangming, barking instructions from the sidelines that day in December 2003, was just getting warmed up. A gruff disciplinarian with thick, arching eyebrows, the forty-four-year-old coach had trained young recruits at Shanghai's Xuhui District Sports School for two decades, including five years teaching the game to a young colt named Yao Ming. Li's daily regimen—a bruising three-hour session modeled on the old Soviet workathons—was not about to change now. The practice would continue into the night, and Li wouldn't let his charges whine about the cold or the darkness or the state of exhaustion toward which he was driving them.

The recruits, all between ages eleven and thirteen, were running a three-on-two fast break drill, a sequence of perpetual motion that constitutes one of the most freewheeling moments in basketball. Anywhere else in the world, boys their age might have been shouting for the ball, cheering a fancy move, or jeering the random air ball. But the young Chinese athletes moved in a joyless silence that shrouded them as completely as the descending nightfall. The only sounds filling the winter air were the thud of basketballs and sneakers pounding the cold asphalt— and the occasional shouted command from the sidelines.

As Coach Li pulled his navy-blue jacket close around his neck, something caught his eye. A long-limbed boy had just clanged a fifteen-foot shot off the rim rather than making the required extra pass to a teammate cutting to the basket. Li blasted his whistle and strode over to the young offender, who bowed his head in anticipation of his punishment.

Earlier in the practice, Li had hurled a ball at a boy for not paying attention, nailing him in the back. Now he stood directly in front of the eleven-year-old, spewing a streak of Shanghainese dialect.

"You can't fool anyone out here!" Li screamed. "How are you going to get any good if you're always taking stupid shots, refusing to pass the ball?"

The boy shifted nervously.

"Use your brain!" Li yelled, leaning closer to the boy's face.

Then in a practiced motion, he rapped the boy hard on the forehead with the knuckle of his index finger.

The other boys didn't react until Li barked out another order. In seconds, they were all in a defensive crouch, zigzagging back and forth toward the opposite end of the court. For the next hour straight, the boys would do nothing but running and jumping drills—wind sprints, frog jumps, shuttle runs. This wasn't punishment per se; this was their normal practice routine, especially in the winter, when the encroaching darkness gave Li few other options. By the end of practice, the boys were bending over at the waist, heaving with exhaustion. Still, nobody complained. No one even said a word.

For all the modern trappings of China today, Confucian hierarchies still prevail in the tradition-bound sports system. From the top of the pyramid (the national teams) to the broad base at the bottom (the 3,500 part-time sports schools training several hundred thousand youngsters), obeisance defines the lives of young athletes. The Xuhui District Sports School may occupy a lowly rung of the system, but even here, the young gymnasts and swimmers and basketball players were taught to see their coaches as a combination of mentor, guardian, and god. Like the several hundred thousand athletes selected for sports schools throughout China, these boys knew they were not here to experience the joy of competition or a passion for the game. Their job was simple: to serve the motherland. Yao Ming's father had learned the same lesson when he trained at Xuhui as a teenager; Yao Ming would learn, too, after arriving in 1989 to start toiling under the vigilant eye of Li Zhangming.

Born on the cusp of China's economic resurgence, Yao Ming was part of the first Chinese generation in forty years that could entertain visions of personal ambition and success. As a child, he fantasized about being an explorer traveling into new worlds rather than retracing the patterns of his parents' old one. "I've always wanted to be an archaeologist, to go looking for adventure everywhere," Yao said, adding ruefully: "It would be hard for me, of course, to crawl in and out of those small caves." It would be even harder, however, to avoid the fate that the Chinese sports authorities had chosen for him years before. Individual desires may have started to mean something in Chinese society—and many of Yao's more conventionally proportioned classmates would choose their own careers—but the sports system allowed no such freedom, especially not for someone destined to be as tall as Yao.

When his parents told him he would have to start basketball training, Yao—not yet nine—didn't utter a word in protest. Ever the obedient child, he agreed to stand outside his primary school, waiting for the man who would control the next five years of his life: Li Zhangming. The floppy-haired coach, then thirty, guided Yao by bicycle through the maze of Shanghai streets to the Xuhui District Sports School, where the boy would train five afternoons a week and on Saturdays. "In the beginning, it was almost like being forced," Yao said later, recalling how he hated basketball with a passion. He would eventually come to criticize the system, saying that "nobody should be forced to play a sport against their will." But at the time, Yao resigned himself to attending practice "purely for my parents, because I respect them so much." He didn't want to make them lose face.

On the first day of practice, Coach Li lined up the recruits to perform a series of frog jumps. As the other boys leaped across the court, Yao bent down into an ungainly crouch, clasping his hands behind his back—and got stuck. He couldn't jump, Li says, because his long, thick legs had no explosive power. That same day, the other boys ran four fast laps around the court. Yao barely loped around the court once before he stopped, gasping for air. "He had no speed or stamina," Li says. "His bones had not developed yet, and his heart was very weak."

Yao's size and clumsiness made him the object of ridicule at first. A group of soccer players at the sports school, led by a pugnacious kid nicknamed "Yellow Hair," picked on him mercilessly. They jumped on his back, mocked his lumbering gait, and raked their knuckles over his flattop head. The bullies also made fun of Yao's physique. With his skeletal torso anchored by thick legs and a protruding posterior, they said, he looked like "a fat penguin."

The teasing embarrassed Yao, but it wasn't nearly as painful as the training itself. Every day, Coach Li made the boys run until they almost collapsed, jump until their legs burned, and shoot baskets until they couldn't lift their arms. With his gangly and uncooperative body, Yao couldn't finish half the exercises, and when he could, he always lagged far behind his more agile teammates. A glance inside the school gymnasium showed that other athletes at the Xuhui school had to endure even more excruciating exercises: the little five-year-old gymnasts sobbing in pain as coaches sat on their legs to force their splits beyond parallel; the tiny, young table-tennis players who had to hit seven hundred shots back and forth in one ten-minute exercise and repeat it ad infinitum the rest of the day; the primary-school weight lifters pushed to clean and jerk more than their own body weight. Every young athlete trudged through practice bordering on exhaustion, keenly aware that they were being trained to become cogs in the machine.

Yao and his teammates quickly learned how to "eat bitterness" without complaint. But what often seemed harder to take than the physical pain was the sheer, numbing boredom of it all. The entire sports system was predicated on repetitive training, a process that the writer Zhao Yu likened to "trying to create a tiger by copying the drawing of a cat." Like nearly every sports coach in China, Li Zhangming marched his young charges through almost the same set of rudimentary drills every day, all year long: stretching, running, shooting, dribbling, fast breaks, jumping, running again. There was no differentiation based on one's size or position or skills; everybody did the same thing. Performing the same exercises over and over again every day was not only deathly boring and, in some cases, counterproductive (team sports like basketball, after all, require much more than the simple repetition of movements), but it also drained youngsters of motivation. Yao reflected on this after he had left the sports schools. "Unlike American coaches, who encourage you to do things because you want to do them, Chinese coaches force you" to do endless drills, he said. "Then you have no interest in doing anything yourself."

It would take nearly a decade before Yao started taking a genuine interest in basketball, an evolution that came about not because of his coaches, but in spite of them.

Back in the 1960s and 1970s, when China was governed by the cult of Mao and the culture of the iron rice bowl, motivating athletes was a relatively simple proposition. Da Fang and her old teammates, for the most part, felt genuinely inspired by "revolutionary spirit," and anybody not moved by Maoist ideals was wise to at least feign enthusiasm, lest they end up on the wrong side of history. By the time Yao Ming started training a generation later, that spirit had dissipated. Communism had lost much of its meaning in China's headlong rush to the market, and the two new "isms" rising to take its place as the motivating forces in Chinese society—nationalism and materialism—seemed far away from the life of a young basketball recruit.

In the aftermath of the June 1989 massacre near Tiananmen Square, as much of the world excoriated the bloody crackdown on students and workers, China's shaken leaders responded by pumping up their nationalist rhetoric. With Communism dead—and the chaos of democracy raising its ugly head—the leadership had little alternative but to cultivate national pride as a way to hold the country together during its rapid, turbulent transformation. Under the slogan "Renewing China," Beijing launched a campaign of patriotic education that focused on the country's humiliating past and lashed out at the licentiousness of American culture, the supposed instigator of the Tiananmen protests. The irony, of course, was that the intense patriotism that emerged ran counter to the nation's growing infatuation with all things American, from KFC to the NBA.

Sports would play a special role in the patriotic revival. For Deng and his aging colleagues, international athletic success—such as the deluge of gold medals in the 1990 Asian Games—would not only help soothe an unsettled society with the salve of nationalist pride. It could also go a long way to help rehabilitate the country's tattered image overseas. From the top of the sports pyramid down to the lowliest schools, patriotic education became intense. Yao and his teammates received *aiguo*, or "love-country," lectures several times a week. Around the country, athletes would regularly march in formation while shouting nationalist slogans that seemed to have little to do with sports. "Carry out the Four Modernizations!" they yelled. "Defend the Nation!"

As a motivating factor, however, patriotism wouldn't prove as powerful as the desire to get gloriously rich. By 1990, China's booming economy was starting to make some businessmen and entrepreneurs fabulously wealthy, and they were revered by many as the role models of a new era. But the prospect of a basketball player earning a decent living, much less deciding his own fate, seemed impossibly remote. Deng Xiaoping's "Gold-Medal Strategy" had brought cash incentives into the old socialist sports system, but they were doled out to individuals who won Olympic gold medals, such as divers, gymnasts, pistol-shooters, even kayakers. The basketball teams didn't stand a chance of winning an Olympic medal, and the sport was neglected. Budgets were slashed, provincial teams were disbanded, and the remaining professional players who still had a team earned only a few hundred dollars a year.

Yao's parents didn't have much hope that their son could make a decent living playing basketball, but once they had relinquished him to the sports school, they wanted to encourage him to do the best he could.

When Yao came home from practice utterly demoralized and wanting to quit, his father took him behind their apartment building to shoot baskets on the iron hoop hanging above the bicycle garage. They didn't play H-O-R-S-E or 21, like fathers and sons across the United States. Their game was simpler. For every basket Yao made, his father promised to buy him little gifts—a small-scale version of the "Gold-Medal Strategy." "My father bribed me into playing!" Yao recalled with mock incredulity.

His mother tried a different tack. One day when Yao was nine, Da Fang snared a pair of tickets to see a visiting team from America billing itself as the Harlem Globetrotters. Never before had they seen basketball played with such joy. The court had the same dimensions as always, but these visitors—almost all African-American—made the sport seem exhilarating and alive. One player spun the ball on his finger, then knocked it to a cutting teammate for a flamboyant slam dunk, a move rarely seen in the land of the dainty layup. The crowd roared with delight. "I think that experience had a strong influence on Yao Ming," Da Fang said. "They turned basketball into a great show, a form of entertainment."

The game may have lifted Yao's spirits, but it couldn't hide the grim reality that he had to return to training sessions with all the fun of boot camp. "Yao Ming didn't want to be here," recalled Coach Li, "but he was obedient and always did what he was told."

Yet even the most dutiful child occasionally feels the lure of rebellion. One day, when Yao was still training part-time at Xuhui, his primary school organized an afternoon outing to the Shanghai Children's Palace, a special state-run venue for after-school entertainment. All of Yao's classmates were going, and his teachers invited him to join the fun. The Children's Palace wasn't far away, so Yao decided to play hooky for an hour or two before heading to practice. But that day, his mother paid a visit to the sports school. When she arrived, Da Fang scanned the dirt courts for her son and then marched up to Xu Weili.

"Where's Yao Ming?" she asked.

"I don't know, I haven't seen him," said Xu.

"Well, aren't you supposed to keep track of him?" Da Fang snapped.

By the time Yao finally arrived, Da Fang was fuming. She understood, of course, that he didn't enjoy practice. But he had disobeyed the school rules and undermined her authority. Da Fang scolded her son sharply in front of the coaches and young players. Then, as the court descended into an uncomfortable silence, she slapped him hard across the face. It was a startling glimpse of the fury that had first emerged during the Cultural Revolution—and the rigid sense of discipline that would govern Yao's life.

When practice resumed, Xu pulled her old friend aside.

"You shouldn't hit your son in front of everybody," Xu said. "You have to give him some face in front of all of his teammates."

Da Fang was silent.

"Yao Ming is just a kid, and kids like to play," Xu continued. "Just once, he goes out to play with his classmates, that's no big deal. It's normal. You don't have to be so strict all the time."

Da Fang didn't back down. "There is a time for class, a time for practice, and a time for fun," she said. "Yao Ming needs to take this seriously. He can't just have fun whenever he wants. And besides, I take him out to the park almost every Sunday."

"Yes, I know," Xu responded. "But has it occurred to you that sometimes he just wants to be with his friends?"

Reflecting later on the incident, Xu reached a conclusion about Da Fang. "She put too many of her hopes on her son." But Da Fang was hardly the only one. Xu had also staked her hopes on young Yao Ming. And soon, so would the entire nation.

The most tragic aspect of China's closed sports system is not the cruelty of the workouts or the resistance to the changes sweeping the rest of Chinese society. It is the fate of the hundreds of thousands of young athletes who don't quite succeed. "Only one in a billion is like Yao Ming," says Wang Qimin, a veteran basketball coach at the Xuhui school. "Most of the rest are left in limbo. They can't make it to the top level, but they aren't let go, either."

During the time that Yao Ming trained at the Xuhui school, one of the best young players in his class was a boy named Li Jun. Unlike Yao, Li was happy to be playing ball. "I always wanted to be the best at something," says Li, the son of a 6'2" deliveryman whose own hoop dreams were cut short during the Cultural Revolution. Li's mother, a textile-factory worker, hoped that sports training would help her hyperactive son let off steam—and, if the coaches' assessments were right, become an athletic hero.

As Yao loped around the court, struggling to find his bearings and catch his breath, the lightning-fast Li mastered the fundamentals of the game. A favorite of Coach Li's, he was one of the few players at Xuhui who seemed to have a chance of reaching the top levels of Chinese basketball. Yao's only talent, at that point, was his size. Li Jun, on the other hand, could dribble through a crowd of defenders, drive the length of the court, and pull up for a soft mid-range jumper—and he seemed to have the energy to do it all day.

After four years of training side by side with Yao, Li joined the Shanghai city sports school and then, at age seventeen, the Shanghai junior team. He played well for a couple of years, eventually earning a starting spot. But his growth topped out at 6'3" (instead of a projected 6'6"), and his slender frame started to break down. Shin splints, sprained ankles, chronic backaches—all the result, he thinks now, of overtraining. Li kept playing through the pain, because that's what Chinese athletes are expected to do. But in 2001, just as he was trying to make the jump to the senior team, he suffered the final blow: an excruciating back injury that took him out of the game for good.

His options now are severely limited, he says, because he missed out on getting a proper education. From the time Li started athletic training, he took a succession of dumbed-down classes in the sports schools that focused less on traditional academic fare and more on the political ideology designed to mold athletes to the nationalist cause. It took nearly two years to complete a normal academic year, and even then, the standards were low. When Li made it to the city's junior team, he was supposed to continue taking classes three times a week at the Shanghai Sports Technology Institute. But after eight hours of practice a day, he—like Yao—was often too tired to go to the evening classes, and few people cared too much if he skipped. "Nobody ever tells athletes how important it is to get a good education," he says. "As long as you can play, it doesn't matter."

Li Jun returned to the Xuhui courts recently to visit his former coach. Standing on the sidelines, he watched silently as Coach Li ran his new charges through the same patterns he had learned by rote a decade before. Li Jun hadn't come to reminisce about his childhood, though; he wanted to talk to his old mentor about finding a job. After spending his youth in the sports system, he now has neither the savvy nor the connections to compete in China's new market economy. The low-level technical degree he was studying for would qualify him for one job: coaching basketball at the sports-school level. Coaching positions, however, are scarce—most coaches at Xuhui have been there for more than fifteen years—and applicants often find that the only spots available are in the desolate Chinese countryside. Even then, the job promises minuscule wages and no real prospect of career advancement. As one coach put it: "Even if I lived a hundred years, I would never be able to be anything but a coach."

When Li Jun was training alongside Yao Ming, he never imagined that this would be his fate. But with his basketball career finished, the best he can hope for now is to end up like old Coach Li, pushing a new generation of kids through the same mind-numbing routine day after day after day.

Failure seemed a very real possibility for Yao Ming. Aside from his spectacular physical growth—by the age of eleven, he was already as tall as his mother (6'2")—he showed little promise on the court. Even after three years of daily training, Yao still dropped easy passes, doubled over in exhaustion after a couple of trips up the floor, and shot with all the touch of a bricklayer. Coach Li eventually helped him develop an accurate set shot—a jump shot was out of the question and, at his height, unnecessary—but his movements remained so sluggish that the coaches worried that he might be suffering from gigantism, an affliction that plagued several of China's tallest players in the 1960s and 1970s.

Da Fang feared for her son's future. Even if Yao suddenly blossomed into a gifted player—if, by some miracle, his mind and muscles caught up with his body—a life in basketball seemed to offer little reward. If China were truly opening up to the world, then Yao needed to prepare to seize the opportunities that would come outside the old socialist sports system. Da Fang's true redemption—her reckoning with the sports establishment that had deprived her of an education and left her living in virtual penury—would be to give her son an education and a chance to lead what she wistfully called "a normal life."

In the name of normality, Da Fang did something quite extraordinary: She made two attempts to rescue her son from the sports system. When Yao was barely ten, she flirted with the idea of sending him to the army team in Beijing, where every Chinese soldier—even a failed basketball player—was assured of a respectable job and a generous pension (and a life far from the grips of the Shanghai authorities, whom Da Fang still distrusted). The Bayi coaches showed interest in Yao, just as they did in Wang Zhizhi. But when Da Fang and her son returned from a surreptitious trip to Beijing to meet with the army coaches, Xu Weili quickly intervened. Yao could not leave Shanghai, the Xuhui school's Communist Party secretary said, because the boy was already on the city's list of "emphasized" athletes, making him the property of the Shanghai sports committee for life. Besides, Da Fang didn't want to further poison her relationship with the Shanghai sports authorities, did she?

Da Fang would have one last chance to pull Yao out of the sports system altogether in 1992, soon after Deng Xiaoping unleashed Shanghai's long-delayed economic revival. With a few encouraging words during his "Southern Tour," the eighty-seven-year-old leader reversed four decades in which Beijing had siphoned off Shanghai's wealth as punishment for being a hotbed of hedonism and capitalism before the revolution. (From 1949 to 1990, more than 84 percent of Shanghai's income was funneled to the central government, buoying the country but leaving the city bereft.) Deng declared that Pudong, the empty swampland across from the city's famous Bund, would become a preferential development zone and that Shanghai would become "the head of the Yangtze dragon." Investment money immediately started pouring into Shanghai—foreign contracts that accounted for $214 million in 1990 would rise to a staggering $5.4 billion by 1995—and young city residents soon began escaping the strictures of the traditional "work units" to become entrepreneurs or employees of high-paying joint ventures. The dream of amassing wealth—or at least of choosing one's own future—wafted through Shanghai again, holding everybody in its thrall.

Even the family of a former Red Guard.

Da Fang had never had control over her own destiny. But now, as a new era was born in China, she became determined to control the fate of her only son. In 1992, when Yao Ming finished sixth grade, Xu Weili put pressure on the family to send him full-time to Xuhui, where rudimentary academics took a backseat to athletic training. But Da Fang was reluctant to consign her son to the harsh discipline of the sporting life and the uncertain future beyond—especially because Yao's schoolwork was already suffering as it was. "His studies were somehow affected by all the basketball training," Da Fang says. "His grades were mediocre, and as his parents, we expected him to gain more in the way of book knowledge."

Da Fang not only rejected Xu Weili's plea to send Yao full-time to the sports school; she pulled him out of Xuhui altogether and enrolled him full-time in a prestigious local middle school known for its academic rigor. The middle school (grades seven to nine) had its own basketball team—which explains why Yao was accepted despite his so-so grades—so her son would still practice in the afternoons, but only after finishing his schoolwork. Xu moved to dissuade her, but it was no use. "Da Fang had already made up her mind," Xu recalls. "She only wanted Yao Ming to study. She didn't care if he played basketball again."

The scheme to pull Yao out of the sports system unraveled in just a few months. Halfway through his first semester, he was floundering in the classroom. His teachers didn't fault his effort or his intelligence. The eleven-year-old loved reading books about foreign lands and China's imperial history. But Yao had started the semester too far behind, and he couldn't keep up with the academic grind. His grades sank to near the bottom of his class.

By the end of the semester, Xu Weili was back. Da Fang had no arguments left. Within a week, she felt compelled to enroll Yao full-time at Xuhui, his experiment with education in the real world a disappointing failure. "Yao loved learning," says one of his close friends in Shanghai. "Leaving school to play basketball was his biggest regret."

Da Fang had to console herself with the hope that basketball could help her son get into a good high school, perhaps even into a university. Under a new government policy, lower-level athletes got an automatic twenty points added to the score of their university entrance exams; the nation's top athletes received an additional two-hundred points, meaning that admittance was almost guaranteed. Da Fang still didn't believe Yao would ever be good enough to make the Shanghai team. In some ways, she hoped he would not. In that case, the sports system might release him when he was still young enough to attend university.

At the Xuhui sports school, Xu Weili tried to make good on her promise to take care of Yao. Children from different grade levels crammed into the classrooms for basic education in the mornings—with Yao, the tallest, always in the back row—but the teachers gave Yao special attention. He returned the favor by cleaning their classrooms and paying them compliments. For the afternoon practices, Xu exempted Yao from carrying any equipment out to the court—balls, backstops, cones—to avoid the risk of a back injury, which had curtailed his mother's career.

Other athletes at the school questioned the fairness of coddling such a mediocre player. "The kids saw Yao Ming getting all this extra care and thought, 'I'm a lot better than him, why shouldn't I be getting that, too?'" says Wang Qimin, the coach. "None of these other kids ever amounted to much, but at least some of us knew that Yao Ming would be something special."

Even at an early age, Yao attracted the attention of the top national sports officials in China. In 1992, the national director of "big-ball" sports—a former national team coach and 1950s-era basketball star named Yang Buyong—came to visit Yao and his mother in Shanghai. A brusque official who carried himself with an air of authority, Yang normally wouldn't interrupt his busy schedule to meet with an eleven-year-old boy. But Xu Weili's reports about Yao's stunning growth had intrigued him, so when he got to Shanghai, he summoned Da Fang and her son to the fancy new Olympic Hotel next to the city stadium. When they arrived, Yang ordered Yao to walk back and forth across the lobby. The blunt Beijing official shook his head disdainfully. Yao's butt was too big, he said, and he looked too clumsy to be an athlete.

Despite his apparent disappointment, Yang says he saw more than a glimmer of possibility in Yao that day. Acceding to Xu's request to assist in Yao's development, Yang decided to increase the Xuhui school's annual budget by 10,000 yuan (about U.S. $1,800 at the time). Yao's parents now say their son never received this money, but coaches and administrators at the school say a portion of the funds went to Yao's care and proper feeding, including a daily lunch stipend of five yuan (about ninety-one cents). It might not sound like a princely sum, but it was more than triple the amount given to most young athletes. Yao's lunch money alone nearly matched his mother's salary and provided him each day with two bottles of milk and as many pieces of meat as he wanted. In a school whose social hierarchy was determined by food, Yao was already on top.

That day in the hotel lobby, however, Yang didn't make Yao feel very special. The gruff national leader quickly dismissed Yao and turned to his mother, abruptly changing the subject. "Da Fang, do you remember Ren Huanzhen, your teammate on the national team?"

"Of course," Da Fang replied.

"Well, she had a son with Wang Weijun, and he is really an extraordinary boy," Yang said. "The boy's name is Wang Zhizhi."

Yao listened intently, absorbing the name for the first time.

Wang was about three years older than Yao Ming, Yang said, but he was already 6'11", and he showed such tremendous talent that he was already on the Bayi junior team. "He's way ahead of Yao Ming in terms of development," Yang said.

Yao's expression didn't change, but inside, he felt a stab of jealousy. "That's when I first set my sights on Wang Zhizhi," he later told the journalist Xu Jicheng. "I wanted to be as good as he was."

Whether Yang had intended to or not, he had lit a competitive fuse in the young player, something that neither financial enticements from Yao's father nor Globetrotter tickets from his mother had been able to do. Yao still didn't have a passion for basketball, but he suddenly had a compelling reason to improve his game: a mysterious boy from the north who was better than he could ever imagine.

Every new recruit in the People's Liberation Army quickly learns to dread the summons, the terse message singling out a soldier for a tongue-lashing from his superiors. So when the request came for Wang Zhizhi to report to his team leader, it was only natural for a little panic to creep in. Not two years had passed since the army men had spirited Wang away from his family in the middle of the night and brought him to this military base on the western outskirts of Beijing. Da Zhi's childhood had ended abruptly that night, and now the sixteen-year-old recruit was trying to prove that he could make the jump from junior high school to the most dominant team in Chinese basketball. His body had cooperated, sprouting several inches—to an astonishing seven feet—without diminishing the speed and dexterity that had first caught the coaches' eyes. But the teenager struggled to adjust to his coaches' authoritarian style—so different from the gentle tutelage of his father—and he feared the punishment meted out to players who showed the slightest hint of laziness or disobedience.

But what had Da Zhi done to deserve the summons today? The ugly custody dispute provoked by his "abduction" that night in 1991 had already been resolved. (Beijing sports leaders had lashed out at Wang's parents and lodged a formal complaint against Bayi for purloining their prized recruit. The quarrel simmered for months before the national basketball administration persuaded Beijing to stand down for the good of the country—and Wang's future.) The summons, then, must have had something to do with Wang's own behavior. Perhaps his coaches felt the stoop-shouldered kid lacked the mettle to become a soldier or the requisite toughness to wear the Bayi uniform. Or maybe he had committed some breach of protocol that had angered the army brass.

Da Zhi had gotten used to the isolated military compound, a walled encampment of gray buildings and sports fields whose dreary physical appearance hardly lived up to its romantic name, Hongshankou, or "Mouth of the Red Mountain." The base still had the mystique of secrecy and power: Some of the country's top military generals were based here, along with the country's most elite military academy, the National Defense University. A sign on the compound's entrance warned: FOREIGNERS' ENTRANCE FORBIDDEN. For Wang, though, Hongshankou's aura also had to do with the athletic excellence it produced. He often walked through the compound with a sense of wonder at the accomplishments of his new comrades. (The Communist salutation "comrade," or *tongzhi*, may have been losing favor in the rest of Chinese society, but it was still a common term in the PLA.) They included world champions and Olympic gold medalists in everything from gymnastics and swimming to table tennis and volleyball—and basketball players were among the most vaunted of them all.

It seemed a lifetime since the days when Da Zhi used to sit in his family's living room making model ships and tanks and pretending to be a soldier. He didn't miss his classes too much—the army was giving him thorough political indoctrination—but he had grown accustomed to biking home from the basketball courts with his father, an hour-long ride that gave them time to chat about life or basketball or the meal his mother was preparing at home. Now he only saw his parents three times a year, and their hours together were so compressed that they barely felt the rhythms of family conversation return before Wang would have to head back to the barracks. His parents were anxious to make everything just like before, but their son was growing up quickly in the long interludes between visits, and a sense of distance grew. As Wang headed back to the military base after these lightning visits, his parents tried to send a reminder of them back with him, plying him with food, new socks, and a few books that he would have little time to read. It took a while before they understood, as Da Zhi already did, that he would never truly be theirs again. The military was their son's only guardian now, and it governed his life with an iron discipline.

The PLA had plucked Da Zhi to play basketball, but like any other army recruit, he first had to go through basic military training: several weeks of boot camp in the boondocks, marching in formation, running in full gear, wriggling through muddy fields under razor wire. The PLA's tallest recruit suffered along with all the other grunts, but there was one activity he excelled in that should have come as no surprise to his army instructors: He could shoot a gun with the same deadly aim as his mid-range jump shot.

For the next several years, Da Zhi and the younger Bayi players would head to the countryside each year for a couple of weeks of military training. The rest of the time, they would don their army uniforms once a week, sometimes less, to march with the regular soldiers. The military training wasn't simply meant to toughen them up. It served to remind them that they were PLA soldiers first—and that athletes had it easy compared to their comrades in the field. The Bayi coaches used this object lesson to push their players to approach every game, every practice, every play with the same spirit of self-sacrifice. If they didn't work that hard, how could they ever earn the right to be called soldiers?

China's sports schools and training centers modeled themselves on the PLA sports machine. But Bayi was the original—and the toughest. In a military camp like Hongshankou, it hardly seemed unusual for players to wake up at 5:30 A.M., run three to five miles, and shoot several hundred jump shots—all before breakfast. Nor did it seem remarkable to have every minute of their lives regimented from reveille to lights-out, from the rushed twenty-minute meal breaks to the endless lectures on patriotism, Communism, and the preeminence of the PLA. This was simply what soldiers did. "Our real advantage was not so much that we had the best players in China, but that we had the strongest spirit," says Fan Bin, a feisty veteran point guard who had fought his way onto the team even after his body had failed to live up to its early promise. (Coaches believed he would reach 6'4", but his body stopped growing at 5'11".) "Other teams also had talented players, too," Fan says, "but nobody could match our grit."

Bayi's training regimen continued every day for the entire year, leavened only by two weeks of competition and one week of vacation. Wang and his fellow recruits lived in a state of permanent exhaustion, but nobody dared to complain. Even back in the dormitories, they watched their words. Like other young recruits, Da Zhi shared a room with a veteran player—his "babysitter"—who was entrusted with teaching him the rules, monitoring his actions and attitudes, and molding him into a soldier-athlete. The center's first two mentors were both over-achieving guards: a balding playmaker from Xinjiang Province named Adi Jiang and Fan Bin. "At Bayi, we are taught to bring a soldier's attitude to everything we do," says Fan, whose use of prescription goggles on court made him look like a World War II bomber heading into battle. "Da Zhi was eager to prove himself. But like everybody else, he was forced to adapt to the rules."

Years later, when asked about how the training at Bayi had shaped him, Wang shrugged a reply: "Round turned into square and square turned into round." Translation: It changed everything.

One of the hardest things for the temperamental teenager was learning stoicism. No matter what the situation—a tense game, a blown call by the ref, a miraculous last-second victory—Bayi players were taught to keep their emotions under wraps. Off the court, Da Zhi tended to oscillate between playfulness and sullenness; but on court, he learned to put on a mask of dull disinterest, making it hard to tell whether he was happy or angry, trying his hardest or just loafing around. The unnerving facade made his most spectacular plays appear even more effortless, but it also made him seem lazy and aloof.

The stoicism went beyond the mere muffling of emotions. Chinese players, especially Bayi's soldier-athletes, were expected to play through physical pain, too. The notion was part of a deeply ingrained idea that nothing—not even a serious injury—should prevent a loyal PLA soldier from making the biggest sacrifice for his team. The most dramatic example involved Liu Yudong, a flattopped 6'8" Bayi forward with a dour demeanor and a warrior mentality. A prodigious scorer, Liu badly injured his knee at the beginning of one season. The Bayi team leaders needed him to bring home another national championship, however, so Liu played the entire season on a busted knee. His bank shot was still pure money and he poured in more than thirty points a game, but Liu hobbled up and down the court in agony. When the season ended—and Bayi had its championship trophy—Liu finally went in for arthroscopic surgery. Ten pieces of broken bone were removed from his shattered knee, and the army doctor held them up as if they were shrapnel pulled out of a wounded war hero. "A normal person wouldn't even be able to walk in such pain," the doctor said. "We can learn an important lesson from such a courageous player."

Da Zhi believed he was being groomed to be a star like Liu Yudong. Nobody talked openly about him being the chosen one; this was still a culture that paid lip service to egalitarianism. But Da Zhi, though as skinny as a pair of chopsticks, was already taller than any other player on the senior team. And everybody knew that the top Bayi coaches were salivating over the prospect of a big man who could run the floor and drain the three-pointer. The last Bayi center to leave his mark on Chinese basketball was Mu Tiezhu, a 7'6" tree trunk so immobile that coaches joked that he spent his entire fifteen-year career planted under the backboard. Bayi's crosstown rival, Beijing, had a couple of bruising centers, including the wide-bodied 6'11" behemoth from Inner Mongolia, Mengke Bateer. But Wang represented a new breed—the agile big man—and Bayi seemed anxious to accelerate his ascent to fill the hole on its team roster. Not long after his sixteenth birthday, in 1993, Wang became the youngest player in army history ever to make the Bayi senior squad.

But if Da Zhi were destined for stardom, why was he summoned by the notoriously prickly team leader? Wang arrived at the administrative building and walked down the corridor to a dimly lit office.

"Comrade Wang, come in," a man's voice called out.

"Team Leader, you wanted to see me?"

"Yes, we've been talking about your situation," the team leader began. "A decision has been made."

Da Zhi took a deep breath, bracing himself for the blow.

"From now on, your birth year will be listed as 1979, not 1977."

Silence.

"It's just an administrative thing, nothing to worry about," the team leader continued. "But if anybody asks, just tell them you were born in 1979, okay?"

"Okay."

Wang didn't know how to respond. He had been expecting some kind of punishment, so he must have been relieved. But this was strange: Somebody had decided to shave two years off his life. Wang had been proud to reach his sixteenth birthday, to finally be on the verge of becoming a man, a soldier. Now, after two years toiling away in Hongshankou, he was being told to go back to the beginning—albeit as a fourteen-year-old with a body that was now nearly seven feet tall.

It would take a while before Wang fully understood the reason for doctoring his age: The leaders wanted to hold him back a couple of years to enhance their chances of winning prestigious junior competitions. When Wang turned twenty, he would still be registered as an eighteen-year-old, and thus eligible to play in most junior championships both at home and abroad. Other Asian countries engaged in the same kind of trickery, but the practice had become (and remains) especially widespread in China, where the inaccessibility of public records helps facilitate the sleight of hand.

There was nothing Da Zhi could do. "In China, you can't control your own destiny," he said later. "Everything is already arranged for you."

In the years that followed, Wang's false age would appear on nearly every public document associated with him: his passport, China's national team rosters, government press releases, official Olympic programs, and newspaper accounts both at home and abroad raving about this prodigy born in 1979. The phony birth date was one of the reasons he started receiving the attention he had always craved—who had ever heard of a slam-dunking fourteen-year-old who could bury the three?—but the deception also made him feel uneasy.

There was one item, however, that bore Wang's true birth date: his official military identification, which he had received upon arriving at Hongshankou. It wasn't clear if Da Zhi's superiors knew he still had this laminated evidence of the deception. But over the years, when he found himself all alone, Da Zhi would sometimes pull the card out and rub his fingers across the smooth face with its PLA insignia. The card was his secret talisman, both a comfort and a reminder of who he really was. He had no idea then that one day this I.D. would also be the key to his escape—not just from the PLA, but from China itself.

6

The Experiment

By the time the men in lab coats arrived at the Xuhui District Sports School, Yao Ming and the other young basketball recruits had already gone down to the gymnasium, a dingy, unheated cavern with a cold draft wafting through a row of broken windows. Bracing themselves for another punishing training session, the boys were relieved when their coach, Li Zhangming, announced that practice had been cancelled. A day off from their grueling regimen sounded almost too good to be true.

The reverie broke the minute Coach Li explained the reason for the reprieve. Doctors from the sports-science research institute were visiting that day, he said, and they wanted to see the young recruits in the main office. The boys groaned. If there was one thing they dreaded as much as an extra twenty laps around the gym, it was the invasive physical exam. In Shanghai, some athletes sneeringly referred to the visiting doctors as "the old perverts."

Yao and the other boys in his class trudged up the stairs of the school's administration building. At one end of the second-floor hallway were the classrooms where athletes of all ages, sizes, and disciplines converged every morning to study a curriculum that was heavy on physical education and political indoctrination. At the other end were the offices of the school administrators, including Party secretary Xu Weili. But the school's most hallowed space was a sterile little room tucked away near the top of the stairs, where the Chinese characters stenciled on the door read: TALENT SELECTION OFFICE.

The boys fidgeted in the corridor as one of the doctors opened the door periodically to call out one name, then another. Finally, it was Yao's turn.

If his exam was like that of the other recruits, Yao was soon standing virtually naked in the middle of the Talent Selection Office, his shorts and underpants around his ankles. Two doctors circled around him, studying his body. The men had been tracking Yao's development more closely than the other athletes for several years, but now the youngster towered over them. At twelve, he was already nearly 6'2", and his physique looked like two different bodies fused together at the waist: thick, pillar-like legs supporting a torso so skeletal that his ribs stuck out.

After making all of the rudimentary measurements, one of the doctors moved in to take a closer look at Yao's genitals. For anyone, much less a shy boy on the cusp of puberty, it would have been a humiliating moment. After searching for signs of incipient pubic hair, the doctor would have then asked Yao, as he had all the others, to squat down. The old man would have then reached in and cupped the testicles in his hand, weighing them gently and then rolling each ball between his thumb and forefinger. This part of the exam didn't last long, but for the boys in this group, it seemed to last an eternity.

And then, mercifully, it was over.

The two doctors who conducted the exam were hardly strangers. By the time Yao walked into the Talent Selection Office that day, they had already compiled a dossier on his growth, the result of more than three years of poking, touching, and measuring. The doctors, in fact, had known about Yao even before he was born. As medical researchers at the Shanghai Sports Science Research Institute, they worked in the same unit where Yao's mother toiled as a clerk. Da Fang's pregnancy in 1980 had aroused great curiosity among the staff. When she brought her oversize infant to the office, her coworkers passed him around and played with him. For the sports doctors who dropped by to take a look at Yao, it was more than just a social visit. The infant would become part of one of their most important experiments: turning a boy with an ideal genetic makeup into the best basketball player in Chinese history.

China's sports system rests on the conviction that a combination of modern science and ancient wisdom can help forge a corps of world-champion athletes. Success, the country's Communist leaders believe, does not depend solely on money or equipment or endless repetitive training. It also requires extensive genetic screening to select future stars at a very young age. Since the mid-1980s, coaches and scouts have scoured the country for potential athletes while clutching manuals with such titles as "The Scientific Identification of Sports Talent" and "The

Principle and Method of Selecting Athletes." Even today, under the glass desktop in the Xuhui school's Talent Selection Office, one can find a chart listing the measurements that Chinese scientists take for athletes age seven and up, including height (both sitting and standing), weight, arm-span, vertical reach, leaping ability (both vertical and horizontal), running speed (sprint and long distance), reaction time, and heart rate.

The ideal physical makeup of a potential athlete depends on the sport. Recruiters searching for potential weight lifters, for example, look for relatively squat children, usually age nine or ten, who have strong legs and short torsos. Swimmers are often selected at age five or six, often before they've even been in the water, based on their strength, height, and speed in the forty-meter dash. Potential divers, also recruited very young, must have flexibility, fearlessness, good leaping ability, and tiny hips to minimize splash on entry into the water.

In basketball, the only measurement that has truly mattered to Chinese authorities over the past fifty years is height. The campaign to cull the tallest children in China has been so thorough that, if you bump into a middle-age man taller than 6'2" walking the streets of Shanghai today, chances are high that he spent his childhood in a sports school. Children in China today have a somewhat wider range of choices—indeed, women's basketball teams are losing prospects to the burgeoning modeling industry—but the very tallest are still under tremendous pressure to train in the sport of the government's choosing.

In the West, the science of tallness is considered fuzzy at best. A person's height is thought to be the result of a complex and occasionally random combination of nature and nurture, in which thousands of genes (controlling everything from bone structure to the production of growth hormone) interact with thousands of environmental factors (from sleep and nutrition to the quality of the water). The best guide for future height, most scientists agree, is to look at a child's parents, but even that is notoriously unreliable: After all, the two tallest men in NBA history—7'7" Gheorghe Muresan and 7'7" Manute Bol—did not have a parent between them who was taller than 5'10".

Chinese sports scientists, however, like to think they have come close to solving the mystery of height. The sports system controls most environmental factors that affect tallness, from athletes' sleeping patterns to their intake of nutritional supplements. All that is left, then, is for doctors and coaches to screen for genetic factors at the earliest possible age, before it is too late to develop the skills and coordination necessary to be a top athlete.

The scientists who arrived at Xuhui Sports School that day had already taken X-rays of Yao's hands and wrists every year to determine what they called his "bone age," or anatomical age: The larger the gap of soft tissue, or cartilage, between the upper three bones on the wrist, the theory goes, the longer the period of growth still left. If measurements continue over several years, scientists can calculate a child's remaining growth period and make a reasonably accurate projection of future height. (Before X-ray machines were available in China—and they remain rare in the poorer provinces today—scientists used only touch and a tape measure to gauge the distance between bones.) Yao, it turned out, still had an extraordinarily large gap between his bones at age twelve, suggesting that he still had many years of rapid growth ahead of him.

The belief in "bone age" is so widespread in China's sports community that it has gained an almost mystical importance. But the practice is hardly foolproof. In Shanghai, scientists found that determining a child's "bone age" was not enough to ensure a precise prediction of future height. By some odd quirk in the genetic code, some players who were projected to become dominating seven-footers barely grew beyond six feet tall. To succeed, Shanghai came up with what its scientists considered to be a better system. "Measuring bone age yields accurate projections only about eighty percent of the time," says Xuhui coach Wang Qimin, sitting at the glass-topped desk in the Talent Selection Office with his daughter, Wang Yun, a former basketball recruit whose growth stopped four inches short of her predicted height of 5'11". In the early 1980s, he says, "a couple of Shanghai scientists came up with another method that, together with 'bone age,' pushed the degree of certainty up to ninety-eight percent. Now it's rare if predictions are more than a centimeter or two off the mark."

The other method, first developed at the same research center where Yao's mother worked, hinges on a close monitoring of athletes' sexual development. The first test measures the growth of pubic hair. The idea, Chinese scientists say, is to determine how quickly an athlete is passing through puberty—and to calculate how many years of growth remain. In sports like diving and gymnastics, where flexible, waiflike bodies are required, puberty can be a career killer—so much so that doping-agency officials believe some Chinese coaches have given athletes special hormone-suppressing drugs to postpone the onset of adolescence. In basketball, where height is the holy grail, scientists have found that maximum growth is usually achieved when puberty starts later and lasts longer. This is precisely what happened to Yao. There is no evidence that sports authorities manipulated Yao's hormones to postpone or prolong puberty. But when the Shanghai doctors examined him on that visit, they found nothing to add to their schematic diagram of pubic hair. And that was a promising sign.

The second test used by Shanghai doctors measures the growth of girls' breasts and boys' testicles. Chinese scientists are a bit vague about the exact methodology behind this measurement—and many athletes simply write it off as doctors copping a feel—but the theory, at least, is similar to the pubic-hair test: By comparing the growth of the testicles in thousands of boys, doctors can determine how much longer the growth period will last. How do doctors weigh and measure the testicles? "It's just like playing mah-jongg," says a former Shanghai volleyball player who was frequently put through the same test, referring to the popular Chinese game involving domino-like tiles. "The best mah-jongg players know what the tile is without turning it over, just by the feel of it."

When the doctors returned to their research center that day, they pored over Yao's file. In all their years of examining athletes, they had never seen a pile of data quite like this. All of the young basketball players at the Xuhui school were abnormally tall for their age, but Yao towered above the rest—and he had not even reached puberty yet. Using the data they collected, the doctors tried to calculate the boy's future height. The first figure they produced was so ludicrously high they thought they had miscalculated. But as they crunched the numbers again and again, the same figure kept appearing. Yao Ming, they reported, would not only grow taller than any other center in Shanghai history. If the conditions were right, they predicted, he would reach the almost mythical height of 2.23 meters. Nearly 7'4".

Incredibly, even that prediction came up short.

The mandarins of Chinese sport have always maintained that their athletes could compete with the best in the world because of their extraordinary ability to *chi ku*, to "eat bitterness." But as the quest for sports supremacy escalated in the late 1980s and early 1990s, the nation's athletic czars also came to put a lot of faith in their charges' ability to *chi yao*, to "eat medicine." Across China, there were coaches and scientists who tried to meet the government's increasingly ambitious targets for gold medals by medicating their athletes, combining the mysterious concoctions of traditional Chinese medicine with the latest—and equally mysterious—supplements and stimulants from the West.

Unlike Western athletes, who used drugs simply to enhance their performance, many Chinese scientists believed their athletes needed to *chi yao* to redress the fundamental physiological inferiority of the Asian body. Chinese athletes were known for being small and agile, qualities that helped them excel in disciplines like table tennis and gymnastics. But their physiques, they believed, left them at a distinct disadvantage in prestigious international sports such as track, swimming, and basketball. That perceived disadvantage had psychological repercussions— many Chinese coaches, for example, felt that their protégés had no chance against black athletes—but Chinese scientists believed it also had physiological roots: North Asian ethnic groups, they contended, had significantly lower levels of muscle-building testosterone than Caucasian or African groups. The imbalance made international sport seem unfair, and some Chinese doctors and coaches felt the only remedy was to pump up their athletes' hormonal levels to just below the allowable thresholds. "The idea was to level the playing field," says one drug expert who has spent more than a decade inside Chinese sports circles. "But sometimes they went too far."

To hone their athletes' bodies, most Chinese sports teams rely heavily on secret homegrown brews that have been passed down from generation to generation. The holistic approach of traditional Chinese medicine is considered effective in improving one's overall health, balancing the yin and yang (the masculine and feminine forces in the body) and ensuring the unimpeded flow of *qi*, vital energy, and *xue*, the blood. When used in the right combination, scientists claim, the potions can also act as powerful stimulants. If athletes need an extra burst of speed, for example, they can mix a little deer-horn powder into their drink. To increase stamina and hasten recovery time between training sessions, they can imbibe warm turtle blood. Some concoctions favored by Chinese coaches have become relatively well known in the natural-food markets in the West: ginseng, sealwort, lingzhi mushroom. But others remain resolutely foreign, such as the tonic made out of dog's kidneys or the popular liquid elixir brewed from seal's penis and testes.

But as China's appetites for sports medals grew, even the miracles of traditional Chinese medicine weren't always enough. Quaffing these secret tonics could enhance the natural qualities that a Chinese athlete already possessed, but they couldn't change his or her essential biological makeup—and that was increasingly what some Chinese coaches and scientists were seeking. At various levels in the sports system—from the provincial schools to the national teams—coaches and doctors started shopping around in the backdoor pharmacies of the West, where they found supplements that could dramatically change an athlete's performance through increased muscle growth and stamina. Beijing didn't necessarily authorize the proliferation of new steroid- and stimulant-enhanced regimens—each sport and province had a degree of autonomy—but independent foreign observers say national-level officials turned a blind eye on the phenomenon for several years as part of the same enterprise: winning medals for the motherland.

The results of this push were astonishing. In the 1986 Asian Games, China edged past their traditional rival, Japan, in the gold-medal count, ninety-four to ninety-three. Four years later, when the Asian Games came to Beijing, Chinese athletes utterly dominated the proceedings, winning 183 gold medals compared to just thirty-eight for Japan and fifty-four for South Korea. The display of Chinese supremacy fueled a surge of national pride that helped shift attention away from the bloody crackdown in Tiananmen Square the year before.

The West's first real glimpse of this brave new Chinese team came at the 1992 Olympics in Barcelona. It was only Beijing's third Summer Games since returning to the Olympic fold, but Chinese athletes snagged sixteen gold medals—more than triple their haul in 1988 in Seoul—along with twenty-two silver and sixteen bronze. The fifty-four medals catapulted China into fourth place in the medal count, behind the United States, Germany, and the Unified Team (a grouping of former Soviet republics). Many of the medals came in events that took advantage of China's small, lithe athletes, such as gymnastics, table tennis, and platform diving. The most stunning victories, however, came in the pool, where a new crew of hulking Chinese women bagged four golds, five silvers, and two world records.

Mainland fans celebrated the news with a display of self-congratulatory nationalism, but the rest of the world no longer shared in the delight. Back in 1984, in Los Angeles, everybody applauded the Middle Kingdom for emerging from its cocoon. But now there were questions about a nation that went from being a first-time participant to sports juggernaut in just eight years. How did the Chinese athletes get so good so quickly? Was it true that they were taken away from their families as toddlers and forced to undergo years of brutal training? And what about the rumors of mysterious elixirs laced with performance-enhancing drugs?

Chinese officials scoffed at the doping rumors, explaining that their triumphs were simply a matter of hard work. "Our athletes have been focused on one goal," said Lin Zhiwei, then chief spokesman for China's Olympic delegation. "For nearly a decade we have planned this—and that is to produce more medals than ever before." Only one Chinese athlete, in fact, failed a drug test in Barcelona, a female volleyball player who had taken a folk medicine that contained the illegal stimulant strychnine. But suspicions about the Chinese team ran rampant. At one press conference, Lin Li, the muscle-bound swimmer who broke one of swimming's longest-standing records when she won the 200-meter individual medley, nearly crumbled under the barrage of doping-related questions. "It is not an issue in our country," she said. "Our country is celebrating because we are doing well in sport. They don't ask the questions you are asking."

The questions would only get tougher as the performances became more incredible. In August 1993, in the midst of China's campaign to bring the 2000 Summer Olympics to Beijing, a band of Chinese peasant girls staged the most astounding breakthrough in the history of track and field. The runners, all protégés of a chain-smoking former prison guard named Ma Junren, burst out of obscurity to sweep the middle- and long-distance races at the World Championships in Stuttgart, Germany. "Ma's Family Army," as the short-haired recruits were known, won six medals of a possible nine, including gold in the 1,500-, 3,000-, and 10,000-meter races. Three weeks later, at the National Games in Beijing, the women ran even faster, obliterating the world records at all three distances—not just once, but fourteen times. The wispy twenty-year-old Wang Junxia smashed the 10,000-meter world record by forty-two seconds, finishing more than a half lap ahead of her second-place rival, who also broke the record.

The world of track and field was stunned. How did a country with no tradition in distance running suddenly produce a crew of world-record breakers? The fact that Chinese men still languished at the bottom of world-class track and swimming while their female counterparts were breaking every significant world record only added to the suspicions. Performance-enhancing drugs were known to have a far bigger impact on women than on men. The details about Ma's Army that trickled out seemed as implausible as the record-setting races themselves. Ma was a maverick forty-nine-year-old coach from Liaoning Province whose experiences as a prison guard and a pig farmer seemed to inform his training philosophy. He recruited the poorest peasant girls, banned all possible distractions (boyfriends, cosmetics, long hair), channeled his mother's "deer spirit" before their training runs, and pushed them through regimens almost unimaginable in the West: more than a marathon a day at high altitude. "All of my runners are from rural areas," said Ma, who rode alongside his athletes in the sidecar of a motorcycle, berating them all the way. "They are used to enduring difficulties. How else would they bear to run a marathon a day at 2,236 meters (7,335 feet)? Who else in the world does this?"

The answer, of course, was nobody. Sports physicians said human beings couldn't follow that kind of regimen without causing serious damage to their legs and spinal columns—unless they were taking steroids or performance-enhancing drugs. None of Ma's runners tested positive in those early years, however, and the coach enjoyed upbraiding his critics. "*They're* the ones on drugs," he said. The truth, Ma insisted, was that he fed his athletes secret potions containing warm turtle's blood and the fungus that grows on the carcass of a dead caterpillar (known as "worm hair"). The potions, he said, were perfectly legal. Yet even as the coach cashed in on his success—marketing the elixirs as "China Turtle Essence" and "Worm Hair King"— track-and-field experts still suspected there was more to the records than tyrannical training and caterpillar-fungus shakes.

Barely a week after Ma's Army's assault on the record books, the International Olympic Committee gathered in Monte Carlo to vote on the site for the 2000 Summer Games. Chinese leaders had staked their nation's prestige on winning the Olympics, suggesting that the IOC couldn't ignore a country that represented one-fifth of the world's population. At one point, a Beijing official directed an IOC delegate's attention to a waving Olympic flag. "You see those five rings?" the Beijing official was reported as saying. "One of those is ours." As part of its all-out charm offensive, Beijing even freed its best-known political prisoner, Wei Jingsheng, just ten days before the IOC vote—nearly fifteen years after locking him up for advocating democratic reform.

By the time the vote took place, most Chinese citizens believed that hosting the Olympics was China's divine right. So when Beijing lost by two votes to Sydney in the final IOC tally, it was a humiliating loss of face—made worse by a broadcasting blunder that left the public believing, for five minutes, that China had actually won. Years later, it was reported that Sydney had bribed two African delegates to win the balloting. But at the time, Beijing laid blame for its loss squarely on Washington, which had lobbied hard against China's bid on human-rights grounds. Within days of the vote, the Chinese government issued a "Four Noes" policy against America, the final "no" warning ominously that "China does not fear confrontation with the United States." Wei Jingsheng was sent back to prison. And the sports system redoubled its efforts to produce world champions—as if to prove to all the critics that, with or without the Olympics, China's ascendancy was inevitable.

The remedy for China's wounded pride, however, would only bring more grief. At the World Swimming Championships the following summer, China's squad of female swimmers replicated the sensational performance of Ma's Army, breaking five world records and hauling away twelve of the meet's sixteen gold medals. The women went on to win all fifteen gold medals at the Asian Games in Hiroshima in October before disaster struck. In December, Japanese drug testers revealed that eleven Chinese athletes at the Games, including seven top swimmers, had tested positive for the anabolic steroid dihydrotestosterone (DHT). China was stripped of twenty-two medals and, though news of the scandal was blacked out in the mainland, Beijing defended itself abroad with a cycle of denial, recrimination, and righteous indignation. China's athletes don't use drugs, officials insisted, so the accusations must have been motivated by jealousy or racism—or a Japanese plot. Japan's only dastardly trick, in fact, was to introduce a new test for detecting DHT, something the Chinese apparently hadn't been expecting.

By the end of the year, thirty-eight Chinese athletes in a variety of sports had failed drug tests. The Chinese Olympic Committee said it was "shocked" to discover that "a few individual" Chinese athletes had gotten juiced up for competitions. But that admission left larger questions unanswered: How did athletes with little freedom of choice or movement get these drugs? Was this the work of a few rogue coaches and scientists, or was China turning into another East Germany, where taking drugs was part of a national sports enterprise?

When the first foreign antidoping officials arrived in China to conduct out-of-competition tests in 1994, they planned their sweeps like a military operation, using absolute secrecy, off-site training, and stealth reconnaissance, all culminating in a surprise incursion at the training site. The problem, however, was that Chinese athletes also trained in virtual secrecy. It was hard enough to put together a reliable map of the various training sites for each sport, much less swoop in and freely test athletes on their hit lists. As a result, there were plenty of wild-goose chases across the countryside followed by meetings in which coaches cheerfully explained that the athletes targeted for testing had gone home to visit ailing grandmothers. Even so, the officials found a disturbing pattern of doping that cut across all provinces and all sports. In the first year, they even found two table-tennis players pumped up on steroids.

Chastened by the drug scandals and the tightened enforcement, Beijing adopted strict antidoping policies in 1995, and the record-breaking track and swim teams began a dizzying decline. Some provincial Chinese coaches, however, found ways around the new restrictions. One tactic was to keep up-and-coming athletes out of sanctioned international competitions so that they would remain unranked—and thus untested by the World Anti-Doping Agency. Like their counterparts around the world, some Chinese officials also tried to stay ahead of the testers by acquiring the latest, as-yet-undetectable stimulants and masking agents.

The public would only get a glimpse of this complicated subterfuge when things backfired. Shortly before the 1998 World Swimming Championships, Chinese swimmer Yuan Yuan was caught in the Sydney airport trying to smuggle in thirteen vials of human-growth hormone—an enormous quantity of a drug for which there was no adequate test. Four other Chinese swimmers were banned during the same competition for using an illegal diuretic. Ten more swimmers and coaches were suspended in 1999, and China's best swimmer, world champion Wu Yanyan, tested positive for anabolic steroids in May 2000. But the biggest news came in late August 2000, just weeks before the Sydney Olympics, when antidoping officials announced that they had approved a revolutionary blood and urine test for erythropoietin, or EPO, a banned substance that boosts endurance. A week later, China dropped twenty-seven athletes from its Olympic roster, including six young runners from Ma's newest Family Army—an unspecified number of them due to failed drug tests. The preemptive bannings may have hurt the prospects of the Chinese Olympic team in Sydney, but they helped Beijing avoid a potentially bigger scandal—and thus boosted the city's chances for winning its all-important bid to host the 2008 Olympics.

Nobody has ever produced a smoking gun to show that Beijing orchestrated a massive East German-style doping program, and top sports officials vehemently deny the suggestion. Dozens of East German and former Soviet coaches had gravitated to China after the fall of the Berlin Wall, looking for work. But their presence didn't necessarily mean there was a wholesale transfer of a centralized doping system. "We're not saying we don't have a problem, but you can't say every time a doping case appears that the Chinese government is involved," Shi Kangcheng, director of the Chinese Olympic Committee's Anti-Doping Commission, said shortly before the 2000 Games. "The problem is that the media overemphasizes the importance of gold medals. Winners become heroes, so athletes and coaches create a culture of gold-medal worship."

Shi's statement fairly captured the shift in Chinese society toward the embrace of individual achievement. Nevertheless, it was a curious statement coming from a top Chinese sports official, not simply because the government itself controls and censors the media, but because China, more than any other country in the world, enshrines this "gold-medal worship" as official state policy. Every four years, China's top sports authorities set targets for the total number of gold medals the national teams should win in the Olympics, and provincial leaders set similar goals for the National Games. These aren't dreamy wish lists, but real quotas backed by incentives and threats. Until recently, coaches and athletes received about $12,000 each for a National Games gold medal, double that amount for an Olympic gold, and even more for a world record. (The dollar awards reportedly climbed into six figures in the most recent Olympics.) By the same token, Beijing also punishes laggards, slashing budgets, demoting coaches, even eliminating entire under-performing provincial teams.

The perks and punishments are an antidote to the old Maoist system in which everyone was treated equally regardless of performance. But they have created an almost unbearable pressure to succeed—especially in the provinces, where coaches' fortunes rise and fall with the National Games. "The leaders remind you every day how many gold medals you must win," says one provincial coach from northern China, who insists on anonymity. "They don't care how you get them, but you're under so much stress you look for any advantage." As China prepares for the 2008 Olympics, the pressure is even more intense, the coach says, especially because it is now accompanied by an equally vehement demand not to cause another drug scandal. "Now the message is: 'Win the gold, but whatever you do, don't fail your drug tests.' "

And what about the athletes themselves? In this age of multimillion-dollar endorsement contracts and cutthroat competition, many athletes around the world—including Americans, as the recent BALCO scandal has shown—are willing to take a banned drug to improve their immediate performance even if it risks a scandal or health problems down the line. But Chinese athletes, even today, have little freedom to choose anything in their lives, much less the kind of performance-enhancing regimen they should follow.

In nearly every sports school and training center around China, athletes are still given daily pills, powders, and potions that they can't refuse—and often can't identify. National table-tennis players training in Beijing line up after practice to drink a cup of blue liquid under the watchful eye of their coaches. Basketball players in Shanghai are given a chocolate-flavored powder that their coaches say will enhance their energy. (During Yao's time, when the supplement didn't have its sweet taste, the players called it "stinky powder" because of its rancid odor.) According to two "big-ball" athletes in Shanghai in their twenties, the stimulants are doled out on a sliding scale: the better the athlete, the more potent the dosage. The most accomplished players, they said, are given red pills whose deleterious side effects—liver, stomach, and kidney damage—are counteracted by a cocktail of traditional Chinese medicines. The other side effect, said one, is not so unpleasant. "The pills," he says, "make you want to have sex all the time, even after a hard practice."

Not long ago, a foreign official attempted to hand out a pamphlet informing Chinese athletes that they had the right to say no both to drugs, whose telltale side effects the pamphlet described, and to the training itself. But Chinese coaches, along with other foreigners who did not want to offend Beijing, refused to let the literature be distributed. "The athletes have no idea what they are being given, and they have been trained from an early age never to say no to their superiors," says one Beijing insider who is familiar with the sports practices in all of the major provinces. " 'Don't worry,' the coach tells them, 'maybe this will give you a bit of a mustache or a deeper voice, but that will disappear after a while.' It's scary, but you have all of these athletes scattered around the country training with a bunch of doctors who will do anything to win."

The thick black notebook always stayed locked up in the middle drawer of the scientist's wooden desk. Only one key to the drawer existed, and Wei Guoping—an associate researcher at the Shanghai Sports Technology Institute—kept it with him at all times, in his front right trouser pocket. When a recent visitor asked Wei about a piece of data, the intense fifty-eight-year-old with thick glasses unlocked the drawer, pulled out the book, and carefully smoothed out the weathered pages covered with his meticulous notes and hand-drawn charts. The black book wasn't exactly Leonardo da Vinci's *Codex,* but to the scientist, it was just as precious, for it represented the culmination of his life's work—and the secret to Yao's success.

The minute Wei finished referring to the book, he locked it back in the drawer and shoved the key back deep into his pocket, lest any prying eyes linger too long on the details of his experiment. He apologized for the secrecy, explaining that he was not authorized to let anybody see the book. "This is confidential information," he said, using one of the most frequently used words in China's bureaucratic lexicon, *neibu,* meaning "internal" or "secret." Then, as he often did at sensitive moments, Wei recited one of Chairman Mao's sayings, this one about how Chinese medicine is the secret for making the people strong and healthy—a secret, presumably, that the Chinese have to hold dear.

Yao Ming was only thirteen when he arrived to live and train full-time at the Sports Technology Institute in the Shanghai suburb of Mei-long. It was March 1994, and the young recruit still had, in the blunt assessment of his former coach Li Zhangming, "no feel for the game of basketball." But he was now nearly 6'6", and city officials, overriding his parents' objections once again, decided he needed a more scientific training regimen to help him reach the full height of his potential—and the full potential of his height. Chinese players under sixteen aren't officially allowed to train with the professional "work" teams, as they are called, but Yao was a special case. The boy knew his age was a sensitive subject—nobody wanted to admit that the team was bending the rules—but he sometimes used it to his advantage. During one practice, he scowled when an assistant coach, the old family friend Wang Chong-guang, pushed him to run more laps.

"No fair," Yao said. "This is child labor!"

As excruciating as Yao's first six months of eight-hour-a-day training were, the Shanghai coaching staff in fact protected Yao as if he were a priceless Ming-dynasty vase. During most of his first two years at Mei-long, the fragile recruit only joined the rest of the junior team for the low-impact shooting and dribbling exercises. Once the practices moved into fast-paced drills or full-contact scrimmages, coaches pulled him off the court. This was partly because he had neither the speed nor the endurance to keep up with his teammates, but also because "we were scared that he would get injured," says Li Qiuping, who coached Yao for eight consecutive years at the training center, going from the junior team to the senior team. "He was growing so fast that we gave him lighter workouts to slowly build up the strength of his heart and lungs."

As the rest of the team practiced, Wang Chongguang took Yao off to the side to work on a series of special drills, just as coaches had done with Yao's mother thirty years before. Day after day, the teenager trained alone in the corner, skipping rope, doing jumping jacks, pivoting around imaginary defenders—exercises meant to boost Yao's endurance as well as his agility. In the afternoons, the coach would often take him to the gymnastics mats next door for a daily dose of somersaults. As gymnasts spun and flew through the air around him, the giant thumped across the mat with all the grace of a tumbling pachyderm.

The crude forms of weight training practiced in China—squats, for example, were performed by lifting a teammate on your back—were off-limits for Yao. The coaches not only wanted to avoid a back injury. There was also a widespread belief among sports scientists, including Wei Guoping, that weight training would channel energy into building muscles rather than increasing height. And if there was one goal that unified the Shanghai sports community, it was the desire to see Yao grow as tall as he possibly could.

The obsession with increasing Yao's height might seem odd, given that he was already taller for his age than anybody the sports leaders had ever seen. But the desire to produce China's tallest basketball player affected nearly everything Yao did—or didn't do. During meals, most of the institute's four hundred athletes—the tapered swimmers, the squat weight lifters, the tiny gymnasts—squeezed onto their own benches in the cafeteria. But Yao was allowed to eat in the "champions' room," an area reserved for top athletes, so he could focus on getting enough nutrition for his growing body.

Coaches didn't let Yao limber up with the rest of the team because they believed "stretching his legs would suppress his growth," says Liu Wei, a fellow player who became Yao's best friend and teammate. Liu, eight months older than Yao, was nearly 6'3" when he arrived at the Meilong campus, only a couple of inches shorter than his new roommate. Over the next eight years, Liu would grow just one more inch, while Yao would add another foot to his frame. The point guard and the big man would become Mutt and Jeff, inseparable friends who pooled their meager weekly allowances (about $1 each) to see how many hours of video games they could play together. But eventually, they couldn't be roommates any longer. "We had to kick Yao out of our room," Liu Wei recalls, "because he was getting way too big."

The team leaders moved Yao next door to room 305, where they installed a custom-made single bed that was 7'10" long. The bed would become one of the most important pieces of equipment at Meilong, for Yao's sleep was considered sacrosanct. China's sports scientists believe that an adolescent's biggest growth spurts come when the body is asleep, so a crucial part of Yao's training, oddly enough, were the long naps he took in the middle of the day. "Whenever we did weight training, Yao Ming was sleeping," says Liu Wei, recalling the unusual arrangement with a smile. "In the afternoons, we started practice at 3:00 P.M. But Yao usually didn't show up for another hour or two. He was always sleeping."

The most radical experiments on Yao Ming, however, wouldn't take place in the gymnasium or the dormitory. They would occur in a room that most athletes only saw briefly, if at all, the realm of gnomish intellectuals bent on creating the fastest, strongest, and tallest athletes in Shanghai. Yao paid his first visit to Wei Guoping's office in the institute's main administrative building in early 1995. The gangly fourteen-year-old had grown quickly over the previous year, but his skills and stamina had shown no marked improvement. Wei led the youngster down the darkened corridor to his office, a narrow space that seemed like the perfect haven for a tinkering scientist. One half of the room was stuffed with scientific equipment that seemed to have fallen into disrepair years before, the other with metal cabinets filled with Chinese-language tomes on everything from medicinal herbs to human-growth patterns. The old wooden desk in the middle groaned under stacks of papers, a thermos of hot water, and a cluster of white medicine bottles.

Wei had arrived at Meilong in 1986, shortly after publishing a thesis on the use of herbal extracts to stimulate the growth, stamina, and recovery of elite athletes. Trained in Russian, the rumpled researcher sought to blend his knowledge of traditional Chinese remedies with the Western science of endocrinology, the study of hormones and the glands that produce them. His work was mostly theoretical and experimental, but he was intent on making practical breakthroughs at the fuzzy forefront of Chinese sports science. Wei's first chance to implement his innovations came in 1990, when he used his own specially developed potions to turn a sluggish, overweight weight lifter into a national champion—and a silver medalist in the Asian Games. "The leaders always give me the cases that are hardest to solve," Wei says. "That's why they entrusted me with Yao Ming."

In Yao, Wei had found the ultimate guinea pig on whom to test his theories about human growth and athletic performance. The central question was how to continue stimulating Yao's growth while making the rest of his body—heart, lungs, kidneys, bones, circulatory system—strong enough to support his enormous size. If that balance couldn't be achieved, Yao would never have the energy or coordination to play top-level basketball.

At their first meeting, Wei asked Yao to stand on the metal scale just inside the door. The contraption only extended to 1.90 meters (about 6'3"), so Wei—himself 5'7"—had to clamber up onto a chair to calculate the final distance to the top of Yao's head. With a blue pencil, Wei scratched a mark on the door frame and wrote next to it: "1995.03: 2.06 m." Six feet nine inches. Yao was only fourteen, but he was now nearly as tall as his father. Wei's excitement, however, was muted by fears. "There were still a lot of doubts about him at the time," says Wei. "He was growing fast, but the rest of his body was lagging far behind."

Wei's first battery of tests revealed a long list of physical ailments. Yao's bones were so deficient in calcium they were vulnerable to breaking and unable to handle the kind of pounding that came during practice. His heart and lungs were dangerously underdeveloped. One of his kidneys was slightly degenerative, and, because of his rice-based Shanghainese diet, he was running low on vitamin B. On top of all that, Yao was more than 60 percent deaf in his left ear—the result, his family thinks, of an allergic reaction to the penicillin he took when he had kidney disease as a child. To this day, Yao feels slightly vulnerable when people—coaches, journalists, translators—stand on his left side.

Wei's greatest fear, however, was that Yao suffered from acromegaly, a disorder also known as gigantism. The condition, caused by the excessive production of growth hormone by the pituitary gland, had afflicted a number of enormous Chinese players recruited into the system. Mu Tiezhu, the national team's 7'6" center during the 1970s and 1980s, was the most prominent example. He had almost no mobility on court, and today, in his mid-fifties, he struggles with heart disease and a painful leg embolism, telling one reporter that his "biggest dream is to be healthy." Wei, who specialized in diagnosing such growth disorders, measured all of Yao's biochemical indicators and put Yao through a CAT scan. Much to everybody's relief, the researcher found no evidence of gigantism. Yao was not normal, certainly, but his growth was the result of his natural genetic inheritance.

Nevertheless, when Wei saw the magnitude of Yao's ailments in those first physical exams—"severe imbalances," he called them—he estimated that it would take five or six years before he could turn the fourteen-year-old into a productive player for the senior team. The city's sports officials, however, were in a hurry. They wanted to have Yao ready to step on the court in the next National Games, in October 1997, just two years away. The games were always a ferocious interprovincial battle for budgets and bragging rights, but this time, Shanghai would be playing host, and municipal leaders wanted to showcase the city's rise to preeminence over its rivals, particularly Beijing, by unveiling the results of Operation Yao Ming.

The rumpled researcher tried to accelerate the usually unhurried processes of traditional Chinese medicine. "The whole point was to bring Yao's body into balance," says Wei, explaining that the body's stored fuel, yin, meant nothing without the spark, yang. "In Western medicine, you treat each problem in isolation. But we try to adjust the whole body according to the individual's needs." Yao's rapid growth, he said, had created such an imbalance of yin and yang that he lacked strength, stamina, and coordination. If Wei could recalibrate the body, then Yao would not only be more agile, strong, and energetic; he would also have a more accurate shot because, Wei explained, balance also governs one's sense of direction.

More importantly, he would grow even taller than anyone expected.

The first thing to change was Yao's diet. Wei urged Yao to "drink milk as if it were water" to add calcium to his bones and help him grow. He fed him double doses of bee pollen for energy. The scientist also made sure Yao got more red meat and vitamin B-enriched wheat, and he asked Da Fang not to let her son gorge on too much sugar, salt, or fat on his Sundays off at home. "Yao's mother was undernourished growing up," Wei says, "so she thought it was good to fatten up her boy."

Then came the nutritional supplements, a series of home-brewed concoctions meant to build Yao's strength and endurance and to hasten his recovery time from strenuous exercise. Wei had developed some of these special compounds out of a variety of herbal extracts before Yao arrived, but the teenager was among the first to imbibe them regularly. "This comes in a powder," he says, pulling out some silver packets labeled #384. "We dissolved it in liquid and gave Yao Ming a dose every day." When asked for the names of herbal extracts it contained, the scientist demurs: "Ah, but that's a secret!"

Wei pulled a white medicine bottle off his desk. This was another supplement he had created to boost Yao's energy and diminish fatigue. Wei was now trying to market the product, whose English-language label read: "Orichem: Energy Supplement for the 21st Century." The bottle, however, listed none of the ingredients in either English or Chinese. "Yao Ming was very curious to know what we were doing to him," says Wei, asking his colleague, Dr. Xu, to pull an illustrated book on traditional Chinese herbs off the shelf. "So I showed him this book to explain the properties of the different herbal extracts." Yao didn't really have any choice but to go along with the treatment, but he never tried to resist. "He was very obedient," Wei says. "He was very good at accepting what we were doing."

Dr. Xu, a young colleague of Wei's with an expertise in Chinese medicine, explained how the potions combine many different herbs to nullify each other's negative side effects and to pack a more powerful punch. He talked about the membranous milk vetch, a plant found in northern Mongolia, whose roots can help increase muscle mass, strength, and endurance; ginseng, the widely used root that regulates the nervous system and bolsters the work of the body's major hormone-releasing glands; and "caterpillar fungus," the rare, grass-like growth found on the carcasses of dead moths and caterpillars high in the Tibetan mountains. The fungus, known in Chinese as *dongchongxiacao* ("winter bug, summer grass") and in English as "cordyceps," is a licorice-tasting respiratory tonic that is supposedly fifty times more powerful than ginseng. As far back as the Ming dynasty, warriors and lovers valued the fungus for its ability to increase endurance, boost energy levels, and eliminate fatigue. In the 1990s, it became one of the secret elixirs fueling Ma's Army—and Yao Ming.

If those who helped engineer Yao's growth were proud of the way they harnessed traditional Chinese medicine, they showed reluctance to discuss a much more sensitive issue: rumors of the use of human-growth hormones. When Xu began to describe the use of *jisu,* the general word for hormones, Wei emitted a guttural sound and started whispering with Yu in the Shanghainese dialect—an exchange captured by a professional translator, also a Shanghai native, who was in the room.

"The hormone treatment," Xu said. "Should we mention that?"

Wei leaned in. "No, no, we shouldn't say anything about that," he said. "Don't confuse them like this."

"But it's a key aspect."

"Yes, but there's no need to say it," Wei said, more gruffly. "Just tell them that there were herbal extracts. That is enough."

The scientists carried on this discussion for a few moments before Xu deferred to his older colleague. In subsequent visits, Wei reminisced about conducting hormone tests in the 1970s as part of his endocrinological research. But he denied ever using hormone treatments on Yao, and he said that he was a staunch opponent of the use of human-growth hormone. Wei also insisted that he never used artificial stimulants on his athletes—he said he had even written a paper condemning their use in the 1980s—and that all of his secret concoctions "would pass any NBA drug test."

Nevertheless, Wei did brag about making Yao taller. "Using my method of nutritional supplement, which is designed to keep a player's biological and chemical factors in balance, a typical player can add two to three centimeters to his height," he says. "But in Yao's case, it was much more than that."

How much more? "Maybe double." An extra two to three inches.

Six months after Wei's experiment began, Yao showed signs of progress. He was still the slowest person on the team by far—he ran the 100-meter "dash" in a plodding seventeen seconds—but he was starting to build up his endurance, covering 2,600 meters (about 1.6 miles) in the twenty-minute timed run. Yao's improvement would continue over the next two years, even as his body shot skyward. In December 1995, Wei clambered up onto his chair again, measured Yao's height, and made another chicken scratch on the wall, this time above the green door frame. He wrote: "1995.12: 2.13 m." Just one-eighth of an inch shy of seven feet. Yao had grown more than six inches in a single year, shooting past his 6'10" father, and he was barely halfway through puberty.

Yao seemed amazed by the changes in his own body. "Sometimes, when I'm lying in my bed at night," he told Wei, "I think I can actually feel myself growing."

The scratch marks in pencil and pen would continue their ascent up Wei's office wall over the following months, signaling the progress of his experiment.

March 1996: 2.13 meters (7'0"). At age fifteen, Yao is somehow allowed to play in the Shanghai Junior High School championships, where he blocks nearly every one of his opponent's shots and seals the victory for the Xuhui school.

August 1996: 2.17 meters (7'1"). In size if not talent, Yao surpasses his future rival, the 2.16-meter Wang Zhizhi.

January 1997: 2.21 meters (7'3"). Now officially the tallest basketball player in China, the sixteen-year-old joins the national junior team's winter training.

October 1997: 2.23 meters (7'4"). Barely seventeen, Yao prepares to make his debut with the Shanghai senior team in the National Games, keeping to the schedule that city leaders had established two years earlier. "By that time, we had been able to establish Yao's biological and chemical balance," says Wei. "We were surprised ourselves that it happened so quickly. But we knew then that Yao would succeed, and that it never would've happened without our work."

Wei has kept the marks on his wall as mementos of his greatest work, reminders of the giant he helped create. But the secrets in his little black notebook would remain locked up in his desk—and the key safely in his pocket.

PART II

EAST MEETS WEST

7

NBA Dreams

The blue Mercedes sedan pulled up to the heavily guarded Beijing head-quarters of China Central Television one day in November 1990. The PLA soldiers stationed outside the state broadcasting monopoly were used to waving through senior members of the Politburo or admiring ambassadors from socialist-bloc countries. But the Mercedes rolling up the circular drive that day was filled with American business executives, including a slightly rumpled man with a fringe of graying hair to whom all the others deferred. This was David Stern, the commissioner of the National Basketball Association. The forty-eight-year-old attorney from New York wore his authority with affable ease, and as he and his small entourage swept into the lobby of CCTV headquarters, he seemed to be in a buoyant mood, exuding his usual confidence and bonhomie—unaware, like so many foreign businessmen in China before him, of the dangers that lurked ahead.

Stern had reason to be in high spirits. The son of a delicatessen owner had become the most powerful man in basketball, widely recognized as a marketing genius who had taken a sports wasteland—a league plagued by bankrupt teams, drug scandals, and a dwindling audience—and turned it into a spectacularly successful business and cultural phenomenon. Stern was fortunate to have timed his arrival with the emergence of Larry Bird and Magic Johnson, the stars of perennial 1980s rivals, the Boston Celtics and the Los Angeles Lakers, along with the rise of a young phenom named Michael Jordan. But among sports cognoscenti, few doubted that the league's real MVP was David Stern. In 1989, NBA team owners rewarded him with a five-year, $27 million contract and a $10 million signing bonus—not bad for a small white guy with a limited vertical leap.

Wags would say that such riches inspired Stern to coin the NBA slogan "I Love This Game." But from the beginning, the commissioner seemed driven to prove that NBA basketball could become the most popular sport in the world. Stern's early critics thought he must've been high—like all too many NBA players at the time. The NBA, they said, was too alien, too menacing, too *black* to sell to mainstream America, much less to the rest of the world. But Stern envisioned a game that defied the boundaries of race and culture and geography just as gracefully as its acrobatic players defied the limits of gravity—a game, in fact, that leaped beyond sport into the realm of entertainment. Stern didn't take his cues from the tradition-bound worlds of American football and baseball. His model was Walt Disney's entertainment empire. "We're not just a sports league, not just a game, we're an entertainment attraction," he said. Disney has "theme parks, and we have theme parks. Only we call them arenas. They have characters: Mickey Mouse, Goofy. Our characters are named Magic and Michael."

Stern turned the league around at home, and soon he was taking the game global. The NBA had made a toe-touch in China back in August 1979, when the Washington Bullets came to Beijing for a pair of friendly games with the Chinese army. (Bullets star Elvin Hayes marveled that the 7'6" soldier Mu Tiezhu was "the biggest man I ever played against!") But Stern's first international deal came in the mid–1980s, when he signed a $5,000 contract with Italian television to rebroadcast NBA games. By 1990, the NBA had expanded across Europe, and the first player from the soon-to-be-former Soviet Union—Lithuania's Sarunas Marciulonis—had made his debut with the Golden State Warriors.

The commissioner had decided to come to mainland China after presiding over a pair of NBA games in Tokyo, the first regular-season games ever played outside of the United States. The Utah Jazz took two games from the Phoenix Suns in front of huge crowds that were enthusiastic, knowledgeable, and unfailingly polite. It was a revelation for Stern. "We may have been the capital of the basketball universe, but we weren't the center," he says, sitting in his spacious fifteenth-floor office with its sparkling view of midtown Manhattan. "It dawned on me that the combination of the global appeal of our game and the growth of television markets around the world meant that NBA games were going to be seen everywhere."

Even in Communist China. Or, as Stern saw it, *especially* in Communist China.

The long-dormant colossus was at the beginning of an explosive economic boom and Stern, like nearly every ambitious Western business executive, found himself nursing his own version of "the China dream." Other global markets were important, Stern says, "but China is an opportunity for the ages." Back in 1990, Stern felt he was arriving at the perfect time to sell the game to a market of 1.2 billion people. Not only did basketball have a fabled history in the Middle Kingdom. But even during his three-day visit to the mainland, Stern could see that the Chinese had an abiding passion for the game. "There were backboards all over the place," he says, "and most of them had kids playing."

Stern traveled with his wife to the ancient capital of Xi'an in western China, where they toured the imperial burial grounds containing the famous army of terra-cotta warriors. When their guide heard that Stern was a big shot with the NBA, she confided that she was enamored with another famous army.

"You know," she said, "I'm a great fan of the Red Oxen."

There was a moment of confusion as the guide tried to explain exactly what or who she meant, but soon Stern found out that Red Oxen, or *hongniu,* was the name the Chinese used for the Chicago Bulls. The woman, it turned out, was hooked on the heroics of the Red Oxen's greatest warrior, whose nickname in China was "Kongzhong Feiren," the "Space Flier." Michael Jordan.

Stern was stunned to see how deeply the NBA had already penetrated China. How, he wondered, had this woman in the Chinese hinterlands become an NBA fan at a time when not a single regular-season or playoff game was being aired in the Middle Kingdom? "This meant she was absorbing the NBA and Michael Jordan in some way, probably through pirated tapes," Stern says. "So I knew that deep in the regions of China, there was a hunger for NBA basketball—and there was NBA television running that was not authorized."

When asked if the piracy bothered him, he smiles. "It was okay," he says, "as long as we could move in behind it."

Stern arrived in China just as CCTV, closed to the West for so long, was tentatively opening up to foreign programming. The network had already aired a few NBA All-Star Games, broadcasting them weeks, in some cases months, after the live event due to delays in the mail—and in the Chinese censors' office. Stern wanted much more, so he had a deputy arrange a meeting for him with the CCTV boss in charge of sports broadcasts.

Because CCTV was a state-run monopoly, Stern knew he couldn't expect the kind of multimillion-dollar rights fees that the NBA commanded in other parts of the world. But that didn't matter too much.

He was desperate to get a foothold in China. Get a few hundred million Chinese to start feeling *I Love This Game,* and all of the other stuff—the merchandising, the multimillion-dollar broadcasting contracts, the NBA games on Chinese soil—would eventually follow. China first needed to air more NBA games, and Stern remembers coming to the meeting prepared to offer CCTV the rights to broadcast the NBA "Game of the Week." The competitive drama, he figured, would surely appeal to the hoop-loving Chinese public throughout the season, not simply during the NBA Finals.

And besides, Stern was offering the games *for free.*

The first inkling of trouble came when the NBA men walked into the vast marble-floored lobby of CCTV headquarters. In most places he visited, the commissioner received the royal treatment: Red carpets, reception lines, and elaborate banquets often materialized magically as the hosts tried to curry favor with one of the most influential men in sports. But the CCTV boss wasn't in the lobby to greet them; he hadn't even bothered to send a minion down to guide them to his office. This was no big deal for Stern. Face wasn't such a crucial issue for the Americans. They could go directly to the office themselves without feeling that their honor had been irreparably impugned.

But when the NBA's interpreter told the secretary that Stern had an appointment, the woman gave a quick look over the calendar and responded curtly: "There is no record of any appointment."

Sandy Brown, the head of NBA television at the time, stepped forward to see if there had been some mistake. The secretary made a phone call, but again, the answer came back the same: no appointment. The Americans pressed further, but the secretary's voice hardened. "The boss is very busy today," she said. "There is no way he can see you."

Even for a group of low-key Americans, this was a humbling insult. Not only had they failed to make it past the dragon lady at the front desk, but, even worse, nobody at CCTV even seemed to know who David Stern was. The NBA commissioner couldn't very well storm out of the office looking to strike a deal with the competition. This was China; there was no competition yet. If the Americans wanted to break into the Chinese market, they would have to wait and try to intercept the official when he emerged from his office.

"We just hung around the lobby," Stern says, recalling how the hours passed with no sign of the executive. "Poor Sandy, he had the boss there with him wanting to know what was going on. It must've seemed like a lifetime for him. I just stood there with my arms folded and said, 'Okay, wise guys.' "

The snub felt particularly galling given the enthusiastic reception Stern himself had given the Chinese just a few years earlier. In the summer of 1985, just a year after he had become NBA commissioner, Stern met with a delegation of officials from Beijing led by Mou Zuoyun, the 1936 Olympian known as the godfather of Chinese basketball. China, at that time, was only a faint blip on Stern's radar screen, but as a courtesy, he extended Mou the sort of breezy invitation most folks would take less as a promise than as a matter of politesse.

"I told him: 'I look forward to one day hosting the Chinese national team as my guest,'" Stern recalled. "And the next thing I knew I got a telex back saying, 'We accept your invitation, the team will be arriving' in a couple weeks."

The hastily organized 1985 NBA/China Friendship Tour, as it was dubbed, was a serendipitous success—and Stern's first significant step toward the globalization of the league. The wide-eyed Chinese players were deluged with new experiences—a major-league baseball game, a visit to the New York Stock Exchange, a lavish dinner with Stern himself atop the World Trade Center—but the truly mind-altering part was facing athletes from another dimension. Though the Chinese players had never seen a real NBA game before, Stern persuaded six NBA teams to interrupt their normal preseason training to practice and play scrimmages with them. He even arranged to have the Chinese team participate in the annual festivities at the Basketball Hall of Fame—on the very site where Mou Zuoyun had studied before the 1949 revolution—playing in an exhibition game against the Cleveland Cavaliers. What Chinese guard (and future national-team coach) Wang Fei remembers most, however, is going up against Michael Jordan, then in his second season with the Chicago Bulls. "I'd never heard of Jordan," Wang recalls. "Every time I tried to penetrate, I lost the ball, and by the time I looked up, he was already dunking on the other end. I thought: 'These players are not human. They are from another universe.'"

Five years later, as Stern cooled his heels at the CCTV headquarters, it was China that seemed like another universe. Hours passed, but the executive still hadn't appeared. Stern was known for having a volcanic temper behind closed doors, but in public he always managed to remain cheerful and upbeat. He had a hard time masking his irritation now. Would the NBA men even recognize their man when he emerged? What if he had already slipped out another exit?

As his patience wore thin, an officious-looking man in a suit came over and asked, with typical Chinese directness, what the Americans wanted. The NBA executives remembered this man as Mr. Li, but it's not clear whether this was the boss they had been waiting for, or whether, as one CCTV broadcaster insists, he was a low-level clerk from the network's international department. Either way, Stern was grateful to have somebody to talk to. With only a few minutes to act—the man's time was short—he launched into his pitch.

The bureaucrat didn't appear overly impressed. China was not interested in sport simply as entertainment for the masses. Perhaps that was acceptable in America, but in China, sports broadcasting had to have the same exalted aim as all CCTV programming, and that was to ennoble the people, to bring honor to the motherland—especially in the aftermath of Tiananmen, just a year earlier. What purpose would it serve China, he seemed to be saying, to promote a league that was composed almost exclusively of American players, a league, moreover, that glorified greed, individualism, and—dare he say it—the dangerous inner-city side of American culture?

Stern hadn't counted on a television executive who disregarded the value of entertainment. Wasn't that the whole idea—to entertain the masses?

Despite the chilly encounter, NBA executives forged their first big deal with CCTV over the next few months. On its face, the contract was a financial bust. The NBA was giving CCTV gratis the same programming that brought tens of millions of dollars in rights fees from Japan, Europe, and Latin America. But the NBA wanted to show its strength to the Chinese, too, to demonstrate what a lucrative partner it could be for CCTV in the future. And that meant keeping face. The first TV deal was "pure cost," Stern says. "We gave them the games and split the advertising." The problem was, he couldn't find advertisers to pay for air time. "We never sold anything," he said. "But we sent [CCTV] a check anyway because we didn't want to indicate the lack of our own prowess."

The experience made the commissioner wary about racing headlong into China. "It's definitely exciting to think about a place with a billion-plus people," Stern says. "But we've watched very closely as one company after another has gone into China and failed. The list goes on and on. They all withdraw, lick their wounds, and say they can't afford *not* to go back." As a result, the NBA has been cautious in its approach to China. It established a regional office in Hong Kong in 1992, but another decade would pass before it set up a one-man outpost in Beijing. In the meantime, there were no NBA clinics, no official NBA tours, no wild promises—just a gradually increasing number of televised games.

Stern knew, however, that he could not afford to ignore the Middle

Kingdom. China's biggest basketball booster, the journalist-cum-entrepreneur Xu Jicheng, caught up with the NBA commissioner a few years later and asked him point-blank: "Do you think China will one day become the second biggest basketball market in the world, behind the United States?"

Stern thought for a moment and then replied with a smile: "You have 1.2 billion people, 1.2 billion! With that many people, you should become the world's largest basketball market, bigger than the U.S."

By a marvelous stroke of luck, the first three NBA finals that CCTV aired on tape delay—from 1991 to 1993—coincided with Michael Jordan's first three championships with the Chicago Bulls. For many Chinese fans, it was love at first sight. Jordan's individual flair, which melded so perfectly with his passion for team victory, struck a chord with a nation struggling to find that balance. They called him "Qiaodan," not simply a Chinese approximation of his name, but a combination of characters—*qiao*, meaning "ingenious," and *dan*, meaning "to carry the burden"—that resonates with Chinese culture.

In one less than scientific 1992 poll, Chinese schoolchildren opined that the two most famous people in all of world history were the revered leader Zhou Enlai and a certain Mr. Jordan from Chicago, Illinois. For a key segment of the NBA's audience, it seemed, Michael was already more famous than Mao. Big Xu loves to tell the story of the visiting American teacher who sought to impart his knowledge of the NBA superstar to his class of Chinese students. When he asked if they knew the name of Jordan's team, the students responded in unison and began to recite his statistics. One student then raised a hand and asked the professor if he knew Jordan's wingspan. When the baffled professor said no, the student replied: "You are the only one in this room who doesn't."

Stern was happy to ride Jordan's popularity, but he understood that the Chinese public—and, more importantly, CCTV itself—would never fully embrace the NBA until one of their own was playing in the league. "David Stern always wanted to find a Chinese Michael Jordan to break open the China market," Big Xu says. "He just hadn't found that player yet."

It would only be a matter of time. On June 8, 1994, the day of CCTV's first live broadcast of the NBA Finals, two young Chinese prodigies sat in front of television sets in their respective training camps—one in Shanghai, the other near Beijing. Yao Ming, then not yet fourteen, and Wang Zhizhi, sixteen but pretending to be fourteen, were given time off from practice to watch the games with teammates. Jordan wasn't playing in the finals that year—he had spent part of the season trying his hand at professional baseball—but the series between the Houston Rockets and the New York Knicks produced a showdown between two of the best big men in the game: Houston's pirouetting center, 6'11" Hakeem Olajuwon, versus New York's scowling thoroughbred, 7'1" Patrick Ewing. The dramatic series went seven games, a fact that Yao remembers happily because it gave him seven glorious mornings of rest, without practice. In the final game, the African-born Olajuwon dipped into his prodigious bag of tricks to roll past Ewing and seal the championship for the Rockets.

After the game, David Stern stepped to center court to present Olajuwon and Coach Rudy Tomjanovich the championship trophy. Half a world away, locked deep in the Chinese sports system, Yao and Wang both watched in awe. The boys themselves had never met; they had only heard scattered rumors about the other, the suggestive murmurs of a future rivalry. Years later, however, both of them would talk about the 1994 NBA Finals as a pivotal event in their basketball lives. It wasn't simply the first time the teenagers had seen big men move with such grace and athleticism. It was also the first time either of them had felt the rumblings of a deeper yearning: Maybe one day they, too, could play in the NBA, perhaps even represent China as splendidly as Nigerian-born Olajuwon had honored his homeland.

At the time, the notion seemed ludicrously unattainable. No Chinese athlete had ever been good enough to play in the NBA, nor would the Chinese government let him go if he were. Even as the economy boomed and private enterprise proliferated—indeed, the first McDonald's in Shanghai would open for business just a few days after the 1994 NBA Finals ended—the Chinese sports system still inculcated its athletes to bring glory to the motherland, not to satisfy individual aspirations. Nevertheless, the seeds of desire were planted in Yao and Wang that day. Before they would come to full flower, another player would have the first shot at the NBA—a cocky, sharpshooting 6'7" guard from northern Hebei Province who seemed almost anything but Chinese.

Ma Jian looked around the huddle at his new teammates on the Chinese national team and saw only deadness in their eyes. Their coach was droning on about how to behave in front of visiting American coaches at practice that day, and the players stared back in dull acquiescence. Ma was only nineteen, a rookie guard, but he had seen that look all his life. It was the numb expression of athletes who had never made an individual choice in their lives, athletes who had followed the strict rules and regimens of the sports system so long that their personalities had been completely ground away, like sandstone made smooth under the torrent of an unrelenting waterfall.

Ma, in contrast, was all sharp edges. He didn't know why he was different, why he had developed this resistance to being told what to do, how he should act, who he should be. He had come up through the same sports system as everybody else. His parents were both basketball players, and his father had become a well-known coach in his home province of Hebei. When Ma was thirteen, sports doctors took X-rays of his wrist, calculated his "bone age," and asked him matter-of-factly whether he had ever *paomo*—or "foamed"—a euphemism for ejaculation. ("I told them I had not, which made them happy because it meant I had a lot more growing to do," he recalls.) By age seventeen, Ma was already near his full-grown height of 6'7", and his deft ballhandling skills and deadly outside shot were good enough to earn him a spot on the national junior team.

Still, Ma wasn't satisfied. When a friend gave him an illustrated basketball manual from the United States, he didn't understand the words, but he treasured the book so much he clutched it while he slept at night. In the 1980s, Ma watched pirated copies of NBA games and started comparing himself to the L.A. Lakers' Earvin "Magic" Johnson, the 6'8" point guard who orchestrated a freewheeling offense known simply as "Showtime." "I thought I still had time to catch up, so I spent every day at the gym," Ma said. In addition to shooting countless baskets, Ma hit the weight room religiously, developing the kind of chiseled physique that was rare among the sunken chests of Chinese basketball players.

Rarer still in China was the rise of a player with a streak of independence. "Ma Jian stuck out like a sore thumb in China," says Jaime FlorCruz, a longtime foreign correspondent in Beijing who struck up an acquaintance with Ma. "Most of the other players looked like robots out there. No expression, no passion. And suddenly here was Ma Jian, full of talent, grit, and a determination to excel at all costs." Ma's coaches never knew quite what to do with him—his ambition seemed so personal, so uncontrollable—but he was too good to ignore. "I wanted to go somewhere, somewhere beyond China, to prove myself," Ma says. "Maybe a lot of other kids had that dream, too, but nobody was just going to hand you an opportunity. I knew I had to be aggressive, to go out and grab any opportunity that came my way."

That day with the national team, Ma thought he might have seen opportunity walking through the gymnasium doors. It was the summer of 1988, and a group of American coaches had arrived to watch the team practice in Beijing's Capital Stadium. One of the men was Jim Harrick,

the young, perfectly coiffed head coach from the University of California, Los Angeles. Ma had never heard of UCLA. He didn't know the
school boasted the most legendary program in the history of American
college basketball, winning a mind-boggling eighty-eight consecutive
games and seven straight NCAA championships under coach John
Wooden while producing stars such as Bill Walton and Lew Alcindor
(later known as Kareem Abdul-Jabbar). Ma had never even seen an
NCAA game. Still, he thought: "This is a big chance for me."

Harrick and his colleagues, however, had come to China trawling for
giants. The national team had a pair of seven-footers and two other
guys over 6'10", and Harrick's eyes seemed glued on the big men.
China's old-style coach, Jiang Xingquan, didn't seem too pleased by the
intrusion, so he ordered his players to run through a couple of plays at
half-speed, showing the visitors nothing. Ma's teammates also figured
there was no reason to play hard. No basketball player in the People's
Republic had ever been allowed to attend a regular university in China.
What was the likelihood any of them would be given permission to go
to college in the United States?

Midway through the practice, Harrick stepped forward and asked if
the players could experiment with a little one-on-one, an individualistic
game that was anathema to the Chinese team concept. The rest of the
Chinese players were nonplussed, but Ma saw his chance. "I played my
guts out," he recalls. "They were all focused on the big men, but I
scored on them inside and outside. We played make it, take it, and I
never gave up the ball."

After practice, Harrick rushed over to speak with Ma. "The only
word I understood was 'America,'" Ma says. "I didn't speak English
then, but I knew what he meant: He wanted me to come play ball in
America." A month later, Ma received a UCLA admissions application.
Harrick was offering the nineteen-year-old a full scholarship.

Ma's coaches were adamantly opposed to his plan to play in America. Both the national team and his provincial team needed him, they
said, and his presence was mandatory. The government, after all, had
raised him: It had given him free training, free room and board, and
now a salary of 150 yuan a month (the equivalent of U.S. $40). How
could he dare suggest that his personal ambition was more important
than the national cause? In any case, the rules stipulated that no Chinese athlete could move abroad to play before the age of twenty-eight.
In other words, Ma would be government property until he was too
old to attend university—too old, indeed, to play much more basketball at all.

Undeterred, Ma composed a formal letter outlining his intentions, including a promise that he would rejoin the national team for the Olympics and other major international competitions. The letter worked its way up through the sports bureaucracy: from the National Team, to the National Team Training Department, to the "Big-Ball" Department, to the Provincial Sports Commission, and to the National Sports Commission. It came back with lots of stamps with the same three characters: *bu tongyi*. Literally, "don't agree."

Ma became a standout starter on the national team, but as the years passed, he couldn't help feeling he was wasting his time and talent in a system that seemed more concerned with saving face than winning games. The team practiced six to eight hours a day, always the same routine. During one long stretch, Coach Jiang even had them doing double sessions on Sundays, their supposed day of rest. Nobody complained, but Ma couldn't stifle his frustration.

"Coach, why do we have to practice on Sundays?" he asked. "We're all feeling a bit run-down. We could really use a day off."

Jiang seemed shocked by the audacity of his star guard. No player was ever allowed to question the coach's decisions.

"We must practice today!" Jiang replied. "What do you think the leader will think if he comes down and sees us training hard on Sunday? He will see that we are training hard seven days a week! Then, even if we lose, it will not be our responsibility. We practiced hard, and nobody can fault us for not trying."

"All he cared about was saving face," Ma said later. "The actual result didn't matter. Tell me, how can you ever get any better with that kind of thinking?"

With the help of some foreign friends in Beijing, Ma began plotting his escape. When the team traveled to the Philippines in 1991 to play a series of games against local all-star teams, he feigned a back injury on the first day—and then sneaked off early the next morning to take the Scholastic Assessment Test he needed for his UCLA application. "My mind was a mess," said Ma. "I couldn't read any English, so I just picked out boxes at random. I think I did okay on the math."

When Ma returned to the hotel around noon, the team leaders were waiting for him in the lobby.

"Where have you been?" asked Yang Buyong, the top-ranking official.

"I just went to the doctor to check my back."

"Why didn't you go to the team doctor?"

"Because I wanted a specialist."

Over the next year, the national team made four more trips abroad, and each time, the team's best young player was mysteriously left behind. Says Ma: "They were afraid I was going to defect."

Ma, however, had found another escape route, and it was a simple matter of *guanxi,* or connections. One of his relatives—a high-level government official who outranked the leaders of the national sports commission—went over everybody's heads and approved his application to go abroad. Ma received his personal passport in June 1992, and soon afterward got a student visa from the U.S. embassy. (His declared major: Chinese.) Basketball officials were furious—Coach Jiang benched him for all but a few minutes in the 1992 Olympic Games in Barcelona—but they were helpless to stop him. Ma finally made it to the United States in the fall of 1992, four years after his first encounter with Harrick in the Beijing gym.

Ma's scholarship to UCLA, however, fell apart almost immediately. His SAT scores were abysmal—his utter lack of English hadn't helped—so the university wouldn't admit him. Determined not to go home a failure, Ma landed at Utah Valley State Junior College, where he improved his English and scored eighteen points a game as a trigger-happy small forward. In one contest, when his coach implored, "Set it up, set it up," Ma responded by drilling a twenty-five-footer and looking over at his coach with a shrug. He hadn't come all the way from China to have coaches put a lid on his talent; he was here to show it off.

When Rick Majerus first heard the name Ma Jian, the famously well-girthed University of Utah coach reportedly thought he was being asked about an order of Chinese takeout. He soon learned differently and invited Ma to enroll at Utah in the fall of 1993, making him the first (and still the only) Chinese player ever to play Division I NCAA basketball. The twenty-four-year-old junior had trouble adjusting to the classes, the language, and the racial divide in the locker room. (Everything was either white or black; where did a Chinese guy fit in?) But he felt at home on the parquet floor. Ma jumped into his role as a starting forward for the Utes, averaging 8.2 points and 3.7 rebounds a game during the 1993–1994 season. "I love him and the players love him," Majerus enthused. "They see the almost insurmountable obstacles he has had to overcome and feel they have a stake in his success."

Ma's playing time shrank during his senior year, a casualty of injuries, an influx of talented players (including current NBA star Keith Van Horn), and his own headstrong ways. During one game, Ma jacked up a wild shot at the end of a half instead of letting the clock run out, and Majerus went ballistic. "Go back to fucking China!" Ma remembered him yelling.

Still, Ma Jian made it clear to anyone who would listen that he had come to America with only one mission in mind. "I want to be the first Asian to play in the NBA," he said. Several NBA clubs *were* listening. The Phoenix Suns invited Ma to play in the 1995 NBA summer league—a proving ground for rookies and prospects—and the Los Angeles Clippers later invited him to show up for its preseason training camp in October.

Ma treated every NBA practice as if it were that fateful game of one-on-one he played in front of Harrick in Beijing. He may have been a step slow on defense, but Clippers coach Bill Fitch loved his ability to bang the boards and bury the outside shot—and the front office was intrigued by the prospect of attracting Asian-American fans to the stadium. Ma survived several rounds of cuts, and he traveled with the team for preseason games. But on the day team rosters had to be finalized, Fitch let Ma go. He was the last man cut.

Ma came back to try out for the Clippers a year later, but again, he missed out on his NBA dream. At twenty-seven, he would never have another shot in America.

When the prodigal son finally returned to China, the sports establishment shunned him for putting personal glory before patriotism. Left off the national-team roster for the 1996 Olympics in Atlanta, Ma would never play for the five-star Chinese flag again. Beijing officials treated Ma like a stranger, a foreigner, and even Ma himself wasn't sure anymore where he belonged. He had married a Japanese-American woman and had two children in the United States, but he still felt he could make a contribution—and a career—in China. The one thing he couldn't do was keep his mouth shut. He bragged about his near-NBA experience, dissed the antiquated methods of the Chinese team, and offered to help teach China how to play NBA-style ball. "He is a personality in a place that does not reward personality," says Terry Rhoads, a former Nike marketing executive in China. "He's like a Chinese Charles Barkley. He has an opinion on everything, and that's what gets him in trouble."

For many people in Chinese basketball, Ma had become insufferably American. Everybody, even the refs, seemed to have it in for him. In one provincial game, the opposing coach, an old nemesis from the national team, told his best defender: "If you let Ma Jian score, I'll kick your ass." A few minutes later, Ma came floating in for a layup and the player hacked him hard across the body. It was a flagrant foul, almost worthy of an ejection, but there was no whistle. Ma accepted the treatment philosophically, quoting a famous Chinese saying: "The first pigeon out of the coop is the one that gets shot."

During his long odyssey, Ma established many milestones. He was the first Chinese basketball player to abandon the national team, the first to earn a scholarship to a university, the first to play Division I NCAA basketball. But there was another distinction that would haunt him for the rest of his life, the asterisk beside his name: Ma Jian would always be the Chinese player who *almost* made it to the NBA.

The buffet-style restaurant off the lobby of the Marriott Hotel in Long Beach, California, was almost empty. Most of the tourists and businessmen had drifted to the sports bar off the lobby, and the members of China's national basketball team—in town while preparing for the 1996 Olympic Games in Atlanta the following month—had all filed dutifully back to their rooms to meet the team's nightly curfew.

All except one. The youngest player on the team, eighteen-year-old Wang Zhizhi, had lingered behind. A jump-shooting Giacometti who now measured 7'1", Wang was just a rookie on the team, and he didn't want to provoke any more jealousy among the veterans than he already had. Even so, on that evening in July 1996, the soldier had a hard time hiding behind his usual emotional camouflage. The man wanting to meet him, after all, was a coach at Georgetown University, a place famous for producing a long line of NBA All-Star centers.

Da Zhi was starting to understand the giddy sensation of being the next new thing. Earlier that year, he had traveled to North Carolina to become the first Chinese player ever to participate in the Nike Hoop Summit, the annual showcase of America's best high-school players. It was Wang's first trip to the United States, and after being hidden away for the previous four years in a military compound, he had delighted in the pulse of American life—the fast cars, the fast food, the tattoo-wearing American players with the extra bounce in their step, and the posses by their side.

The coaches, for their part, were intrigued by Wang. It didn't mean much to them that he had helped lead the People's Liberation Army team to the Chinese national championship or that, the year before, he had become the youngest player ever invited to join his country's national team. The coaches were simply looking for a hidden gem who could enliven a college-recruiting ritual that had become mired in predictability. With the proliferation of scouts and all-star camps, top American prospects were often identified—and shamelessly courted— by the time they were freshmen in high school, sometimes even earlier. Wang, on the other hand, was an utter unknown. And when he took to the court at the Hoop Summit, coaches gathered to watch the beanpole display his blazing speed, good ballhandling skills, and mouthwatering jump shot—all extraordinarily rare in a big man. Best of all, according to the official roster, Wang was only sixteen years old.

By the end of the three-day Hoop Summit, several universities showed interest in bringing Wang to America, including Marquette and Louisiana State University, where Shaquille O'Neal had played college ball. Now Georgetown was making its move. Head coach John Thompson, a 6'10" former NBA center who had helped mold some of the best big men in the game—Patrick Ewing, Alonzo Mourning, and Dikembe Mutombo—dispatched his thirty-nine-year-old assistant coach, Craig Esherick, to track down the Chinese prospect. Esherick, a heavyset man with a walrus-like mustache, found that China's team policy forbade players from leaving their hotel, so he agreed to meet Wang in the café off the lobby. Chinese players also weren't allowed to meet with foreigners without a government official present, so when Wang met Esherick that evening, he was accompanied by the director of Chinese basketball, Liu Yumin.

Any other Beijing official might have rebuffed Esherick altogether. But Madame Liu was a close friend and former teammate of Wang's mother, and she looked upon Wang as her godson. Liu had been aided in her career climb by her father's stature as Mao's former minister of railways. But she always seemed to show up in the family's time of need—finding sports shoes for the growing teenager, for instance, or talking down angry Beijing authorities after he was "abducted" by the army team. Now the fifty-year-old basketball chief was curious to hear what the American coach had to offer Wang and, by extension, Chinese basketball.

Despite her long career in the Communist system, Madame Liu had a deep fascination with America that stretched back more than two decades to her first visit with the Chinese national women's team in 1975. Before the trip, the team leader instructed players to be suspicious of the Americans—if you leave a room with your water glass half full, he warned, don't drink from the same glass when you return, lest it be poisoned—but Liu says she couldn't help admiring the freedom she saw in America. She went to Disney World, saw the World Trade Center, and shared Thanksgiving dinner with an American family. Liu was also impressed by a kindergarten she visited, where each child pursued a different activity. "Each kid was allowed to develop his own personality," Liu recalls. The delegation also met President Gerald Ford—the *Philadelphia Inquirer* even ran a front-page picture of Liu and her teammates posing with Ford—but she was shocked later to hear her American hosts arguing about his presidency. "I was surprised they could talk so freely about their leader," she says. "We couldn't speak like that in China."

As a player, coach, and administrator, Liu had returned to the United States several times since then, and each time she had come away thinking that Chinese basketball could benefit from closer ties with America. If China was ever to become a world basketball power, the hothouse environment of the Chinese sports system would have to be opened up, like the rest of the economy. Chinese basketball players needed exposure to the best competition in the world, and that meant coming to America. Thus the men's national team's appearance in the NBA summer league and the meeting with Esherick. For Madame Liu, it was worth exploring, even tentatively, the idea of letting China's top young players hone their skills in the NCAA as a way to raise the level of the national team.

Wang would be the logical candidate for such an experiment. With the proper instruction and inspiration, the teenager could become the first Chinese player to truly compete on the world stage. One of the first Americans to see Wang play had been Tom McCarthy, a Boston native who had once coached another tall teenager who went on to NBA stardom. "Wang Zhizhi is Patrick Ewing in disguise," said McCarthy, who conducted clinics for some of China's most promising players for his Hong Kong–based sports-marketing company. "The only thing holding him back is he's not playing every day against the brothers in the city. He'll only wither on the vine if he stays in China."

That summer of 1996, Wang had already had a chance to test himself against some of his American hoop brethren in the NBA summer league. The games' frenetic pace wore down many of the slower Chinese players. But Wang loved the run-and-gun style of play, for it highlighted his open-court speed and three-point shooting—and masked his disdain for defense. With each game, Wang's confidence seemed to grow, like a sprout in nutrient-rich soil.

Fueling Wang's ambitions even more were two games against the U.S. Olympic team, a squad so loaded with NBA superstars that it was simply known as the Dream Team. Two years earlier, Wang had been just a junior army cadet watching Hakeem Olajuwon on television twirling his way to the 1994 NBA championship. Now he was going head to head with Olajuwon and two other All-Star centers, David Robinson and Shaquille O'Neal. In the first game, an Olympic warm-up played in Phoenix, the Americans pummeled the Chinese squad, 119–72, but Wang acquitted himself well, netting twelve points, seven rebounds, and even blocking one of Olajuwon's shots. A month later,

Wang would lead China against the Dream Team in Atlanta before the biggest crowd in Olympic basketball history. The game was another rout, 133–70, but the moves of the youngest starter on the floor—including a sweet little jump hook over Robinson—would draw high praise from the Americans.

Back at the Marriott in Long Beach, Esherick eased into his pitch, his words translated by Nike's sports-marketing director in China, Terry Rhoads, who had helped set up the meeting. After expounding on the quality of a Georgetown education and the line of famous big men who had trained under Thompson, Esherick tried to assure Madame Liu that letting Wang play college ball didn't have to mean a betrayal of China's interests. The youngster would receive a college education and the best basketball training anywhere—and he would be free to return home to play for the national team in important competitions.

Esherick glanced up at Wang. The shy eighteen-year-old had been listening to the conversation, but he kept his head down and rarely made eye contact. The coach needed something flashier to grab the kid's attention.

"You know, your game reminds me a lot of another guy we used to have at Georgetown," Esherick said. "Have you ever heard of Patrick Ewing?"

Back in his room that evening, Wang allowed himself a moment to dream about adding his name to the Georgetown legacy: Ewing, Mourning, Mutombo . . . Wang. The soldier yearned to make it to the NCAA, to follow the path of Ma Jian to America, without incurring the kind of wrath that left the talented forward off the Olympic team. Wang was one of the few people in China who still spoke admiringly of Ma Jian. "His courage in facing the challenges of the outside world is worthwhile for me to study," he would say later. "It is not easy for Chinese to make it in America. I learned from [Ma] that, even if you have the talent, you need to prepare yourself for hardship."

Ma's shadow, however, hurt the chances of every player who wished to follow him, including Wang. Madame Liu might be willing to entertain the idea of letting her godson go to an American university, but her bosses on the national sports commission—still fuming over Ma's end run around their authority—seemed even more intent on clinging to the talent they had. If that realization wasn't enough to spoil the reverie of that night's meeting, one more immovable reality surely was: Wang was a soldier bound by an oath of loyalty to the People's Liberation Army, and the generals who measured their pride in Bayi basketball victories would be loath to let their rising star go play in the West.

There seemed to be no immediate way out for Wang unless he considered the unthinkable: defection. Chinese authorities had structured the sports system to virtually eliminate this possibility, controlling nearly every aspect of athletes' lives and deeply inculcating in them a sense of national pride. Nevertheless, there had been a trickle of cases over the years—from the disgruntled table-tennis world champion who disappeared and turned up in Japan, competing under a Japanese name, to nineteen-year-old tennis player Hu Na, who had slipped away from her teammates during a tournament thirteen years earlier in the nearby city of Santa Cruz.

In Wang's hotel room that night, Nike's Rhoads talked to the Chinese prospect about his future. "Coaches and agents were all whispering in my ear, 'Hey, any chance this guy will jump?'" Rhoads said. "I had to ask what he thought."

Da Zhi sat in a chair in his room, surrounded by random piles of shoes, socks, and uniforms, still wearing his national-team sweats.

"Look, you could play college basketball or pro basketball here," Rhoads told him. "What do you want to do?"

"I just want to play basketball," he said, seeming puzzled by the question.

"Okay, but a lot of people are asking about you," Rhoads said. "Have you ever thought about just staying here and, you know, defecting?"

"What?" Wang erupted, seeming almost terrified by the mere mention of the word. The 7'1" giant recoiled, leaning way back in his chair as his eyes grew wide. "I could *never* do that!" he insisted. "I have no interest in doing that. I would never put my family in that kind of position!"

Wang shook his head angrily and fixed his gaze on the Nike executive. After a few seconds, he ended the conversation with a warning: "Promise me you will never say that word in my presence again!"

8

The New Evangelists

The Western evangelists who have ventured into China over the ages have often carried symbols of their faith, signs of the higher power with which they sought to enlighten the souls of the Middle Kingdom. For the YMCA missionaries who came in the dying days of the Qing dynasty, there were crosses and "The 13 Rules of Basketball." For Terry Rhoads, a young American who arrived a century later, there was another symbol altogether: a tiny blue swoosh tattooed to the back of his left calf. The Nike swoosh.

Rhoads's tattoo was not simply a stylistic flourish. As Nike Inc.'s sports-marketing director in China, he decided to get branded, as it were, on a 1996 visit to corporate headquarters in Beaverton, Oregon, as a way of showing his devotion to the Nike cause. When the tousle-haired Oregon native, then thirty, returned to China a few days later, he gathered his coworkers around and, pulling up his pant leg with a mischievous wink, revealed the tattoo. "My Chinese colleagues were scratching their heads," says Rhoads, a fluent Mandarin speaker whose enthusiasm for Nike gushed out in a torrent of words in any language. "But I always took seriously my role as an evangelist for Nike."

Like many of his colleagues, Rhoads saw Nike not just as a company, but as a religion. He was not simply an employee trying to help the world's biggest athletic-shoe company sell a few million more waffle-soled trainers. He was a missionary sent out to preach the gospel according to Nike, a hyper-American vision of sports as a noble expression of freedom, competition, and individual human achievement. It was, of course, a vision that ran counter to nearly fifty years of socialist sports development in the People's Republic. China's sports factories churned out athletes who were subjugated to the glory of the Chinese nation and the supremacy of the Communist Party. Nike, on the other hand, was in the business of hero worship. It believed in the power of star athletes to inspire the kind of emotional bond that gave people the urge to cheer, to scream, and—ultimately—to fill their closets with a lot of really cool stuff.

If the looming cultural collision between East and West seemed ominous and inevitable, Nike approached it with the same sense of cheerful manifest destiny that has fueled generations of Western missionaries. China needed the Nike gospel, just as certainly as Nike needed the booming Chinese market. "My job was to make Nike become part of the fabric of China sports," Rhoads says.

Nothing could seem further removed from the warp and woof of Chinese reality than the Nike World Campus in Beaverton, the pristine seventy-four-acre corporate oasis where Rhoads received his formal initiation in January 1994. Inside the earthen wall that separates the world of Nike from everything else lies an idyllic shrine to fitness and fame: Freshly mowed playing fields and wood-chipped jogging trails mark the perimeter, a large cluster of low-rise, glass-sheathed buildings encircles a tranquil man-made lake at the center. The clean-cut, casually dressed employees striding across the corporate quad all seem remarkably young, and fitness is so fetishized that the company offers free physical evaluations to all employees and a bonus to anyone who bikes or roller-blades to work instead of driving. Who could resist a place that actually encouraged you to take a two-hour lunch break to play hoops in the Bo Jackson Fitness Center?

Rhoads's official introduction to "Nike thought" consisted of a five-day training program that was designed, in his words, "to Nike-ize us." "It's like joining the cult," Rhoads recalled. "You're indoctrinated into the world of Nike." Not that he needed any brainwashing. Rhoads had been steeped in Nike lore ever since he was a kid growing up in Eugene, the university town a few hundred miles south where a middle-distance runner named Phil Knight and his track coach first started hawking running shoes with soles they made by pouring molten rubber into a waffle iron. Inspired by the story of how Knight had turned a fly-by-night operation into a trend-bending $4 billion company, Rhoads did everything he could to become "a Nike guy." As a sophomore at the University of Oregon, he heard a Nike executive talk about Knight's vision for growth in Asia—and he therefore headed to Taiwan to learn Mandarin Chinese (even teaching English to Nike's Taiwanese employees while he was in Taipei). As a senior, Rhoads interned at the Nike Research Lab in Eugene. After graduation, he got rejected for a Nike production job in Asia. Four years later and another degree wiser, Rhoads applied for a Nike position that was more suited to his penchant for putting on a show: sports marketing.

Nike was built on sports marketing, and Phil Knight himself was its ultimate guru. An eccentric entrepreneur who allowed virtually no visitors into the inner sanctum of his Japanese-style office, Knight was one of the first to understand not only how to create sporting heroes but, more importantly, how to connect those heroes to the consuming public through a pipeline of fantasies. Building that magical emotional bond between athlete and consumer, a process that reached its apotheosis with Michael Jordan in the early 1990s, was the real secret of Nike's success, the engine that propelled its revenues beyond those of the NBA, the National Football League, and Major League Baseball combined.

Soon before Rhoads arrived at Nike, *The Sporting News* called Knight "the most powerful man in sports," edging out the NBA's David Stern. The red-haired recluse in rumpled khakis and aviator glasses would've gone unnoticed on most streets in America, but inside the company, his gnomic proclamations—often written on Post-it notes— took on a mythical force as powerful as any of Mao's sayings in his *Little Red Book*. As Rhoads arrived, Knight was commanding his troops to turn Nike into "the first truly global company in our industry"—a vision that hinged, to some extent, on the company's success in the biggest and fastest-growing market in the world, China.

Knight had been hooked on the China dream ever since his first visit in July 1980, two months before China and the U.S. opened their ports to each other. Jogging around Tiananmen Square early one morning—a red-haired "barbarian" weaving around the elderly men and women practicing tai chi—Knight told colleagues he longed to put every Chinese foot, all 2.6 billion of them, in Nike shoes. Manufacturing, though, came first. It took more than five years before the company could even make a white shoe in China—the state-run plants were so poorly maintained that the shoes came out a dull gray—but the combination of low wages and high productivity eventually made China the ideal place to manufacture for export. Nike was already making two million shoes in China by 1994, when Rhoads arrived, and the company was poised to shift more than a third of its production to the mainland. In the early 1990s, Knight turned his attention to China's burgeoning domestic market. What would happen, he wondered, if Nike could become the ultimate status symbol in a nation of 1.2 billion people experiencing double-digit growth rates and a new binge of consumerism? "There's no telling what can happen to the business," Knight said, "if China truly catches fire."

It was Rhoads's mission to light the Nike flame in China, and as he walked around the Beaverton campus on his first day of work in January 1994, he felt more than a twinge of anxiety. How could he help Nike inject its uber-American culture of individual hero worship into a nation that was still mired in group think? China was growing fast, but it still didn't have any of the usual hooks for a company like Nike: no personality-based marketing tradition, no professional sports leagues, no individual heroes in mass-participation sports—indeed, no real hero worship at all since the death of Mao.

There was another problem, too. Rhoads had never lived on the mainland before. He spoke good Taiwanese-inflected Mandarin, but he had no contacts in the Chinese sports system, and he didn't really know enough to offer an assessment of the market, much less a strategic vision for Nike. He hoped nobody would ask.

On that first day, Rhoads remembers being shown around by an international sports-marketing manager named Martha Hill. He chatted and joked amiably with his new colleagues, thrilled to finally be part of the exclusive Nike club. But as they continued their tour through the McEnroe Building, Hill noticed a smallish, red-haired figure in the corridor ahead.

"Oh look, there's Phil Knight," she said.

Rhoads looked up and saw the most powerful man in sports. For a moment, he stared at the reclusive Nike boss—now *his* boss—before he turned away, keeping his head down.

"Do you want to meet him?" Hill asked.

"No, no, no," Rhoads whispered urgently. "Not now."

"Why not?"

"Because I know he's going to ask me about China."

Hill shrugged her shoulders and let Knight pass without making introductions. "It should've been a dream come true to meet Mr. Knight," Rhoads says. "But I'm sure he would've walked away saying, 'Great, we hired an idiot for China!'"

Nike's newest evangelist only needed a little more faith.

Rhoads landed in China at the perfect time. All around him in the southern city of Guangzhou, the site of Nike's lone China office in 1994, there were signs of an incipient consumer explosion. Formerly known as Canton, Guangzhou served as the gateway into China, a chaotic, sprawling city at the heart of the sweltering Pearl River delta, just 150 miles upstream from Hong Kong. It was here that Deng Xiaoping had initiated his grand reform experiment, creating special economic zones that had, by 1994, sprouted thousands of factories—many of them joint ventures between state-owned companies and foreign firms. The industrious Cantonese workers, along with a massive influx of migrants from all over China, produced an ever-increasing percentage of the world's goods, from children's toys and computer parts to Nike shoes.

Most of the products were bound for export, but the rush of jobs and investment was also putting cash in Chinese pockets, and the masses were starting to make up for nearly half a century of material deprivation. By the mid-1990s, more than half of the $300 billion invested in China was chasing Chinese consumers rather than manufacturing for export. The Middle Kingdom still didn't have anything that could rightfully be called a middle class, and the decade of rapid economic growth in the southeast could hardly be felt in wide swaths of the Chinese interior where the country's nine hundred million peasants lived. Even Shanghai was only just emerging from the darkness. But in Guangzhou, the epicenter of China's boom, residents were madly buying refrigerators and television sets, Big Macs and Western-style suits, often leaving the labels ostentatiously attached. It was a peculiar habit, especially in an ostensibly classless society, but it signaled the beginning of a brand consciousness that Nike could only hope to further stoke.

The rapid urbanization of a largely rural society—along with the Chinese public's growing fascination for all things American—made the Middle Kingdom ripe for the arrival of the boys from Beaverton. When Rhoads landed in early 1994, there were already an estimated eight hundred million Chinese with access to television sets ready to receive the proliferation of Nike imagery. So in mid-1994, Nike executives leaped at the chance to sponsor China's new pro soccer league—the country's first in any sport—beating out their European rivals at Adidas.

But soccer wasn't Nike's specialty—indeed, Rhoads says some Chinese players complained that the company's newly developed soccer cleats gave them blisters—and the company soon realized that its signature sport, basketball, would be its best bet for infiltrating the China market. The game "skewed young and urban," in marketing terms, and hip teenagers in Beijing, Shanghai, and Guangzhou would surely define the tastes and values of the next generation of Chinese consumers. In Chinese schools and playgrounds, the trendsetters were easy to spot with their long streaked hair, baggy pants, and—every so often—a pair of leather Nike Airs. These teens were ahead of their time: More than 95 percent of Chinese athletes at that time still wore canvas shoes, including players inside the sports system such as Wang and Yao, and the rest often wore cheap knockoffs. Nike's sales in China barely pushed $8 million per year, a figure the company passed in U.S. sales once every twenty-four hours.

Rhoads and his colleagues, however, followed the Nike mantra: "Sell the sport first, and the profits will follow." Over the next few years, the company would try to become, as Rhoads put it, "the Johnny Appleseed of basketball in China." Nike sponsored streetball contests, high-school leagues, and new outdoor-basketball complexes in China's major cities, even splashing the walls with ghetto-style graffiti. NBA stars and coaches came to China to headline Nike-sponsored events, while the biggest star of them all, Michael Jordan, soared in the Nike ads airing on Chinese television, leaving many Chinese fans with the impression that Nike *was* the NBA. Already seduced by KFC and Chicken Mc-Nuggets, Chinese youth longed for anything made in the U.S.A., so Nike gave them a game that was hip, urban, and unabashedly American. Later, as the company sponsored three-on-three tournaments and slam-dunk contests, the action was almost always fueled by the driving beat of American hip-hop music, a marriage of hoops and pop culture that delighted teenagers—and rankled the Chinese sports orthodoxy.

What Nike truly craved was a hero, a local icon who could do for the swoosh in China what Michael Jordan had done in the rest of the world. China's best players, however, were all stuck behind the walls of the old socialist sports system, toiling away in a rigid regimen that seemed to stifle their ambitions and stunt their development. If Nike wanted to become "part of the fabric of China sports," as Rhoads put it, the company would have to find a way to bring its message into the heart of the Chinese sports machine, a machine that had largely been off-limits to the West since the 1949 revolution.

To penetrate the system, Nike couldn't simply rely on its brand name or marketing savvy. Like any other businessmen trying to crack the China market, Rhoads and his colleagues would have to rely on *guanxi*, the intricate network of mutually beneficial "connections" that lubricates all political and commercial transactions in China. The foreign executives racing into China in the 1990s were often saddled with misconceptions: Either they thought the Middle Kingdom was still a monolithic system controlled by an authoritarian central leadership, or they believed the country had magically transformed into a freewheeling capitalist paradise that abided by no rules except the laws of supply and demand. The reality, of course, was a far more confusing muddle in which one could never be certain who in the thicket of competing interests would be throwing up roadblocks and who could make them disappear. Foreigners trying to find their way quickly learned that they needed *guanxi*. So it was that visiting executives spent the vast majority of their time shaking every hand, enduring every twelve-course banquet, and drinking every glass of *baijiu*—all in the hopes that this particular contact had just the right *guanxi* to make a business deal happen.

Nike got a lucky break in the fall of 1994, when the vice director of Chinese basketball, Liu Yumin, called Rhoads's boss in Guangzhou, Nike China's general manager, Dan Loeb, with a small crisis on her hands. Despite her Communist upbringing—her father was Mao's minister of railways—Madame Liu had developed a grudging admiration for the swoosh. She had visited Nike headquarters with a Chinese coaches' delegation back in 1983, long before the storefront operation had transformed into a sleek corporate empire. At a Nike youth clinic, Liu was amazed to see NBA coaches standing in line at the water fountain *behind* the kids. The trip also marked the first time she had ever heard what she called "capitalist thinking." "This Nike guy told the kids that if they played hard and well, they could live a luxurious life," she recalled. "I thought about it a long time and decided that our players needed more incentives, too."

On that day in 1994, Madame Liu was looking for some incentives of her own. The Olympics-obsessed sports administration had slashed the basketball budget in recent years, forcing Liu and her colleagues to seek outside sponsors to survive. The Asian Games in Hiroshima were just a few weeks away, but another major shoe company that had verbally agreed to sponsor the team was unwilling to supply shoes and uniforms until the contracts were finalized. Given the red tape in China, that could take weeks. Liu worried that the teams wouldn't get their new uniforms in time. Could Nike help out? Loeb knew this kind of invitation didn't come around every day, so he seized the opportunity. Within a week, a shipment of Nike shoes and uniforms arrived for the national team, sewn and stitched to specifications. "We were so desperate to get into China," Rhoads says, "that we were ready to pounce on any opening."

Soon after the Asian Games ended, Beijing rewarded Nike with a long-term contract to sponsor the national basketball team. Nike had outfitted the Chinese track-and-field teams competing in the 1984 and 1988 Olympics and supported the mainland tennis federation. But the company had never been so deeply involved that it could exert control over a nation's top athletes and shape the course of a sport's development. And that's what it hoped to do with Chinese basketball.

Nike burrowed in more deeply at the beginning of 1995, when Beijing hastily decided to launch its first professional basketball league, the China Basketball Association (CBA). The rush was owed partly to commercial interests—CCTV's new director of sports programming wanted to spice up his desultory winter lineup—but also to historical symbolism: The leaders of Chinese sport wanted the semicommercial league to debut on the 100th anniversary of basketball's arrival in China. Following in the footsteps of their YMCA forebears, Nike's clean-cut emissaries eagerly jumped into the venture, paying $2.5 million to outfit all eight original teams and nurture the league over its first four years. International Management Group (IMG), the Cleveland-based agency run by sports-marketing legend Mark McCormack, administered the league. But Nike was the lone title sponsor in that first trial season, and it had a strong influence on the top officials in the sport. "IMG had more control over the games," recalls Madame Liu. "But Nike had a broader vision. It wanted to change the culture of basketball."

Many of China's top sports officials, steeped in the solemn traditions of Communist sport, were resistant to new ideas. "For their entire lives, the leaders' only concern was to win honors for China," says Xu Jicheng, the veteran Xinhua journalist. "They never thought about the need to make money or provide entertainment. But suddenly, here come these young American guys telling them to lighten up. It was hard to adjust." Madame Liu was not much easier to crack. She often chastised Rhoads for trying to introduce an in-your-face dunk culture that was too American, too rebellious. Every new idea required a monumental effort of persuasion. "Madame Liu busted my chops for two years," Rhoads says. "I was completely intimidated by her."

At the inaugural CBA game in February 1995, a nervous Rhoads sat next to Liu in the VIP section. Nike had rushed to prepare all of the league's shoes and apparel in just one month, and Rhoads hoped that Liu would finally go easy on him. "The players had been wearing those tight Tarzan shorts," Rhoads says. "We decided to bring them up to date." When the players took off their warm-ups to reveal loose-fitting Nike jerseys and long, baggy, NBA-style shorts, Liu scowled and leaned over toward Rhoads.

"Look at those shorts," she said. "They look like dresses!"

"You don't like them?" Rhoads replied, mortified.

"The players can hardly run in them," Liu said, shaking her head. "This is not going to work. This is China basketball. This is unacceptable."

Rhoads's mind reeled. How would he ever find enough tight, 1950-style shorts in Nike's inventory to outfit an entire league? They probably didn't even exist anymore. After the game, Rhoads followed Liu down to the locker rooms, where she chatted with a couple of players still in their uniforms.

"Those shorts are terrible, huh?" she said. "You can't run out there, can you? It's like wearing a dress."

"No, we love 'em," raved one of the players.

"Yeah, they look great and they're comfortable," said another.

Madame Liu turned to Rhoads and raised an eyebrow. He had been saved, and the director of Chinese basketball let the uniforms remain. The same pattern seemed to follow every innovation: initial resistance followed by gradual acceptance and grudging respect. "Madame Liu came to a crossroads," Rhoads says. "She had to decide whether she was going to stay in the old system or open up, letting foreigners come in and create something new."

The dingy old Jing'an gymnasium in downtown Shanghai hardly seemed an auspicious place to mine for athletic gold. Tucked away down a side street off Nanjing Road, Shanghai's main thoroughfare, the gym was located behind a row of electrical shops and food vendors, its entrance hidden by a kiosk selling dozens of newspapers trumpeting government propaganda.

Rhoads certainly didn't expect much that day, in the fall of 1996, when he slipped into the bowels of the dimly lit gym. This was supposed to be a casual get-together to welcome the Shanghai Sharks basketball club to the CBA's first division. The hapless Shanghai team, jointly owned by the city sports commission and state-run Shanghai Oriental Television, had finally climbed out of the "B" division dungeon, but it was still considered one of the CBA's weakest squads—hardly the kind of powerhouse that either Nike or Shanghai's leaders expected in the once-and-future commercial capital of China. The ambitious city government, after all, had just erected (in 1994) the tallest building in China on the banks of the Huangpu River, the 1,535-foot Oriental Pearl Television Tower, a construction of needles and spheres that looks like a rocket ship set to take off into the twenty-first century. And now, just a few hundred yards away, construction had already begun on a luxurious skyscraper that would soar even higher, the eighty-eight-story Jinmao Tower. Why shouldn't a city aiming for world-class status have a basketball team to match?

Nothing about the motley crew of players that shuffled onto the court that day seemed remotely world class. Rhoads remembers thinking that the skinny players arriving in their hodge-podge of different uniforms looked more like a random pickup team than a professional squad. But then, just as he and his Nike buddies were starting to lose interest, the last player walked out of the tunnel into the gym. Swaying slightly as he walked, like a young giraffe, this boy kept rising and rising until he stood a foot above the rest. His upper body looked almost emaciated, but he had long, thick legs—and sweatpants that were about eight inches too short. This, Rhoads would learn, was Yao Ming: Barely sixteen years old, he was already 7'2". "When Yao walked into the gym, my jaw dropped," Rhoads recalls. "I had never seen or heard of him before. I said: 'He's a big boy, but does he have any skills?'"

Yao picked up a ball and started shooting around at the basket on the other end of the gym. His form was a bit unorthodox—he cocked the ball far back over his head and released it with very little spin—but nobody could block that kind of shot. Yao gradually moved out from the basket, extending the radius to twelve feet, fifteen feet, eighteen feet. Most of his shots settled into the bottom of the net. "Finally, he went out beyond the three-point line and he drained a few more from there," Rhoads recalls. "I turned to my colleagues on the sidelines and said: 'Boys, we have just seen the future of Chinese basketball.'"

For Rhoads, this wasn't just a bit of idle conversation. The teenager shooting hoops in the Jing'an gym would soon become the central focus of his life and a cornerstone of Nike's Asia strategy. But first Rhoads and his colleagues had to take care of a practical matter: The future of Chinese basketball was wearing a pair of worn Adidas shoes. During the shootaround, the Shanghai coaches introduced Yao to the Nike reps, who gazed up at him incredulously before cutting to the chase.

"Hey, this is a Nike party, why are you wearing Adidas?" one Nike executive asked.

"They were the only ones my mother could find that were big enough," Yao replied shyly. The old shoes, in fact, had been donated by the 6'8" center on the women's national team, Zheng Haixia, an old acquaintance of his mother's. "We can never find anything my size."

The next morning, Rhoads e-mailed his colleagues in Beaverton and requested a pair of size-18 basketball shoes. A few days later, a package arrived with a brand-new pair of Nike Airs made for NBA star Alonzo Mourning. Rhoads's colleague Jimmy Qin shuttled the shoes out to Meilong and hand-delivered them to Yao in his dorm room. It was the first of many gifts, each with a set of invisible strings attached.

For Rhoads, the appearance of Yao Ming seemed like a stroke of blind luck. Here was a 7'2", sixteen-year-old basketball prodigy emerging in a city of sixteen million people that was exploding economically. Nike had moved its sports-marketing operation to Shanghai a few months earlier, as the focal point of China's economic boom shifted north from Guangdong. Barely five years had passed since Deng Xiaoping had pulled the shackles off of Shanghai, but the city was already caught up in the biggest building frenzy the world had ever seen.

All around Nike's new Shanghai office, the jumble of construction cranes testified to a boom that would, over the decade, give the city an average of one new skyscraper (defined as more than thirty stories) every twelve days and one new high-rise (eight stories or more) every twenty-four hours. The advancing armies of fanciful glass-and-chrome towers would wipe out scores of historic neighborhoods, sending residents scurrying to new high-rise satellite cities on the outskirts of town. Even the old Xuhui sports-school gymnasium where Yao trained as a youngster was torn down in 1996, replaced by a cluster of thirty-story residential buildings. Few people in Shanghai bemoaned the past, however, for this was a city—and a country—hurtling into the future, a place whose sense of pride and destiny turned the words *xiandai,* "modern," and *fazhan,* "development," into the two most cherished utterances in the Chinese language.

Those words, of course, were also music to Nike's ears. By 1997, the company's edgy, modern style had caught on so thoroughly that some television stations even aired Nike's Air Jordan ads for free, using them as bait for other advertisers. Shoe sales climbed slowly, however, and some Nike executives wanted to start pushing more local stars to strike a chord with the patriotic masses. But how could Nike create heroes in a nation that for half a century had virtually none—save the Chairman himself?

Ever since Mao had become the greatest icon in Chinese history, the few individuals who had emerged in China were not really heroes at all, but archetypes created and exploited by the Communist propaganda machine. True, Beijing had lionized many of its sports stars, but almost always as teams rather than as individuals: the volleyball team, the table-tennis team, the interchangeable peasant girls in Ma's Army. (The "team first" culture in Chinese sports was so strong that the CBA only grudgingly agreed to compile players' individual statistics; even today, CBA teams don't market their star players, lest it disrupt the harmonious team emphasis.) Even if the government shunned individual heroes, Nike's research showed that the Chinese public longed for them—so the company decided it would pick up the slack.

Nike's first step was to sign unprecedented individual deals with

Wang Zhizhi and two Chinese teammates, veteran playmaker Adi Jiang and prolific scorer Hu Weidong. The one-year contracts were a pittance by international standards—a few thousand dollars a year with some product thrown in—but they nearly doubled the players' annual salaries (more in Wang's case, because his rookie salary was only a few hundred dollars). The contracts, moreover, opened a slight crack in the socialist armor of Chinese sport, where the promotion of individual stars had long been seen as counterrevolutionary. Rhoads persuaded Madame Liu that the cash-strapped basketball administration could use these deals as a lever of control. "Chinese officials are always looking for an edge over their athletes, ways to motivate and control them, punish and reward them," said Rhoads. "We try to make them understand how footwear and individual deals can actually be such a tool." It was a remarkable leap: Capitalist Nike was suddenly part of the machinery of the socialist sports system.

In early 1997, Nike launched a series of print and television ads featuring the three Chinese players. The "Local Heroes" campaign was designed to inspire Chinese pride, and Rhoads felt confident that the combination of local stars and edgy American advertising would resonate with the Chinese public. Wang's ad showed the 7'1" soldier as a man-mountain swatting away every shot that came near the basket. The voice-over intoned: "Not all of the tallest mountains are in the West."

The Chinese public, however, didn't buy it. "The viewer surveys all came back reading: 'Jiade. Fake,'" Rhoads recalls. "They all said: 'We know that an athlete has to be a real star to be in a Nike ad, so why are you trying to cheat us?' We were shocked." Nike quickly dropped the "Local Heroes" campaign and retreated to the comfort of Michael Jordan and the "real stars" of the NBA. "It was apparent then," Rhoads says, "that the idea that Chinese players couldn't compete on the world stage wouldn't disappear until one of them actually went to the NBA."

For Rhoads, the task was now blindingly clear. He had to find and develop a talented player and guide him on the long journey to the NBA—all the while keeping him shod in Nike shoes. The first Chinese player in the NBA would surely become an instant icon, the kind of true local hero who could carry the gospel of Nike into the farthest reaches of the Middle Kingdom. If this realization had come three years earlier, when there was no professional league and few hot prospects, Rhoads might've felt completely demoralized. But he had already identified not just one, but two gigantic kids who, with the best training and competition, might have a shot at becoming NBA-caliber players: Wang Zhizhi and his young admirer, Yao Ming. The potential reward for getting either of them into the NBA would be huge. "Once a Chinese player gets to the NBA," Rhoads said, "this market will explode."

That is, if Rhoads's plan didn't implode first. Even within the CBA, no trades or transfers were allowed; players stayed with the same team from recruitment to retirement. Aside from Ma Jian's quixotic run at the NBA, two other NBA dreams had also fizzled fast. In 1987, the Atlanta Hawks used their last draft pick to select a 6'8" leaper named Song Tao, and, in 1996, the Orlando Magic offered sharpshooting 6'6" forward Hu Weidong a ten-day contract. Both overtures seemed more likes gimmicks than gimmes, and both players were NBA no-shows, ostensibly because of injuries. The only Chinese hoopster ever to play abroad was the female player, Zheng Haixia, a hulking 6'8" center who would spend two seasons on the WNBA's Los Angeles Sparks. By the time Zheng was finally allowed to leave China in 1995, however, she was already twenty-eight, near the end of her career, and so gimpy-kneed that she was reduced to a shadow of her former greatness.

Persuading the mandarins in Beijing to let Wang and Yao go to the United States would require some high-level *guanxi*, the only currency in China that has never lost its value. Rhoads had a close ally in Madame Liu, but her influence waned after she ran afoul of the national sports commission for opposing the formation of a competing basketball league. Her demotion in 1997 coincided with the Asian financial crisis, which forced Nike to slash its staff in China from 325 to 75. Chinese demand, however, was one of the few things that wasn't mortally wounded by the crisis. Rhoads needed a new pipeline to power, so he hired a couple of local *guanxi*-makers. In Beijing, an aggressive young sports-university graduate named Xia Song became Nike's government liaison. Using a combination of cunning and connections, Xia forged close ties to the basketball hierarchy and to the secretive military team, both of which enabled him to ensure that Wang—and China—remained loyal to the swoosh.

In Shanghai, Rhoads came to rely heavily on a soft-spoken Shanghai native named Frank Sha. The 6'3" former high school and college basketball player had started as an intern at Nike in the fall of 1996, but Rhoads hardly paid any attention to him until a year later. At a staff meeting in the fall of 1997, Rhoads mused aloud about how Nike was going to get the inside track on Yao.

"Any ideas?" he asked.

The room was silent until Sha, for the first time ever, spoke up.

"Yao's a friend of mine," he said quietly. "I grew up with him."

"You what?" Rhoads exclaimed.

"My father used to be his mother's coach," Sha said, explaining that Da Fang played for his father, Sha Feng'ao, when she first joined the Shanghai team in the early 1970s. "Yao Ming's family lived downstairs from us in the sports compound. I used to carry him around the hallways when he was a baby."

"Are you kidding me?" Rhoads asked.

Sha shook his head.

"Frank, you've been working at Nike for almost a year now," Rhoads said. "How come you never told me this before?"

"You never asked."

From that day on, Sha had a new job added to his portfolio: deepening his friendship with Yao Ming. Over time, Sha would take on a wide variety of other responsibilities as Nike's main basketball representative—coordinating public events, closing endorsement deals, even helping strategize marketing campaigns. But his most crucial role was to build relationships with key people at every level of the basketball hierarchy, from top officials to club owners to rising stars.

Guanxi-making came naturally to Sha. Though still in his early twenties, much younger than most sports officials, his background as a former player—and as the son of a former Shanghai coach—made him part of the club. In the sports world, as in the rest of China's business world, relationships were built not so much in the boardroom as in the restaurants and nightclubs springing up all over the country. After CBA games, coaches, owners, and veteran players would often head out to the neon-lit clubs and karaoke bars. In the privacy of special VIP rooms, many of the men selected their companions for the evening from a lineup of young, heavily made-up women, many of them fresh from the countryside. The *xiaojies,* as these working girls are known, are paid to sing and laugh and drink with their hosts. But if a client so desires, sex can also be negotiated. Sha, who was single, never let things go too far, but the long evenings of carousing helped create a bond that would prove its worth when contracts were on the line.

Keeping Yao and his parents happy was also Sha's job. Ever since he and Yao used to play together in the hallway outside their apartments—the toddler Yao was "naughty," Sha remembers—he had felt like an older brother to Yao. Now, fifteen years later, Sha resumed that role. He called his childhood friend nearly every day, played video games with him after practice, and took him out for meals—often at the American chains that had started to pop up in Shanghai in the late 1990s. Yao learned to love American-style steaks at the Hard Rock Cafe, baby back ribs at Tony Roma's, and, later, grande Frappuccinos at Starbucks. Sha would often invite the parents out, too, chatting amiably with them about Nike's desire to help expose Yao to a higher level of coaching and competition.

With Sha's *guanxi,* Nike could court Yao and his family directly, without having to navigate through the thicket of the Shanghai sports bureaucracy. "From the outside, this probably looks like a conspiracy," Rhoads says. "But I swear, it was pure coincidence that we had Yao Ming's best friend already working for us."

Nike's courtship of Yao's family reflected a subtle shift in the balance of power in China between individuals and the state. In the past, nobody ever bothered to curry favor with basketball players or their families, for they had no influence over their own fates. But now, Chinese parents were beginning to assert more control over the futures of their children, especially in places like Shanghai, where economic advancement awaited youngsters with an education. Da Fang may have been unable to prevent the sports system from taking her only son. But she was still determined to do everything in her power to help Yao Ming make the most of his life—and Nike helped her see what that could be.

In 1997, Rhoads proposed taking Yao to that summer's Nike Euro Camp in Paris, a gathering of the best young players in Europe. Perhaps recalling her own eye-opening trip to Paris more than two decades before, Da Fang agreed that the experience could broaden Yao's horizons. But the heirs of her old nemesis, Zhu Yong, intervened to thwart the plan. Shanghai's brusque deputy sports commissioner, Yao Songpin, called the Paris trip "a boondoggle." There wouldn't be any real coaching, he told Da Fang, and besides, why would a long-standing Communist Party member like herself let a money-hungry multinational wield such influence over her son?

Da Fang wouldn't back down this time. The Nike camp, she told the bureaucrat, would expose her sixteen-year-old to the kind of competition that could inspire him to be a great player. How could that be bad for Shanghai? Yao Songpin eventually relented, and Da Fang relished her first little victory over the sports commission since the Cultural Revolution. In the end, the 1997 Paris trip not only helped open up her introverted son; it gave him a sense of what was possible. As Da Fang put it: "He started to have more faith in himself."

That faith would be tested soon after his return to Shanghai, when the seventeen-year-old walked onto the court for his first showdown with Wang Zhizhi. It was October 12, 1997, and Shanghai was playing host to Bayi in the 8th National Games. The 7'3" rookie, unveiled as the special project of Shanghai scientist Wei Guoping, was still as raw as they come: a bony 220-pounder who had only played one game with adults in his life. The crowd tittered when Yao came off the bench into the game, and he tried not to be intimidated by the sight of a scowling Wang. "Nobody had ever seen Yao Ming before," recalled Da Fang. "Wang had already made a big name for himself, but this was Yao Ming's first real appearance."

In one of the first sequences of the game, Wang darted past his man down the baseline for one of his patented drives, only to have Yao swat the ball out of bounds. A few minutes later, Yao blocked another of Wang's shots. The Shanghai crowd erupted, and Yao couldn't prevent a smile from spreading across his face as he loped back down the court. Bayi cruised to victory that day behind Wang's nineteen points, but Yao was walking on air after the game. He had not only survived his first encounter with Wang; he had showed a glimmer of his potential, and even he seemed surprised at its brightness.

Back at Meilong, Yao began to walk and talk like a star. When a teammate invited him to play a game of one-on-one, Yao responded with mock toughness: "What? You want to challenge me? But I blocked Wang Zhizhi!"

The rivalry had begun, and Nike wouldn't have wanted it any other way.

9

Strangers in a Strange Land

The staccato blasts of the coach's whistle echoed through the gymnasium in suburban San Diego, and the basketball court went deathly still. Coach Rle (pronounced Ar-lee) Nichols had finally run out of patience, and the teenagers on court—all members of his Nike-sponsored "High Five America" youth team—knew that one of them, maybe all of them, would be paying for it. The coach, standing just 5'5", arched a bushy eyebrow and glared up at the towering Chinese kid under the basket.

"I've already told you a hundred times," Nichols said, shaking his head. "You've got to go for a dunk *every* time you touch the ball!"

Yao Ming had arrived in the United States just a few weeks earlier— a 7'4" package delivered personally by Terry Rhoads—and the seventeen-year-old would be spending the summer of 1998 playing on Nichols's traveling squad. The High Five America team was an odd assortment of wealthy white suburban kids, inner-city toughs, and some of the best athletes in California. And now, a Chinese giant. Yao was a foot taller than anybody else on the team, nearly two feet taller than his coach, and he showed some promise—soft hands, a delicate fadeaway jumper, fearsome shot-blocking. But he also had an infuriating habit: He refused to dunk.

The slam dunk, of course, is the most glorified shot in the American game, a rim-rattling exclamation point that can delight the crowds and demoralize an opponent. It also happens to be the highest-percentage shot in basketball, especially for players over seven feet tall. And yet each time Yao got position inside, he laid the ball in gently off the glass or spun away from the basket for a soft fade-away, just as he had been taught to do in China.

For a week, Nichols had been insisting that Yao dunk the ball every chance he got. And for a week, Yao had been resisting. Was something getting lost in translation? Nichols didn't speak any Mandarin, but he wasn't completely unaware of Chinese culture. He had toured China in the early 1980s as the coach for Athletes in Action, a traveling Christian missionary squad that had played several games against the national team while surreptitiously bringing in hundreds of Bibles for China's underground churches. Nichols's Chinese hosts had informed him in advance that the Americans wouldn't be allowed to win any televised games against the national team; the referees would make sure of that, if they had to, because it was a matter of face.

But Yao was displaying the other, gentler side of face. His reluctance to dunk came from a deeply inculcated aversion to showing off and hurting other players' feelings. "He thought dunking was too flashy," Nichols said. The Christian coach didn't ever think he'd ever have to say this about a player, but Yao was simply too nice. How were they supposed to win any games against the best high-school teams in America if their big man was so polite?

To convince Yao to dunk, Nichols had cheerfully chastised his big man. No luck. Then he made Yao run laps every time he failed to dunk. That didn't do the trick, either. Finally, in frustration, Nichols came up with a new rule that exploited Yao's sensitivity to his teammates' feelings. "If you get the ball in close and don't dunk it," the coach explained, "all of your teammates will run laps."

Now Yao had flubbed up again, missing a weak layup attempt when he should've slammed the ball home. It was time for Nichols to make good on his threat. After lacing into his Chinese center, he ordered all of the players except Yao to run penalty laps around the gym. As the team carried out his punishment, Yao stood at the center of the court, hanging his head in shame.

It took Yao many more such humiliations, with his teammates begging him to dunk, before he finally started going strong to the hoop. "I couldn't help it," Yao said. "I was very accustomed to laying the ball in the basket." But after a few weeks in America, Yao was dunking nearly every chance he got.

He even started to enjoy it.

Nobody could blame Yao for not fully appreciating the slam dunk. He'd been brought up in a team-first system that was far removed from America's in-your-face playground culture. Indeed, the distance between American and Chinese basketball could be measured by the polar extremes of the two shots each culture favored: the dunk and the three-pointer.

In the United States, the slam dunk is the ultimate expression of freedom, creativity, and power—a gravity-defying shot that can turn a game or make a name. Thanks to the sky-walking wonders of the NBA, the dunk has become so popular that it has even spawned its own vernacular, from the "tomahawk" (a one-handed slam thrown down away from the body) to the "alley-oop" (a pass caught in the air and dunked in a single motion). "Three-sixties" are wonders of twirling grace, while a "thunder dunk" can bring down the house—and the backboard along with it. The most devastating dunks, however, can "posterize" opponents who are caught under the basket just as the slam comes down and the flashbulbs go off. These instances of hoop humiliation, delivered in the grill of opposing players, also have a name: "facials."

Chinese authorities, ever sensitive to matters of face, have always had a hard time embracing the slam dunk. When Yao was growing up, his coaches dismissed dunking as a self-aggrandizing flourish that detracted from team unity and subjected opponents to an unnecessary loss of face. Curious nonetheless, Yao attempted his first dunk when was thirteen years old—and well over six feet tall—but he pinned the ball against the iron. He waited a few more years before trying—and failing—again. He didn't worry about it, he said, because his coaches didn't either. Basketball, they taught him, was about skill and teamwork, not chest-beating aggression. It required more talent, they said, to sink a turnaround jumper or to kiss the ball off the glass. In those early days, entire seasons went by in China without a single dunk.

In the late 1980s and early 1990s, as America's fascination with the dunk intensified, Chinese basketball authorities became obsessed with the three-point shot. Having decided that their players would never match the speed of the Americans or the size of the Eastern Europeans, they tried to spawn a nation of gunners. During training, coaches instructed their young players to take hundreds of shots in a row from beyond the 20'6" three-point arc. To encourage more long-distance barrages, the authorities even experimented with a scoring system that rewarded four points for every three-point shot (starting with the team's fifth of the game). By the time Yao reached the CBA, this rule had been dropped. But even at his size, Yao—like Wang before him—still learned the game from the outside in, starting with his perimeter shots before moving inside, years later, to learn post moves.

Much of the Chinese game feels like a throwback to American basketball of the 1950s—except that it is trapped under a thick lacquer of ancient Confucian culture and half a century of Communist Party rule. The CBA may sound like the NBA, but while the American league is a paean to the competitive free market, the CBA remains wedded to the "iron rice bowl" as one of the only pro sports leagues in the world run by the central government. Even as the rest of China has been hurled into a brutally competitive environment over the past decade, the sports system stands as one of the last redoubts of socialism, where the state takes care of everything from food and lodging to the political ideology athletes are expected to hold dear. The CBA clubs, almost all of which are owned by government sports committees and state-run companies, draw their players from the local sports schools and control their lives with the same combination of coddling and coercion employed by the old *danwei,* or "work units." The factory-like training, virtually unchanged in the past half-century, produces athletes who are obedient, hardworking, and highly skilled—even as it sands away the individual qualities required to reach the highest level of team sports.

The Chinese model of repetitive training has yielded dazzling results in disciplines that require almost mechanical perfection, such as gymnastics, diving, and pistol-shooting. China has largely dominated those events in recent Olympics and world championships. But the model breaks down in creative team sports like basketball or soccer, where everything is, by design, in a constant state of flux. Chinese basketball players are known as good outside shooters in part because they take nearly one thousand practice shots a day. But the changing contours of a single game, or a single play, demand creativity and spontaneity and variety—qualities that are still anathema to the Chinese system. "In some sports, you can just close the door and practice to perfection," says Sun Baosheng, a veteran sports reporter at the *Beijing Evening News.* "But in basketball, you need the doors to be wide open to creativity and international competition. The leaders are used to doing things their way, and everybody down through the ranks has been taught to please their superiors. It's such a Chinese way of thinking, it's hard to change because nobody dares to question it."

When Nike and IMG helped launch the CBA in 1995, they tried to breathe new life into China's hoop culture. This meant introducing snazzier atmospherics, from baggy shorts and gyrating dancers to emcees who pumped up the crowds with chants of "*jiayou!*"—literally, "add oil," meaning "let's go!" (As hip as they were, the emcees stopped short of using the cheers Chinese fans have traditionally used to spur on the home team—*xiongqi,* meaning "erection"—or to ridicule their opponents' mistakes—*langwei,* meaning "impotent.") The Westerners also persuaded the CBA to take the radical step of recording individual statistics, which up until then were largely taboo in China. To jazz up the game, they even added a statistical category not tallied in the NBA: dunks.

The top dunkers, in those early years, came from the league's small coterie of foreign players, mostly African-American journeymen whose pro careers had taken a detour through China. Each CBA team was allowed two foreign imports—with the exception of Bayi, whose army regulations prohibited the presence of outsiders. The foreign players were limited to no more than five quarters between them (about half a game each) lest they dominate the games. CBA coaches tended to crave high-flying black players, especially those who had even a few minutes of NBA experience. "China is still blinded by the myth of the black player," says Bruce O'Neil, a former University of Hawaii coach who sometimes helps CBA teams acquire American players. "They think, 'Chinese players are like white guys; we need something different, the sheer athleticism of a black guy.' They often end up going after the kind of player who will never fit in."

Fitting into such an alien environment was never easy for these soldiers of fortune. One of the earliest foreign arrivals was Juaquin Hawkins, an intense 6'7" guard who had been prowling the lower reaches of the global basketball food chain ever since the Los Angeles Lakers cut him during their 1996 training camp. Raised in a single-parent home in South Central L.A., near one of America's most crime-ridden ghettos, "Hawk" chased his NBA dream around the world, with stints in Taiwan, Japan, and the Philippines. He also spent a year with the Harlem Globetrotters and several seasons bouncing around the American semi-pro leagues. (Almost miraculously, he would land a spot on the Houston Rockets in 2002, where he would share rookie chores with another newcomer, Yao Ming.) In 1998, the unfailingly polite twenty-five-year-old arrived with his girlfriend (now wife) in Chongqing, central China's largest city. The poverty of daily life there, far worse than he had seen in South Central, "was a real wake-up call," Hawkins says. "It helped me see that I needed to make sacrifices to survive." Unlike some other foreign players, Hawkins didn't seem to mind the crowds that always gathered to stare at him as he flailed his chopsticks in the local restaurants. "They weren't being malicious," he says. "They'd just never seen a black man before."

For his mercenary work, Hawkins received $7,500 a month—more than ten times the highest-paid Chinese player on the "B" Division team—along with free lodging in a four-star hotel that served, mercifully, American breakfasts. His Chinese teammates all stayed in a sports-compound dormitory, hemmed in by minders and managers from morning to night. The lack of privacy or free time away from the team—a condition that begins the moment a child-athlete enters the full-time sports school—was meant to reinforce the idea that players are not individuals so much as a part of a larger organic whole. It also ensured that athletes wouldn't go astray, especially when traveling abroad.

As a foreigner, Hawkins was exempt from the more insidious impositions of "group think." But he still trooped through the team's two-a-day practices, sometimes conducted in gyms so cold that he had to keep his parka on until halfway through practice. The training sessions were both grueling and tedious, as the coaches ordered them to shoot jumpers for three hours straight and then ran them endlessly through a single play until all mistakes—and all spontaneity—had been squeezed out of it. After practice, the spindly players would undergo some primitive strength training: lifting each other on their backs, heaving bamboo rods fitted with metal weights, strapping themselves into jiggly, 1950s-style vibrator machines. "It was definitely old school," Hawkins says.

For Hawkins, who had fought his whole life to play basketball, there was something strangely unsettling about the Chinese system. The polite, hardworking players always did exactly what they were told, but they trudged through practices and games with a curious detachment. Hoops had offered Hawkins an escape from South Central, and he pursued it with passion and perseverance. In Chongqing, he averaged eighteen points and seven rebounds a game, with a few thirty-six-point games as well, but he knew it was his defensive tenacity that could get him to the next level, so even in China, he lunged for steals, dove for loose balls, and sacrificed his body to take the charge. The players in Chongqing had never seen such intensity before. They had been going through the same routine since they were young kids, mostly with the same group of teammates, and they would continue until they were too old or injured to play anymore. "These kids didn't have any passion," Hawkins says. "There was no light at the end of the tunnel."

The early CBA games, not surprisingly, were notable mainly for their stultifying dullness. It wasn't just that the quality of play was low. The Chinese players, raised in a system in which it was considered blasphemy to scowl at a ref or pump a fist in self-satisfied pride, displayed all the emotion of automatons. "For forty years, the sports leaders wanted you to forget about your feelings," says the journalist Xu Jicheng. "It was hard to get them back right away." The army team's utter dominance also deprived the league of any compelling drama or rivalry. "Bayi was almost robot-like in its dismantling of opponents," recalls Nike's Terry Rhoads. "You don't get a lot of chest-bumping or high fives when you're up or down by fifty. We couldn't do anything without players who showed some emotion. As a sports marketer, it was infuriating."

The only glimmer of fun and excitement in those early years came from the foreign players. Some imports, like former Howard University star John Anthony Spencer, played up their role as Globetrotter-style entertainers, bantering with the crowd, patting referees playfully on the butt, and whooping with glee after a big play. The fans would reward him with hoots and hollers—with only occasional racial epithets about the "black monkey" beating up on the locals. Hawkins was always more low-key, the kind of player who, in America, was known for his businesslike approach to the game. In China, though, everything about him struck the locals as novel and entertaining: the tattoo on his left arm (of a hawk, naturally), the headband he wore over his tight Afro, and the extra relish he added to his breakaway slam dunks. But what the home fans really appreciated was the ferocity of his man-to-man defense.

None of that competitive fire seemed to rub off on the Chinese players. In an effort to jack up the excitement, Nike persuaded Madame Liu to let the company stage a show of unapologetic individualism: an all-star game. The 1997 game was a smashing success—literally. Lured by Nike advertisements, Chinese fans busted through the glass doors of Shanghai Stadium, sending Nike employees scurrying to avoid the stampede. That night, in front of a capacity crowd of fourteen thousand rapt fans, an American named James Hodges won the slam-dunk contest with a maneuver that involved leaping over his team mascot. A Lithuanian sharpshooter outgunned a Chinese player in the three-point competition. And nineteen-year-old sensation Wang Zhizhi led a hotly contested game in which the CBA all-stars seemed to have been freed from their straitjackets.

The game's most enduring impact, perhaps, would be felt by a sixteen-year-old boy who had bicycled to the stadium that day with his father. Yao Ming, then a player on the Shanghai junior team, soaked in the excitement of the game, thrilled to see Wang—who was now emerging as the best center in Asia—going head-to-head with the high-flying American players. Nike had staged the all-star extravaganza to arouse

China's fans, leaders, and players—and Yao rode his bicycle home that night feeling utterly inspired. More than anything, the game intensified Yao's desire to be as good as his older rival in Beijing. "Wang," he said later, "gave me this new idea of what I could become."

Before Yao's American road trip in the summer of 1998, his decade-long relationship with basketball had been decidedly antagonistic. He hated the game as a child, not simply because he was forced to play or because, for years, he couldn't get his body to cooperate with his mind. Basketball represented everybody else's expectations of him—expectations that he had heard in a constant, uninterrupted stream from the moment he could understand the words of friends and strangers who marveled at him as a toddler. As Yao later put it matter-of-factly: "I've been reserved since the day I was born."

Even as Yao matured into a passable player, basketball hardly seemed like a game. It was his job, and the young teenager approached it with the joyless determination of a factory worker. He toiled hard and long, but there didn't seem to be any real prospect of fame or fortune or fun—just a dutiful trudge through the ranks until he could end up, like his parents, in some dead-end job. His first season on the Shanghai Sharks senior team had more than its share of difficulties. In one of his first CBA games, a powerful opposing center knocked him to the floor fifteen times—a pattern that would repeat itself so often that season that if statistics were kept for falling down, the seventeen-year-old would have easily established a new league record.

But the summer after that season, something changed in Yao. As he crisscrossed an unfamiliar new land, free from the rigid restrictions of China, Yao began to see the world—and the game—in a different light. Hanging out with his fun-loving American teammates—including his best friend on the team, Teyo Johnson (now a tight end for the National Football League's Oakland Raiders)—the once painfully shy teenager came out of his shell. On court, Yao's self-confidence began to match his towering physique. The angles of the game seemed to come into sharper focus, and his body—now reaching full maturity—responded more quickly to the commands of his mind, producing shots and passes and, yes, dunks that surprised even him. During the All-America Camp, he even kept up with some of the top-rated American players, including 7'0" prep star Tyson Chandler (who would become the number two overall pick in the 2001 NBA draft). During one game, Yao swatted a Chandler dunk attempt almost back to half-court.

Yao's most thrilling moment, however, came at the end of one scrimmage. With his team down by a point with just three seconds remaining, Yao reached over three defenders to catch a full-court pass, took one dribble, and rattled home a dunk as the clock ran out. His American teammates raced madly onto the court and jumped on Yao to celebrate their one-point victory. It was just a scrimmage, but Yao experienced a rare and wonderful sensation that day: The basketball court, a place that had brought him so much grief and pain, at that instant was bringing him only pure, unfettered joy. It was a perfect moment, only more so because it was triggered by a dunk.

By the end of the Nike All-America Camp in Indianapolis, Yao was rated the second-best center out of the forty who had been invited, and an *Indianapolis Star* columnist, reaching for a metaphor, dubbed him "the eighth wonder of the world." Yao began to realize that he could one day be as good as, if not better than, the most highly touted teenage stars in America. "That summer," Yao recalled, "I began to think maybe I really could play in the NBA."

That heady realization was reinforced by the big-name coaches and scouts suddenly vying for his attention. John Thompson, the Georgetown coach who had tried to recruit Wang Zhizhi two summers before, exchanged cards and posed for photos with Sharks' deputy general manager Li Yaomin. San Francisco mayor Willie Brown wrote a letter inviting Yao to come play for the University of San Francisco, the alma mater of the winningest center of all time, Bill Russell. Nike's head of basketball, Ralph Greene, who had dismissed Terry Rhoads's earlier boasts about Yao, was now a big fan. Wandering around the camp with a proprietary air, Greene asked: "Where's my big kid, where's my boy?"

Later in the summer, Nike's venerable camp director, George Raveling, arranged for Yao to visit Michael Jordan's "Flight School" in Santa Barbara, California. Yao could hardly control his nerves when he met and posed for photographs with The Most Famous Athlete in the World, whose poster-worthy smile beamed next to Yao's dour game face. Yao settled down by the time he took the court for a playful scrimmage with Jordan. At one point, Jordan sank a three-pointer, and Yao immediately countered with a three of his own. Jordan's eyes grew wide. "The big boy can really shoot!" he said, his famous grin spreading across his face. "I'm going to call [Chicago Bulls' General Manager] Jerry Krause and tell him to get a contract ready."

Jordan may have been half-joking, but other NBA suitors were starting to swarm around Yao. Dennis Lindsey, a scout for the Houston Rockets (and now head of player personnel), couldn't keep his eyes off the "big kid from China." At summer's end, when Yao visited Nike headquarters, Portland Trail Blazers president Bob Whitsitt interrupted high-stakes negotiations in Seattle to fly down to Portland to greet Yao in person. Nike canceled the meeting at the last moment, however, saying it felt uncomfortable giving the Blazers preferential treatment over the company's other NBA clients. An angry Blazers executive fumed at Rhoads: "I can one hundred percent promise you that the Portland Trail Blazers will *never* go to China to see Yao Ming." (Two years later, a Blazers scout would arrive in Shanghai eager to get back into the Yao Ming sweepstakes.)

For Yao, the canceled meeting was an unexpected reprieve, giving him one final rest day in America. Leisure had always been an alien concept for Yao. Back home, he'd had very few days off from training in the previous four years, and when he did, he usually spent them sleeping in his family's apartment or playing video games. He knew that he would soon return to a life dictated by the sports system, where even on trips abroad with the national team, officials hold onto all of the players' passports so there is no chance of defection. Now, for the first and perhaps last time in his life, he had the freedom to be just another teenager. Traveling around America that summer, Yao stared in wide-eyed wonder at the glittering panoramas of Disney World and Las Vegas. He and Liu Wei went to a baseball batting cage, where Yao whiffed on every swing. They played a game of touch American football on a beach in San Diego, then lounged in the sun at a multimillion-dollar mansion overlooking the Pacific Ocean, where a teammate's parents had invited them over to enjoy a swim and a barbecue. When they got back to China, Liu Wei said, "All of our teammates called us 'black monkeys' because we had gotten so tan in America."

On that day in late August, with a few extra hours to burn, Yao, Liu Wei, and Teyo Johnson went down to the Columbia River near Portland for one last outing. None of them had ever ridden a jet ski before, but that didn't stop them from renting a few and zooming out wildly onto the open water. About half an hour later, Yao wiped out—and for some time, the future of Chinese basketball flailed around in the middle of the river, unable to get his enormous body back onto the jet ski. Exhausted and exasperated, Yao finally grabbed onto the back of Liu Wei's machine and, with his enormous legs splayed out behind him, the sheepish giant was towed safely back to shore.

*　　*　　*

The halcyon memories of Yao's dream summer lingered for weeks after his return to Shanghai. Yao had seen so much of America—a place whose main feature, he decided, was "open space"—and yet the biggest changes were inside him. Not only did he now know that he had a chance to make it to the NBA, but the game he'd always struggled against had finally won him over. Now when he looked at the court, he didn't just see a prison of white lines and hash marks; he saw hidden arcs and angles and possibilities. The game had meaning now, and that gave it all the beauty of a perfect philosophy.

On his eighteenth birthday—September 12, 1998—Yao wandered over to the courts outside Shanghai Stadium, where Nike was holding a three-on-three tournament for local youth. Only eighteen months earlier, Wang Zhizhi had demonstrated his prowess here at the CBA All-Star Game. Now Yao was a star in demand, too. Rhoads and Yao's old friend Frank Sha were there to greet him with backslaps and bear hugs, introducing him to two visitors who'd just flown in from America: Dallas Mavericks assistant coach Donnie Nelson and the team's international scout, Tony Ronzone.

The gregarious son of the Mavs' head coach, Nelson was one of the NBA's pioneers in finding talent—and spreading enthusiasm for the game—in the farthest corners of the earth. Back in 1989, he had recruited the league's first former Soviet player, the Lithuanian Sarunas Marciulionis. Now with the advent of satellite television and the Internet, the NBA had gained a truly international audience—and a new generation of youngsters across the globe who wanted to be like Mike. Nelson had just drafted a young 7'1" German center named Dirk Nowitzki; now he was hoping to find another hidden gem, this time in the Middle Kingdom.

That afternoon, Nike presented Yao with a birthday cake, and Yao's mother, Da Fang, returned the favor by inviting the Nike folks and the NBA visitors over for a Shanghainese meal. The group barely fit around the card table in the family's tiny apartment, but the atmosphere was buoyant. Yao recounted the highlights of his trip to America, letting Rhoads fill in the more salacious details, while Nelson and Ronzone talked about the unnerving experience of eating snake in a Chinese restaurant for the first time. All the while, Da Fang and Da Yao smiled and listened, making sure their guests always had enough to eat and drink.

At one point during the dinner, the group posed for a picture at the table. The photo captured everyone beaming, their faces flushed from laughter and a day in the sun, their arms entwined in a group embrace.

The moment, in which two worlds came together to delight in each other's company and dream about the possibilities, was one that Nike's most fervent evangelist had imagined for years.

"That's my favorite photo from all of my time in China," says Rhoads. "Everyone was so happy then."

The feeling wouldn't last for long.

10

The Gathering Storm

Gazing down on the Shanghai skyline from the fifty-fourth floor of the city's tallest building, Li Yaomin must have felt on top of the world. Here he was, a fifty-five-year-old former manual laborer in a Windbreaker and a bad comb-over, standing in the lobby of the loftiest hotel in the world, the Grand Hyatt. It was Friday night, and all around him, elegant Shanghainese women in the season's most fashionable designs swept past as foreign businessmen discussed their latest China deals. Normally, a person from Li's background might have felt uncomfortable in such rarefied surroundings. But like many strivers in the new China, Li had made a journey that paralleled the rise of Shanghai itself, morphing from manual laborer into television cameraman and, finally, into the deputy general manager for the Shanghai Sharks basketball club.

He was now a *laoban*, a "boss."

On that evening of April 30, 1999, no location seemed more perfectly suited for the realization of Li Yaomin's ambitions than the Jinmao Tower, the just-completed eighty-eight-story skyscraper that had come to define Shanghai's global aspirations. The Grand Hyatt, which occupied the building's top floors, was nothing if not a symbol of status and power, with its vertigo-inducing crow's-nest bar, eightieth-floor swimming pool, and cylindrical atrium that spiraled gracefully to the top like the inside of a conch shell. The rest of Shanghai spread out far below, from the somber procession of neoclassical buildings on the Bund to the vast thicket of skyscrapers and construction cranes beyond. From where Li stood, the teeming metropolis must have seemed peaceful and quaint, like a miniature city of toy building blocks that could be held in the palm of one's hand.

Li had not come that night to admire the views, but rather to grasp what now seemed in the palm of his hand: the Jinmao Tower's closest human counterpart, the 7'4" Yao Ming. The foreign businessmen sitting in the Grand Hyatt's lounge, hungrily talking about a country in which everything was suddenly a commodity to be bought or sold, would surely underestimate the unassuming little man in the Windbreaker. But how could they know that Li Yaomin had control over the biggest commodity of all—and that his plan to export Yao to the United States was now being set in motion?

The final maneuver had begun barely an hour before, when Li phoned Yao's parents at home and told them to meet him and their son immediately at the Grand Hyatt. It was an emergency, he told them.

Like many former athletes, Da Fang and Da Yao were simple folks who spent most nights cooking in their modest apartment and going to bed early. Taking a taxi ride across the Huangpu River to the Grand Hyatt late on a Friday night would seem an extravagant inconvenience, and they would surely feel uncomfortable in such a glamorous setting. And that's just how the Sharks' boss may have wanted it.

When Yao's parents finally arrived, Li strode up to them with a beneficent smile. "Congratulations!" he said. "Your son has been taken care of for life."

Li Yaomin had been waiting for this moment for nearly three years. When he first became the Sharks' deputy general manager in 1996—a post given to him by an old schoolmate who was now the city's deputy Communist Party chief—Li knew nothing about either basketball or business. "I had no experience in this," Li said. "But the leader had such trust in me, so I thought I should try."

As a Shanghai native, Li was born with an entrepreneurial zeal that seems almost genetically programmed into the city's citizens, helping them turn a drab city blunted by Mao's socialist vision into the Paris of the Orient once more. One day during his first season, the former cameraman read an article about how the Los Angeles Lakers had become the NBA's most lucrative franchise, and he soon became consumed with the idea of turning the Sharks into a Chinese "Showtime." Li envisioned a world where Sharks fans flocked to buy season tickets, major multinationals lined up to pay huge sponsorship fees, and everything that could possibly be sold was emblazoned with the Sharks' logo: caps, shoes, apparel . . . hell, why not even a new stadium?

It was a beguiling vision, even if the prospects at the time looked bleak. The Sharks, after all, were hardly the L.A. Lakers, who had rolled to five NBA championships in the 1980s in front of packed houses. The

Shanghai team wasn't even close to making the CBA playoffs, and their performances didn't exactly excite the denizens of a city preoccupied with fattening their wallets. For one home game that first season, Li sold a grand total of nine tickets. He had to bus high-school students in to stave off the embarrassment of an empty stadium.

Li kept crashing into the reality of modern China, a place caught halfway between the old socialist hierarchy and high-flying capitalism, where the rules for neither ideology seemed to apply. The CBA might have been sponsored by Nike and run by IMG, but the league had been grafted onto a socialist sports system in which there were no drafts or trades or recruiting wars. Players were owned in perpetuity by their local clubs, an arrangement that would benefit the Sharks—they would never have to fear losing Yao Ming to another Chinese club—but which Li saw as an impediment to fielding the best possible team. Shanghai, for all its size and soaring ambitions, produced few tall basketball players. And as the city's economic fortunes rose—the average income in Shanghai had quadrupled over the previous decade (from $700 to nearly $2,700 per year)—fewer urban parents wanted to send their only sons into the black hole of the state sports system.

Getting around the restrictions required ingenuity, and Li had plenty to spare. Traveling to the northern province of Liaoning, where the harsh conditions spawned strapping peasant boys accustomed to "eating bitterness," he oversaw the construction of the Shanghai Sharks' basketball academy near the town of Anshan. The year-round camp was one of the first private sports schools ever set up in the People's Republic, and it functioned almost exactly like its traditional counterparts—except that its tallest, most talented prospects would all be funneled to Shanghai. Within a year, more than eighty boys from China's impoverished "rust belt" were living and training full-time at the facility, including a ten-year-old who already stood 5'11" and was projected to reach 7'2".

Such a plan, however, would take years to come to fruition, and Li's entrepreneurial spirit chafed at the more immediate commercial roadblocks in the CBA. The Shanghai Sports Commission, which owned the club jointly with Li's bosses at Shanghai Oriental Television, took most gate receipts for itself. The CBA chiefs in Beijing, meanwhile, signed all major sponsorship deals on behalf of the league, denying clubs a share of the proceeds or the right to sign independent contracts. Li reserved his greatest ire for the league's most powerful sponsor, Nike. "Nike wanted to monopolize the China market," says Li, bemoaning the company's initial four-year $2.5 million deal with the CBA. The clubs "didn't get any money, but we had to pay a penalty if we didn't wear the shoes. So basically, we were just providing the company free advertising."

Fueling Li's animosity was what he saw as the overbearing attitude of Nike's sports-marketing director. Terry Rhoads spoke fluent Mandarin, but his breezy, backslapping manner was pure American. Rather than defer to the *laoban,* as Chinese decorum would dictate, the loquacious Rhoads offered endless lectures on how to improve the marketability of the Shanghai team. The Sharks' manager didn't like taking dictation from Rhoads. "He always acted like your boss," Li says. "He just didn't talk to us as equals." Eventually, Li would lead a revolt against Nike, forcing the CBA to let local clubs sign separate sponsorship deals with any shoe company they desired.

The CBA's marketing revolution, however, never fully materialized, and Li would be forced to think of other ways to build his juggernaut. There was hope on the horizon: Yao Ming. During Yao's rookie year, 1997–98, his uneven performance gave Li little indication of the powerhouse he might become. Li didn't realize what he had in his hands until the summer of 1998, when he joined Yao and Rhoads at the Nike All-America Camp in Indianapolis. The *laoban* had initially voiced skepticism about the trip, balking at the $20,000 in expenses that Nike wanted the club to share. But as he stood on the sidelines watching Yao's games, a steady stream of college coaches and NBA scouts approached him. They wanted to know if China would ever let go of Yao, and Li wanted to know how much it would be worth to them. The answer was staggering: Yao, they told him, could be worth tens of millions of dollars if he decided to jump to the NBA. The NBA had very few centers as tall as Yao, the scouts explained, so even with his rudimentary skills, Yao could probably be a top-ten pick in the following year's NBA draft. One NBA team, Li claimed, even offered to pay the Sharks $1 million to secure Yao's release.

When the Sharks' manager returned to the hotel that evening, bursting with ideas, he found Rhoads chatting with Yao's interpreter that summer, Brock Wilson.

"I've been talking to NBA guys all day," Li blurted.

Rhoads stared back. He didn't have much patience for the Sharks' manager these days. Li had embarrassed him throughout the trip by sidling up to Nike executives, including one prestigious board member, and pointing down at his feet: "Tell him I'm a size 7."

"It's amazing the level of interest there is in Yao Ming," Li continued. "I've decided that I want to do all I can to help him realize his dream of playing in the NBA. He's definitely going to need an agent."

Rhoads flashed a horrified glance at Wilson. "Really?" he said, trying to maintain his composure. "Hmmm, well, that's interesting."

When Li left, Rhoads let loose a tirade. "Here's this guy, saying he wants to personally handle Yao Ming's future, when all summer he's just been hounding us for shoes and apparel," he said. "I didn't think he had Yao Ming's interest at heart."

A few weeks later, back in Shanghai, Li sat in his office flipping through the stack of business cards he had collected over the summer: coaches, scouts, managers, media outlets. The cards were proof that the NBA's intense interest in Yao wasn't a figment of his imagination. Li knew he would need high-level government approval to let this designated *rencai,* or "person of talent," leave the motherland that had raised and developed him. He would also need a trustworthy intermediary who could shepherd Yao to the NBA and help the Sharks get their just financial reward. As he mulled over the dilemma, Li received an unexpected phone call. A powerful official in China's central government— somebody who outranked the sports administration and the Shanghai municipal government—wanted him to meet an American friend who was keen on helping Yao get to the NBA.

Somebody, it seemed, had been reading Li's mind.

Michael Coyne arrived at the Shanghai Sharks' offices in October 1998. A fresh-faced, thirty-four-year-old lawyer from Cleveland, Ohio, he hardly exuded the image of an international wheeler-dealer with high-level government connections. But this was Li Yaomin's chance, and as they sat around the enormous mahogany table cut to resemble a basketball court in the Sharks's conference room, he listened intently as Coyne described his company, Evergreen Sports Management, and his search for the world's tallest basketball players. Coyne had traveled to some of the globe's most remote places prospecting for potential stars. He had found young giants in Brazil and Tanzania and the Sudan, placing several of them in American college programs.

Coyne's most famous client up to that point was Ri Myong-hun, a North Korean player who, at just under 7'9" was one of the world's tallest humans. Ri—who adopted the name Michael, as in Jordan— could barely outrace an oak tree, but he had a soft shooting touch and he could nearly dunk with both feet on the ground. In 1997, with the help of a Korean business associate, Coyne persuaded the paranoid leaders of the Hermit Kingdom to let Ri, then twenty-eight, try his luck in the NBA. The Korean Goliath didn't get any farther than Canada, however, because Washington—in the middle of acrimonious negotiations with Pyongyang over nuclear weapons—refused him entry under the "trading with the enemy" act that prevented American companies from doing business with North Korea. After eight months training in Ottawa, Ri returned home, never to be seen again.

Now Coyne had his eyes set on Yao Ming, and he was determined not to let this deal become another victim of international politics. Coyne had begun at the top of the pyramid, spending months meeting with officials in the central government and the Communist Party, as well as a member of the Chinese Olympic Committee. Li Yaomin wasn't interested in politics. He just wanted to make sure that in return for losing a future star, Shanghai would receive a substantial windfall. Not a problem, said Coyne. The team's percentage could be structured into Yao's contract. Li Yaomin didn't need to hear much more. "At that time, we didn't depend on Yao Ming," he says. "Why not let him go?"

The two men marveled at their mutual good fortune. In Li Yaomin, Coyne had found an entrepreneurial Chinese manager who, unlike many bureaucrats, seemed unafraid of making decisions. In Coyne, Li had discovered a bright young American intermediary who seemed eager to help Yao without neglecting the interests of the Chinese club that had developed him. Best of all, Coyne came with no strings attached: Because he had arrived on the recommendation of the central government, he was beholden neither to the CBA nor to Nike. Indeed, when the two men agreed to make Coyne's company the team's exclusive advisor on all international matters, nobody else in the Chinese sports world even knew that he was in the game—or, for that matter, that the game had begun. Not even Yao himself. Coyne left Shanghai that October having never met the eighteen-year-old center or his parents—a situation he found unsettling."The dealing with the family was very limited," Coyne said. "It seemed strange to me."

The time to meet the family would finally come on the evening of April 30, 1999. "This is the man I wanted you to meet," Li told Yao's parents, introducing them to the young American agent in the Grand Hyatt. "He's got your son's future all figured out." For the next several hours, as Yao and his parents sat in confused silence, Coyne guided them through a thick presentation booklet that outlined his three-year plan for turning Yao into an NBA star. Like a teacher conducting a high-school class—NBA 101—Coyne explained certain concepts, like the NBA's salary structure, by drawing diagrams in magic marker on a whiteboard at one end of the room. He made a long list of specialists he said he would hire to guide Yao in his development: a coach, a nutritionist, weight trainers, practice partners, even academic tutors. He also promised to provide Yao with a car, an apartment, English lessons, and a laptop computer.

At one point, Coyne elaborated the steps Yao needed to take to enter the 1999 NBA draft, then just two months away.

"Wait a minute," Da Fang interrupted. "I don't understand why this has to happen so fast. Yao Ming is not good enough to play in the NBA yet."

That was just the point, Coyne told her. Once the NBA buzz around Yao got too loud, the government might want to hold onto its national treasure.

"He's not physically ready yet, but we have all the approvals we need," Coyne recalled telling the family. "Yao is just on the cusp, he's not on the radar now. When he gets more noticed, more valuable, it will be harder to get released."

Moving fast made sense financially, too. The sooner Yao entered the NBA draft, Coyne said, the sooner the money would start to flow—and the longer he would make an NBA salary. Moreover, Yao would then be three years closer to the biggest payday of all: Once his restrictive rookie contract expired, he would be in position to sign a massive free-agent contract that could be worth tens of millions of dollars. "Why don't you have [an NBA team] pay him $3 million a year to get him in shape?" Coyne remembered asking. "Then by the time he's twenty-two, he'd be done with me and he could sign a $77 million contract."

Numbers and dates and diagrams still seemed to be swirling around the room when Li Yaomin pushed a crudely typed, two-page document in front of Yao's parents. It was an agreement that would give Coyne's company, Evergreen, the right to represent Yao for three years, until July 31, 2002.

Yao and his parents knew nothing about the mysterious workings of the NBA, and Coyne's tutorial had been more dizzying than illuminating. But now, as they tried to make sense of the contract's legalese, one line stuck out above the rest: Evergreen would garner fully one-third of Yao's earnings over the course of the agreement. Had Yao's parents been prepared for this meeting, they might have known that the NBA's limit for agents' commissions was just 4 percent—less than one-eighth the figure on the document. But even in their relative ignorance, they sensed that something wasn't quite right.

Li Yaomin only deepened their doubts. According to a source close to Yao's parents, the Sharks' manager told them that, from the remaining two-thirds, the family would receive a graduated amount over three years: $150,000 the first year, $250,000 the second, and $500,000 the third—for a grand total of $850,000. It was a huge amount of money, more than the modest Chinese family had ever contemplated before, but suddenly it seemed miserly. Even if Yao's initial NBA contract earned him an average of $1 million a year—a figure Coyne had made seem very feasible if Yao became a top-ten draft pick—this figure amounted to less than 30 percent of the total. If Coyne got a third and the family got less than a third, what would happen to the rest?

"I'm sorry, but we need to think this over carefully," Da Fang said. "We'd like to take this home and get back to you."

Li Yaomin insisted on finishing up then and there. Coyne had a flight to catch in the morning, he said, so this was the only chance to sign such a deal.

The clock crept past 2:00 A.M. They had been going at it for several hours now, and the walls seemed to be closing in around them as it came down to a standoff between Da Fang and Li Yaomin. In the end, according to a source close to the family, Li lashed out in frustration, calling Da Fang "a peasant" and asking how she dare question his authority.

"This is your last chance," he reportedly shouted. "If you don't sign this, your son is *never* going to the NBA!"

Li would later deny threatening the family. But at the time, a shaken Da Fang told friends she felt she and her family were being forced to sign. The pressure was too much. She didn't want to jeopardize her son's chances of fulfilling his NBA dream. Nor did she want to become the target of the *laoban*'s enduring animosity. She had already spent a lifetime learning about the consequences of hatred—and the price of revenge.

Da Fang picked up the pen and handed it to her son. It was nearly 3:00 A.M. when Yao signed the contract—and the family, drained and dispirited, made their way home through the empty streets of Shanghai.

The phone on Frank Sha's bedside table trilled to life just after dawn the next morning—May 1, 1999—jolting him out of a deep slumber. The twenty-four-year-old Nike basketball rep was expecting to sleep in that Saturday morning. It was, after all, May Day, when workers of the world were supposed to snooze. Who could be calling so early?

Sha answered the phone groggily and heard the voice of Yao Ming's mother. Da Fang sounded weary, as if she'd been crying.

"Auntie, what's wrong?" asked Sha, wide awake now. "Are you okay?"

It was barely light out, but he agreed to meet at her place of work, the Shanghai Sports Science Research Institute. Da Fang arrived alone, her eyes puffy and red. Sitting in the courtyard, surrounded by old pines and sycamores, Da Fang recounted the details of the contentious meeting with Li Yaomin and the unknown American agent, her torrent of words occasionally melting into a flood of tears. Sha tried to comfort her—and himself—for this was his mess, too. His primary job was to ensure that Yao and his parents remained within the Nike family—and now, it seemed, he might have failed.

Sha called Terry Rhoads, and within minutes, the Nike executive was on his way over in a taxi, pleading with Sha on the phone: "Please tell me they didn't sign!" They had signed, of course, and by the time Rhoads got to the courtyard, there was not much that he or Sha could do but try to lift Da Fang's spirits—and figure out how to forestall this American interloper who had swooped in under their noses to cut a deal with Yao Ming.

"We'd been there for several years, laying the groundwork with Yao," Rhoads says. "Who was this guy flying in?"

It was, in basketball parlance, the ultimate backdoor play.

Twenty minutes later, back in the Nike office, Rhoads started working the phones. He called Xia Song, his man in Beijing, to see if the CBA could declare the contract null and void. Then he placed a call to Walnut Creek, California. He needed to relay the news to Bill Duffy, the NBA agent he had introduced to Yao and his parents barely two months before. A former college basketball star with a spit-polished style, the 6'4" Duffy had an almost magical gift for putting people at ease, and both Rhoads and Yao had fallen easily under his spell. Da Fang didn't sign a contract with Duffy—citing the possible political repercussions of signing with an American agent—but she did agree informally to let Duffy be Yao's lone representative. To Nike's matchmaker, it seemed like a cosmic convergence. "All of the stars were aligned," Rhoads said.

But now, everything seemed out of whack.

Duffy listened in shock as Rhoads broke the news about the Evergreen contract. Who was this Coyne? And what had happened to all of the goodwill that Duffy had built in China?

Looking at a faxed copy of the contract, Duffy couldn't believe what he saw. Evergreen wanted a 33-percent commission, when the NBA limit was 4 percent. The contract also seemed to violate another NBA rule stipulating that players earn their salaries for themselves, not for foreign governments or business entities. Moreover, Duffy checked and found no record of any Michael Coyne being registered as an NBA agent.

"This is extortion," Duffy told Rhoads. "It'll never hold up in the NBA."

Just to be sure, Duffy faxed a copy of the contract to NBA Players' Association president Billy Hunter in New York, who, he said, later confirmed that the contract would not be acceptable in the NBA.

The following week, after listening to the advice of Nike, Duffy, and a local lawyer, Da Fang composed a letter to Evergreen reneging on the contract, saying she and her family were coerced into signing an invalid document. Her voice was soon joined by that of Yao Songpin, the deputy commissioner of the Shanghai Sports Commission, who said that the deal had been done without government approval. Getting Yao out of China would require many more signatures up the Chinese bureaucratic chain. The Evergreen contract seemed dead on arrival.

Li Yaomin's backdoor play hadn't resulted in the easy layup he had imagined. But the Sharks' boss wasn't about to give up. He insisted that the contract remained valid and that Da Fang and her family had signed of their own free will. "Da Fang thought the club was selling off her son," Li says. "But it was a huge misunderstanding." In any case, Li knew that anybody who wanted to bring Yao to the NBA would still have to go through him first.

Coyne, for his part, was crestfallen by the turn of events. "I thought I was wearing a white hat," he says. "I tried to do it the Asian way, starting with the central government and working my way down. Duffy did it the American way, winning the player over first." Coyne blames Duffy for weaving a web of half-truths and distortions to turn Yao and his family against him. Evergreen was not acting as an NBA agent, Coyne says, but as a management company that would help Yao in every aspect of his career development—a distinction, he says, that made the high commission fee legal. Moreover, it was the Chinese authorities—not Coyne himself—who requested that the fee structure be set up so that Evergreen received a third of Yao's earnings. The idea, he said, was for him to funnel 98 percent of that money to various Chinese government entities, including the Shanghai Sharks, to buy out Yao's contract and gain permission to represent him. That explanation only added to the mystery, however, and Da Fang vowed never to deal with Evergreen again.

The trauma of May Day had barely dissipated by the time Frank Sha visited Yao's parents in their apartment a month later, on May 31. Though deeply shaken, Da Fang and Da Yao showed gratitude to Sha for trying to extricate the family from the mess. For a long time, they had seen Sha simply as the coach's son, the little boy upstairs who used to play with their son. Now the twenty-four-year-old Nike rep was one of the few people they could trust.

Sitting on the rattan-covered sofa in their living room sipping tea, Sha seemed more businesslike than usual that day. And when he laid a sheaf of papers in front of Da Fang and Da Yao, the purpose of his visit became clear: Nike wanted Yao under formal contract.

Sha's boss, Rhoads, had been spooked by what he called the Evergreen "train wreck," and he wanted to ensure that Yao would never again be taken out of Nike's control. Despite all of the foreign trips and the efforts to gain the family's trust, the company still had no formal relationship with Yao. Before, there had been no real sense of urgency. But now it was time, Rhoads decided. "We didn't want to get caught with our pants down," he recalls. "It was still not one-hundred-percent clear what would happen with the Evergreen deal. But if it stood up, at least Yao was going to be under contract with Nike."

In the living room that day, Sha explained to Yao's parents that Nike wanted to show its commitment to Yao by paying him to continue wearing the shoes he loved. Only one other Chinese athlete had ever received a bigger endorsement contract—and that was Wang Zhizhi, who was three years older than Yao and already recognized as the biggest star in Asia. The baseline number wasn't too big—less than $20,000 a year to start—but it was already more than ten times what the eighteen-year-old center was making on the Sharks and twenty times the average salary in China. Performance bonuses would also be added if Yao led the CBA in scoring or won the league MVP award. The numbers, moreover, would increase every year of the contract— and if Yao made it to the NBA, he could negotiate a separate, far more substantial bonus.

Da Fang looked over the document skeptically. The financial terms didn't seem to bother her so much; Yao couldn't expect to receive more than Wang. But she was worried about the length of the contract: four years. That meant Yao Ming would be bound by this deal until May 31, 2003. Far too long, in her opinion.

"Is there any way to shorten the time period?" she asked.

Four years was standard, Sha told her. Wang's was the same length. Beaverton didn't offer shorter-term contracts because it needed time to work with its clients on ad campaigns without worrying about renegotiating all the time. The terms, in other words, were not negotiable.

Once again, Da Fang found herself in the unnerving situation of being pushed to sign on the dotted line. All of these legal terms—endorsement contracts, individual rights, representation agreements—were still largely alien concepts in China, and the former Red Guard didn't know exactly what they meant or how they worked. On the other hand, Da Fang didn't want to spoil the goodwill that had been built up over the years with Sha and his boss.

Da Fang picked up the pen and, without smiling, looked over at Sha.

"I'm only signing this," she said, "out of respect for your father because he was my coach."

Yao was now officially a Nike client, a cog in a new machine. It should have been a happy occasion: the union of two families, the marriage of a company and its new hero, the coming together of East and West. Nine months earlier, on Yao's eighteenth birthday, his family and the whole Nike crew had beamed for the camera, arm in arm, after Da Fang's home-cooked meal. But something new and uncomfortable had now intruded into the relationship, something that nobody wanted to acknowledge. It was the seed of doubt.

11

Mavericks and Mandarins

H. Ross Perot, Jr., didn't know anything about basketball, and he wasn't afraid to admit it. When the only son of Texas's most famous billionaire plunked down $125 million to buy the Dallas Mavericks franchise in 1996, he bluntly confessed that he had not done it to indulge any affection for the sport, but to expand his real-estate empire in downtown Dallas with a massive new arena complex. But on June 30, 1999—the day of the NBA draft—the clean-cut forty-one-year-old property developer sat in the Mavs' draft-operations center in Dallas's Reunion Arena and couldn't help getting caught up in the excitement.

The "war room" buzzed with activity. Mavs coaches scribbled names on a big board, while scouts and assistants manned the phones or scanned television screens, computer terminals, and sheafs of scouting reports. And then there was what, for Perot, in his regulation dark suit, white shirt, and tie, must have been the nearly incomprehensible banter of hoop vernacular: "serious ups" (excellent vertical leap); "pick 'em on the come" (draft on potential); "he's a preemie" (not ready for the NBA).

Perot might not have known all the slang, but like his eccentric father—the little Texan with a buzz-saw twang who had made two rambunctious runs at the U.S. presidency—he knew how to identify historic business opportunities. And one visitor in the room that day was testament to those instincts: a young, broad-shouldered Chinese man with a wolverine-style buzz-cut. The war room was a place for secret strategies and negotiations, a preserve in which strangers were normally viewed with suspicion, if not outright hostility. But Perot and the Mavs front office had invited this man, Xia Song, as their special guest. Perot had only just met Xia, but the mere presence of the Chinese visitor infused the proceedings with a dose of international intrigue.

Perot had been born with global ambitions. The only son in a famous

household that played host to a constant flow of astronauts, military heroes, and former prisoners of war, "Junior" got his first taste of overseas adventure when he accompanied his father on trips to Southeast
Asia during the Vietnam War. After graduating from Vanderbilt University in 1981, he set the speed record for an around-the-world helicopter
flight, circumnavigating the globe in twenty-nine days. Perot went on to
serve as an Air Force fighter pilot, but he was never as quirky or charismatic as his father, nor did he have the rebellious streak of the wild-
living son of another Texas dynasty, George W. Bush, who had also
recently bought part of a professional sports franchise, the Texas
Rangers baseball team. "Rebelling wasn't a big option in our household," Perot said.

Junior would instead become the leading real-estate developer in a
state where builders often wield more power than politicians. And as his
property and computer businesses expanded, he started looking for
large-scale projects around the world, from the Middle East to China. It
was in 1997, during a trip to the Far East, that Perot first heard Wang
Zhizhi's name. He was attending a meeting in Hong Kong for one of his
companies, Perot Systems, when a Chinese business associate cornered
him with a question about basketball.

"When are the Mavs going to draft a Chinese player?" the man
asked.

Perot looked at him quizzically. He didn't know much about basketball, but this sounded like a crazy idea. Did China, a nation not known
for its people of stature, even have basketball players? He decided to
humor his colleague.

"Well, who shall we draft?" Perot asked.

"Wang Zhizhi," the man answered. "He's the Michael Jordan of
China."

Perot quickly got an earful about the hoops-playing army lieutenant.
Most of the basketball talk meant little to him, but he was intrigued by
the business possibilities. The first team that drafted a Chinese player
would surely reap a windfall, not just in terms of increasing the team's
marquee value—but, more importantly for Perot, in building goodwill
with Beijing. Keen to expand his computer and real-estate empire into
the Middle Kingdom, Perot sensed that basketball could help pave the
way.

Back in Dallas, Perot didn't have to look far to find somebody who
shared his enthusiasm for a soldier stuck in a Communist sports system
halfway around the world. Mavericks assistant coach Donnie Nelson,

the globe-trotting thirty-five-year-old son of head coach Don Nelson, had already been tracking Wang for several years. A former player with the traveling Christian basketball team, Athletes in Action, Donnie had made internationalizing the game his NBA mission—a modern-day incarnation of the YMCA missionaries who spread the game around the world a century before. It was in St. Petersburg, Russia—not far from where Nelson had recruited Lithuanian sharpshooter Sarunas Marciulionis in 1989—that he caught his first glimpse of Wang in 1993. The youngster was participating in his first international junior tournament, and though he didn't get much playing time, Nelson remembers him vividly. Wang was built like a pair of chopsticks, but the seven-footer possessed a silky jump shot and the slightest hint of a swagger—"a little edge," Nelson recalls, "something that was just near the surface." Even more memorable: The Chinese junior team roster listed Wang's year of birth as 1979, making him just fourteen years old.

Three years later, Wang emerged from behind the curtain of the Chinese sports system to make his debut in the 1996 Olympics in Atlanta. It would be another two years, however, before Nelson finally met Wang in person at the 1998 Goodwill Games in New York. Looking for a place to sit in the crowded athletes' cafeteria, Nelson barged in on the Chinese team as the players, coaches, and minders wolfed down their supper. "Hi, my name is Donnie Nelson!" he blurted. Wang and the others stared up blankly from their plates, never changing their expressions. "That was the icebreaker," Nelson says, laughing.

When Nelson landed in Beijing for the first time in late August 1998, the Chinese coaches and officials who'd previously given him the frosty reception welcomed him like a long-lost friend. One reason for the turnaround, aside from Nelson's unrelenting enthusiasm, was his guide through the Beijing bureaucracy: Xia Song, the beefy, twenty-six-year-old Nike rep whom Terry Rhoads referred to as "our bulldog in Beijing." Rhoads had hired Xia the year before in part because he saw the former athlete as the perfect embodiment of new China, a restless striver with a lot to prove. As Xia led Nelson and his sidekick, Mavs scout Tony Ronzone, around Beijing, he regaled them with stories of growing up in the remote, coal-mining province of Guizhou, where he upgraded his dreams of basketball stardom for an even grander ambition: becoming the David Stern of China. Inspired by old copies of *Sports Illustrated* and NBA Yearbooks that a sister living in America had sent him, Xia enrolled in Beijing Sports University, the breeding ground for China's athletic top brass. When Nelson arrived in Beijing, Xia had been working at Nike for only a year. But thanks to his gift for making *guanxi* —

and the fact that many top officials shared his alma mater—he had already earned people's trust in the most sacred precincts of Chinese sport.

With Xia smoothing the way, Nelson and Ronzone ingratiated themselves with their Chinese hosts. They conducted basketball clinics and endured long Chinese banquets, where they learned the dubious pleasures of knocking back endless cups of rice wine—with the most prized cups laced with bright-green snake bile. Somewhere amid all the toasting and *guanxi*-making, the visitors got a glimpse of China's hoop potential. "The thirst for basketball in China was incredible," says Nelson, recalling a Nike three-on-three tournament in Beijing that had a limit of three hundred teams, but for which twelve hundred teams showed up. "In all my travels, I've never been so blown away as on my first trip to China."

Even more surprising for the two visitors was the mother lode of basketball-playing giants that China was producing. Ronzone, who would spend much of the following two years coaching in China, said he saw twenty seven-footers between the ages of sixteen and twenty. The tallest was a raw and ungainly Shanghai native, Yao Ming, but the most polished by far was Wang, the dominant player in the Chinese league—and Xia's biggest client at Nike. Watching the center glide across the court and shoot with pinpoint accuracy from every angle, Nelson believed he had found a rough-hewn diamond with NBA potential. Still, he tried not to get too excited. Nelson didn't know if a player sequestered his entire life in the Chinese system could learn to compete with the best in the world. And if a Chinese player were drafted, would the country's top officials—for all their generosity with the snake and wine—ever allow him to leave for the NBA?

The most ticklish question of all revolved around Wang's age.

Over the years, Xia Song had developed a close rapport with his client—taking him out for steak dinners at the Hard Rock Cafe, delivering Nike sweatshirts and shoes to his parents, nurturing his dreams of making it to the NBA. It was during one of their nightly conversations that Wang made a startling confession. The birth date printed in his passport and all team documents, he told Xia, was fabricated. He was not born in 1979, but in 1977. The authorities had manipulated his age, he said, so that he could play two more years—and win more prestige for China—in international junior tournaments.

Age-fixing among athletes was common in international basketball—so common, in fact, that many basketball insiders felt there was nothing wrong with China's engaging in a little manipulation to level the playing field. But it would slowly dawn on Xia just how critical the difference of two years would be for Wang's future. Poring over NBA draft rules, Xia found that players were automatically eligible to enter the draft during the calendar year in which they turned twenty-two years old. That meant that if Wang were born in 1979, he could not enter the NBA draft until 2001—*unless* he had the prior written consent of both the PLA and the CBA, which was unlikely given that both institutions viewed him as property of the state. But if Wang was actually born in 1977, then he would be automatically eligible for the 1999 draft just a few months away; an NBA team could select him without getting explicit permission from Beijing.

The truth about Wang's age put Xia in a position to make Chinese sports history, and perhaps some money on the side, and he wasn't about to let the opportunity slip from his grasp. Xia was an entrepreneur at heart, not a company man, and the cloak-and-dagger plan that began to form in his mind compelled him to go behind the backs of everybody he worked with: his Nike boss Rhoads, the NBA agent Bill Duffy, his friends at the CBA, and his carefully cultivated contacts in the People's Liberation Army. Without informing his superiors, Xia rang up Donnie Nelson and told him about Wang's revelation. The Mavs coach seemed intrigued. The information gave him the inside track on a little-known talent who could make the Mavs the most popular team in the biggest market in the world. Even so, Nelson wondered if they should speak first with Chinese government officials, just to make sure that the Mavs wouldn't be wasting a valuable draft pick. Xia demurred. "If you announce that this guy is draftable, that he was actually born in 1977, then Wang is going to be stuck in a very ugly situation," Xia recalls telling Nelson. "He may never get out."

It would be better to draft Wang first, Xia said. Then the officials would be under pressure to let him go. A media campaign—orchestrated, naturally, by Xia himself—could trumpet the historic event to China's patriotic basketball fans and persuade government officials that this was an extraordinary honor for China. Facing the reality of Wang's selection and the fervent popular response, how could Beijing deny Wang the right to play in the NBA?

Nelson conceded that Xia knew more than he did about the Chinese bureaucracy, but the coach had one further concern. So far, Xia had provided no proof that Wang was actually born in 1977. Did the Nike rep expect the Mavericks to make a multimillion-dollar decision based simply on his word?

As the June 1999 NBA draft loomed less than a month away, Xia focused all of his energy on getting incontrovertible proof of Wang's age and delivering it to Nelson before the draft. By coincidence, China's national junior team was scheduled to be in Dallas during the week of the draft, practicing under Nelson's supervision. Rhoads had assigned Xia to cover a Nike soccer camp in Europe in late June, but Xia announced that he would be skipping the camp. He wanted to use his personal vacation time to act as official interpreter for the Chinese junior team. It was, he said, part of his "patriotic duty."

Obtaining official evidence of Wang's age would require more subterfuge. Bill Duffy, the NBA agent whom Nike had brought to China, was trying to orchestrate a deal with the Vancouver Grizzlies, who showed interest in selecting Wang to help boost the team's flagging home attendance in the most Asian city in North America. Duffy and Rhoads had heard about Wang's true birth date—Xia had told them as much—but they didn't have documentation, and Xia took steps to ensure that their efforts to obtain it went nowhere. He wanted the proof for himself, for his own private shot at making history with the Mavericks. Time was running out, however, and Wang wasn't even in Beijing; he was with the national team practicing in seclusion in the northeastern city of Changchun.

Xia called him one evening in the team compound. "Da Zhi, remember what you told me about your age?" Xia asked. "I'm going to need some proof."

Wang was taken aback. This was a sensitive issue that he almost never discussed anywhere, much less inside the team compound where everyone assumed that, as the Chinese say, *geqiang you er*—"the walls have ears."

"What for?" Wang asked.

Xia explained that he was heading to Dallas just before the draft, and he wanted to persuade the Mavericks to make Wang the first Chinese player in the NBA. There was only one hitch: The Mavs needed evidence of Wang's true age.

"It's only on my old military I.D.," Wang said. "But I don't have that with me. It's back in my room at Hongshankou"—the army compound near Beijing.

"Well," Xia said, "we need to get it."

It was a devilish dilemma for Wang. Though eager to be drafted by an NBA team, he seemed worried about letting his I.D. card get into the wrong hands. If the truth leaked out, China's basketball leaders would be exposed as cheats—and they would know that he had broken his promise to conceal his real birth date. Such a loss of face, moreover, could push Chinese officials to prevent Wang from ever going to the NBA. Heightening the sensitivity of the situation was China's angry reaction to the NATO bombing of the Chinese embassy in Belgrade just a few weeks earlier, in May 1999. The anti-American protests outside the U.S. ambassador's residence in Beijing had subsided by now, but graffiti still scarred the building—and Sino-American relations remained extremely tense. NBA basketball, the ultimate symbol of American culture, had even gotten caught in the crossfire: As part of its retaliation, Beijing canceled all NBA broadcasts for the rest of the season (and halfway through the following season). How would Chinese officials react now if the Americans, using evidence of age-fixing, chose their best player behind their backs?

Xia sensed Wang's trepidation. "Listen, Da Zhi," he said. "I would never do anything to put you in a bad situation. You've gotta trust me on this."

Finally, Wang relented. But how was he going to get the I.D. card to Xia Song? A civilian like Xia couldn't wander into his barracks at Hongshankou and filch the card himself. After a moment's thought, Wang promised to arrange for a friend to pick up the card and get a copy to Xia before he left for Dallas.

A week before the June 30 draft, Xia Song landed in Dallas with the Chinese national junior team, clutching the precious copy of Wang's military I.D. card. At the first opportunity, the Nike rep pigeonholed Nelson in the Mavs' administration offices at Baylor University's Landry Center and handed him the proof he thought the Mavs needed.

Nelson looked at the piece of paper and registered no reaction. The poker face, so uncharacteristic for a coach who never seemed at a loss for an enthusiastic slap on the back, unnerved Xia. Perhaps the Mavs, then a middle-of-the-pack team in the NBA's Western Division, had another plan that didn't involve a largely untested army lieutenant from China. Dallas only had two direct draft picks that year and Wang, even with an amended age, was a risky choice.

Xia asked Nelson what the Mavs were going to do, and Nelson's response sounded less than hopeful: "We don't know."

Draft day came, but Xia had still heard nothing. He joined the junior team for an evening practice, tormented by the knowledge that the draft was taking place in New York—and that his gambit may have failed. But then, shortly after 9:00 P.M., a Mavs staffer rushed into the gym and told Xia he had been instructed to drive him to the Mavs' draft-operations room in Reunion Arena downtown. A few minutes later, Xia was ushered into the war room, where everybody was gathered: the silver-maned head coach Don "Nellie" Nelson, his goateed son Donnie Nelson, the impish Tony Ronzone, and the lone man in a white shirt and tie, Ross Perot, Jr. They were all beaming.

"We did it!" Donnie shouted. "We picked your boy!"

On the television set, a live transmission from New York's Madison Square Garden showed NBA deputy commissioner Russ Granik receiving the envelope that contained the Mavs' second-round selection. Xia pulled out his cell phone to call Wang. It was almost 10:00 P.M. in Dallas, nearly 11:00 A.M. at the national-team training camp in the northern Manchurian city of Changchun. The team's morning practice had just ended.

"Listen, boy," Xia told Wang over the crackly connection. "In about thirty seconds, your dream is going to come true."

Wang was speechless. "I thought it was impossible," he said later. "I'm halfway around the world in China. They hardly know me. They've never really seen me play."

Xia placed the phone down next to the television and turned up the volume so Wang could hear the announcement. Together, Xia, Perot, and the two Nelsons watched the look of surprise cross Granik's face as he opened the Mavs' draft envelope. Here was a name the NBA executive might never have seen before, a name he surely didn't know how to pronounce. He said: "The Dallas Mavericks, with the thirty-sixth pick in the draft, select Wang Zee-Zee from the People's Republic of China." The ballroom at Madison Square Garden broke into polite and baffled applause, but the Mavs war room erupted in cheers.

Xia picked up the phone. "Did you hear that, Da Zhi?"

Wang didn't say anything. He seemed to be crying.

"You should go and tell your parents," Xia said.

"No, I can't tell them now," Wang said. "They will never believe it. Now even I don't dare to believe it is true."

Nellie grabbed the phone out of Xia's hand. "Keep working hard," he said. Donnie then got on: "Congratulations, Dodger, you have just made history." And finally, Ross Perot, Jr.: "We'll be coming over to get you real soon."

Outside the bubble of the war room, confusion reigned. Nobody in Dallas had ever heard of Wang Zhizhi; his name had never appeared on any draft list. Long-suffering Mavs fans ripped into the Nelsons' Chinese gamble. At one basketball Web site, Hoop-la.com, a writer moaned: "Some unknown player from China? I think Don Nelson has gone insane!" ESPN, grading the draft, gave the Mavs an "F," saying "Don Nelson just doesn't get it." Even the cognoscenti had their doubts. "I've seen Wang play and for a big man, he can really run the floor," said former NBA coach Hubie Brown. "The big question, though, is about his age; I'm not sure if this draft pick will be eligible."

Xia's coup left Duffy and Rhoads dumbfounded. Even without proof of Wang's age, the Grizzlies had been primed to take Wang with the thirty-seventh pick—the one directly following Dallas's selection. Neither Duffy nor Rhoads knew exactly what had happened, but it wouldn't be long before they discovered that someone—someone inside Nike—had orchestrated this unexpected turn of events. (When Rhoads and his superiors in Beaverton finally learned of Xia's subterfuge, they were livid—marking the beginning of a spiral that led to Xia's departure from Nike to start his own private company a few months later.)

Back in China, the news traveled fast. Xia had alerted friends at CCTV and Xinhua News Agency to broadcast reports almost instantaneously, making Wang's draft a fait accompli. Most Chinese fans reacted gleefully, flooding Web sites formerly filled with anti-American vitriol over the Belgrade embassy bombing with a gentler form of patriotic pride. For Yao and the Shanghai leadership, however, there was only envy and disappointment. Sharks coach Li Qiuping, in Dallas leading the junior team, grumbled to Donnie Nelson the next morning: "We wanted Yao Ming to go to the NBA first."

But if there was jubilation in Beijing and disappointment in Shanghai, there was only an ominous silence from the military brass cloistered in the Hongshankou base. No one knew how the PLA generals would react.

The four-man rescue mission led by Ross Perot, Jr., landed in Beijing on a hazy afternoon in the middle of August 1999. For the previous seven weeks, ever since the draft, the Mavericks' owner had monitored the mixed reports coming out of China. The initial silence had been followed by a flurry of hopeful dispatches in the Chinese press predicting that Beijing would soon release Wang to play in the NBA. Army officials denounced these stories as fabrications, and another round of silence followed. In the last week of July, the Mavericks sent a fax to the Chinese national sports commission, announcing their intention to come to Beijing to negotiate Wang's release. The message was relayed to Wang's team, the Bayi Rockets, and to the top generals of the People's Liberation Army. There was no reply.

It was time, the Mavs' owner decided, to launch the sort of international rescue operation that had made his father famous. Ross Perot, Sr., had spent the better part of three decades sponsoring quixotic missions in dictatorships throughout the world, starting in 1969, when the brash young billionaire carried out an off-the-books operation to airlift food and medicine to American prisoners of war in North Vietnam. Perot Sr. was so obsessively committed to rescuing POWs that he even brought along his teenage son, Ross Jr., on one of his fact-finding trips to refugee camps in Cambodia and Laos. Now, a quarter-century later, Junior was bringing his own sons along to spring a player from China's Communist sports system.

The most striking similarity to his father's exploits was the old white-haired man who was walking next to Junior in the Beijing airport. Harry McKillop was a former Braniff Airways vice president who had worked behind the scenes on nearly every special operation Perot Sr. funded, from the 1969 Vietnam airlift to the daring 1979 rescue of two Americans caught in a Tehran prison during the Iranian revolution (an operation lavishly recounted in Ken Follett's 1984 bestseller, *On Wings of Eagles*). This wasn't McKillop's first mission to China. Back in the 1970s, the Irish-American had led a Perot-financed team to rescue 175 refugees from Vietnam who were being detained by Chinese authorities on Hainan Island. More than a decade later, again at Perot's behest, McKillop returned to China in search of an American woman who had been held prisoner as a presumed CIA operative for more than forty years. McKillop reportedly tracked her down in Manchuria and won her release—again under mysterious circumstances.

After all the hair-raising missions he had undertaken, McKillop—now close to eighty—must have thought saving Wang was rather straightforward. The People's Liberation Army, after all, had 2.5 million soldiers. Surely the generals could spare one tall lieutenant who happened to have a sweet running hook shot.

Perot's rescue team, however, didn't seem to fully appreciate the significance of Wang's role as a soldier in the People's Liberation Army, the most reclusive, intransigent segment of Chinese society. It was the PLA generals—not the national sports commission, to whom the Mavericks had directed their original fax—who held the final say over Wang's fate, and they harbored the deepest suspicions about the Americans' intentions. The PLA couldn't fathom how a group of foreigners, without China's knowledge, had laid claim to the player the army had so carefully cultivated. Wasn't this how the Middle Kingdom had lost its greatness in the nineteenth century, by ceding its most valuable assets to marauding Westerners?

Part of the confusion may have simply been a matter of translation. The word "draft," after all, carries a different meaning for the average Western sports fan than it does for a Chinese army general. "China didn't understand what the draft was," says Cheong Sau Ching, public-relations director for the NBA's office in Hong Kong. "People thought it was some kind of coercive recruitment like an army draft, when it was simply an invitation to play in the NBA. Chinese officials kept asking me: 'Why didn't you go through us first?' But *we* didn't even know. Nobody knew Wang was going to be drafted until that day."

Feeling that they had suffered a loss of face, Wang's military bosses refused to meet the Mavericks' delegation. Xia Song, after keeping PLA officials in the dark in the months leading up to the draft, now tried to convince them that having a player selected by the NBA was an honor, not an insult. But he ran into a wall. "Wang was Chinese army. That was it," says Xia, who acted as the Mavs' guide in Beijing. "Politically and practically, nobody knew how he could go from the army to the NBA. That was the thing nobody wanted to touch."

The Americans tried not to lose faith, but they couldn't help but wonder: Had they wasted a valuable draft pick?

On their first morning in Beijing, Perot and company dropped by the national-team training center near the Temple of Heaven. After practice ended, Wang jogged over to the sidelines with a shy smile. He accepted hugs and handshakes from the Nelsons, in their matching scruffy goatees, and then met the clean-shaven capitalist in khakis who wanted to become his newest boss, Ross Perot, Jr. At the other end of the court, eighteen-year-old Yao Ming looked on jealously as Donnie challenged Wang to a shooting contest and Perot presented him with a ten-gallon cowboy hat.

The media trumpeted Perot's arrival, and Chinese basketball fans treated the Nelsons like rock stars, following them around as they conducted seminars for Chinese coaches and clinics for Beijing youth. Donnie never missed a chance to sell his audience on the wisdom of letting Wang play in the NBA, often framing it in terms of national power and pride. "If you want to be great basketball players, don't just be the best in your city or country, go and compete against the best in the world," Donnie urged the Chinese players, before adding: "It would be a shame if the first Asian to play in the NBA was not Chinese."

Beijing sports officials also seemed remarkably welcoming. The Americans sipped tea with the national sports director and dined with the national team coach. On Perot's final day in Beijing, he had a lunchtime chat with Beijing's deputy mayor about how their two cities could help each other achieve their mutual dreams of hosting the Olympic Games—Beijing in 2008, Dallas in 2012. But for all the friendly talk and smiling photo ops, there was one inescapable truth: Nobody had any sway over the military, and unless the PLA agreed to release Wang, nothing else mattered.

Moments after Perot left for the airport that day, Xia Song's cell phone rang. It was Xin Lancheng, the CBA director.

"Get over here as fast as you can," Xin told him. "The army leaders are waiting for the Americans."

Within fifteen minutes, the two Nelsons, Harry McKillop, and Xia were sitting in the CBA's second-floor conference room across from two somber-looking officials wearing the crisp uniforms of the People's Liberation Army. One of the officials was Qian Limin, the deputy director of Bayi sports. The other, a woman with an extra stripe on her epaulet, was Chen Zhaodi, the director of the PLA's politics, arts, and sports bureau—the highest-ranking military official involved in sports. Neither of them looked happy to be there.

Xin sat at the head of the wooden table, and he made his introduction brief. "I think you all have something to discuss," he said.

There was an awkward silence. The military officials didn't nod or smile; they just stared coldly at the Americans over their cups of bitter tea. Donnie Nelson spoke up first. "We understand that the draft may have come as a surprise to you," he said. He explained that the draft was simply an invitation for Wang to play in the NBA. There was no prior notification, he explained, because an NBA team, much like an army, tries to hold onto its secrets to keep a competitive advantage over other teams in the league. "We didn't mean any disrespect to you," he said. "We see the draft as a recognition of the talent in China, a great chance to bring our countries closer together."

Qian Limin frowned. In a gruff voice laced with sarcasm, he said: "You know, your team is quite famous now in China." By drafting Wang, the Mavericks had suddenly become one of the best-known teams in China, and that, Qian seemed to be implying, must be worth a lot of money in merchandise sales and other business opportunities. The subtext was clear: *You capitalists are only in it for the money.*

Nellie stepped in, smiling. "Well, you are very famous in America now, too." China finally had a player in the NBA draft, and he was a PLA soldier.

The officials didn't crack a smile.

"The first time we sat down with the army was pretty unnerving," Donnie recalled later. "The atmosphere was very chilly. There were pre-

Hong Nanli

The lifelong rivalry between Wang Zhizhi and Yao Ming gains new intensity in 2001, when the two centers—both heavily pursued by NBA agents—face off in the finals of the China Basketball Association Championship.

In 1954, as Chairman Mao's massive sports system begins to take shape, a basketball game in Beihai pits the People's Liberation Army squad against a team from the Beijing Sports Institute.

Before a "friendly" 1974 game with Albania, China's 4'11" Vice Premier Deng Xiaoping (*second row, left*) stands behind the kneeling 6'2" captain of the Chinese women's national team—Yao Ming's mother, Fang Fengdi (*bottom row, center*).

Near the end of the Cultural Revolution in 1974, the Shanghai women's basketball team gives a demonstration of Communist spirit to peasants at a collective farm outside of the city.

Yao Ming, age nine, towers above his class of young basketball recruits at the Xuhui District Sports School in Shanghai. In another year, Yao will be as tall as his first coach, Li Zhangming (*far left*).

With his body growing so fast he can feel it in his sleep, a teenaged Yao struggles to build his stamina on the sports-school track.

Young gymnasts at the Xuhui District Sports School follow the same rigorous— some would say torturous—routines that have produced dozens of Olympic champions.

Yao Ming takes a rare day off from his full-time basketball training to enjoy his mother's home cooking in the family's cramped Shanghai apartment.

Yao seventeen, stands with Shanghai sports-institute researcher Wei Guoping, who believes his regimen of traditional Chinese medicine helped the teenager grow an extra few inches.

A party celebrating Yao's eighteenth birthday brings together two worlds in the family's apartment: (*from left*) Yao's parents; Nike's former Beijing rep Xia Song; Yao; Terry Rhoads; the Dallas Mavericks' Donnie Nelson; scout Tony Ronzone; Frank Sha; and Nike's Jimmy Qin.

Wang Zhizhi stands with his parents and the Dallas Mavericks' Donnie Nelson in Beijing shortly before his long-awaited departure for the NBA in April 2001.

At the height of his popularity as a national basketball star, Wang rubs shoulders with Chinese president Jiang Zemin during an official reception.

Wang pumps his first in a rare display of emotion after scoring his first NBA basket, a perfect swish from the top of the key.

Agence France-Presse

Yao Ming waits in line with other visa applicants outside the United States Embassy in Beijing in October 2002.

Agence France-Presse

Yao bids farewell to his parents at the CNN office in Beijing after the June 2002 NBA draft. The 1968 propaganda poster above the door reads: "Down with the American imperialists!"

Yao Ming and Wang Zhizhi battle for a rebound in their first NBA game against each other in November 2002, barely a month after Yao arrived in America—and Wang got kicked off the Chinese national team.

Agence France-Presse

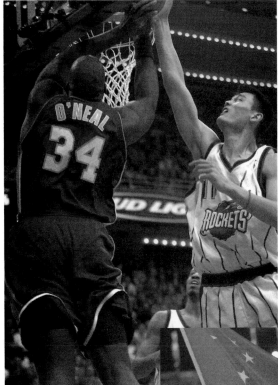

Yao Ming snuffs Shaquille O'Neal in the opening minutes of their highly anticipated clash in January 2003.

As China's flag bearer, Yao looms over other athletes during the opening ceremonies of the 2004 Olympic Games in Athens.

With basketball growing in popularity across China, aspiring players like these Beijing boys don't let an improvised hoop stop them from soaring.

conceptions on both sides. They must have thought: 'What's going on here with this NBA team laying claim to our property?' And we thought: 'This Red Army is old-style Communism, treating its players like a piece of property.' "

The Nelsons ended up doing most of the talking, while McKillop quietly watched the proceedings, his facial expression as coldly impenetrable as his counterparts' across the table. "We are not trying to steal your player," Donnie continued. "We would like to build a relationship with you, to sit down with you and understand the situation. We'd like to get Wang to the NBA as soon as possible, but we respect your point of view."

The PLA's perspective was unwavering. Wang would not be allowed to go to the NBA, Qian explained, because Bayi needed its star center to maintain the team's dominance within China. Moreover, PLA leaders were frightened by the muscle-bound brutality of the NBA game. What if Wang's frail body couldn't withstand the blows? If he came back injured, how would that help anybody?

Near the end of the meeting, Qian's boss, Chen Zhaodi, spoke up. "We appreciate your interest in our player, but this is out of our control," she said. "We have to make a report to our superiors, and they will make any final decision." Chen's superiors were the generals in charge of the PLA's political department, the most powerful members of China's military.

How long might that final decision take? The generals hadn't even started to discuss the matter, she said. The military brass, apparently, didn't like to be pressured, especially not by some fast-talking Americans. Chen concluded by reciting a famous Chinese adage that counsels infinite patience: "Only when the canal is dug will the water flow."

The Americans puzzled over the proverb for a minute, with Xia trying to interpret, before the brush-off was clear: *Don't call us, we'll call you.*

Realizing there was no sense in pushing further, Donnie reached down and rummaged around in his bag. "You should know that regardless of what happens, we've come here to create goodwill," he said. "We figured you probably didn't know much about our state of Texas, so we wanted to give you some mementos that would make you feel like honorary Texans."

Donnie pulled out a pair of embroidered cowboy hats—big, white, wide-brimmed—and presented them with a broad smile. The Chinese army officials seemed baffled. Didn't this American see that they had their own peaked military caps with their single red Communist stars?

"Go ahead, try 'em on!" Donnie urged.

Goaded on by the enthusiastic American, the PLA officials placed the hats tentatively on their heads. It wasn't a good look—outlandish cowboy hats on top of dark-green PLA uniforms—but for Donnie, it represented a minor victory: For that brief moment, China and America were united.

"I'm sorry," Chen Zhaodi said, "but we don't have anything for you."

The Mavericks would leave China empty-handed. There would be no daring rescue of Lieutenant Wang Zhizhi. But at least now there was a ray of hope. If Donnie could get Chinese army leaders to put on cowboy hats, maybe he had a chance of one day convincing them to try on the NBA for size.

12

Hoop Diplomacy

Fans swarmed up the steps of Shanghai's Luwan Stadium, lured by the promise of an epic showdown. It was a chilly night in November 2000, half an hour before game time. As the raucous crowd packed the arena, it was easy to forget that the games in China weren't always like this. A decade before, as the CCTV apparatchik had reminded David Stern, the entire Chinese sports system was designed to ennoble the nation, not to entertain the masses. Even after the CBA league began in 1995, Chinese hoopsters still looked like Soviet-era automatons performing out of a somber sense of duty. The Shanghai Sharks were one of the worst offenders, playing games so completely devoid of drama and emotion that they would sometimes have more players on court than paying customers in the crowd.

But this was the opening game of the 2000–2001 CBA season, and the Sharks, as well as the league's top officials, were determined to make the leap from no-show time to Showtime. A gaggle of heavily made-up cheerleaders in plastic miniskirts and bare midriffs revved up the crowd—a remarkable transformation in a nation where three decades before women were forced to wear androgynous Mao suits and crop their hair into a sexless bob. Then a Chinese rap group called "Point Zero" took center stage, belting out the CBA's new anthem, *Xiangxin Ziji*—"Believe in Yourself."

The real hoopla began when the Shanghai players burst onto the court through the mouth of a massive plastic shark to face their archrivals, the glowering soldiers of the Bayi Rockets. The army team had swept Shanghai in three games to win its fifth consecutive CBA title the previous season, and CBA officials figured staging a rematch of the championship battle would start the new season with a flourish. The game was more than just a confrontation between China's two best teams. This time, it was personal: a battle between the country's two biggest stars, gifted seven-footers whose brewing rivalry mirrored the struggle between old and new China.

Wang Zhizhi had now reigned over Chinese basketball for more than three years, roaming the hardwood with an almost feline grace. In the CBA, where he poured in nearly thirty points a game, Wang scored a rare trifecta, winning the Most Valuable Player award for the regular season, the playoffs, and the All-Star Game. "Wang is ready to play in the NBA right now," said Louisiana State University coach Dale Brown, who had tried, over several trips to China, to make the PLA soldier his second-most famous recruit after Shaquille O'Neal. "In Asia," Brown said, "he is a man among boys."

Getting selected in the NBA draft had only added to Wang's aura of invincibility in China. "Da Zhi was the Chinese fans' true idol," says the journalist Xu Jicheng. "Yao at the time was just a little brother, a small potato. But Da Zhi was the ultimate *shuaige*—handsome, smart, cool." Nike played off that image in an ad campaign entitled "I Dream." In one poster, Wang stood tall in his red national-team uniform, palming a basketball with his left hand and looking off into the distance. The tagline: "Today you dream about being somebody else; tomorrow somebody else will dream about being you." The double meaning was inescapable. Wang dreamed of being an NBA star, while everybody else in China—including Yao—dreamed of being Wang.

But even kings can be tormented. After leading Bayi to the 2000 CBA title—his fifth in as many years—Wang had hoped the generals might let him leave for America. Sports fans and journalists all clamored for him to go, but there were no assurances—indeed, no word at all—about whether leading Bayi to yet another CBA championship would guarantee his passage out of China. Now, another CBA season was beginning, and Wang had no choice but to lace up his shoes again for Bayi. The prospect of beating up on China's sluggish, second-rate centers rather than honing his game against the world's best players seemed pointless. "It's very hard for a young kid to face two opinions on one thing—fire and ice together," says Big Xu. "He had the fire and enthusiasm of the media and fans behind him. But in front of him was ice."

The only remaining challenge for Wang in China stood before him on that night in November 2000. Not, of course, that he considered Yao Ming much of a threat. Yao, now twenty, had no doubt come a long way in the year since Da Zhi treated him like a kid brother on foreign trips, peeling off a bill from his wad of hundreds so Yao could buy a pair of shoes at the Big Foot Shoe Store in Portland, Oregon, while Wang himself walked off with a dozen pairs. Yao had almost reached his full height, 7'5" (more than 7'6" in his shoes). He had his own Nike contract now, albeit smaller than Wang's, and he no longer lumbered awkwardly up and down the court like a giraffe pulling free of a sinkhole. During the 1999–2000 season, Yao averaged twenty-one points a game and led the CBA in blocks, rebounds, and dunks—a sign that Rle Nichols's forced-dunking exercise was paying off.

Already, Yao had begun to steal some of Wang's limelight. Politics had kept him out of the Nike Hoop Summit in March 2000—China's national team coach moved up Olympic training by a week, effectively foiling such individualistic pursuits—so Yao's international debut didn't come until the Sydney Olympics in September. As the Games opened, *Sports Illustrated* ran a cover story on the three Chinese big men: Wang, Yao, and Mengke Bateer. Wang was privately irked at having to share top billing with the upstart Yao, who had a full-page photo and the best quip of the article. When the photographer suggested posing the giants on the Great Wall, Yao replied: "Why do you need to do that? When we're all together, we *are* the Great Wall."

Great or not, the Chinese wall could withstand only a few minutes of serious attack from the U.S. at Sydney, but the brief interlude was glorious. Soon after the opening tip against the Dream Team (version 3.0), Wang beat Kevin Garnett down the floor for two fast-break layups and then buried a three-pointer. Yao, just five days past his twentieth birthday, had two quick hoops underneath, and then, within the space of ninety seconds, stuffed an attempted slam by Vince Carter and swatted a curling Gary Payton layup into the fifteenth row. Three minutes and twenty-nine seconds into the game, China led 13–7.

Then the wall came crashing down. Over the next ten minutes, the three big men committed twelve fouls and spent most of the rest of the game on the bench. Wang ended up with thirteen points, Yao just five, and the Americans cruised to a 119–72 victory. The Chinese team finished in tenth place, two places worse than in 1996. Wang was by most measures the best player on the team, but the world suddenly seemed fixated on his 7'5" teammate. After the U.S.-China game, American head coach Larry Brown singled out Yao, not Wang, for effusive praise: "In four years, he could be one of the best players in the world."

When Yao returned to Shanghai, he reflected on all the attention. "I found more people fixing me with hungry eyes," he told his friend, the Chinese journalist Yang Yi. "I was just twenty years old and I knew how much I was worth." By then, Yao knew his future should be in the NBA, but his more immediate target was Wang Zhizhi. Yearning to surpass his old idol, Yao started spending extra hours improving his footwork and agility. When nobody else was looking, he also worked obsessively on a secret weapon: the three-point shot, 20'6" out from the basket, where a 7'5" center should never dare to go.

That night in Luwan Stadium, the battle began from the opening tip. Just a few possessions into the game, as Shanghai brought the ball downcourt, Yao stopped outside the three-point line. Wang hung back, waiting for the big man to come in to establish position on the post. But Yao didn't move. Instead, he just caught the ball, squared his shoulders, and launched an arching three-point shot. It ripped the net cords, and the fans went wild, stomping their feet.

For Wang, the only seven-footer in Asia who could count on that kind of range, Yao's trey was a brazen affront. The PLA lieutenant raced down the court and jacked up a three-pointer of his own. The shot caromed off the rim. A few minutes later, Yao again lingered outside the three-point line. Once more, Wang let the big man stand unguarded. Yao drained another three and then raised both his arms in excitement and amazement. The 4,200 faithful in Luwan Stadium—including a stooping, oversize couple that called Yao their son—leaped to their feet, screaming deliriously. "Yao has lost his mind!" yelled someone in the crowd. "He's gone mad!"

Yao's second three-pointer seemed to break Wang's spirit. Desperate to prove that he was still the king, Wang abandoned Bayi's game plan to pursue his own personal vindication. During the rest of the game, Wang attempted an astonishing eleven three-pointers—nine in the first half alone—and missed them all. He even muffed a slam dunk. Behind Yao's 22 points and 21 rebounds, Shanghai pulled out an improbable 101–96 victory. Wang walked off the court in a stupor. Bayi had never lost a season-opening game before; indeed, this was only its fourth defeat in six seasons, and nobody doubted that Wang was to blame.

Balances of power in sports are enigmatic forces in which ineffable swings in the pendulum can suddenly propel a supremely confident player into a downfall. For Wang, the energy shifted that night, and in sickening disbelief, he locked himself in his hotel room. As the rest of the team went out to dinner, the morose center stayed in bed, turning off his cell phone so he wouldn't have to speak to friends or journalists. He didn't play in the next three Bayi games, and in a single fortnight, the army team lost as many games as it had in the previous four years. The team's official explanation for Wang's absence was that he had a serious cold, but Chinese reporters suspected that it was more a feverish reaction to the drubbing he had suffered at the hands of Yao Ming.

Yao, on the other hand, only grew more dominant. As Bayi slumped, Shanghai reeled off eleven consecutive victories and the "Little Giant" started thumping the rest of the league. In one game against the Shenyang Army team, he poured in thirty-eight points in just thirty minutes, shooting a perfect 11-for-11 from the field and 16-for-19 from the free throw line.

China's sports media turned Yao into their new darling, and the foreign press was quick to crown the heir apparent, too. In December 2000, *ESPN: The Magazine*—the hip new competitor to *Sports Illustrated*—splashed Yao on its cover as the top athlete of its annual "Generation Next" issue. "As we approach the halfway point of the Age of Shaq, the search for a successor has extended to the least likely of places: China," wrote former All-Star center Bill Walton. "Simply put, the twenty-year-old Yao has a chance to alter the way the game of basketball is played." In the entire ESPN cover package, Wang's name was only mentioned a few times, and even then, just in passing. "Wang is a good player," Walton wrote. "But it's Yao who has the NBA truly excited."

Wang slid more deeply into despair. "I talked to him in the middle of that season and he no longer wanted to talk about going to the NBA," says Xu Jicheng. "He was so frustrated, he was no longer interested in learning English. That entire season, he just went quiet." One day, during that long winter of Wang's discontent, Bayi coach Wang Fei went into his hotel room and tried to shake him out of his malaise. The disconsolate center was sprawled out on his bed, wearing an emblem of his thwarted desire: a Dallas Mavericks sweatsuit. "Listen, Da Zhi, you gotta face reality," Wang Fei told him. "You have to pull it together and play your best. If you don't, then you might never have a chance to go to the NBA."

It is perhaps the most shopworn cliché in Chinese philosophy that every crisis carries within it the seeds of opportunity. The idea is embedded in the Chinese language, where the word for crisis—*weiji*—contains the characters for both danger (*wei*) and opportunity (*ji*). Wang Zhizhi almost certainly didn't reflect on this nuance during his crisis of faith in the winter of 2000; he was more focused on the danger of Yao Ming's rise and his own stagnation. But Xia Song, the hoops operator who had helped orchestrate Wang's draft the year before, was, as always, looking for an opportunity.

Xia had no real reason to be optimistic when he traveled outside of

Beijing to the Hongshankou military compound in the fall of 2000 to meet the deputy director of Bayi sports, Qian Limin. More than a year had passed since the NBA draft, and even after donning those cowboy hats, the Bayi leaders had rebuffed all attempts to release Wang. Moreover, Xia had left his Nike job earlier in the year, so he could no longer offer army leaders shoes and apparel and coveted trips abroad. Now, Xia was trying to make it on his own as one of China's first sports entrepreneurs, hoping to escort to the NBA all three pieces of China's Walking Great Wall —Wang, Yao, and Bateer—whom he referred to as "my three big boys."

The rumor that Shanghai might let Yao participate in the 2001 NBA draft gave Xia some unexpected leverage. He now planned to appeal to the one thing that motivated the Chinese army more than money, perks, or connections—their sense of pride. To get Wang out, Xia wanted to ignite a race for glory between the PLA generals and the civilian leaders of Shanghai—between old and new China. The PLA may have been reduced in size and importance over the previous decade, but it was still the foremost institution in China—and it didn't like coming in second place to civilians, much less the arrogant arrivistes from Shanghai.

"If Yao goes to the NBA first, all the honor of making history will go to Shanghai," Xia told Qian. "The army should be getting that glory."

Qian allowed that the PLA had already been considering letting Wang go after the National Games in November 2001. This was the first encouraging news Xia had heard. But it still wasn't enough.

"That will be too late," Xia said. "Shanghai will have already stolen your thunder at the draft. Anything Da Zhi does will be overshadowed by Yao Ming."

"What option do we have?" Qian said. "We need Da Zhi to help us win another championship this season. He is our only center, the only player who can neutralize Yao."

"Then wait until after the CBA season is over," Xia suggested.

The NBA season lasted until mid-April, he explained. Assuming Bayi made it to the CBA finals in March, Wang would still have about three to four weeks to make his NBA debut—and perhaps more, if the surging Mavericks made it to the playoffs. It would just be a toe-touch, but Bayi could claim the honor of having the first Chinese player in the NBA a full two months before Yao could be selected in the NBA draft.

Qian seemed intrigued. "Why don't you write up your proposal?" Qian said. "I'll pass it on to my superiors."

It was a minor breakthrough, but it felt as though a door had just been opened. Xia called up Mavs assistant coach Donnie Nelson and announced the news as if it were a fait accompli: the army was willing to let Wang go at the end of March 2001. "I was working both sides at once," Xia recalled. "I couldn't tell either side the whole truth. I told the PLA that, of course, the Mavs would take Wang. I told Donnie that the PLA would release him. But I didn't really know if either of these things would happen. If either side backed down, I was screwed."

Xia knew, of course, that Donnie Nelson had been working toward this very moment for three years. The thirty-eight-year-old globe-trotter had been flying to China every summer to build his *guanxi* with the basketball authorities and to win Wang's release. Nelson consulted quickly with his father, the head coach, and with Mark Cuban, the outspoken dot-com billionaire who had bought the team from Ross Perot, Jr., in 2000. The response was clear: "Go for it."

Now it was up to the generals in Beijing. For weeks after Xia's meeting with Qian, there was only silence—and both Xia and the Mavs started to sweat. Things got even stickier in early March, when the Shanghai Sharks announced that the club was opening up a search for the best agent to represent Yao in the upcoming NBA draft. Perhaps chastened by the news, the PLA generals finally replied two days later: Wang would be free to go to the NBA, on a trial basis, when the CBA season ended.

The irony of what had transpired escaped few who monitored the battles between old and new China. The conservative Communist army, long considered immune to outside pressure, had beaten the Shanghai capitalists to the punch. What had changed their minds? One army insider said it hinged on a patriotic high-ranking general in the political department who happened to be a basketball fanatic. Another source said it had more to do with the influence wielded by the father of Wang Zhizhi's girlfriend, a retired Air Force general. But according to Xia, Wang's release came because a small group of generals had the same goal: burnishing the PLA's reputation. "In many ways, it was simpler for Bayi to make this decision than for Shanghai," Xia said. "Yao Ming's case is a lot messier because there are too many people trying to guide the game. With Wang, there are only a couple of army guys—and I'm the only guy speaking to them."

But there was something else that was perhaps even more vital to China's sense of pride and manifest destiny. The vote on Beijing's bid to host the 2008 Summer Olympics loomed less than four months away—and after the humiliation of losing its previous Olympic bid in 1993, China was now staking its national honor on success. Just two weeks earlier, in February 2001, the International Olympic Committee had come on an inspection visit, and Beijing had put its best face forward, closing smog-producing factories, spray-painting dormant grass an artificial green, and painting all building facades visible to the IOC delegation a happy rainbow of colors, from canary yellow to Pepto-Bismol pink. Now, it seemed, the nation's leaders—along with the most powerful PLA generals—were adding Wang's release as one element in their diplomatic offensive. Surely such a positive gesture would help Beijing's bid in the court of American public opinion.

But even as Wang suited up for the CBA finals against Yao in mid-March 2001, there were still lingering doubts about whether he would really be allowed to leave. Wang had started to pull things together on court—raising his season scoring average to 29.6 points per game, more than two points better than Yao Ming—but the championship was all that mattered. It was, after all, the reason Bayi had kept him in China these past two years. What might happen if he lost it now? "In China, everything is so political, every step is so treacherous," said one NBA official who has dealt closely with mainland officials. "Every time, you ask for it to be black and white. But there's no such thing; it's always shades of gray."

The CBA finals against the Shanghai Sharks began disastrously for Wang. Yao thoroughly outplayed him in the first two games of the best-of-five series, which the teams split. It was in the third game that Wang finally caught fire, defending fiercely (a rarity for him) and reeling off seven points late in the game to carry Bayi to victory. In the fourth game, with a single victory standing between him and freedom, Wang was simply unstoppable. He scored forty points (nearly double Yao's twenty-one), including twelve clutch points in the fourth quarter to stave off a Sharks comeback.

When the buzzer sounded, his long wait was finally over, his passage to America assured.

A week later, on the morning of his historic departure, Wang shambled into a brightly lit conference room packed with all of the people who were counting on him to bring glory to the motherland and build a bridge to America. Sitting in the front row were army generals, political leaders, national sports directors, the head of the Beijing Olympic bid committee, the director of NBA Asia, and, naturally, the Mavs' assistant coach Donnie Nelson, who had flown in for the final negotiations. The seats behind them were filled with several dozen local and foreign media. Standing in the back, inconspicuous as ever, was the white-haired Harry McKillop, Ross Perot's rescuer-in-chief, here to bring one more soul back to America. Presiding over it all was Xia Song, the hoop impresario who had finally made history. "This is just like Ping-Pong diplomacy," said Xia triumphantly, "only with a much bigger ball."

Dressed in a tattered old sweater, Wang seemed taken aback by all the fanfare. The taciturn soldier had never felt comfortable being portrayed as a role model, and though he said he wanted to be "a good ambassador," he preferred to let others reflect on the deeper meaning of the day. A colonel from the People's Liberation Army, which reserved the right to bring Wang back at any time for reasons of national defense (or, more pointedly, for Bayi's *offense*), voiced hope that "America will support our bid for the 2008 Olympics."

He didn't have to look far for reassurance. Donnie Nelson, wearing a gold Beijing 2008 pin on the lapel of his black suit, milked the moment for its symbolism. "This is more than just a basketball player going to the NBA," he said. "Wang Zhizhi is synonymous with the spirit of China. He has great potential, and he's on the rise." Then, nodding to the Olympic bid committee leader, he added: "It would be my dream to come here in 2008 to participate in the Olympic Games. You have our full support." Later, Nelson took his public relations a step further. He presented both Wang and the mayor in charge of Beijing's Olympic bid committee with Mavericks jerseys emblazoned with "Beijing 2008" on the back. The soldier put it on over his ragged sweater and posed for the cameras—the perfect image of a loyal patriot.

Later that afternoon, Nelson and his small entourage had a celebratory meal at Beijing's Great Wall Sheraton Hotel. There was no snake or stinky tofu to choke down at this send-off, just a Hawaiian pizza accompanied by a $120 bottle of Veuve Clicquot. Now dressed more comfortably in blue jeans and cowboy boots, Nelson was in a buoyant mood. Even though the deal Xia had brokered was tentative—the army offered no guarantees that Wang would be allowed to play the following season—the Mavericks were making history. "Wang is going to put on an NBA jersey," Nelson exulted, "and that will be going to Springfield"—home of the International Basketball Hall of Fame.

Nelson hoped that the relationships he had forged with the Chinese authorities could also give the Mavs the inside track on future Chinese ballplayers, including the one they had been eyeing all along—Yao Ming. Seven months earlier, standing courtside in Dallas as the Chinese national team prepared for the Olympics, young Nelson confided to an American reporter: "Wang might turn out to be okay, but the next great player in the NBA, and the world, is that one over there." He pointed toward the nineteen-year-old Chinese beanstalk shooting mid-range jump shots on the other end.

"Can you get him?" the reporter asked.

"Yes," Nelson answered.

Now, sitting in the hotel restaurant, taking a sip of bubbly, Dallas's true maverick laughed about the possibilities.

"The sky's the limit, man, the sky's the limit."

As the Mavericks' entourage—now including an exhilarated 7'1" soldier—headed off on their flight to America, a middle-aged Chinese coach sat in his dilapidated office behind Beijing's Workers' Stadium. "It's been a long struggle," Wang Weijun said, "but my son has finally made it." Da Zhi had come by earlier that day for a brief farewell. "We only had a short time to say good-bye, and his mother was crying the whole time," said the coach. "We're happy for him, but we're also worried. How will he adjust to a new environment?"

The old coach paused, caught up in the emotion, and the question lingered in the air. "I can't always hold my son by my side," he said, "but I hope the people in America will treat Da Zhi like their own son."

He spoke the last so softly it sounded almost like a prayer.

The buxom blonde waitress in electric-orange hot pants and a low-cut T-shirt leaned suggestively over Wang Zhizhi.

"Y'all want some beer with that?" she asked, smiling brightly as she set down a plate of Hooters' hot chicken wings.

Had the 7'1" soldier turned his head at that moment, he would have caught an eyeful of Texas hospitality. But Wang's attention was fixed on the big-screen television, which was broadcasting an NBA game between the Houston Rockets and his new team, the Dallas Mavericks. Wang and Xia Song had landed at Hooters by default. It was the only place near their hotel that broadcast the Mavericks live, and Wang—just five days into his American adventure—desperately wanted to catch the game, the last he'd watch before formally joining the team the following day. In forty-eight hours, Wang would no longer be a spectator but the center of attention. All of the fans in this Hooters—and hundreds of millions in his homeland—would be watching him step onto the court as the first Chinese man ever to wear an NBA uniform.

When asked if he wanted some *pijiu* (beer) along with his burgers and wings, Wang, without turning, shook his head and said in broken English: "Coke. *Big* Coke."

The young waitress took a closer look at the Chinese giant in the navy blue Mavs sweats. "Isn't he that basketball guy who came all the way from China?" she asked Xia, crinkling her nose. Xia nodded, and the waitress bounded away to spread the news.

Wang remained enraptured by the game, punctuating each bite of chicken and cheeseburger with comments about the NBA stars who were now, miraculously, his teammates: Michael Finley ("the second Michael"), Steve Nash ("pretty fast for a white guy"), and the 7'1" German forward Dirk Nowitzki ("just like me, he likes the three"). At one point, Juwan Howard, the goateed power forward, coolly drained three consecutive turnaround jumpers. "Wow, Howard is good, like a tai chi master!" Wang said. "How much does he make?"

"Twelve million American," Xia replied.

Wang nodded thoughtfully, as if calculating how much he might be worth someday if everything went his way.

During a break in the game, Wang pulled his eyes away from the television screen and swiveled on his stool to take in his surroundings. Hooters was a far cry from the army mess hall back home in Beijing, and it wasn't simply the extra-juicy burgers or the oversize wooden tables carved in the shape of Texas. (Wang displayed a keen interest in U.S. history by recounting how the Americans stole the territory from Mexico, then bragging about how Xinjiang—China's westernmost province, which Beijing appropriated in similar fashion from the peoples of Central Asia—was four times as big.) The lanky lieutenant wiped his fingers and noticed—for the first time, it appeared—the copiously endowed waitresses in their less-than-copious T-shirts.

Bewildered, he asked: "What does 'Hooters' mean, anyway?"

Wang still had a lot to learn about the finer points of American culture. But he was asking all the right questions. When he finally understood why the sign on the door read NOBODY UNDER THE AGE OF TWENTY-ONE ADMITTED, he laughed. "Then Yao Ming wouldn't be allowed in here!"

The game ended, and Wang was preparing to leave when several waitresses scurried over to give him an extra-large Hooters T-shirt and a miniature Hooters basketball to sign. The women wanted to lean in for a friendly kiss and a photograph to put up on their "Wall of Fame," but Wang shied from the attention. On the way out, several frat boys in the restaurant started yelling, "Wang! Wang!," saying his name as though it rhymed with "twang" (rather than, as it should be pronounced, "wahhng"). A few fans rushed toward him to get his autograph. Wang was so flustered by the commotion that he barged right into the women's bathroom, thinking it was the exit. A man who had been quietly following Wang all night went in to rescue the rookie, who emerged sheepishly shaking his head.

Wang's rescuer, in fact, was not another Hooters patron but an undercover agent who had been assigned to protect Wang in the wake of the spy-plane controversy that had thrown U.S.-China relations into a tailspin. On April 1, less than thirty-six hours after Wang had landed in Dallas, a Chinese fighter jet had collided with a U.S. Navy EP-3E surveillance plane flying close to the coast of southern China, resulting in a crash that killed the Chinese pilot, Wang Wei. The EP-3E was forced to land on China's Hainan Island and its twenty-four crew members were still being held prisoner by the Chinese, sparking the first foreign-policy crisis of George W. Bush's new administration. Beijing and Washington were now at a standoff, and Wang's comrades in the People's Liberation Army were on high alert. Wang checked the Internet every day for news. But he said nothing publicly about the confrontation, except to confide in friends that, had he tried to leave two days later, he might never have made it out of China.

Chinese newspapers and Web sites were filled with anti-American diatribes that week, and the Mavericks feared that rising anti-Chinese sentiment in America—particularly in Bush's patriotic home state of Texas—might put Wang in a dangerous situation. So they hired three plainclothed retired FBI agents to guard him around the clock, stationing two of them at night across the hall from his suite in the Hyatt Regency. The man who followed Wang to the restaurant that night in his unmarked cruiser—he identified himself only as Dwight—sat a few tables away, sipping a Coke, trying to act inconspicuous while keeping alert for any hecklers or worse. The one thing he hadn't counted on was having to rescue Wang from the ladies' room at Hooters.

The following morning, Wang traded in his ratty old sweater for a $4,000 cream-colored, designer suit with his name stitched into the silk interior. On the lapel, he attached a little red Mao pin, a good-luck charm his aunt had given him before he left Beijing. At the Mavs' offices that morning, Wang signed his first NBA contract with owner Mark Cuban. The prorated $317,000 salary was a pittance by NBA standards, but it was more than four times what Wang earned in China, and he stood to earn $420,000 if he returned the following season. Then Wang stepped into the bright lights of the Mavs' biggest-ever press conference, jauntily telling reporters in Mandarin how he would handle the trash-talking ("I'll pretend not to understand"), bad officiating ("I'll remember the ref's number"), and the pressure of representing 1.3 billion people ("I try not to think about it").

Within thirty-six hours, Wang Zhizhi was standing on the court in Reunion Arena, facing the American flag as the U.S. national anthem played before his first NBA game. He glanced up to see several Chinese flags in the crowd, including one held by his girlfriend, who had just arrived that day from Beijing. She also waved a placard that carried a message in Chinese characters: "Da Zhi, China is proud of you!" Late in the first quarter of the game against the lowly Atlanta Hawks, head coach Don "Nellie" Nelson yelled down the bench. Wang sprang to his feet and ripped off his warm-ups, and the crowd cheered in anticipation of his debut. But Nellie wanted Juwan Howard—"Juwan, Juwan!"—and Wang sat back down. (Wang insisted that he hadn't misunderstood Nellie's command; he said he simply got overheated in all the excitement and had to take his warm-ups off.) With 26.8 seconds left in the first half, Nellie finally did call for Wang, and the sellout crowd erupted in a rafter-shaking roar.

Somebody unfurled a banner: WELCOME TO WANG'S WORLD!

Although the first half ended uneventfully, Wang returned in the fourth quarter for nearly eight minutes and proved that he could play in the NBA. After his first shot—a perfect swish from the top of the key—the usually blank-faced soldier pumped his fist as he ran down court. He coolly sank two free throws and then hit a short baseline jumper to push the Mavs over the 100-point mark. The crowd burst into a frenzy, and the players on the Mavs' bench started waving their towels and giving each other chest bumps. "Chalupa!" yelled the P.A. announcer. Wang didn't realize it until later, but by pushing the team over a hundred points, he had entitled all 18,187 spectators to free chalupas at Taco Bell. Amid the raucous cheers, one fan waved a sign that read: "Wang's first English lesson: CHA-LU-PAS!"

The cacophony of cultures was music to the ears of Mavs owner Cuban, the Internet entrepreneur who had put together a team that was a virtual United Nations, with players from five different continents. "Tonight was a dream come true," Cuban said after Wang's historic appearance. "There were so many things that could have gone wrong, and everything went right." Wang was equally ecstatic. "I can score on an NBA floor," he said, with a hint of wonder in his voice. "A Chinese player can play against the best players in the world."

Over the next few weeks, Wang learned what it meant to be a symbol of the biggest nation on earth. Tens of millions of his compatriots watched his first NBA game on television, and the Chinese media sang paeans to their national hero—even as it mourned the death of the "martyred" pilot killed in the collision with the American spy plane. As that crisis continued to simmer—Beijing insisted on a formal U.S. apology, while Washington demanded the return of the aircraft and its twenty-four crew members—former U.S. president Bill Clinton suggested in a speech in Hong Kong that Wang, whom he called "China's biggest export," could help heal fractured Sino-American relations.

Aside from a few boos during a stop in San Antonio, fans and media around the United States embraced Wang as a peaceful antidote to the spy-plane controversy, an innocent soldier whose only long-range missile was a three-point jump shot. (A team of American players touring China, however, could've used his security guards. During a game in Hunan Province, Chinese players angered by a flagrant foul attacked the Americans with fists flying while fans chanting anti-American slogans pelted the visitors with bottles—an incident that was immediately blacked out on Chinese television.) The ongoing spy-plane imbroglio, in fact, ensured that Wang would become a media darling far beyond the American sports pages. Features about the hoops ambassador appeared in *Time, Newsweek, People,* and *Fortune.* Comparing him to the fallen pilot, Wang Wei, *New York Times* columnist Thomas Friedman lauded the NBA rookie in a column entitled "The Two Wangs."

Even as the political crisis hovered around him, Wang delighted in all the little things about life in America. He rushed to give extravagant tips to the hotel bellhops. He gaped in awe at the glass elevator that rose through the hotel's atrium lobby. And during practice, he barked out with undisguised pleasure the English names of the Mavs' offensive sets: "Red, Blue, Split." "Already, you can see such a big change in him," Xia Song said as he watched a practice. "I haven't seen anything like this from him since he was drafted. He's smiling!"

On his way to practice one day, Wang happily ticked off the names of every luxury-car dealership he passed—"BaoMa (BMW), Benchi (Mercedes-Benz), Linken (Lincoln)"—even as he made merciless fun of a friend's compact rental car. For the 7'1" center, size *did* matter. Later, when a Mavs assistant pulled up to the hotel in a wide-bodied $50,000 Lincoln Navigator, Wang whistled: "Now this is a real car!" Wang already had a vehicle in Beijing—a Jeep Cherokee—but his fantasy of owning a luxury car would have to wait a few more weeks. That day, however, Wang did something that, after a decade of living in barracks with other male athletes, seemed nearly as liberating: He moved into a $2,400-a-month town house with his girlfriend, Song Yang.

That evening, Wang invited a few friends to join them for dinner at a local steakhouse. Gobbling down an eighteen-ounce T-bone, a side order of chicken, and two Caesar salads, Wang talked animatedly about everything from the eating habits of his Chinese teammates ("Yao Ming eats like a bird compared to me") to one of his favorite movies, *Forrest Gump*. Picking up a baguette from the table, he strummed on it like the guitar-playing Elvis Presley in the movie before swinging the bread around wildly as if it were the paddle Gump used in the movie's famous Ping-Pong scene. Everybody laughed. Even Wang's girlfriend, in her expensive pink twinset, smiled demurely. At the end of dinner, after signing autographs for a few fans, Wang proudly pulled out two crisp $100 notes to pay the bill. "It's not a problem," he said. "I can afford this."

During that first week in America, Wang spent a lot of time at Donnie Nelson's house in Plano, Texas, a freshly scrubbed all-American suburb with big brick houses and green lawns. Nelson treated Wang like another son, just as Wang's father had hoped, and the Chinese center seemed perfectly at home playing on the driveway hoop out back with Donnie's six-year-old son, D.J., and a group of awestruck neighborhood kids. After dinner, D.J. led the Chinese rookie around their home, teaching him the names for different objects in English. "D.J.'s my best teacher," Wang said, patting the boy on the head.

Later, when D.J. scooted off to bed, Wang slipped into the hot tub in the backyard with Donnie and Xia Song. Leaning back, he pointed at the lights of a plane moving slowly across the star-filled sky. It would have made sense if he made a reference to the spy-plane crisis that had his fellow Chinese soldiers on red alert at that very moment. But instead, Wang just started singing, in broken English, the theme song from Michael Jordan's film *Space Jam*.

"I believe I can fly. I believe I can touch the sky."

13

The Battle for Yao Ming

Like so many old orchards in California, the grove of fruit trees in Walnut Creek had made way for a nouveau riche paradise. The latest monument to the American way stood on the cul-de-sac at the end of Ashley Lane: a million-dollar mansion whose seven thousand square feet boasted seven bedrooms and a multilevel recreation room with, naturally, seven televisions built into the walls. A $350,000 landscaping makeover would soon transform the grounds outside with a lush garden, a swimming pool, and twin rock formations with cascading waterfalls on either side of the driveway. But in early 2001, the only fully completed outdoor feature was, for the owner, also the most important: a top-of-the-line basketball court with a high-tech rubberized surface and a pro-style plexiglass backboard. What better symbol could there be for a sports agent who had finally hit the big time?

Propping his feet up on his polished hardwood desk, Bill Duffy couldn't help letting a satisfied smile spread across his face. The 6'4" NBA agent was feeling just fine, thank you. At age forty-one, he had climbed to the top of his cutthroat industry without ever raising his voice—and built the ultimate dream home for his wife and children, including the five-year-old daughter who had just bounded into his office for an after-school hug. But on that day, Duffy had other news to celebrate. He had recently returned from China, and now, after two years of maneuvering through what he called "uncharted territory," he felt on the verge of clinching the deal that would bring Yao Ming to the NBA.

The 2001 NBA draft was just three months away, and if he could pull this off, Duffy believed that Yao would not simply make basketball history as the first foreign-trained player to become the number one pick. The Chinese center, he averred, could transcend the sport itself. "I don't want to overstate it, but I think you'll be talking about this in the same breath as when President Nixon went to Red China," Duffy said, referring to the 1972 diplomatic mission that opened up the People's Republic to the world. "He's going to be the window of America into China, and the window of China into America."

To hear Duffy tell the story, his own quest to pry open that window was almost preordained—from his early childhood years in Taiwan to his adolescent desire to model himself on Kwai Chang Caine, the preternaturally calm avenging hero of the *Kung Fu* television series. Duffy attributes his sense of discipline and painstaking politeness to his father, an African-American U.S. Army colonel who used to punish him for forgetting to say "Yes, sir!" But Duffy developed a coolness of his own as a basketball standout at the University of Minnesota (where he roomed with future Celtic star Kevin McHale) and Santa Clara University (where he played with future Laker center Kurt Rambis). His Zen-like approach became even more useful when his own NBA dreams were dashed—and he decided to turn his childhood knack for memorizing sports statistics into a career as an NBA agent.

By the time Duffy first heard about Yao Ming, in 1998, his business was just starting to take off. A devout Christian who spoke proudly of his wife's family connection to Martin Luther King, Jr., Duffy had a twinkle-in-the-eye charm that worked on the women in prospective players' families as much as on the players themselves. He also had a feel for business, and, seeing that the game was going global, he had expanded his recruiting into Eastern Europe. When he saw Yao, then just seventeen, play in an exhibition game in California in the summer of 1998, he wondered about the mysteries that must be hidden within the Middle Kingdom. A few weeks later, by coincidence (though Duffy himself would surely call it Providence), Yao's translator that summer dropped by his house with a message from Nike's Terry Rhoads: Would Duffy be interested in coming to China to guide Yao and another seven-footer, Wang Zhizhi, to the NBA?

On his first visit to Shanghai in February 1999, Duffy focused his energies on wooing the wide-eyed Yao and his more skeptical parents. His inability to speak Mandarin blunted some of his natural charisma, but he found that, with Yao at least, he could establish rapport on the basketball court, where the leather ball they shared could fill in for the words they couldn't express. At one point, Duffy backed up and drained a shot from NBA three-point territory. Yao dribbled over and replicated the three, flashing Duffy a little smile. Surely, this was luck: no 7'4" center could really have three-point range. The American moved out and drilled another three. Again, Yao matched him. The third time, it was the same: Duffy made, Yao followed. By now, they were both laughing in a fit of mutual admiration. After the session, Duffy gushed about the Chinese teenager: "He'd already be a number one draft pick!"

Yao's parents were harder to crack. When Rhoads first introduced them, Duffy eagerly shook Da Yao's hand and leaned in to give his wife a peck on the cheek. Da Fang stiffly extended her hand. (A few nights later, Duffy would see another side of China when, awakened by a knock on his hotel-room door at 3:00 A.M., he found himself being propositioned by a Chinese girl who didn't seem shy at all about strangers.) With Rhoads acting as his interpreter, Duffy talked about the special bond he felt with China—the years in Taiwan, his half-Chinese sibling, his *Kung Fu* fascination. But the African-American agent told them that his deeper sense of connection with China came from his almost Confucian belief in the primacy of personal relationships. His business, he said, was based on being a mentor to his players and a respectful friend to their families.

"It's all about building bridges," he said.

Yao's parents smiled politely. It would take many more months—and lots of long, awkward dinners—but the smooth-talking Californian eventually softened the couple's defenses. Da Fang would never sign a formal contract with Duffy, claiming that it would be too politically sensitive, but he says she agreed informally to let him represent their son.

In America, where the consent of the individual player and his family was all that mattered, Duffy's work would have been all but completed. But in China, where the rights of individual athletes had never mattered before, his odyssey was just beginning. The secretive generals in old Beijing may have decided Wang Zhizhi's fate with a simple nod of the head. But in Shanghai, the booming commercial capital of the new China, Duffy would discover that every step forward required a tenuous transaction guided not by written rules and regulations, but by greed and *guanxi,* pride and political power. This was "capitalism with Chinese characteristics," a strange hybrid of lawless frontier and authoritarian straitjacket.

For all of his professed kinship with Chinese culture, Duffy often felt lost as he tried to navigate the treacherous landscape. It wasn't simply that none of the rules in America—open competition, legal contracts, transparent proceedings—seemed to apply in China. There was also a dizzying array of local Chinese characters laying claim to the nation's basketball stars: old-school bureaucrats, grasping new capitalists, a crop of ambitious young agents. It was hard to know who, if anybody, was in charge. Duffy didn't fully understand the intricate hierarchy that defines business in China, the hidden order among the seemingly inter-changeable bureaucrats crowding each meeting—no matter how many Western-style coffees were fueling the proceedings. Shaking hands with the wrong person first can doom business relations in China, and Duffy didn't always know which hands came first. And then, always hovering in the background, there was Yao's potential significance as a national icon. What patriotic Chinese official would leave Yao's safekeeping in the hands of an American, and a black one at that, given China's barely concealed racist tendencies?

During his early trips to China, Duffy had often locked horns with the Shanghai Sharks' Li Yaomin, who blamed the American for scuttling the Evergreen deal in 1999 and planting notions of independence in Yao's head. Li wasn't about to make it easy for Yao to get the approval he needed to participate in the NBA draft. He insisted that, regardless of what Duffy or the NBA might say, the disputed Evergreen deal was still valid in China. As time wore on, Li also drew up a list of extrava-gant demands that would make Yao's financial burden almost unbear-able. To Duffy and to Yao's family, the predicament hardly seemed fair, given that the Chinese army generals had let Wang Zhizhi leap to the NBA for little more than a handshake. "The club has Yao Ming over the barrel," Duffy said. "They're saying, 'You go under our conditions or you don't go at all.' With that choice, what will Yao do?"

By early 2001, Duffy decided that the only solution would be to avoid the middleman altogether. With the help of former Arizona con-gressman Matt Salmon, the son of American missionaries in Taiwan who claimed to have good contacts with the Chinese leadership, he arranged meetings with the powerful Shanghai mayor and the Sharks' owners at Shanghai Television. This would be Duffy's last chance to persuade the leaders to let Yao go before the June 2001 NBA draft, and he did his best to stroke their egos and challenge their pride. "If an army soldier can go to the NBA," Duffy asked them, "why can't a guy who represents the most dynamic, open, and outward-looking city in China?"

Shanghai's then-mayor, Xu Kuangdi, voiced one reservation: Yao was still so young, he said. Nevertheless, Xu—an ambitious official who spoke excellent English—seemed intrigued by the idea that an NBA star could symbolize Shanghai's reemergence as a world-class city.

By the time Duffy returned home from China, he was convinced that all of his hard work had finally paid off. He had effectively cornered the market on Chinese giants. The first piece of the Great Wall, Wang

Zhizhi, was on his way to the Dallas Mavericks with Duffy as his agent. The second piece, Mengke Bateer, also Duffy's client, was getting nibbles from a couple of NBA teams. And now, the biggest piece of all, Yao, was only one step away from getting the green light. The Shanghai officials had led Duffy to believe that the final answer on Yao's release would come soon, and it would almost assuredly be a resounding "yes."

But nothing in China was as simple as it sounded. Back in Walnut Creek, on that day in March 2001, a visitor from Shanghai arrived at Duffy's home with some troubling information. Li Yaomin, it seemed, had been so incensed by the American's latest attempt to go over his head that he had launched a search for an agent who could represent the interests of both Yao and the Sharks. Over the previous few weeks, in fact, the Sharks' deputy general manager had been meeting with scores of NBA agents and Chinese-American businessmen who seemed more willing than Duffy to entertain the club's demands.

The most chilling part for Duffy, however, was the name at the top of Li Yaomin's list. It was the "super-agent" who had turned Michael Jordan into a global icon, the power broker whom Duffy saw as his biggest rival in the business: David Falk. Even in China, Falk was renowned as the most influential businessman in basketball, a fierce negotiator whose parent company, SFX Entertainment, had revenues that surpassed the GDPs of many small countries. As Jordan's agent, Falk also had star power. And, according to Duffy's visitor that day, he was gearing up for a trip to China the following week.

The rumor of Falk's imminent arrival in Shanghai ruined the reverie of the sun-dappled afternoon. All this time, Duffy thought he had been operating alone. Nobody else had invested two years of his life—and a half-million dollars of his own money—laying the groundwork and cultivating relationships with Yao, his family, and everyone who mattered in Chinese basketball. Nobody else had set up a company in Beijing—with Xia Song at the helm—to maintain exclusive access to China's three big men. After all that effort, how could Duffy just let Falk muscle in and walk away with the big prize?

He picked up the phone and dialed Beijing. "I gotta talk to Xia."

As a devout Christian, Duffy almost never swears, and he prides himself on staying calm even in the face of crisis. His coolness under fire has won him and his clients a lot of money at the negotiating table. But when he reached Xia on the phone, he had a hard time masking his irritation.

"What the hell is going on over there?"

*   *   *

A few days later, Duffy heard even more disturbing news.

Falk hadn't barged into China on his own. He had been invited by the very person whom Duffy had courted for more than two years—Yao Ming's mother—and a pudgy Chinese-American whiz kid who had surreptitiously assumed the role of Da Fang's closest confidant.

The story of how Erik Zhang landed in Yao's life revolved, fittingly, around a pair of Nike shoes. Though foreign companies manufactured millions of basketball sneakers in China, Da Fang struggled for years to find a suitable pair for her growing giant, who quickly blew out the two pairs of canvas sneakers he received when he joined the junior team. In desperation one day in early 1996, Da Fang wrote a plea for help to one of her niece's former middle-school classmates, a girl named Angie, who was studying in the United States at the University of Wisconsin, Madison. It was a shot in the dark, but Angie, who had never met Da Fang, shared the letter with her boyfriend, Erik Zhang. The twenty-two-year-old economics major knew almost nothing about sports, but he saw all sorts of possibilities in a basketball prodigy from his old hometown who was 7'3"—and still growing.

Zhang's family had moved from Shanghai to Madison, Wisconsin, in the early 1980s, when he was just ten years old. Zhang adapted quickly to the American heartland, learning to speak English in a flat Midwestern accent, but he still spent his summers in China. More nerd than athlete, the little Chinese kid with the pocket protector also developed a Shanghainese nose for business. In college, he started up a software company with a few friends, which he says they sold a few years later for several million dollars. After hearing about Yao's predicament, Zhang (pronounced "Jahng") scoured the malls of the Midwest until he finally found a pair of size-18 white Nike Airs. Price: $92. It was the best investment he would ever make.

After delivering the shoes to Yao and his family in Shanghai, Zhang stayed in touch with Da Fang through a regular stream of polite letters and phone calls. One of his first suggestions was that Yao attend high school in Madison for a year or two before moving on to the University of Wisconsin. "Yao's parents didn't even think he would make it in [Chinese] professional ball at that time," Zhang says. "They wanted their son to get a good education." But the Wisconsin basketball coach didn't seem impressed by the grainy videotape of the spindly Shanghai giant, and soon it was too late. In the fall of 1997, Yao joined the Sharks' senior team. He earned barely $60 a month, but he was a full-fledged professional now, and college ball was out of the question. If he played in America, it would have to be in the NBA.

Zhang kept writing letters to Da Fang, and by late 2000, when she turned to him for help, he enjoyed a level of family trust that Duffy and Rhoads, for all their years of trying, had never been able to establish. Zhang was Da Fang's secret friend, an independent voice who was beholden neither to an American company nor to the Chinese state.

For a protective mother who feared getting burned, again, by the people circling hungrily around her son, Zhang must have seemed like a godsend. A young entrepreneur who moved comfortably between Chinese and American cultures, Zhang claimed to have no financial interest in Yao and, as he couldn't resist telling everyone he met, his family had *guanxi* to spare. His grandfather had been a "good friend" of Deng Xiaoping. His father was close to then-premier Zhu Rongji. And his "uncle"—actually his grandmother's cousin—was China's former vice president, Rong Yiren, who had become the fabulously wealthy head of the Citic investment group. "It was a process of earning respect with Da Fang," Zhang says. "I told her my intentions were honorable, that I would not take compensation. I made it clear that I would not manage [Yao's] basketball career in any way or form."

What Da Fang needed was not a manager but an unbiased guide who could help her navigate the conflicting worlds of American business and Chinese politics in which her son was stuck. Up until that point, in late 2000, Da Fang had relied on her friends at Nike for most of her advice and information. Terry Rhoads and Frank Sha were constantly in touch with the family, and their handpicked agent Bill Duffy also made periodic visits. Duffy had helped Da Fang wiggle out of the Evergreen contract, but his public criticism of the deal, along with his disregard for the finer points of Chinese hierarchy, had turned Li Yaomin into his mortal enemy. How was Duffy going to get her son out of China if he wasn't even on speaking terms with the gatekeeper? Now that Yao was a potential top draft pick worth tens of millions of dollars, Da Fang needed to take control of the situation and find her own way through the thicket of competing interests.

Da Fang's first assignment for Zhang seemed deceptively straightforward—much like a question on the business-school applications he was filling out at the time. The list of NBA agents he says Yao's mother wanted him to evaluate, after all, only contained two names: David Falk and Bill Duffy. Zhang recognized the name of Michael Jordan's agent. He had never heard of Duffy, though, and Yao's mother neglected to tell him that the family had already been dealing with him for two years—an omission that he says deeply angered him when he later found out.

Zhang left messages for both agents. Duffy never returned the call, he says, but Falk responded quickly, telling Zhang that he envisioned Yao becoming a truly global icon not unlike Jordan. The conversation left the twenty-six-year-old Chinese-American feeling giddy. Falk, after all, was a legendary agent, a man whose company represented one of every six players in the NBA. Moreover, there was the tantalizing prospect of having Yao playing with Falk's most famous client. As part owner of the Washington Wizards, a struggling team assured of a top draft pick, Jordan was toying with the idea of making another comeback as a player. Could Falk, so renowned for his ability to orchestrate deals that steered players toward their desired teams, align the planets so that Yao would play in the nation's capital alongside the greatest player in history?

Zhang quickly set up a three-way call with Falk and Da Fang, and she, too, was intrigued. He also put Falk in touch with Michael Coyne, the Cleveland lawyer who still had a claim on Yao through the disputed Evergreen contract. Coyne denies making any buyout agreement with Falk, but as an official advisor to the Shanghai Sharks, he was happy to recommend that the club work with the super-agent—telling Li Yaomin that "as part of a $40 billion company, Falk is the guy with the resources to help the team."

A solution to Yao's imbroglio finally seemed within reach. For two years, Da Fang and Li Yaomin had been unable to get past their anger with each other over the Evergreen fiasco, and Duffy had only seemed to inflame the tensions. But now another possibility had emerged. By mid-March 2001, both sides were ready to meet with the best-known agent in American sports.

Duffy's two-year head start in China appeared to vanish in an instant. The man who modeled himself on the righteous avenger in *Kung Fu,* however, wasn't about to give up without a fight. From his home office in Walnut Creek, Duffy tried to rally the forces against Falk's unexpected incursion. One of his first calls went to Terry Rhoads.

The situation presented the Nike executive with a ticklish dilemma. Falk had excellent relations in Beaverton—his most famous client, after all, had helped make Nike outrageously profitable—but Rhoads felt committed to Duffy. Moreover, he seemed convinced that Falk's involvement would spark an ugly public battle over Yao that could turn the Chinese establishment against the idea of letting him go. "We definitely didn't want to have these two American agents fighting over Yao like he was a bone and they were two junkyard dogs," Rhoads recalls. "Only bad things were going to come out of that."

Rhoads and his associate Frank Sha decided to talk with Yao directly about the predicament. Normally, Da Fang made the decisions for the family, but the Nike duo knew that the twenty-year-old center felt a bond with Duffy, and they wanted to make sure Yao was on their side.

"Don't let Falk in the door," Rhoads advised Yao. "It's not good for you, or for China, to have two *laowai* (foreigners) fighting over you in public."

Yao seemed flattered that Jordan's agent had expressed interest in him. But if what his Nike friends were saying was true, Falk's arrival might jeopardize his chances of going to the NBA that year—and it would certainly ruin his relationship with Duffy. Yao agreed to resist Falk's advance.

Rhoads then raced across Shanghai for an uncomfortable meeting with Yao's parents. Da Fang listened to his "junkyard dogs" argument, but this time, instead of going along with him, she strongly disagreed. "It was the first time I saw Yao's mother arguing against Nike," Rhoads says. "She really wanted to bring Falk in. She'd heard about what he'd done with MJ, and she thought it would be best to compare" him with Duffy. Rhoads then delivered a bigger surprise: Yao had already said he didn't want to deal with Falk.

Apparently miffed that her son would make a decision without her, Da Fang went to talk to Yao, but he held firm. "This was the first time that Yao Ming had ever stood up to his mother," Rhoads said, and Da Fang blamed the family rift on Nike. "That was where she suddenly thought, 'Nike, you have too much influence here. This is not a good thing.' She really held it against us. From that moment on, she was cold toward us." (Rhoads's bosses in Beaverton were also upset; they didn't understand why he would work against a Nike-friendly agent like Falk.)

On March 25, 2001, barely ten days after Duffy had heard the news about Falk's maneuvering, Yao signed a letter to NBA Players Association president Billy Hunter that rejected the advances of Jordan's agent and lambasted "the corruption of commercialism and selfish greed." The blistering letter, of whose authorship Duffy coyly pleaded ignorance, read in part:

> "Recent developments in this complicated process to bring me to the NBA has [sic] alarmed my family. Rumor has it that I have already retained the service of Mr. David Falk as my agent. This is absolutely false. I am on record here to state that I have never met Mr. Falk, nor have I signed, or have any intention of signing, any representation agreement with Mr. Falk. I take the liberty of writing you to emphasize the damaging nature of such a rumor.

Although many kind-hearted people have labored tirelessly on my behalf, but [sic] a few, I feel, have taken the futile path of enticing or forcing the Shanghai Sharks and my family into an unfavorable arrangement. I resent such unethical behavior. But rest assured that I will stand up for my rights at any cost."

The letter went on to say, in a bit of misdirection, that Yao would not hire a sports agent before he arrived in the United States. He and his family, it said, would work "without outside interference" to negotiate his release to play in the NBA. This clause was meant, in part, to appease local officials who believed that Yao's fate should be decided among the Chinese without the influence of American interlopers. But it also enabled Duffy to choke off the challenge from Falk and other NBA agents. Falk's associate, David Baumann, was heading to Los Angeles International Airport for a flight to Shanghai when he received a call about Yao's angry salvo. Baumann boarded the plane anyway, but when he got to Shanghai, Yao's family refused to meet with him. Falk, who was reportedly planning to fly in to Shanghai from Paris, canceled his trip.

Duffy's gambit had worked. By blocking out other American agents, he believed he had set himself up to be Yao's exclusive agent when the big man arrived in the United States. After a few conciliatory talks with Da Fang and Erik Zhang, he resumed his role as the family's principal outside advisor—only now he gave his counsel in secret, flying under the radar so as not to provoke the ire of either the Chinese authorities or his iced-out American rivals.

Nobody, however, derived as much of a kick from the letter as Yao Ming himself. Near the end of the letter, which Yao signed alongside his dorm-room address ("Rm 803"), there was an almost defiant statement. "My family and I," it read, "will resist any attempt to infringe upon our inalienable rights of exercising free will." The phrase may have been just a verbal flourish rather than a veiled swipe at the system that had controlled Yao's steps from the time he was a child. But to many ears back in China, it sounded like a dangerous declaration of independence.

The Chinese authorities hardly thought it was time for Yao to start exercising free will. If there was anything his family should have learned after all these years, it was that every aspect of Yao's development as a basketball player—including the choice of an agent—was meant to serve the nation's needs, not his individual aspirations. That Yao might be in a position to earn tens of millions of dollars in the NBA didn't change that basic equation. It simply raised questions that deeply divided officials on all levels of the Chinese hierarchy: How could Yao best serve the collective good? Would it be better to keep him in China, where, in Wang Zhizhi's absence, he could prop up the fledgling pro league and lead Shanghai to its first national championship in fifty-three years? Or would it be more beneficial to let him go to the NBA, where he could bring the nation glory, honor—and loads of cold hard cash?

The first item on the agenda, so far as Shanghai's pragmatic officials were concerned, was to figure out exactly how much cash was at stake. A private dinner with two top NBA executives in April 2001 gave them a chance to suss out the possibilities. It was a rare appearance for the NBA honchos, who usually stay away from clubs carrying out negotiations with individual prospects lest they appear to be favoring particular players. But China was a special case that, as one NBA official noted, "needs a little more hand-holding than other places." More than a decade had passed since David Stern had struggled just to give away NBA games to CCTV. The NBA broadcasts had helped generate a massive wave of interest in basketball, but the league was having trouble turning the excitement into profits. The broadcast fees that China paid were still negligible, and rampant counterfeiting made selling authentic NBA merchandise difficult. "Most businesses think, 'How do I create demand for my product?' " says Andrew Messick, the NBA's senior international vice president. "But we say: 'We've got demand, now how do we unlock it?' "

Yao provided one obvious key. The arrival of Wang in Dallas earlier that month had yielded a burst of positive publicity in America and huge television audiences in China. If Yao came to the NBA as the league's top draft pick, as many believed he could, the executives could imagine the kind of impact he could have enlivening the league—and opening up the market in "basketball's final frontier." Yet even for NBA executives steeped in the ruthless global business of sports, the mercenary tone of the Shanghai dinner conversation was astonishing. "It was all about measuring the value of their investment," said one NBA official who attended the dinner. "It could have been a Boeing 727 they were talking about. They treated Yao Ming strictly as an asset."

During the meal, one of the NBA executives raised the issue of Yao's contract. No outsider had ever seen his agreement with the Shanghai Sharks, and many people around the NBA wondered about his status. This was an important point for the Americans. The number of seasons remaining on a contract often affects the price of any buyout; and if a player's contract expires, there is no need for the NBA team or the player to negotiate a buyout.

But one of the Shanghai officials dismissed the question. "That is irrelevant," he said, "because we own his rights in perpetuity."

The visitors stared at the man in disbelief. Did China really think it could assert its claims on Yao throughout his entire career?

Yes, in fact, it did. A few weeks earlier, the Sharks had announced that Yao would only be allowed to go to the NBA "at the appropriate time, with the appropriate team, and under the appropriate conditions." The "three appropriates," as this quintessentially Chinese formulation became known, hinged on the last, and Li Yaomin now laid out for the NBA visitors just what they meant by "appropriate conditions." In return for losing their star center, Li explained, the Sharks expected to receive a raft of benefits: NBA-caliber replacement players; exhibition games in Shanghai; special television rights for NBA games; professional coaching clinics and exchanges; a new basketball school to train young recruits; and, most surprising of all, financial assistance to help build a new modern stadium.

"Yao Ming is China's Michael Jordan," Li explained. "We cultivated him from childhood, made him what he is today. If we're being asked to give him up, don't you think we should get a high price?"

The NBA officials demurred. It wasn't their business to get involved with negotiations. All they could do was explain that the limit any NBA team could pay as a "transfer fee" was $350,000. Conducting clinics or helping find replacement players would be no problem. But any further cash contribution would have to come not from the NBA team but from the player himself.

Undeterred, the Chinese moved on to their next question: If China decided to let Yao enter the draft, would Yao be guaranteed the number one spot? And if so, how much might that be worth? The 2001 draft pool was not too deep, the NBA executives admitted, and 7'5" centers with true ability seldom come along. Indeed, most of the NBA's best centers were fading from the scene—Patrick Ewing, Alonzo Mourning, and Hakeem Olajuwon were all on the verge of retirement—so Yao stood an excellent chance of being the top pick.

There was, however, a crucial caveat. If Chinese officials left any doubt about Yao's freedom to leave the country to play in the NBA, his draft position could fall sharply. One of the Americans pulled out a chart and showed his hosts that, under the league's collective-bargaining agreement, the top draft pick would earn about $9.9 million over three years versus $4.2 million for the number ten pick—a difference of $5.7 million even before the option on the fourth year was added.

The Shanghai officials nodded thoughtfully, as if understanding for the first time that their predilection for secrecy and control could cost them millions of dollars.

Li Yaomin knew that such salary figures only hinted at Yao's true value. All spring, the Sharks' *laoban* had been meeting privately with agents and businessmen eager to get the inside track on Yao. The giant's blistering letter to the NBA may have forced Falk out of the race, but it hadn't slowed Li's search for what was known informally as the "fourth appropriate": the "appropriate" agent who could deliver a package of lucrative benefits to Shanghai. Several of Li's contacts had told him that Yao's salary over the course of his career could reach $200 million. But even that paled in comparison to the potential endorsement income he could earn from companies keen on using him as a conduit to a booming market of 1.3 billion people. Yao's endorsement income, the agents told him, could push his overall earnings close to one billion dollars.

One billion dollars. The number sounded almost mythical, but it would soon set into place an immovable reality: Shanghai wasn't about to let its star player traipse off to the NBA without making sure that the city got a healthy portion of the billion-dollar pie.

As the May 13 deadline for declaring Yao's eligibility for the 2001 NBA draft approached, Li Yaomin upped the ante. He insisted that the Evergreen deal, which would give at least two-thirds of Yao's income to agents and third parties, was still valid. He also stipulated that Yao pay tens of millions of dollars from his future earnings to buy out his Sharks contract. And this was on top of the long list of demands—the "appropriate conditions"—aimed at the NBA and the team that selected Yao. "Some of Li's ideas are off the wall," said Tom McCarthy, a sports-marketing consultant in Shanghai who has dealt extensively with China's sports authorities. "But if I were on the Chinese side, I'd be squeezing as much as I could because I have something the NBA wants."

As outlandish as the Sharks' demands might have seemed, they reflected the natural tension that arises when foreigners hoping to strike it rich in China collide with deeply rooted local interests. Nike's Terry Rhoads would witness this kind of collision often from his perch in Shanghai, and the one constant seemed to be that foreigners, blinded by a naive enthusiasm for China's booming market, would come away shaken. "You see starry-eyed foreigners coming in here all the time dreaming about making millions," says Rhoads. "But for every one of those, there are many more Chinese thinking: 'If I can just scalp one gullible foreigner, I'll have it made.' Frankly, I think the Chinese will always have the better odds. They've got the home-field advantage."

Li Yaomin was not about to lose his edge. Just days before the deadline, on Duffy's advice, Da Fang made the Sharks a lump-sum offer of just under one million dollars, but Li waved her off. "If Yao Ming wanted to go to the NBA, he needed to abide by our conditions," Li recalled later. "If not, okay, but he wouldn't go to the NBA. We weren't forcing him to do anything. But from our perspective, we had done everything we could to cultivate him as a player. Da Fang should have thanked the club for doing so much work. If she didn't recognize this, then there was nothing else to talk about."

Indeed, there was nothing else. On May 11, after two months of speculation, the Sharks called a press conference to announce that Yao Ming would *not* be entering the NBA draft. As a grim-faced Da Fang stood by his side, Li Yaomin's boss Bai Li ran through all of the official reasons for holding Yao back: He was too young and immature to play in the NBA; the still-growing CBA couldn't afford to lose its two biggest stars in a single year; and, most important of all, Shanghai needed him to claim its first national championship since the 1949 revolution. At no point did the Sharks' manager mention the raging financial dispute between Yao's family and the Sharks; nor did he hint at the Chinese government's wariness about doing any favors for the United States in the wake of the spy-plane controversy. Bai Li simply expressed confidence in Yao's loyalty and obedience. "On big things like this," he said, "Yao Ming will consider the collective good."

The government's decision deeply embittered Yao and his family, along with the cluster of supporters who had been pushing for his release. Da Fang toed the party line—"No matter when he goes [to the NBA], he will repay the kindness of the homeland," she said—leaving the sharper rejoinders to her advisors. "He's a slave to his club," said one. "He has no individual rights." Another moaned: "Greed overcomes everything. I keep hoping things will change. But in China, how much longer can you hold out for things to change?"

One businessman even tried to entice Yao into defecting to the United States. The "d" word scared Yao, just as it had frightened Wang years before, and he requested that his advisors never contact that person again. "China is almost asking for Yao to defect," said one insider, noting that Yao wouldn't dare enter the draft without official permission, as Wang had done in 1999, out of fear that the government would turn against him. "Yao knows his future in the NBA is tied to the future of China, because that's where all of his endorsements will be. If he defects, he kills all of his chances in China."

Yao himself seemed more on the verge of depression than defection. He had refused to watch Wang's debut with the Mavericks—"I'm jealous as hell," he told a friend—and now he would avoid tuning in to the NBA draft as well. "Ever since I was young, everything in my life seemed to be preordained," he said later, reflecting on the deep funk he fell into when it became clear that he would not be leaving China anytime soon. "But once your heart gets broken, once you feel like your dream passed you by, you can really grow up. For that period I was very depressed. When I faced the TV camera I smiled, but that was a cover-up."

After believing that he, not Wang, would be the first to go to the NBA, Yao now had to face the grim reality of spending another year, maybe more, in China. It was easy to believe that the Shanghai giant was now, as ever, simply a pawn of the powers that be. But as Yao came to accept his predicament, he focused on the one thing that remained in his control: his performance on the basketball court. If he could lift his game and lead Shanghai to its first national championship in fifty-three years, there would be nothing in China he hadn't achieved, no obligation he hadn't fulfilled. And, he hoped, no real reason the Chinese authorities could concoct to keep him from going to the NBA.

Nearly a year later, on April 19, 2002, the Shanghai Sharks' team bus rolled through the rain-shrouded streets of the southern coastal city of Ningbo. Yao usually zoned out on these bus rides, stretching his 7'5" frame over two or three seats and listening to the Backstreet Boys (favorite song: "Larger than Life") or sending text-phone messages to his girlfriend, a willowy 6'3" forward on the Shanghai women's team named Ye Li. Yao had kept quiet about his first and only girlfriend, even shielding her from his parents, but the blossoming romance was the one thing that helped mitigate the frustration he felt at being left behind while Wang suited up for the Dallas Mavericks.

It had been a bittersweet year. In July 2001, Beijing had been awarded the right to host the 2008 Olympic Games—a moment that sparked delirious nationalistic celebrations in Tiananmen Square but which only confirmed for many athletes that the sclerotic sports system would not undergo any serious reform for at least another seven years. The September 11 terrorist attacks on New York and Washington, which came just one day before Yao's twenty-first birthday, provoked mixed feelings among the Chinese. Some saw it as a karmic comeuppance for an arrogant superpower, but Yao, who desperately longed to go to America, only knew that, as a result, the NBA had to cancel its scheduled clinics in Shanghai and postpone its plans to hold an NBA exhibition game on Chinese soil. The news that left him feeling most torn, perhaps, came when Mengke Bateer, the bruising 6'11" center from Inner Mongolia, joined the NBA's Denver Nuggets in February 2002 to play out the rest of the season. Yao was happy for the good-natured Bateer, but his departure made Yao's own situation even starker. He was the last piece of the Great Wall still stuck in China.

As the bus turned off Ningbo's main road that evening, the twenty-one-year-old giant could catch a glimpse, beyond his own reflection in the glass, of the Bayi Rockets' home stadium looming in the distance. Yao had never won a game in the so-called "graveyard of hope"—four years of futility against a team that dominated Chinese basketball. Bayi had won six straight CBA titles, the last two over Shanghai, and it had never lost a game on its home court. Even without Wang, the soldiers of Bayi had extended their home winning streak to sixty-five games. Under Yao's leadership, the Sharks had established the CBA's best record that season, but its only two losses—the last game of the regular season and the first game of the championship finals—had both come in this arena.

Driving toward the PLA stadium that night, Yao knew he needed a win over Bayi not only to give Shanghai its long-coveted national title—but, more importantly, to clear an important hurdle in his quest to get out of China. All season long, the pressure on Shanghai leaders to let Yao play in the NBA had been rising steadily. It wasn't just that, in Wang's absence, Yao thoroughly dominated the CBA, averaging 29.7 points, 18.5 rebounds, and nearly five blocks per game during the regular season. The backlash against Shanghai's decision to hold onto its star the year before had reverberated through the local and international media, making the glimmering modern city seem distressingly like retrograde Communist China. With the 2008 Olympic Games bid awarded to Beijing the year before, Shanghai wanted to grab its share of the international limelight. But first, it had to beat Beijing in its quest for a national championship.

In the first three games of the CBA finals, Yao played with the ferocity of a man on a mission—racking up more than forty-five points and twenty-two rebounds per game, including one astounding performance in which he made all twenty-one of his shots from the field. Having given the Sharks a 2–1 advantage, Yao knew that if he could lead the Sharks to one more victory, he would be one step closer to his dream. Before he got off the bus that night, Yao made a promise to Ye

Li that he would bring her back the championship. And he wasn't about to renege. That night, in front of a phalanx of CBA leaders and five thousand foot-pounding Bayi faithful, Yao played all forty-eight minutes of the game and piled up forty-four points and twenty-one rebounds. It almost wasn't enough. Only a miraculous tip-in at the buzzer would ensure the Sharks' 123–122 victory—and Yao's vindication.

The "graveyard of hope" had become the birthplace of a dream. Once the hostesses in their red *qipao* had handed out the championship trophies, the Sharks' general manager Bai Li spoke live on Shanghai TV. "Now I would like to deliver a piece of good news," he said. "The club has decided that it will no longer keep Yao Ming from going to the NBA. Yao has opened the door to the NBA with his own hard work . . . From now on, the club will take an active part in the discussion with NBA teams on Yao's transfer. I promise that the club will not hinder Yao from going to the NBA anymore."

The announcement, made live on television instead of in a sober communiqué, surprised a lot of people in Chinese basketball—including the CBA leaders in Beijing, who had not given their approval. Yao himself seemed strangely subdued, more relieved than ecstatic. He stayed out late that night drinking with his teammates and his vanquished Bayi rivals, but he couldn't help thinking about all the distress his family had endured—and the new pressures that awaited.

Just ten days later, on April 29, Yao boarded a plane for the United States, where he would face one of the most public job auditions in sports history. The top coaches and executives from twenty-six of the twenty-nine NBA teams—along with hundreds of media—were converging on Chicago to watch the little-known giant display his skills in a specially arranged predraft workout. Erik Zhang, who had spent weeks organizing the tour, despite earlier promises not to manage Yao's career, hoped all the hype would keep the pressure on China to let Yao go.

But as the big man hurtled across thirteen time zones, accompanied by Li Yaomin, it was hard to avoid thinking about another more worrisome scenario: If Yao didn't dazzle the NBA executives enough to earn the number one draft pick, there was a chance he might not be allowed to go to the NBA at all. China's leaders, after all, wouldn't agree to let go of their national treasure just so he could come in second or third. Nothing less than number one would do.

Nothing less than total control would do, either. Just a few days earlier, the Shanghai *Morning Post* had reported on tough new CBA regulations that seemed targeted specifically at Yao. The rules covered nearly every aspect of a player's transfer abroad, from the duty to give China face ("The receiving club or the player himself shall not do or say anything to harm the dignity of China") to the obligation to hire a registered Chinese agent who has passed a special test. Up until that moment, there were no basketball agents in China, and many observers suspected that the CBA had instituted the new rule simply to keep Yao under its thumb. "The CBA is doing this so it can control Yao," said a close associate of Yao's family. "But this isn't the 1960s! How can they have such a backward point of view?"

The restriction that provoked the greatest outcry, however, was an existing regulation tucked away in "Provision 5 (4)" of an obscure document called the "Notification on Problems Related to the Standardization of Work in Sport Management Centers." Under this regulation, Yao would be required to hand over a full 50 percent of his foreign earnings to the Chinese government: 30 percent would go to the national basketball center, 10 percent to the Shanghai provincial sports authorites, and 10 percent to the national sports bureau. The other 50 percent would be shared by "the player, coach and others who contributed."

Suddenly, it seemed that the Sharks were not the only ones who wanted to take a bite out of Yao; the national sports authorities wanted their pound of flesh, too. That the CBA in Beijing would trot out this old rule just days after Shanghai gave Yao the green light also seemed to carry a political message: It served notice that Beijing, and not Shanghai, had the ultimate power to decide whether Yao would go to the NBA.

American sports columnists railed against the Chinese regulations. The NBA also expressed reservations. "Agents only get four percent," said Billy Hunter, NBA Players Association president. "What makes the Chinese government any different from agents?" Even a few Chinese media criticized the regulation. YAO MING ROBBED! read the headline of an article in *Titan Sports Weekly*, which went on to note that Wang, Bateer, and several Chinese soccer players abroad had never been subjected to such draconian conditions. Yao didn't comment publicly on Beijing's new stratagem, but when the *Titan* article came out, he asked a reporter: "Who wrote that article? Because I would like to invite him out to dinner!"

Money was hardly the only lever of control. Chinese officials also seemed intent on guiding the process toward the agent and team of their choice—a fact that Yao would be reminded of even before he landed in Chicago. During their long layover in Los Angeles, Li Yaomin introduced Yao to an American man who offered to fly them directly to Chicago in his boss's private jet.

Yao looked at Li quizzically. Who was this guy?

The man, in fact, was an associate of Nicholas Rockefeller, a forty-five-year-old scion of one of America's wealthiest families. A Los Angeles–based lawyer with investments in China, Rockefeller had been meeting privately with Li to plot out Yao's future, even offering, Li says, to be Yao's "godfather" in America. (At the time, Li was also entertaining other potential agents, including Lee Steinberg, the man who inspired the title character in the movie *Jerry Maguire*.) Sensing that something was amiss, Yao refused the offer of a private jet. Two days later, when Li tried to escort Rockefeller into the locker room after the Chicago workout, Zhang kicked the American out, telling him to stay the hell away from Yao—the first shot in the family's looming battle with the Shanghai establishment.

Li's more intricate plan, however, involved trying to steer Yao to the team of China's choice, the New York Knicks. The NBA sternly discourages draft picks from dictating where they will or will not play. It had happened before; Kobe Bryant, for instance, had forced the team that drafted him, Charlotte, to trade him to the Los Angeles Lakers. But such manipulation had never been attempted by a foreign government. Yao himself didn't seem to care strongly about where he landed, but Shanghai officials wanted him to play in a major metropolis with a vibrant Chinese community and a massive media market—the better to reflect China's growing importance. That, Li said, meant New York. "The city is more like Shanghai than any other in America," Li explained. Under the neon lights of Broadway, he figured, Yao would become a major star overnight.

A day before the public workout in Chicago, the Knicks arranged a private session with Yao. The shootaround wasn't simply an opportunity to see Yao up close—general manager Scott Layden had seen Yao play in China several times before—but a chance for the Knicks to put on a show for Yao as well. A full contingent of twelve team officials, including star guard Allan Houston, flew in to meet him. That evening, the team threw a banquet for Yao at the posh Fairmont Hotel, presenting him a Knicks jersey along with a video featuring prominent New Yorkers imploring: "Come to New York, Yao Ming. We welcome you!"

Other NBA teams fumed about the favoritism shown to the Knicks and, a day later, to the Bulls. But by the time his black stretch limo rolled up to Loyola University's Alumni Gym, the biggest names in basketball were all waiting for him inside, including the Miami Heat's spit-polished head coach Pat Riley; the Chicago Bulls' rumpled general manager Jerry Krause; and Lakers legend Jerry West, newly named the Memphis Grizzlies' president of basketball operations. All told, more than sixty-five NBA coaches, scouts, and executives filled the courtside seats, while at least 150 reporters and cameramen hung over the second-floor balcony to get a good look at the big man. As Yao jogged a few warmup laps, the gym went virtually silent—except for a small cluster of officials from the local Chinese consulate, who applauded gently as he passed.

When former NBA coach P. J. Carlesimo started putting Yao and his 7'2" practice partner, University of Oregon center Chris ("I'm not the singer") Christofferson, through a series of drills, there was one person who seemed to have walked into the wrong audition: the chubby 5'6" Chinese translator out on the court in pressed khakis and a pink, button-down Ralph Lauren shirt. Erik Zhang, now twenty-eight, was making his first public appearance after more than a year of working in the shadows—and he looked like a wreck, the bags under his eyes barely obscured by his wire-rimmed glasses. Over the previous two weeks, Zhang had been juggling a full-course load at the University of Chicago business school along with endless meetings, negotiations, and late-night phone calls to China. He wasn't Yao's agent per se, nor was he a relative, though he introduced himself as Yao's "cousin" to make everything seem all in the family. But Zhang was the only person Da Fang trusted to speak on the family's behalf in China and the United States, so he was working both time zones at once. "I realized during that period that I couldn't handle it on my own," Zhang said. "I wasn't getting any sleep at all, chugging Cokes like you wouldn't believe. I didn't want to screw things up. I needed a team to back me up."

To help smooth things with the NBA, Zhang had asked Bill Duffy to come to Chicago, though the agent stayed behind in his hotel room so as not to rile Chinese officials or raise eyebrows among other NBA agents. Zhang would soon bring his graduate-school professors on board, too. As part of his penance for cutting class that week, the deal-maker had invited his statistics professor to the workout, and he, in turn, had brought along the business school's assistant dean, a basketball nut named John Huizinga. The flaxen-haired economist knew little about the NBA, but Zhang would later hire him as Yao's official NBA agent, relegating Duffy to an advisory role both because the Chinese government wouldn't accept him and because Zhang himself wanted to control the process. Later, Zhang would involve his marketing classmates in one of the coolest projects on campus: devising a marketing plan for Yao in China. The strange confederacy that would become known as Team Yao was beginning to take shape.

Out on the court that day, several hundred pairs of eyes followed Yao's every move. His heart fluttered nervously and his legs felt heavy, but his hands remained steady. Displaying a remarkably soft touch for a big man, he sank seventeen of his first twenty-five perimeter shots, nine of fifteen with a hand in his face, and then twelve free throws in a row. But he looked soft in other ways, too. Instead of finishing strong and fighting for rebounds against the slow-footed Christofferson, Yao settled for a few too many ten-to-twelve-foot fadeaways. At one point, Christofferson even blocked one of Yao's shots, sending a murmur through the audience. It wasn't long before the jet-lagged Yao was bending over and tugging on his shorts, grateful for a water break.

And then, suddenly, the forty-five minutes were up.

It wasn't clear if Yao had locked up the number one pick. He sounded slightly disappointed about his performance. "By the time I could catch my breath and get in the right state of mind, the workout was over," he said. The NBA coaches and executives, however, were more generous. "This is an unprecedented circus to bring someone into, and he handled it all very well," Carlesimo said. "He has the ability to be a very special player in this league." Houston Rockets general manager Carroll Dawson was even more upbeat. "Very impressive," he said. "I think you'd have to think about him if you've got the first pick." Three weeks later, in fact, the Rockets—though relative long shots— would win the NBA draft lottery and make it clear that they wanted Yao Ming—if, that is, China would let him go.

Yao's new entourage whisked him away soon after the session ended in Chicago, leaving reporters with a playful statement that seemed a world away from the typical swaggering of a top draft pick. "I would like to express my sincere gratitude to all NBA teams for showing interest in me," Yao wrote. "I am honored by your presence. And I hope I have not disappointed you with my performance today." Then he buttered up the media before joking: "I look forward to taking each and every one of you to dinner sometime in the future. But the check is on you if your reporting makes me look bad."

He signed off, almost goofily: "Let the good times roll!"

PART III

WEST

14

Soldier Gone AWOL

The rumor ricocheted across the globe, from the basketball courts in downtown Dallas to the glass-enclosed executive suites in Manhattan to the austere halls of Beijing's secretive military compound. With each phone call, the voices expressed more alarm, the expletives flew more freely. Wang Zhizhi, the 7'1" basketball ambassador from the People's Liberation Army, the first Chinese player to make the leap to the NBA, had disappeared.

The loyal soldier had gone AWOL in America.

Lieutenant Wang had been scheduled to fly back to China immediately after the Dallas Mavericks finished their season in mid-May 2002, according to an agreement the Mavs had made with the Chinese government the year before. But nearly three weeks had passed since the Mavs' final game on May 13—a playoff loss to Sacramento in which Wang played just six minutes—and the Chinese center was nowhere to be found. He had missed a team meeting and ignored directives from Chinese authorities demanding that he report without delay for national-team practice in Beijing. Now, powerful men on both sides of the Pacific were starting to panic.

The Mavs' swashbuckling owner, Mark Cuban, said he had been trying to get in touch with Wang for a couple of weeks. Worried about jeopardizing the team's privileged relationship with Beijing, he sent Mavs staffers to bang on the door of Wang's two-story town house in Turtle Creek, a gated community where Wang's teammates Dirk Nowitzki and Steve Nash also lived. Nobody ever answered Wang's doorbell, and through the windows, the town house looked strangely empty. There was no sign of Wang's girlfriend, the elusive Chinese beauty with the pinched smile and the expensive tastes. Gone, too, was the Mercedes

SL500 that Wang normally parked out front. "We do not know where he is or how to get hold of him," Cuban said. "It never occurred to us that Wang wouldn't do what he was asked or what the possible consequences might be." Baffled and angered by Wang's disappearance, Mavs personnel dialed Wang's cell phone every few hours. There was no answer. All the callers heard was a strange voice recording, in English, before the beep:

"His name is Wang."

His name in Beijing suddenly became a byword for disloyalty. For China's sports authorities, Wang's vanishing act was the ultimate indignity: They had spent more than a decade raising him to be a basketball star, and now, after being granted the rarest of privileges, to play in the NBA, he was openly defying them. Wang's refusal to come home was precisely what Chinese officials had feared all along, a principal reason they had been so reluctant to let him go in the first place. Officials resisted lashing out at Wang publicly at first, limiting themselves to vague statements that only fueled more media speculation. "Wang Zhizhi has not come back to train with the national team," CBA spokesman Xu Minfeng would finally admit in mid-June. "He should have been back more than a month ago, but he has not returned. We don't know where he is."

Wang's status as a PLA soldier made the situation immeasurably worse. Barely fourteen months earlier, when the military brass joined civilian leaders at his farewell press conference, everybody assumed that Wang's decade of submission to the army's rigorous indoctrination had made him an unshakable patriot. But his disappearance was tantamount to desertion, an offense punishable by military court-martial. Even more troubling, however, was the specter of defection. "Wang is still an active employee of the military, a lifetime employee," said one Beijing source with close ties to the Chinese army. "He's not allowed to have a personal passport. He's not allowed to stay abroad without an explicit agreement with his military boss. The only way for him to stay overseas is to defect."

Before news of his disappearance broke, Wang was still considered a hero in China. His games with the Mavericks had drawn television audiences that numbered in the tens, perhaps hundreds, of millions in his homeland. San Francisco mayor Willie Brown had declared a special "Wang Zhizhi Day" and the African nation of Liberia had immortalized him on a series of collector stamps. Wang's respectable performance with the Mavs showed that he was not just a marketing gimmick for a league hungry for the China market, but a legitimate NBA player with undeniable potential. He averaged 5.6 points a game, coming off the bench mostly during "garbage time" at the end of blowout games. But after Wang poured in eighteen points in a win over Memphis—then his career high—Dallas head coach Don "Nellie" Nelson lavished him with praise, saying that, even with their explosive lineup, "Wang is as good an offensive player as I have."

As the season drew to a close, however, the Chinese soldier had grown deeply fearful about his future. His two-year contract with Dallas was set to expire at the end of June, but the Chinese army had given no clear indication that he would be allowed to continue his NBA career. Indeed, the PLA generals couldn't mask their irritation at seeing their star center on the Dallas bench even as their depleted Bayi team lost the CBA title for the first time to Yao Ming and the Shanghai Sharks. The Mavs' front office had made no promises about a contract extension either. "If Dallas does not extend my contract," Wang said, "then my career in the NBA may well be over." His dream, so long deferred, was now on the verge of ending prematurely, and he laid some of the blame on the Chinese government. "If I had been able to come [to the NBA] when I got drafted in 1999, then I would probably not be so anxious," he said. "But the reality is that I have wasted two years, and I cannot waste any more."

Beijing's continuing restrictions only deepened Wang's anguish. After his first stint in Dallas in early 2001—a period in which he had only nine games and a total of fifty-one minutes on court to get used to the NBA—Wang longed to hone his skills in the NBA summer league, as most young players did. One game in the summer league, he was told, was worth ten games in China. Nevertheless, he obediently trooped back to China for the East Asian Championships and three months of monotonous training for the World University Games. During that tournament, opposing coaches groused about the presence of a twenty-four-year-old NBA player who had never set foot in a college classroom, especially after Wang led his team to a semifinal squeaker over a squad of U.S. college players—China's first triumph ever over an American basketball team. What the foreigners didn't understand, of course, was that China's honor was at stake, and Beijing wasn't going to let a few rules get in the way of international prestige.

In October 2001, as every other NBA player went through training camp and the start of the regular season, Wang was again stuck in China, dutifully practicing with the army team for the National Games in November. This was the first time a foreign government, much less a

Communist army, had ever dictated the schedule of an active NBA player. The Mavs and the NBA accepted the intrusion as the price for maintaining smooth relations with Beijing. But Wang chafed at the delay. Tracking the Mavs' progress on the Internet from halfway around the world, he couldn't help thinking that his own skills were deteriorating against inferior Chinese competition. Bayi pulled out a last-second victory over Yao Ming's Shanghai team to win the national title. Wang, however, could only think about catching the next plane out. He arrived in Dallas two months late, not suiting up in a Mavs uniform until the nineteenth game of the season. Coach Nelson gave him few opportunities to shine, but Wang understood: He couldn't expect much more playing time in the NBA when he was always forced to play catch-up.

The growing frenzy over Yao left Wang even more unsettled. By the spring of 2002, his longtime rival was being hyped ad nauseam as the best basketball prospect in the world, a surefire top pick in the upcoming NBA draft. It was difficult for Wang, China's first NBA player, to be overshadowed by the twenty-one-year-old upstart he had long dominated in China, a kid who had never played a single game of pro or college basketball in the United States. Moreover, Wang worried about the CBA's new regulations—the so-called "Yao Ming Rules"—that required Chinese players abroad to hand over 50 percent of their earnings to the government. Wang's salary was relatively modest by NBA standards—$420,000 that season—but Beijing didn't get a penny. If he returned to China or signed a new contract, he wondered if he'd be forced to surrender half of his salary to the CBA. Wang felt he had already paid his debt to China with the two wasted years and the missed training camps. Why should he have to pay any more?

A week after the Mavs' season-ending loss in Sacramento—on the very day that the Houston Rockets announced their intention to make Yao the NBA's top draft pick in June—Wang arranged a meeting with the Mavs' assistant coach Donnie Nelson to discuss his future. Nelson and Wang still shared the mutual affection that was forged in those first few heady weeks in 2001, when the ebullient Mavs coach escorted the soldier out of China and embraced him as part of his family, putting him up in the extra bedroom in his home and joining him on late-night refrigerator raids for leftover chocolate cake. But the two had inevitably drifted apart. Nelson, now elevated to the job of Mavs vice president for basketball operations, had assumed a gravitas that seemed to diminish his gregariousness. Wang, for his part, had settled down with his girlfriend—now fiancée—Song Yang, spending most of his free time with a handful of her wealthy Chinese friends or with the twenty-nine-year-old Chinese-American hoop fanatic sitting beside him during his meetings with Nelson.

Simon Chan had never imagined he would end up working as Wang's closest advisor. A year earlier, the Columbia University graduate had been working as a video archivist at NBA Entertainment, studiously avoiding a career in law, when his bosses asked him to go to Dallas to help film a promotional video of Wang. The two quickly became friends, playing cards late into the night and swapping stories about their upbringings in Beijing and Brooklyn. On his periodic visits to Dallas over the following year, Chan helped Wang with everything from running errands to mediating his relationship with the Mavs' front office. It was a role full of potential conflicts for an NBA employee, and at Wang's prodding, Chan quit his job in May 2002 and moved to Dallas to become his full-time advisor. "I was just so proud that a Chinese player had made it to the NBA, and I wanted to see him become a success," Chan says. "He needed somebody to help him."

Normally, a professional sports agent would help a player negotiate his future, but Wang could no longer count on the two people who had helped him get this far. Bill Duffy, the NBA agent who had always seen Wang as a stepping-stone to Yao Ming, ended their relationship in early 2002 following a financial dispute with Xia Song, Wang's longtime handler. And now, Wang had fired Xia as well. At their final meeting in March, Wang had broached the possibility of staying in America to play in the NBA summer league. Xia quickly shot down the idea, saying that Beijing probably wouldn't allow it. Perhaps Xia was simply giving sound advice, but Wang believed the young deal maker—who still worked closely with the national team—would be reluctant to endanger his relations with Beijing. It was the last time the two old companions would speak to each other. From then on, Wang refused to accept Xia's phone calls, and the relationship withered. By jettisoning his advisor, one NBA official said, "Wang severed his last remaining tie to China."

By the time Wang sat down with Nelson that night, with Chan acting as his translator, the soldier was, both literally and figuratively, "a restricted free agent." In basketball terms, this meant that even if the Mavs didn't re-sign Wang before his contract expired on June 30, they still had the right to match any other team's offer. In political terms, of course, it meant that Beijing could bring him back whenever it deemed necessary—and the PLA generals seemed to be running out of patience.

Nelson couldn't say at that point whether the Mavs would extend Wang's contract; for all of his offensive skills, Wang's defense was still lackadaisical, and his English was so minimal that it only accentuated his natural aloofness.

Wang, for his part, couldn't tell Nelson that he had already resolved not to return to China. He wanted to gauge the team's commitment to him—and to get Nelson's support for his plan to spend the summer bulking up his slender frame, toughening up his defense, and sharpening his skills against top-level competition. It was the kind of individual initiative any American coach normally would have embraced, except for the niggling fact that Wang was a Chinese soldier, restricted by the kind of laws and logic that applied to no other NBA player.

"I want to play on the Mavs' summer-league team," Wang said, getting to the point quickly. "Can you guarantee me a spot on the roster?"

Nelson was taken aback by the question.

"Da Zhi, you know you're supposed to return to China right after the season ended," he said. "That's the agreement we made with the CBA."

Wang bristled. The Mavs had secured his release from China only after promising to send him back whenever the Beijing authorities saw fit. Xia Song had made a similar pact with both Bayi and the CBA. Midway through Wang's second NBA season, Xia had managed to stave off the army's overtures to pull Wang back to play in the CBA finals against Yao and the Shanghai Sharks. But the episode deeply troubled Wang, for he himself had never signed a single piece of paper agreeing to such terms—even though it was his life and career on the line.

"I understand, coach," Wang said. "But this would help the Mavs *and* China. Isn't it in everybody's interest to see me improve?"

Nelson must have sympathized with Wang's plight. The youngster's NBA career might be over if the Mavs didn't extend his contract or if he couldn't showcase his talents to other teams in the summer league. But the goateed assistant coach couldn't afford to undermine the trust he had built up in Beijing, a trust he hoped would pay dividends for the team far into the future.

"If you really want to play in the summer league," Nelson suggested, "you'll have to get written approval from the CBA."

"No problem," Wang said. "I can get you the approval letter. Give me five days."

Wang's confidence might have seemed misguided. The Beijing bureaucracy had always been excruciatingly slow, especially when it came to making changes in its rigidly established procedures. How was Wang going to cut through all the red tape?

Wang apparently believed he could count on two things: the good will he had built up in Beijing after six years of fulfilling every obligation ever asked of him—and the political pull of his fiancée's father. The retired general, the former chief acquisitions officer for the air force and a member of the powerful Committee of National Defense Technology and Science, had weighed in during the negotiations for Wang's release in 2001. Now, according to a high-level Chinese basketball source in Beijing, he tried to use his *guanxi* with the director of the PLA's political department to persuade CBA director Xin Lancheng to let his future son-in-law stay in America.

It wasn't clear whether this lobbying effort actually softened Xin's attitude, but when Wang talked to him a few days after his dinner with Donnie, the basketball chief seemed to offer a hint of flexibility. Xin began by explaining that it was Wang's patriotic duty to join the national team as it prepared for the World Championships in August, just as it was for all international players.

"When their countries need them, they must return home," Xin said.

Such a request from a top authority in China would normally have been met with automatic submission. But Wang quietly resisted. He tried to explain that the NBA summer league would make him a better player for the sake of China—and that it would still leave him six weeks to train with the national team before the World Championships. He wouldn't miss a beat.

Xin suggested that Wang first return to China to discuss these issues. When the soldier remained noncommittal, according to one of his close friends, Xin offered a cryptic response. "Well, you won't get any letter of approval from me," he said. "But if you do stay, nothing better get into the press."

Was this tacit consent? Or a veiled warning? Having already made his decision, Wang chose to believe that Xin was giving him silent approval to stay through the NBA summer league, which ended in mid-July. Perhaps it was wishful thinking, but he presumed that Xin would let him stay—as long as he didn't attract attention—even if the basketball chief couldn't publicly endorse his plan. In any case, the Chinese soldier seemed to understand that he was now operating on his own, without the public support of his team or his country. Rather than report back to Nelson, who seemed intent on doing everything by the book, the PLA soldier simply packed up his belongings, slid behind the wheel of his Mercedes, and started driving west across the plains.

Wang had disappeared without the knowledge of his superiors once before. But this was different from that night, more than a decade earlier, when the fourteen-year-old prodigy was trundled off in the back of a van by the men from the military. Now, the twenty-four-year-old was trying to take control of his own destiny. He was heading to Los Angeles, site of the NBA summer league, where he hoped to prove himself and secure a new contract. The road trip across the American Southwest wasn't exactly a Kerouac moment, but it marked a definitive break with his past, a point in time when China receded behind him and the lure of America lay just ahead. The freedom of the open road was intoxicating, the scenery so vast and empty that it seemed a broad canvas on which Wang could create anything of himself, just like the American pioneers in whose path he was traveling.

Wang arrived in the City of Angels in the last week of May and moved into a temporary apartment in Westwood, just down the road from the campus of the University of California, Los Angeles. With the help of Simon Chan, who had moved out with him and his fiancée, Wang began working out with a private trainer at the UCLA track and playing pickup games with a group of second-tier NBA players. Chan, a health-and-fitness nut, also set Wang up with a nutritionist who would help the Chinese center reduce his body fat while bulking up his slender frame. Like his American peers, whose will and determination to shape their own destinies he so admired, Wang vowed to do everything in his power to reach the NBA's top echelon, where he felt he belonged. "Before, in my home country, I had neither the time nor the opportunity to think and decide for myself," he said.

Following a self-imposed training regimen wouldn't be easy for a soldier used to following the dawn-to-dusk dictates of the Chinese army. In China, where his height and natural ability had carried him effortlessly to the top, Wang was known for his rather casual approach to practice. In L.A., he tried to train with a newfound intensity, with nothing to support him but his own ambition. "After so many years in the system, he's like a tiger being released from his cage," says Xu Jicheng, the veteran basketball commentator. "But it's been so long that he doesn't really know how to hunt."

During that interlude, Wang says, he sent a couple of faxes to his CBA bosses detailing the wonders of protein shakes and interval sprints. He thought he might enlighten the old-school basketball leaders even as he persuaded them that he was improving his game for the sake of China. The tone of the faxes was always cheerful, but Wang made sure never to give his bosses in Beijing any of his contact numbers. Eventually, the CBA ran out of patience, and Xin—disavowing Wang's interpretation of their earlier conversation—sent two letters demanding that Wang return to China at once. Da Zhi ignored them.

Perhaps nothing, at this point, could have prevented the coming collision between the maverick and the military. But the catalyst that Wang says set it in motion was an article that appeared in the *Dallas Morning News* on June 6, 2002 under the headline: CENTER MISSES DEADLINE TO RETURN TO CHINA, MAY BE MULLING DEFECTION. Wang's mysterious disappearance, the story explained, was "leading NBA sources to speculate that Wang's rebellion against the Chinese government may end in defection to the United States."

There it was, the word that had so spooked Wang five years earlier, the word that he had made Terry Rhoads promise not to say in his presence again. It frightened him even more now. "Da Zhi just panicked when he saw that article," Chan says. "As a member of the army team, as a soldier, he was afraid of what might happen to him if he went back. He could be court-martialed, or maybe China would never let him come back to play in the NBA. He didn't know, but he was scared." Many basketball experts in Beijing suspected that the anonymous Chinese source quoted in the article was deliberately trying to sabotage Wang's career. Whether a "black hand" was present or not, the *Morning News* piece, says the Beijing-based journalist Su Qun, one of Wang's few contacts back in China, "put Wang Zhizhi on a road with no return."

Within twenty-four hours, the original "defection" article spawned dozens of similar stories across America, and the reports filtered back into Chinese newspapers and Web sites. Angered by what he called the *Morning News's* "false reporting," Wang told reporters, through Chan, that he was not defecting and had no plans of giving up his Chinese citizenship. He was simply training hard to participate in the NBA summer league, where he would join the Golden State Warriors roster. "I need to play more high-level games if I want to be like the other NBA players, and the summer league is a very good opportunity," Wang said. "I hope people can understand my intentions. I want to become stronger as a player, and make Chinese basketball stronger."

To American fans, this paean to personal improvement made perfect sense. To Chinese authorities, however, it seemed more like the justification of a man who has been infected by the greed and selfishness of American culture.

Wang's refusal to return to China represented a staggering loss of face for Beijing, and both the CBA and the army scrambled to reassert control over their erstwhile star. CBA officials knew Wang was somewhere in Los Angeles, but until the summer league began in early July, they didn't know his exact whereabouts and they had no way to contact him directly. In the meantime, they tried to put the squeeze on anybody who might be able to exert influence over the missing star.

The Chinese consulate in Los Angeles reportedly received orders to prevent Wang from getting an extension of his visa or a renewal of his passport, which he would need if he were to stay in the United States. At one point, CBA officials even urged Yao's agent, Erik Zhang, to intervene on their behalf, intimating that the crisis, if allowed to fester, could hurt his client's future. They also talked to Xia Song, who insisted he knew nothing of his former client's plans or whereabouts. In the first days after the "defection" article came out, Xia strongly suspected that Chinese police were tapping his mobile phone. On two occasions, his phone rang but nobody was on the other end. When Xia dialed back the number that appeared on his screen, he found himself connected both times to the Beijing public-security bureau, the headquarters of China's secret police.

Far greater anguish, however, befell a pair of middle-age former athletes living in a small apartment near Beijing's Temple of Heaven. Wang's parents were stunned by the rumors about their son. His mother, Ren Huanzhen, the former national-team player, had already been punished for letting her son go to Bayi—an act that left her stuck for more than two decades in the same miserable job as the sports compound's gate attendant. But nothing in her life had stung more than the accusations now being hurled at her only son.

For the previous year, Ren and her husband had basked in the glow of Wang's success. Friends and former teammates dropped by the family's apartment to congratulate them on their son's latest NBA performance or to ask in wonderment about his American life. But now, the kind words and admiring looks had disappeared along with their son. When Ren walked through the old sports compound, some of her neighbors and lifelong acquaintances averted their gaze or—when contact was unavoidable—greeted her with a grimace or a pitying shake of the head. Wang's slump-shouldered father soldiered on with his coaching duties, but Ren stayed in her apartment most days, crying constantly and avoiding the world outside. Their home, however, was no refuge. Reporters bombarded them with phone calls, asking indelicate questions about their son's supposed betrayal. "When is Da Zhi coming home?" they would ask. "Is it true that he has defected?"

The pressure became so excruciating that the couple moved out of their apartment for several weeks just to avoid further harassment. The truth was, they didn't know the answer to any of these questions. Their son hadn't communicated with them since he had gone AWOL, and many months would pass before they spoke again. The silence only deepened his mother's torment. When friends urged Wang to call and comfort her, he refused, saying he wanted to save his parents from having to lie when officials hounded them for information or pressured them to beg him to return. It was equally true, however, that Wang simply didn't know what to say to his parents. He had caused them shame and humiliation, and now he didn't know if he would ever be able to go back to China again—or if they would ever be able to leave.

If this were another era, perhaps Wang's parents would have been thrown into prison as punishment for their son's offense against the state. But now, they simply had to suffer the inevitable questions from the Chinese authorities, and they could truthfully reply that they had not heard from their son.

One of their visitors during those weeks was Ren's old friend and protector, Liu Yumin. The former CBA director was no longer as influential as she once was, but she was Ren's closest friend in the basketball hierarchy. Once again, Madame Liu was dealing with conflicting emotions. She wished Wang would return to China for the sake of both the family and the Chinese government. But she couldn't bring herself to exert much pressure on Wang's family. It was clear that Ren and her husband had no information about their son's whereabouts—and little influence over his behavior even if they did. So Liu just sat at the table in their spartan home, trying to console her heartbroken old friend.

When Wang's mother stopped crying enough to speak, she just repeated a single phrase over and over, a mantra that seemed as much a plea to her visitors as a reminder to herself.

"My son loves China," she said, weeping quietly. "My son is a patriot."

15

Houston, We Have a Problem

Nobody in China had more to lose from Wang Zhizhi's disappearance than Yao Ming. This was supposed to be his crowning moment. The NBA draft loomed only three weeks away, on June 26, and a delegation from the Houston Rockets, the team that held the top draft pick, would soon be arriving in China to negotiate his release. The sports authorities in Shanghai and Beijing, for all their rumblings about compensation, had agreed to promote Yao as the NBA's number one draft pick, the first time such an honor would ever be bestowed on a foreign-born prospect who had never played competitive ball in America. After three years of false starts, the twenty-one-year-old Shanghai star finally had his dream within reach.

But now, Yao's old rival had thrown everything into question. The relationship between the two Chinese big men had always been so intensely competitive that some of Yao's supporters believed that Wang was deliberately sabotaging his younger rival's coronation. Yao didn't believe the conspiracy theories himself, but that did little to diminish his worries over the timing of Wang's decision to go AWOL. When the news first reached the national-team training center in Beijing, Yao called up his friend Frank Sha in a state of near panic.

"Will this hurt me?" he asked.

Sha, who had quit Nike four months earlier to help prepare Yao and his family for the draft, tried to calm the big man down.

"Don't worry," Sha said. "Your situation is totally different. He's army, you're civilian. Besides, you've already proven that you're a good boy."

The reassurances weren't wholly convincing. Perhaps Yao had shown a degree of loyalty by accepting, without public complaint, his leaders' demand to postpone his NBA dreams by a year for the good of his city and his nation. But the same could have been said of Wang's unwavering loyalty before he disappeared. Further clouding the picture were the so-called "Yao Ming Rules" that Beijing had issued to control—or was it to complicate?—every step of his possible transfer to the NBA, from the share of income the state demanded (50 percent) to the number of signatures required at all levels of China's byzantine bureaucracy (at least six) to the kind of agent allowed to negotiate on his behalf (only a certified Chinese national who passed a government test and coughed up the steep, $8,300 application fee). Most insiders had assumed that the Shanghai Sharks, with their calculating front man, Li Yaomin, posed the main obstacle to Yao's release. But now, in the wake of Wang's defiance, there were questions about whether the sports leaders in Beijing—the ultimate authorities—would want to let Yao go at all.

China's sports czars, after all, faced a wrenching dilemma. If Beijing blocked Yao's shot at the NBA this time, when the hype surrounding the 7'5" star had already begun in the American media, there would surely be an international outcry about the lack of freedom in China—and few things grated on Chinese leaders than Western lectures about human rights. But if the top draft pick ever defected, the repercussions could be far more devastating. Nobody wanted to be the bumbling bureaucrat blamed for losing the most valuable athletic treasure in Chinese history—least of all CBA director Xin Lancheng, who was already catching heat for letting Wang slip out of his grasp. A slender man with a lid of neatly combed hair, Xin (pronounced "sheen") was barely in his forties, but he had already calcified into the career apparatchik: resistant to change, averse to risk, fearful of *shikong*—losing control. Suddenly, his future seemed to depend on bringing Wang home and preventing Yao from following the same road to rebellion.

To reassert the CBA's control over Yao, Xin took aim at all of the outside influences on Yao, beginning with his mother's trusted advisor, Erik Zhang, and the business-school dean whom he had brought along to Beijing as Yao's new NBA agent, John Huizinga. Team Yao's only experienced NBA hand, Bill Duffy, remained in the background while the twenty-nine-year-old Zhang invited his business-school professor, who had no prior exposure either to China or the NBA, to play out his sports-agent fantasies. It was a curious lineup, but Duffy, who represented several other top draft picks, was still seen as a polarizing element in China. And despite Huizinga's steep learning curve—at his first meeting with Yao, the professor had asked the only child if he had any brothers or sisters—he was a tough negotiator and, more importantly, in lockstep with Zhang. In Beijing, Zhang went through the motions by hiring a government-approved agent named Lu Hao, but the Chinese-American maintained full control over the process as the only person authorized to speak on behalf of Yao's family—even if the Chinese government didn't recognize that authority.

In May, Zhang sent Xin a cordial letter to open the negotiations. "We definitely will work closely with the CBA," he wrote, "and we won't do anything against the CBA's interests."

"Who are you?" Xin responded testily. "If Yao wants to go to the NBA, he needs a Chinese agent. We won't deal with you."

Zhang had presented himself as part of Yao's family—a distant cousin living in the United States—but that "white lie," as he called it, did little to ease Chinese officials' minds. The leaders blamed Wang Zhizhi's Chinese-American friend, Simon Chan, for filling the soldier's head with thoughts of defiance, a charge Chan himself vehemently denied. Now they feared the same might happen with Yao. When the motley crew from Team Yao showed up to negotiate Yao's release—Zhang, Huizinga, and Lu Hao—Chinese officials refused to meet with the American and vigorously objected to Zhang's presence.

"We don't trust you to protect our rights," Xin told Zhang bluntly.

"Well, of course not, because I'm here to protect Yao's rights," Zhang responded, sounding perfectly American. "I don't have your interests as a top priority, but in order to protect Yao's interests, I have to consider yours. That's only logical." Then he added: "It's like in a divorce. You can't have the same lawyer represent both the husband and the wife."

Divorce might not have been the most reassuring example to use, even if it did neatly illustrate the gulf that separated Chinese and American views on legal rights. Chinese officials were looking for something more like a legally binding marriage contract that would continue until death—or, in Yao's case, retirement—do them part. Within days, the basketball authorities began pushing Yao's family to "divorce" Zhang. The campaign against the young business-school student would be particularly fierce in Shanghai, where the Sharks' Li Yaomin insisted that he still had the prerogative to pick Yao's agent. At one point in May 2002, Li called Yao's parents into an emergency meeting to announce that Yao's new agent would be Xia Song, the former Nike employee whose early separation from Wang Zhizhi had preserved his good relations with Beijing.

"We need somebody who can represent both the club's interest and Yao Ming's interest," Li explained.

Yao's father abruptly stood up and walked out of the meeting. Yao's mother was, as usual, more defiant. "If you want Xia Song to represent the club, go ahead," Da Fang said. "But we will *not* use him as our son's agent." Then she stormed out of the room.

Erik Zhang hardly cut an intimidating figure. With his belly sliding over his belt, his jawline fading into a double chin, the bespectacled 5'6" graduate student seemed too soft to play hard, too young to take on China's old guard. But the kid in khakis and Docksiders possessed nothing if not self-confidence, and he clearly relished the rough-and-tumble world of high-stakes negotiations, where, like a young poker player on a roll in Las Vegas, he could assess the risks, raise the ante, call his opponents' bluffs, and—when the situation called for it—let his normally jovial demeanor give way to cold-blooded brinksmanship.

It didn't hurt, of course, that Zhang was holding an ace in his hand.

By late May 2002, the family's talks with Li Yaomin stumbled once again over the issue of compensation. Zhang acknowledged that the Shanghai Sharks, in return for losing their star center, deserved more than the $350,000 limit that NBA teams were allowed to pay in transfer fees. Other NBA imports had gone down this path, buying out their contracts with future earnings. Memphis Grizzlies star forward Pau Gasol had paid $2.5 million to get released from his Spanish club, Real Madrid. The Sharks, however, had come into the negotiations demanding a whopping $30 million from Yao over the course of his career, not including a separate six-figure settlement for the disputed Evergreen contract, which Li insisted was valid until July 31, 2002. The mention of the Evergreen deal especially infuriated Da Fang: As if gouging them were not enough, the club was asking them to pay to undo a deal that had caused them years of distress.

Angered by the continuing stalemate, Zhang and Da Fang arranged to meet with Li Yaomin's boss, Bai Li, at his office in Shanghai Television headquarters at No. 651 Nanjing Road. Thirty-five years earlier—in the same year that the young television executive was born—Da Fang and her fellow Red Guards had imprisoned, humiliated, and deposed their sports leaders on the training grounds at this very location. The graceful clubhouse where she had helped conduct struggle sessions during the Cultural Revolution had long since made way for Shanghai Television's thirty-two-story steel tower. As Da Fang zoomed up the elevator to Bai Li's twentieth-floor office, she may have been too preoccupied to contemplate the historical ironies. But the fate of her family would be determined, then and now, on the same parcel of land on Nanjing Road.

The meeting started off cordially. Bai Li was an easygoing executive who had a family connection to Da Fang. His late uncle, the basketball sage Bai Jinshen, had been Da Fang's national-team coach in the 1970s. Bai Li himself came to sports as a journalist rather than as an athlete, and though he was nominally the Shanghai Sharks' general manager, he readily admitted that he had been so busy launching his own sports-television channel that he had left the club—and the negotiations—in the hands of his deputy, Li Yaomin. As he spoke that day, however, Bai Li mumbled something about the Evergreen contract. Da Fang and Zhang had been waiting for just this moment. Zhang pulled out a copy of the contract and placed it in front of Bai.

"Tell me, where in this agreement does it say that the Shanghai Sharks will receive any money?" Zhang asked.

Bai Li looked down at the document. The contract clearly stipulated that Evergreen would receive a third of Yao's earnings, but it said nothing about what the Sharks would get.

"Where does two-thirds of the money go?" Zhang asked. "You either have no agreement here, or there is some kind of funny business going on and you are taking advantage of Yao's family."

The color drained from Bai's face. It seemed to Zhang, at least, that the executive had been caught by surprise; he had apparently never studied the contract closely and was unaware of just how murky the conditions were.

Then Zhang went in for the kill: "I hope you never bring this up again."

From that moment on, Bai Li took charge of the negotiations for the Shanghai Sharks, and Li Yaomin was relegated to a supporting role. The Evergreen contract was never mentioned again.

The most difficult part of the negotiations remained: settling on a buyout figure. Even with Bai Li in charge, Shanghai still insisted on garnering more than $18 million from Yao's future earnings. For anybody in America, that figure would have been hard to fathom. But for Yao and his family, steeped in the austere world of the Communist sports system, it was almost unimaginable. Yao's first pro salary was only $61 a month, and his biggest take—nearly half comprised of his Nike contract—was about $60,000 during his last year in the CBA. But the family had entered a different universe now.

Two weeks before the draft, Da Fang and Zhang made the Sharks a counteroffer worth several million dollars. Days passed, but the Shanghai authorities offered no response. During the agonizing wait, Yao's parents set up a "war room" in the new apartment their son had bought them in a modern high-rise building across the boulevard from Shanghai's Luwan Stadium. Fueled by Da Fang's cooking, the odd assemblage of visitors—Zhang, Frank Sha, John Huizinga, Chinese agent Lu Hao, and lawyer Wang Xiaopeng—gathered around the dining-room table for marathon strategy sessions. At times, the tension got so thick that his father, Da Yao, a gentle port worker who suffered from hypertension, would retire to the bedroom. Yao himself was off training with the national team in Beijing, keeping in contact by cell phone but hardly participating in the discussions.

As draft day approached, Da Fang could take the stonewalling no longer. "If we don't reach an agreement, Yao Ming will never play basketball again," she warned less than a week before the draft. "He will go to university, and that will be the end of his career. That's okay, because that's what we wanted from the start."

The CBA broke its silence on June 21 with discouraging news: Yao, the leaders said, would *not* be permitted to travel to New York to attend the NBA draft, making him the first presumptive number one pick in NBA history not to be present. The official excuse was that Yao was too busy training for the World Championships. But few could doubt the influence of the Wang Zhizhi affair. The World Championships, after all, were more than two months away, but Wang's defiance was barely two weeks old and the wounds were still fresh.

The canceled trip cast a pall over the NBA draft—David Stern had hoped to preside over the culmination of his China dream at the ceremony in Madison Square Garden—and pushed Da Fang over the edge. That day, she finally agreed to go along with Zhang's last-ditch gamble to force Shanghai's hand. Reserving a room at Shanghai's Regal International Hotel, he and Frank Sha alerted thirty media outlets that there would be an "important announcement" about Yao's situation the following evening, June 22, at 9:00 P.M. Zhang then told the Shanghai leadership that the clock was ticking. If the team didn't make a good-faith effort now, he warned, the family would tell the world that Yao was not going to the NBA—and that Shanghai's greedy officials were to blame. Get prepared, he said, to be pilloried in the press for abusing Yao's rights.

"It was a big gamble," Sha later said, "but we had no other leverage."

The maneuver incensed the Sharks' owners at Shanghai Television, who saw it as a breach of etiquette that verged on blackmail. Rarely in the People's Republic had an individual or a family tried to use such coercive methods against a government institution, much less gotten away with it.

"You can call the press conference if you want, but remember, we *are* the state media," the club's lawyer seethed at Zhang. "We can ruin you."

Zhang held his ground. He reminded the lawyer that, even in China, the media's purpose was "to shine a light into the dark corners of society."

The following morning, June 22, a chastened Bai Li arrived to hammer out a deal with Zhang. Nothing was formalized, but in return for Yao's release from the club, the family agreed to pay the Sharks between $8 million and $15 million over the course of his career, based on a sliding scale determined by the size of his NBA contracts. The tentative pact still required the approval of several top city officials, but Zhang went ahead with the press conference anyway to announce that Shanghai had agreed to let Yao go to the NBA. It was an insurance policy, a way to prevent Shanghai officials from reneging on a deal that Zhang believed "fairly distributed the risks and rewards" of Yao's career.

Zhang's game of hardball may have saved Yao's family several million dollars, but the whole situation—the bruising tactics, the tentative deal, the huge financial stakes, the continuing uncertainty in Beijing—seemed to weigh heavily on Da Fang as she sat in front of the assembled reporters that evening. Her husband had stayed home, too nervous to make a public appearance. The journalists had grown to expect that, but they found it curious that none of the top club or city officials was there to announce the supposed deal. As Yao's Chinese agent Lu Hao spoke almost apologetically about the agreement's financial burdens— "I hope this pact won't be copied in the future," he joked, "because I don't want to be considered a criminal in Chinese sports history"—Da Fang sat off to the side, looking drained and dispirited. She didn't speak until a reporter asked her how she felt.

"Every parent gives his sweat and blood for his children," she replied. "I am very happy to see the results today."

"But you don't look happy. Why not?" the reporter asked.

"Am I unhappy?" Da Fang asked, considering the question. She paused for several awkward seconds, as if taking an internal reading, before she responded weakly. "I am sorry . . ."

Her voice trailed off.

The Chinese journalists were too polite to ask follow-up questions, and Da Fang spent the rest of the press conference sitting in silence, her pinched smile dissolving into a vacant stare. Her new group of advisors kept repeating the upbeat message to the crowd, but the woman at the center of it all now seemed far away, as if, after all these years of emotional turmoil, she could barely feel a thing.

*   *   *

The theatrics in Shanghai were merely a prelude to the real drama in Beijing, where the specter of defection seemed to paralyze authorities just when they needed to decide whether to let Yao Ming go to the NBA.

Money and material benefits, along with a dose of brinksmanship, had been enough to convince Shanghai officials to release their homegrown star. But persuading the shaken bureaucrats in Beijing to give Yao their final approval would take more than the promise of glory and riches. It would require trust. And as the NBA draft drew near, trust was in dangerously short supply in Chinese sports circles. CBA chief Xin Lancheng couldn't be sure that Yao wouldn't defect—after all, the youngster had followed in Wang's footsteps most of his life—and until he could bring Wang home and be convinced of Yao's loyalty, he seemed to prefer not making any decision at all.

Strictly speaking, the Chinese government couldn't stop Yao from entering the NBA draft. He would turn twenty-two later that year, so, according to NBA rules, that made him automatically eligible. The CBA's endorsement, however, was indispensable. Without it, Yao would never be able to retrieve his passport from the national team leader or get the necessary visa to leave the country and play in America. Moreover, the Houston Rockets would not want to squander their first top draft pick in eighteen years on a prospect who had no formal clearance to play in the NBA. The uncertainty surrounding the number one pick threw the entire draft into confusion. By the time the Rockets' delegation arrived in China to negotiate Yao's release on June 9, nearly everybody in the NBA was watching closely.

The Rockets landed in the middle of a maelstrom they could only dimly comprehend. None of the four men—the team's general counsel Michael Goldberg, general manager Carroll Dawson, coach Rudy Tomjanovich, and press officer Nelson Luis—had ever been to China before, and they seemed as disoriented by the country's gleaming skyscrapers as by the mysterious maneuvering of their Chinese interlocutors. Goldberg, the delegation leader, was a forty-five-year-old senior partner at the prestigious Houston firm, Baker Botts, who prided himself on his international practice, having negotiated major deals in Brazil, South Korea, and Saudi Arabia. Despite his affable demeanor and thick-lensed glasses, Goldberg enjoyed a reputation as a pit bull with cast-iron cojones. On the bookshelf in his thirty-seventh-floor office in downtown Houston sits a plaque for the "How Sweet It Is" award that Baker Botts bestowed on him "in recognition of his intensity, tenacity, and obvious pleasure in kicking ass."

Nevertheless, Goldberg was out of his element in China, and he found himself clinging to the few snippets of advice he had received before boarding the transpacific flight. Erik Zhang had been so worried about the Rockets' ignorance—"It is a bigger culture shock for the Rockets to go to China than for Yao to come to Houston," he said—that he had arranged for a noted Sinologist to give them a pretrip tutorial on China's cultural sensitivities: the concept of face, the penchant for secrecy, the reflexive suspicion of outsiders. Goldberg also consulted his law partner, former secretary of state James A. Baker III, who cautioned that Chinese negotiators tend to build trust slowly and make abrupt changes at the last minute. None of it boded well for the blunt Americans, who had only a few days, not years, to wrest a deal from the Chinese authorities.

During the first meeting with Xin Lancheng, the CBA director sat as still as a stone carving, eyeing his visitors warily. Goldberg had come bearing a letter of introduction from former president George H. W. Bush. He even had Tomjanovich carry his briefcase to enhance his aura of authority. But none of that seemed to matter. Xin remained silent. The awkwardness, Goldberg suspected, came not so much from the language barrier as from the unresolved crisis of the missing soldier. "Xin was caught in a box because of Wang, so I didn't want to push too hard," he says. "We felt that we had to show that we were not the kind of team that would encourage a defection, since one of my goals, both for the Rockets and for Baker Botts, was to be number one in China. It would be a disaster for us if Yao defected. I told them: 'You may not trust me, but look at our American self-interest.' "

But American self-interest was precisely what Xin feared most. It was self-interest, after all, that had led Wang down the path toward defection. Xin had grown to trust the Mavericks, whose self-interest also included developing a long-term relationship with Beijing, but they had failed to deliver on their agreement to return Wang to China. How could he trust the Rockets, whom he had only known for a day, with the player who was China's Michael Jordan? Before negotiations could move ahead, Xin requested that the Rockets sign a guarantee ensuring Yao's safe return to China anytime the CBA deemed it necessary.

Goldberg politely demurred. "We told them that Rudy, of all people, knows what national duty means," he said. "Rudy was the U.S. Olympic coach, and he would do everything possible to keep Yao Ming returning to play for the national team." But the Rockets couldn't sign an agreement that would keep their top draft pick at China's beck and call during the regular season. "It was a cultural difference," Goldberg says. "We needed a full release, but the CBA saw this as a temporary loan that could be rescinded at any time."

The clash over competing demands sent a chill through the conversation. Goldberg asked if the delegation might arrange a visit with Yao, but Xin shook his head and responded coldly: "Let's see how our meeting goes first." Xin eventually let the Rockets see Yao at a national-team practice, where they bantered briefly and snapped photos, but the basketball chief balked at giving a formal release—and the delegation left Beijing empty-handed.

Back in Houston, the pressure on Goldberg mounted. It was bad enough knowing that if he failed to win Yao's release, the Rockets' long-suffering fans—indeed, the entire NBA—would blame him for botching a historic opportunity in China. But the escalating threats were almost too much. During the previous three weeks, Goldberg said he had received "dozens of phone calls" demanding that he stop dealing with Erik Zhang. The callers, he said, were mostly Chinese or Chinese-American, several of whom said they were calling at the behest of mainland officials. On one occasion, Goldberg even received a visitor in his office who warned him tersely that the Chinese government would not let Yao go if Zhang were involved.

A few days before the draft, the same man called again. "If you don't get rid of Zhang, Yao Ming will *never* go to the NBA," he said. "You'll never get the deal done."

"I will tell people that you told me this," Goldberg responded icily. "Then when we don't draft Yao, you'll get all the blame, okay?"

Up to this point, Goldberg had tried to reason with Chinese officials. Reining in his natural eagerness to make a deal, he had sat through long meetings of tea-sipping and relationship-building, reassuring his hosts about their mutual interests in developing both Yao and Chinese basketball. So far, the sweet-talking had been greeted with threats and stonewalling, but no formal assurances that Yao would be free to play in the NBA.

As the countdown to draft day ticked past thirty-six hours, Goldberg ran out of patience. Through an intermediary, he delivered a sharp warning to Xin.

"If we don't get the full release before the draft, we won't pick Yao Ming," Goldberg's message went. "And if we don't draft Yao, everybody in the NBA will know there's a problem with the Chinese government—and Yao's stock will plummet. He would drop several places, maybe a lot more. He might not even get drafted. You don't want that to happen, do you?"

Xin fumed at the display of American arrogance. First one NBA team had failed to fulfill its promise to send Wang home; now, less than a month later, another team was trying to bully China into relinquishing the rights to the most valuable player in the nation's history without any guarantee of his safe return. As draft day loomed, the CBA chief made an unusual appeal to NBA headquarters, requesting the league's written guarantee that Yao would return to China whenever the national team needed him. The NBA, however, did not have the power to intervene. Unlike the dictatorial Chinese sports hierarchy, the NBA ran the league at the behest of the teams, and its rules were mostly designed to protect—not to proscribe—the rights of individual players.

The cultural rift left both sides shaking their heads. How, the Chinese asked, could the world's most powerful league have so little influence over its players? And how, the Americans wondered, could the CBA control Yao so tightly? David Stern made no comment, but he recalled warning Chinese authorities not to fall into the trap of letting politics interfere with sport. "Do you know how to spell Arvydas Sabonis?" Stern said he had asked a Chinese official, referring to the Soviet-era Lithuanian center who had to wait nine years after he was drafted before he arrived in America. "If that's what they want, a player who doesn't come to the NBA in his prime to learn the game and ultimately to perhaps even help his country attain a medal, then that's their decision to make."

Lacking any firm guarantee, the CBA chief apparently hoped to slide through the crisis without making a firm decision—letting Yao get drafted but waiting until Wang's situation was resolved before discussing the details of Yao's release. The Rockets, however, were now forcing China's hand, and officials in Beijing were so irked by Goldberg's warning that they were tempted to call off the negotiations. "That threat almost doomed the whole deal," Zhang said. "At that point, everything was hanging by a thread."

It was a gamble, Goldberg admitted, but he was betting that China's obsession with being number one would prevail over all other concerns. It was not enough that Yao was the greatest player the Middle Kingdom had ever produced. Yao's boosters in China claimed that he was already more talented than the NBA's most dominant player, Shaquille O'Neal. The claim was ludicrously premature—Yao's inflated statistics had come against relatively feeble Chinese competition—but it showed that China would only be satisfied with the top draft pick. "They absolutely wanted the number one draft pick," Goldberg said. "Number two or number five wouldn't do. Only number one. It was all about face."

As the Rockets wielded a stick—the threat of pulling out of the Yao sweepstakes—Yao himself decided to offer Chinese officials a carrot. For the previous three years, the young giant had stood outside the drama of his own life, watching helplessly as others haggled over his fate. But on June 25, with less than thirty-six hours remaining before the draft, Yao had grown so frustrated by the stalemate—and frightened about letting his best opportunity to play in the NBA slip away—that he volunteered to give Xin a "loyalty pledge." The Chinese leaders "did not ask for [this pledge]," Zhang said. "We want to reassure the CBA that Yao's commitment to the national team is unwavering and unconditional."

In the document he signed that day, Yao promised to conduct himself in a manner that made China proud. He said he felt honored to wear the uniform of the Chinese national team and would return to play for the five-star flag whenever the leaders deemed it necessary. It was the least he could do to repay his debt to the sports system that had so painstakingly developed him. The tone of the pledge was respectful and optimistic, but the subtext was clear: Yao would not become another Wang Zhizhi. Though the pact never mentioned Wang by name, it amounted to a denunciation of the behavior that led to his disappearance—and an assurance that Yao would never do the same.

Even with Yao's loyalty pledge in hand, Xin gave no indication about what the government might do. Hours passed, the silence persisted. Draft day, June 26, arrived and Yao—instead of being in New York for a big celebration—was grinding through another practice in Beijing, trying to pretend it was a normal day. His mother remained in Shanghai, wondering if a lifetime of preparation—and three years of roller-coaster negotiations—would come to nothing. Even if she was unschooled in the ways of the NBA, the former Red Guard understood how the Chinese government worked. She knew that silence was just as likely as salvation.

Half a world away and half a day behind, Michael Goldberg sat in the darkened den of his suburban Houston home. It was well past midnight, nearly two hours into draft-day morning. His wife and three children were all fast asleep, but Goldberg stayed near the phone and the fax machine in his office, waiting for the final word from Beijing. With only hours remaining before the Rockets needed to submit their selection to NBA officials, Goldberg still didn't know if his threats had killed the deal—or saved the day.

Shortly before 2:00 A.M. Houston time, Goldberg's fax machine sputtered to life, spitting out three pages of scribbled Chinese characters. It hardly looked like a formal document: There was no letterhead, no signature, and—strangest of all, for a society built on bureaucracy—no official seal or stamp. Goldberg faxed the letter to Zhang in Shanghai and to a Chinese colleague in Hong Kong to get it translated. Xin was agreeing, at last, to make Yao available to play in the NBA through the regular season and the playoffs, if necessary. This was the news Goldberg had been waiting for, but his elation was tinged with doubt. The fax didn't contain the one sentence Goldberg had demanded, the confirmation that Yao had been freed of his playing contracts in China. Moreover, no Chinese bureaucrat could ever be held accountable for the patently unofficial document.

Were the Chinese truly committed to letting Yao go or were they just fudging it to ensure Yao's selection as the number one pick?

Goldberg rang up Rockets owner Les Alexander and delivered the news. Alexander, Yao's most enthusiastic booster on the Rockets, asked Goldberg if the document was strong enough to let them select Yao that evening. The onus would be on Goldberg to pull Yao out of China; losing a top pick in the morass of Chinese negotiations would be a setback that Houston fans might never forgive. Nevertheless, in his hope and optimism, Goldberg said yes. "It wasn't a release, per se," he says, "but it was enough to give me comfort to make the pick."

After all, in the three weeks that he had been dealing with the Chinese authorities, this was the first time he had seen them blink.

The military guards standing at attention outside the Jianguomenwai diplomatic compound in Beijing normally don't allow Chinese citizens to enter the leafy foreigners' enclave without a stern inspection of their identification cards and an interrogation about the purpose of their visit. The walled-in cluster of fifteen-story apartment buildings is one of the few foreign reserves in China, a place designed both to keep the diplomats and journalists living inside under close surveillance and to keep out any Chinese who might unfavorably influence them. But when a van pulled up to the gate shortly after dawn on June 27, 2002, the soldiers in their high-peaked hats waved the vehicle through without delay. The man reclining in the passenger seat, his enormous square head nearly brushing the van's high ceiling, was the 7'5" basketball star whose image was all over television. As Yao Ming arrived, even the stern-faced young soldiers couldn't help breaking out in smiles.

The NBA draft was scheduled to begin at 7:30 A.M. local time, and Yao's parents, who had flown up from Shanghai the night before, met their son on the top floor of Building #12, inside the Beijing bureau of

CNN, whose affiliate, TNT, would be broadcasting the draft. Much had transpired since Yao had last seen his parents more than a month before—Wang's act of defiance, the showdown with Shanghai authorities, the last-minute reprieve—but he expressed little emotion upon greeting them, limiting himself to an almost imperceptible nod of the head. Yao and his family knew the day they had all been striving for had finally arrived, but they felt, just as keenly, that a new kind of pressure was about to begin. The assembled photographers, anticipating a photogenic moment of catharsis from the family reunion, were compelled to lower their cameras.

Even as the other top prospects gathered in the Madison Square Garden ballroom, decked out in custom-made suits tailored for the occasion, Yao sat under the lights on a hard-back chair in a pair of brown corduroys and an untucked white T-shirt. There was only an audio feed of the TNT broadcast, but at 7:36 A.M., Yao and his parents listened as the disembodied voice of NBA commissioner David Stern announced the first draft pick. The message traveled in milliseconds from the world's most vibrant commercial metropolis to a Communist capital where fleets of bicycles were stuck in morning rush hour. "With the first pick of the 2002 NBA draft," Stern said, "the Houston Rockets select Yao Ming from Shanghai, People's Republic of China."

Three years of intensive international diplomacy had led to this milestone moment, but the pro-American—and decidedly pro-Jay Williams—crowd met the announcement with only light applause and a smattering of boos. Leading the chorus was the TNT announcer and former NBA all-star Charles Barkley, who wondered aloud why the Rockets were choosing an untested behemoth stuck in a recalcitrant Communist state. "They've lost their minds!" he crowed.

Back in Beijing, the atmosphere was strangely deflated as well. Yao's parents clapped lightly while showing only the faintest of smiles. "They had felt tortured by this whole process," says Frank Sha, who accompanied them that day, "so they didn't have much emotion left." The NBA personnel on hand prompted the family to show some excitement for the cameras, and the trio proceeded to make one of the most ungainly group high-fives in television history. "The parents were very stoic," recalls Jaime FlorCruz, CNN's Beijing bureau chief. "It seemed very Chinese, or at least very much a piece with their generation in China. This was supposed to be one of the best moments of their lives, and yet they couldn't show any emotion on the outside."

FlorCruz knew better than most foreigners how to analyze Chinese emotions. A Filipino who had come to China in 1971 as a starry-eyed

Marxist on a three-week tour, he was prevented from returning home by the Marcos government and ended up stranded in China as an exile. Having undergone "reeducation" in mountainous Sichuan Province during the Cultural Revolution (before joining the Peking University basketball team as a backup point guard), FlorCruz understood how a turbulent history had caused the Chinese to blunt their most extreme feelings. But as a television man, FlorCruz had an eye for drama, and he was disappointed at the Yao family's reaction. "It was frustrating," he says, "because we were more excited than they were."

Hoping to inject some historic resonance into what was turning into a rather desultory event, the CNN bureau chief at one point led the trio past a huge floor-to-ceiling portrait of Chairman Mao so photographers might capture China's two greatest icons together. The oversize family blocked out Mao's face, however, and one of the resulting photographs beamed around the world recorded something far more intriguing. Above the heads of the three giants hung another of FlorCruz's collector's items: a 1968 propaganda poster from the Cultural Revolution with three figures—a soldier, a worker, and a peasant—drawn in brawny socialist-realist detail. The peasant and the soldier both carried rifles, while the worker held up Mao's *Little Red Book,* the same collection of guiding principles that sparked Da Fang's own revolutionary zeal more than three decades before. Below the figures, a slogan exhorted: "People of the world, unite! Defeat the American imperialists!"

The photograph infuriated many Chinese, who felt that their country's glorious moment was marred by a useless—and perhaps malicious—dredging up of the past. The *Houston Chronicle,* which splashed the photograph across its front sports page the next morning, would feel compelled to remove the photo from its late editions after receiving a flood of angry calls from Chinese readers—including a subscriber or two at the local Chinese consulate. Rockets officials, for their part, were at pains to soothe the wounded egos of their Chinese counterparts, explaining that this was not an intentional slight but an unfortunate accident.

On the morning of the draft, however, history could be seen in a different light. The juxtaposition of the NBA's new poster boy with the old propaganda poster only served to show how far China—and Yao's family—had come. Yao was on the verge of becoming a capitalist icon in America, moving as far away from the Maoist past as any Chinese could imagine. In the moments after the draft announcement, as he juggled congratulatory cell-phone calls from his new bosses halfway around the world, an NBA official put a Rockets hat on his massive head. It was four sizes too small. Even the NBA had no idea just how big this Chinese star would be. There would be plenty of struggles ahead, but in his live postdraft interview, Yao reached across the ocean to greet his new world with a simple phrase, in broken English:

"Houston, I am come!"

16

Summer of Discontent

Two veteran members of the People's Liberation Army walked briskly through the arrivals lounge at Los Angeles International Airport, intent on carrying out their covert mission: finding Lt. Wang Zhizhi and bringing him home. The two officials—national-team leader Kuang Lubin and Bayi head coach Adi Jiang—had been delayed in San Francisco following their transpacific flight, and their late arrival in Los Angeles threatened to foil their plan for tracking down the wayward soldier. At that moment, on the evening of July 17, 2002, the Chinese center was playing in his final NBA summer-league game for the Golden State Warriors at the Pyramid in Long Beach. The sporting complex was about a twenty-minute drive from the airport on a good day—which this, it seemed clear already, was decidedly not.

Wang had been AWOL for nearly two months now, and the Beijing authorities, exasperated by their inability to contact him directly, had turned to the two men who had known the prodigy since his early years at the Hongshankou military compound. Kuang, the taller and more senior of the two, was a 6'4" former Bayi standout who had coached Wang on the army's junior team and now, at age forty-six, served as the leader and chief disciplinarian of the Chinese national team. Adi Jiang, a decade younger and more than half a foot shorter, had only recently hung up his high-tops as Wang's teammate on both the Bayi and national teams to become the Bayi head coach. A native of China's westernmost province of Xinjiang—his balding pate, long sideburns, and light-brown eyes marked him as a member of the Muslim Uighur minority—the crowd-pleasing point guard had dished out so many assists to Wang that many considered him partly responsible for the young star's rapid rise. Off the court, he had also played a vital role: As one of Wang's first roommates, he became a mentor whose sense of honor and style the young soldier sought to emulate.

Up until that moment, when the two men lurched through the snarling L.A. traffic to intercept their former protégé, China's basketball authorities felt they had been patient with Wang. His act of insubordination deeply angered them, but aside from a bit of unscripted criticism from national-team coach Wang Fei on the day of Yao's draft, nobody had denounced Wang publicly. The leaders at Bayi and the CBA hadn't stopped him from playing in the NBA summer league. But the two-week competition was ending that night, and while Wang had shown off his skills admirably—averaging 14.4 points and 6.8 rebounds per game up to that point—the time had come for him to return home. There were no more excuses now, and indeed, Wang's public statements had led people to believe that he, too, was willing to come back to Beijing to make amends with the basketball leaders. "I will try to rush back immediately after the summer league ends in late July and join the national team," he told a Chinese reporter for *Titan Sports Weekly* on July 1. "I must find an opportunity to explain my position to CBA director Xin and Coach Wang, and apologize to them, because I caused the misunderstanding. I should have actively sought them out to talk."

In the intervening three weeks, however, something had made Wang change his mind. By the time the two army men reached Long Beach, the Warriors' game had ended—and Wang had already sped away in his Mercedes. Simon Chan, Wang's Chinese-American advisor, sounded evasive. Speaking Mandarin with the imprecise drawl of a second-generation *huaqiao* (overseas Chinese), Chan told the two army men he had no way to reach Wang; the player's mobile phone was turned off. Skeptical, Kuang asked Chan for Wang's latest number, but the Chinese-American refused. Wang had instructed him not to reveal his phone number to anybody, and Chan wasn't about to hand it over to a pair of officials who had come to take Wang home.

It was a startling setback for the two visitors. The leaders in Beijing had entrusted them to travel several thousand miles and bring back a young player over whom they'd always had unquestioned authority. But now they couldn't even find him, much less persuade him to return home. Sitting in his L.A. hotel room that week, Kuang felt humiliated having to plead for a meeting with Chan, a twenty-nine-year-old with an Ivy League degree and perfectly moussed hair but, to Kuang's mind, little understanding of what was at stake. "I didn't believe that anything Chan told us was what Wang really thought," Kuang recalls. "I needed to talk to Wang himself." It wouldn't happen. Kuang returned to Beijing a week later without having spoken a word to the defiant soldier.

Adi Jiang would have a bit more luck. A few days after the missed connection in Long Beach, Wang agreed to meet his old mentor for dinner at a Korean restaurant. Wang may not have trusted Kuang, but he and his former point guard had forged a close bond through years of living, eating, and playing ball together. They had even been featured together in the Nike "Local Heroes" ad campaign six years before. Still, this wasn't like old times; Wang was skittish and paranoid now. Adi Jiang may have been an old friend, but he was acting, on this occasion, as an emissary of the powers in Beijing. When the Bayi coach asked to meet with Wang alone, Da Zhi insisted on bringing along what passed for his posse—his fiancée, Song Yang, and Chan—and, during the meal, he repeatedly looked to them for guidance.

As the group sat around eating beef and kimchi, Adi Jiang tried to ease Wang's mind, just as he used to do on the basketball court years before. He said he understood that Wang's decision to stay in America wasn't meant as a betrayal of China but as an attempt to secure his future in the NBA. But the center had forgotten that his NBA dream only existed because of the care and support of his country; he was nothing without his motherland. Nevertheless, the coach said, Wang still had a chance to set things straight with Bayi and the CBA before either side did something that made the situation irreversible.

"Nobody will punish you when you return to Beijing," Adi Jiang assured him. "I will back you up all the way, you have my word."

Wang appreciated the voice of support, but he no longer believed, if he ever did, that he could return to his homeland without being severely punished. To his mind, the newly appointed Bayi coach, for all his good intentions, did not have the power to stop that. "Adi Jiang was not the principal decision maker at Bayi or the CBA," Chan says. "Wang looked at him as a friend, a mentor, but he didn't think he could protect him back in China."

For Wang, the conversation over Korean barbecue served not as a prelude to his return so much as an opportunity to plead his case. Like his parents, the taciturn soldier had never been gifted with words or *guanxi*-making, and his initial response to crisis had always been to burrow into isolation. During the previous six weeks, Wang had lurked on Chinese-language Web sites watching people debate his predicament. Though some applauded his courage—most Chinese youth were making decisions for themselves, so why shouldn't Wang?—thousands of posts excoriated him for spurning his homeland to chase the all-mighty

American dollar. Now that he had come out of hiding, the first thing Wang wanted Adi Jiang to know was that his motivations were honorable.

"You know, I'm not doing this for the money," Wang said.

Adi Jiang nodded, but he must not have looked convinced, for Wang's fiancée broke in to offer supporting evidence.

"He doesn't need the money," Song said. "My family is very rich."

Adi Jiang was taken aback by the blunt assertion, but he must have heard the stories about Song and her family that had rippled through the Chinese basketball community. Song was several years older than Wang, and her air of wealth and worldliness—along with her passing resemblance to *Crouching Tiger, Hidden Dragon* movie star Zhang Ziyi—had undoubtedly appealed to the unsophisticated soldier when they began dating two years earlier. As their relationship grew, Da Zhi began spending more time with her circle of wealthy friends and businessmen—a fact that many attribute to his growing sense of aloofness and arrogance. Wang had been, by Chinese standards, a wealthy athlete, earning nearly $75,000 a year on salary and endorsement contracts combined, but that hardly compared to the riches of Song's family. Her father, the retired air force general, had been in charge of military acquisitions, and now the family was moving into private enterprise. Song's brother reportedly controlled a large amount of assets whose value had risen in China's stock and property markets, and Song now managed some of that money in America. One of Wang's friends recalled how Song liked to brag that she had given Wang a Mercedes-Benz even before the basketball star could afford one himself.

Now, Song took her assertion one step further: "Da Zhi doesn't even need to play basketball anymore if he doesn't want to."

The table went silent, and the odd interruption—part boast, part threat—hung in the air. Nobody really believed that Wang would quit playing basketball. It was the one thing he had been raised to do, and when the pressure wasn't too intense, the one thing he enjoyed more than anything else. What people around the table understood to be Song's implicit message, however, seemed more pointed. It wasn't that Wang didn't need basketball anymore; it was that he didn't need China. Now that he was in the NBA—and living with Song—he had the financial means to be make independent decisions about his future without the impositions of the state.

After the awkward moment passed, Wang explained that all he really wanted was what every other NBA player already had: the freedom to prove himself. His first two NBA seasons were cut short by obligations to China, and now Beijing expected him to play in the Asian Games in October, forcing him to miss another NBA preseason training camp. Although Wang looked forward to playing in the World Championships in August, he didn't see why he should have to play in tournaments that were either irrelevant or disruptive to his NBA career. The Asian Games, to his mind, were both.

The conflict over schedules, however, was merely a cover for Wang's greatest fear—that Beijing would never allow him to play in the NBA again. Bayi had already been stalling on this issue before he made his escape in May; he could only imagine what the generals wanted to do with him now. Adi Jiang attempted to assuage Wang's fears. "Don't worry," he said. "I've been assured that you will be able to come back to the NBA. It's just a matter of coming home, giving the leaders some face, and getting things squared away."

Even if his old mentor was right, even if the CBA and Bayi embraced him as the prodigal son, going back to China at that moment might still end his NBA career. His performance in the summer league—where he sank 56 percent of his shots and more than half of his three-pointers—had boosted his stock among NBA coaches. But he was still in limbo, a player without a contract for the following NBA season. The market for the NBA's restricted free agents had opened that week, and Wang's new sports agent—Jeff Schwartz of the Artists Management Group—wanted to shop him around the NBA.

As the evening progressed, Wang asked his old teammate a question he had been mulling over the whole time: What would happen if he didn't go back?

The Bayi coach's demeanor darkened. If Wang didn't reconcile with his bosses at Bayi and the CBA, the conflict would hurt not only his future in China—but also in the NBA. Part of this was simple economics. No matter how big an attraction Wang became, China would always be bigger. Wang's value to the NBA was not simply measured in three-point shots and field-goal percentages, but in his role as a gateway to doing business in China. Why did he think the Mavericks pursued him so doggedly for three years?

The bigger calculation, however, was political. If Wang didn't return soon, he could be expelled from the Chinese national team and face even stiffer punishment from an army tribunal. The bosses in Beijing were so angry that there was talk of pushing the NBA to prevent any team from signing a contract with Wang. The specter of the Chinese government reaching into the United States to thwart his NBA dream terrified Wang. The NBA commissioner, Wang knew, couldn't stop a team from signing any player it wanted. But the Mavericks had caved in to Beijing without even a whimper of protest. What if everybody else in American basketball did, too?

As Wang sullenly contemplated his future, the coach's cell phone rang. He answered and then extended the phone to Wang.

"It's your mother."

Wang froze. He hadn't spoken to his mother in nearly two months. A journalist friend had told him that Ren had been devastated by the sudden backlash against him, spending most of her days crying at home. His silence hurt her most. Wang said he tried to get messages to his parents to let them know he was all right, but he didn't call directly for fear that they would be drawn into a nasty political struggle that they couldn't handle.

With his mother on the cell phone inches away, Wang must have wanted to hear her voice, to reassure her that he was doing everything he could to make her proud. But the doubts took over again. Why was she calling now, during his first encounter with Beijing authorities since he went AWOL? Wang's mother clearly had been in touch with Adi Jiang, and they had prearranged to have her call at this time. Was his mother being used to persuade him to come home? And would he crack when he heard her voice?

Wang's response was adamant.

"No, no, I don't want to talk to her," he said quietly, turning away from the phone. "I'm sorry, I can't talk to her."

It was shortly after four o'clock in the morning on August 22, 2002, when the silver Mercedes-Benz gunned up the ramp onto the Los Angeles freeway. The predawn sky hung heavy and dark over the empty ribbon of asphalt, and Wang Zhizhi was speeding north toward his last shot at redemption.

Even at eighty miles per hour, it would take more than five hours to reach Oakland, where Wang hoped to intercept the Chinese national team at a morning practice before their game that evening against a squad of NBA stars. Traveling by plane would have been faster, but after a summer spent in paranoid seclusion, the 7'1" soldier wanted to avoid the gawking crowds at the airports and, more pointedly, the Chinese travelers who might hurl epithets at him in public. So here he was behind the wheel, his friend and confidant Simon Chan in the passenger seat and, thrown across the backseat, a duffel bag full of good intentions: a few basketball jerseys and shorts and his favorite pair of Nike Airs. If everything went right, Wang hoped this would be the day when he played his way back into the good graces of the Chinese authorities—and back into the embrace of the NBA.

Wang's sudden decision to drive through the night had come after waiting in vain for a phone call from Beijing inviting him to rejoin the national team. For the previous month, Wang had been trying to find a way out of his predicament, a middle ground that would help him protect his future in the NBA and restore his relations with his homeland. So far, he had failed, and now he was running out of time. Oakland was the last stop for Yao Ming and the Chinese national team before the World Championships began in Indianapolis the following week. In just two days, the CBA would have to submit its final roster for the tournament, a prestigious competition second only to the Olympics. All of Wang's hopes hinged on one tenuous supposition: that the leaders' need to field the best possible team would outweigh their desire to punish him for defying orders.

In just a few hours, Wang would learn if the supposition was right. He stepped on the accelerator, nudging the needle past eighty-five.

The signals from Beijing over the previous month, like so many communications from China's capital, had left room for interpretation. CBA leaders had included Wang's name on the alternate list for the World Championships, making him eligible to play if he rejoined the team before the upcoming enrollment deadline. Nike had even prepared uniforms with his name stitched on them. Soon after Adi Jiang's visit to L.A., the CBA sent a letter addressed to "Comrade Wang Zhizhi." "Now is the most critical time that your country needs you," read the July 26 missive. "As an elite basketball player brought up by the country over so many years, it is your honor and high duty to return to China for training with the National Team and to represent your country in international competitions." The letter went on to promise that Wang would not be punished by the CBA or the Bayi Rockets. "You can still sign a contract with any NBA team and play in the NBA," the letter read. "Please free yourself from all unnecessary worries."

The letter's upbeat tone hardly cheered Wang. The soldier now seemed to appreciate that a full-scale conflict with Beijing could ruin him professionally. But he still believed that returning to China would endanger his NBA career—either because the authorities, despite all their promises, would prevent him from returning to America or because he would miss his chance to sign with an NBA team. Two weeks after receiving the CBA letter, in mid-August, Wang instructed Chan to propose two possible scenarios to CBA director Xin Lancheng. One was for Da Zhi to meet the team in Denver when it arrived for training on

August 17; the other was to join the squad in Vancouver two days later before a game with the Canadian team. Neither scenario involved returning to China, as Xin had requested.

Despite his irritation at receiving Wang's demands via Chan—"Why won't Wang Zhizhi call us himself?" he asked—the CBA chief agreed to let Wang join the team in Vancouver on one condition: that he return to China immediately after the World Championships to sign a loyalty pact and play in the Asian Games. Wang, however, never showed up in Vancouver. It remains unclear whether he couldn't accept the terms of Xin's offer or whether, as Chan contends, Xin later told him to hold off, neglecting to help him obtain a Canadian visa. In any case, the standoff continued. For the next six days, Wang waited for the green light to rejoin the national team, but no one called. He would have to take his future into his own hands.

The Chinese national team hadn't yet arrived at the Oakland Arena for their shootaround when the silver Mercedes rolled into the parking lot at 10:20 A.M. A Chinese reporter, however, was waiting for Wang. On the drive up, Da Zhi had called his friend Su Qun at the *Titan Sports Weekly* in Beijing to inform him about the plan, and Su had dispatched the young sportswriter, Yang Yi, to meet him there. "This may be my last chance," Wang told Yang, pulling his duffel bag out of the car. "Now my only option is to come here and tell them I am ready and available for the game. I have always said I am willing to work for the country; now it depends on the decision of the CBA."

Wang waited for the team on the stadium steps, pulling the sleeves of his Windbreaker over his hands and covering his face. Perhaps the weary soldier was simply fending off the cool morning breeze, but he also seemed to be bracing himself for the looming encounter with his former teammates and with national-team leader Kuang Lubin, the very man he had snubbed just a month before in Los Angeles.

By the time the Chinese team bus pulled up outside the stadium twenty minutes later, Wang had already disappeared inside. The Chinese coaches, alerted to Wang's arrival, had called a special team meeting that morning to advise players how to behave when the defiant star showed up at the shootaround. "We [the team leaders] will deal with him," head coach Wang Fei had told them. "But none of you should talk to him freely. Be careful about what you say to him." Yao Ming glanced around anxiously as he walked into the vast empty arena. Later that evening, the number one draft pick would make his American debut in that very stadium against a team of NBA stars. But at that moment, he was simply looking for his former rival, the one player whose fate, now as ever, was inextricably linked with his own.

All summer long, Wang's rebellion had hung like a cloud over Yao. After the draft, which the soldier had almost derailed, Yao continued to hound friends and journalists for updates, showing an intense interest in resolving the crisis. It wasn't simply his desire to play alongside Wang in the World Championships, creating an inside-outside tandem that would improve China's chances. Wang's continuing defiance had also brought the negotiations over Yao's own future to a virtual standstill. By late August, nearly every NBA draft pick—including Jay Williams, the number two selection, against whom Yao would play that evening—had already signed contracts with their teams. But Yao was still stuck in limbo. The rivalry between China's twin towers seemed to boil down to a bleak equation: If Wang's case was not resolved, Yao might not be allowed to go to the NBA.

Yao didn't see any sign of Wang as he walked through the arena to the locker room. But as he changed into his practice clothes, a hand touched him on the shoulder.

"How are you doing, number one draft pick?" Wang said.

The two big men smiled and shook hands. There was no time—or permission—to talk. The players had to report immediately to the court, and Wang had to steel himself for his meeting with Kuang Lubin.

The practice had already started by the time Wang shuffled out to the court. Kuang led him over to a pair of seats in the stands, and the two old acquaintances—they had been coach and pupil at Bayi more than eight years before—started talking in low voices. Kuang upbraided Wang for going into hiding, leaving him stranded in a hotel room for seven days without having the decency to give him a proper response. Wang apologized. He had gotten scared, he said, but now he wanted to make things right. Wang pointed down at his duffel bag. "I've brought my shoes and socks," he said. "Just give me a jersey and I can play."

It wouldn't be that simple. Kuang advised Wang to return to Beijing first to sign a pledge to play in the Asian Games; only then could he rejoin the team. Wang reiterated his position that the Asian Games would interfere with the NBA season, something he was not willing to do for the third season in a row. "He seemed contrite," Kuang said later. "But he kept wanting to add conditions. That's not right. He can't negotiate the conditions."

After fifteen minutes, Kuang abruptly ended the conversation. "I have to report this to Beijing," he said. "I'll let you know the response as soon as possible." For the remainder of the practice, the two men sat on opposite ends of the floor, watching in silence as the team ran through its drills.

When the practice ended, some veteran players came over to say hello to Wang. The big Mongolian center, Mengke Bateer—who had made his own moderately successful debut with the Denver Nuggets the previous season—gave him a big bear hug. Another old teammate playfully squeezed Wang's biceps, joking about how buff he had become during his California summer. Yao came over, too, and Wang teased him about the red woven bracelet around his left wrist. "So who gave it to you?" he asked. It wasn't long, however, before the head coach, Wang Fei, broke up the reunion. "Let's go," he said, and all of the players filed obediently into the locker room—except for Wang.

Alone on the court, Wang picked up a basketball and began tossing up desultory three-pointers. At another time, he might have considered this a moment of pure delight: shooting baskets on a perfect parquet floor in an empty NBA arena, nothing but the sound of a basketball to concentrate his mind. But Wang had driven through the night to be reunited with his old teammates, and now he was lost again, shooting only because he didn't know what else to do. When the players emerged from the locker room a few minutes later, they walked straight to the team bus. None of them came over to say good-bye. At the door, Yao turned around for one last glimpse of his old rival. The 7'1" soldier, for so long celebrated as the best player in China, looked strangely diminished in the cavernous arena, launching his lonely, meaningless threes.

Seven hours later, the atmosphere in the Oakland Arena crackled with electricity as a rollicking crowd of 19,783 anticipated Yao's debut against the stars of Team USA. Nearly two-thirds of the crowd was Chinese or Chinese-American—all of Chinatown seemed to have emptied out for the occasion—and they flew banners everywhere welcoming their native son. A large contingent of NBA agents and coaches was on hand, including Bill Duffy and Rockets skipper Rudy Tomjanovich, and they would be watching Yao closely. So, too, would the American players, who seemed eager to give the number one draft pick a proper introduction to NBA-style basketball. "We're going to beat him up pretty bad," promised Detroit's muscle-bound center Ben Wallace. The trash-talking American players even put together a betting pool—$400 a player—for the first person to throw down a slam dunk on the Chinese giant.

Sitting in the locker room before the game, Yao tried to focus on the challenge ahead. But his concentration wavered when somebody informed him that Wang's attempt to rejoin the team had failed. Yao bowed his head and stared at the floor for a full minute. "Well, if they're not going to let him play," he said finally, "then there's nothing we can do."

Minutes later, steeled for battle, he strode through the tunnel into a swirl of noise and light. Yao proved his mettle that night with a solid game, racking up thirteen points, eleven rebounds, and six blocks against a swarming defense. He even prevented anyone from dunking on him until he let number two draft pick Jay Williams blow by him in the closing seconds of the Americans' 84–64 victory.

Even before the first half ended, however, Wang Zhizhi was already more than a hundred miles away, racing back to Los Angeles. The only bright lights for Da Zhi that night would come from the high beams of the northbound traffic, the only roar from the straining engines of the eighteen-wheelers hauling their cargo. Wang had called Kuang Lubin one last time two hours before the game. The team leader said he still hadn't gotten through to Beijing; it wasn't clear if he had even tried. Wang asked if he could accompany the team back to Denver, where it would complete its training for the World Championships. The answer was no.

Not long after hanging up, Wang tossed his duffel bag into the backseat of the Mercedes and, with Chan by his side, started heading south. There was no reason to drive fast now, but for a man who had run out of options, there was no reason not to, either.

When the Chinese national team rolled into Indianapolis for the World Championships a week later, few outsiders noticed that Wang Zhizhi was missing. Yao Ming had arrived, and that was all that mattered.

The American media swarmed around the number one draft pick, hungry for a glimpse of the Chinese big man. Erik Zhang, the family friend now in charge of Team Yao, ushered his client into press conferences, print and television interviews, promos for ESPN, even a cover shoot for *Sports Illustrated*. As Yao's teammates rested between games, the Chinese star posed patiently for the photographer with both arms outstretched, palming a basketball in each hand. The "cross" position was a form of punishment in the Chinese sports schools, but now it was merely a sign of faith that Yao would soon be arriving in the NBA—and that he would become, as the magazine cover promised, "The Next Big Thing."

The arrival of Yao Ming, NBA phenomenon, seemed perfectly on track. But behind the scenes, a fierce battle still raged over Wang, and Yao's future was directly in the line of fire. On August 26, four days after Wang's failed attempt to rejoin the team in Oakland, the Chinese government lashed out publicly against him in an official statement: "How could we imagine that someone fully absorbed by his own wills and preferences, ignorant of the requirements of the nation that brought him up, someone who regards his personal interest as higher than anything, could fight devotedly for the honor of the nation?"

After two months of silence, in which they threatened to shut down at least one newspaper that dared to publish sympathetic reports about Wang, the nation's sports leaders were now determined to publicize their version of events. China's state-run press launched a vitriolic campaign against "the ungrateful traitor," turning a private dispute into a public test of wills. To set the foreign media straight, the CBA even translated its blistering August 26 communiqué—"A Fact on Wang Zhizhi's Failure to Return"—and stacked copies in the press center in Indianapolis.

The CBA's anger only seemed to grow as the Chinese team, without Wang, floundered at the World Championships. Yao couldn't win games single-handedly, and the team, which had arrived hoping to make the top six, finished a dismal twelfth. After an early victory against lowly Algeria, the Chinese team suffered six consecutive defeats, including a devastating collapse against New Zealand in which it squandered a twenty-four-point first-half lead. Yao's stat line for that game was unblemished: He went 8-for-8 from the field and 11-for-11 from the line for twenty-seven points in just twenty-six minutes. But when the final buzzer sounded, he stomped off the court without shaking the victors' hands, kicking tables in the locker room in fury and frustration. "Why spend six months training six hours a day?" he asked. "We worked so hard all year and won only one game!" Dispensing with his usual charity, he laced into his teammates for failing to get him the ball. "How can a gun show off its firepower without bullets?" he asked.

Few people in Indianapolis, though, had run out of ammunition more than the Americans who had come to negotiate Yao's future. Rather than hammer out the final deals, the different parties—Zhang and John Huizinga for Team Yao, Michael Goldberg for the Houston Rockets—spent most of the ten-day tournament getting stonewalled by CBA director Xin Lancheng. Fewer than three weeks remained before the start of the Rockets' training camp on October 1, and the Americans became increasingly alarmed at the lack of progress. At one point in Indianapolis, Huizinga pushed Xin to resolve the issue of Yao's release—to live up to the agreements they had made before the draft—and the Chinese bureaucrat responded imperiously.

"Yao Ming will go to the NBA exactly when and how I say he can go," Xin said, "or else he will not go at all."

Huizinga could barely contain his exasperation. After the meeting, the blunt-spoken professor sought out the reporter Yang Yi, who, despite his relative youth, understood the convoluted psychology of the Chinese bureaucracy. "What would happen," Huizinga asked Yang, "if we just asked Yao Ming to stay in the United States when the tournament is over?"

The question shocked the young reporter. It wasn't clear if Huizinga was raising this as a real option or simply as a theoretical exercise, like an economics professor exploring another angle of a knotty equation. But the consequences of keeping Yao behind were incalculable. Yao would not only become a political pariah, but all of the commercial possibilities Team Yao had been dreaming about would be worth nothing because Yao's relationship with Beijing would be ruined.

"You absolutely cannot do that," Yang warned. "If you do, Yao would become a second Wang Zhizhi—and that would be a disaster for everybody."

Nobody connected to Chinese basketball left Indianapolis satisfied. Zhang and Huizinga had watched over the birth of a new NBA sensation, but they were no closer to getting Yao released than before. Goldberg returned to Houston, having to face fans, reporters, and bosses who were wondering whether the team had wasted its precious number one pick. Yao had been named to the all-tournament first team, but that was hardly consolation for the dreadful results and the continuing impasse over his future. As the Chinese delegation slunk back to Beijing, Kuang Lubin stayed behind to try one last time to bring Wang home. A week later, in mid-September, he, too, came home empty-handed.

Now, after two months of trying to lure Wang back, the exasperated Chinese authorities decided to make the soldier pay for his defiance. It wasn't enough to see the former hero's name smeared in the nation's newspapers; they wanted to make sure his little rebellion didn't succeed, so they appealed to the NBA to prevent Wang from signing a contract with any NBA team. Even if Chinese officials understood that their appeal had no legal or political authority, perhaps they hoped that it would have a psychological impact. After all, any team that considered signing Wang would have to realize that it would be iced out of the massive China market now and forever. Whether intimidated by that prospect or not, several NBA teams that had expressed an interest in the restricted agent earlier that summer quietly withdrew.

But on October 1, just as every NBA player around the league (except Wang and Yao) gathered for the first day of preseason training, something remarkable happened. The Los Angeles Clippers stepped forward and offered Wang a three-year, $6 million deal—far more than the $740,000 he had earned over the previous two years in Dallas. The timing of the offer may have been pure coincidence: October 1, after all, marks China's National Day, the holiday that commemorates the birth of the People's Republic in 1949, when Mao's troops "liberated" the country from the Nationalists after a brutal civil war. But Chinese officials couldn't help but see the link as an extra slap in the face. Wang, however, was just happy to have landed a contract. He might not have won his battle with the establishment—his name had been sullied and his commercial appeal all but destroyed—but he had earned the right, at least for a while, to continue playing in the NBA. And, unlike Yao, he wouldn't have to pay a penny to the Chinese government.

In an unexpected twist, the Clippers' contract seemed to offer an escape—liberation, as it were—to *all* parties embroiled in the "Wang Zhizhi Affair." The Dallas Mavericks had the right to match the Clippers' offer on the restricted free agent, but they seemed almost grateful to wash their hands of Wang. Mavs owner Mark Cuban, who had once praised the soldier's potential, sniped: "We're not going to miss him. We'll find the two or three points from someone else." (Wang, to be fair, averaged 5.6 points a game for the Mavericks.)

Beijing, for its part, used the Clippers' offer as added justification for kicking Wang off the national team. On October 9, the CBA formally dismissed him for showing an "absence of professional standards, indiscipline, and indifference to the interests of the nation." While Yao and the rest of the national team were in South Korea playing for the five-star flag, Wang was in America negotiating a seven-figure deal. "Participating in international competitions—winning glory for the country—is every athlete's honor and obligation," the CBA statement said. "But when the motherland needed him, he did not care about what was good for the country and was unwilling to serve."

It was the first time a Chinese player had been booted off the team so unceremoniously. Even the original rebel, Ma Jian, had been quietly left off the team list without any public fuss. Bayi leaders who learned of the dismissal after the fact were upset by the very public—and virtually irreversible—decision involving their soldier. But Chinese fans, influenced by the patriotic state-run media, applauded the move. In a poll on Sina.com that canvassed more than two hundred thousand Internet voters, nearly 48 percent felt that Wang deserved the punishment; only 22 percent felt that Wang had been dealt with too harshly.

When the Clippers presented their newly signed Chinese center to the media a few days later, Wang tried to justify his actions. "My decision [to stay in America] hasn't satisfied everybody," he said. "But I know that I am doing what is good for both China and the national team." His differences with Beijing, he said, were like a family quarrel. "Sometimes a mother and a son might have disagreements, but that doesn't mean the son doesn't love the mother," he said. "I really love my country." The feeling, however, was no longer mutual.

The news of Wang's dismissal shocked and saddened Yao Ming, even if he knew that it ultimately broke the logjam in his own struggle to get to the NBA. Yao and Wang might have been rivals since childhood, but they had always shared the same dream—and, it had once seemed, the same destiny. Now everything had changed. Wang, the soldier from tradition-bound Beijing, was now cast irrevocably in the role of the rebel, while Yao, the civilian boy from the modern, commercial capital of Shanghai, was the loyal, obedient son. Wang's sacking wouldn't change the situation in South Korea, where Yao and the national team were competing in the Asian Games, but the finality of the decision made Yao seem even more alone at the top, the only player with the talent to carry China into the highest ranks of international competition.

Even at the Asian Games, where Yao and his teammates rolled over such bantam-weight opponents as Hong Kong and Malaysia, Wang would be sorely missed. The Chinese men's basketball team had won five straight Asian Games gold medals, and this time, in the finals against host South Korea, the squad once again seemed to be cruising toward victory, enjoying a seven-point cushion with barely a minute to play. But a series of egregious ballhandling errors by China and a flurry of Korean three-pointers pushed the game into overtime. Somehow, despite Yao's twenty-three points and twenty-two rebounds, the Chinese managed to lose, 102–100. It was another stunning collapse, even more humiliating to Chinese leaders than the World Championships, for this came in China's backyard where the team was supposed to dominate. Head coach Wang Fei would be sacked after the defeat, but many Chinese fans pinned the blame on Wang Zhizhi, whose presence would have surely changed the outcome.

Yao, too, was crushed, but his disappointment was eased by the fact that the various parties involved in his case—the Rockets, Team Yao, the CBA, the Shanghai Sharks—were now negotiating madly to hasten his departure to the NBA. The simplest deal, because it required no government stamp, was the four-year, $18.03 million contract Yao signed with the Houston Rockets. The number fell within the predicted range of the NBA's collective-bargaining agreement, but to a family that had pulled in less than $4,000 a year just a few years before, it must have seemed like fantasy money.

The sum that Yao agreed to pay the Shanghai Sharks to buy out his contract was without precedent in basketball history—between $8 million and $15 million over the course of his career. Nevertheless, it was still less than half of what the Sharks had originally demanded, and Zhang says he and Huizinga structured the deal to minimize the pain. Under the agreement, Zhang says, Yao would immediately start paying a minimum of $500,000 a year into a trust fund. If he played less than three years in the NBA, he would keep the kitty. But if he kept playing beyond the third year, his contributions would increase—and the Sharks would receive a growing percentage of his earnings up to a maximum total of around $15 million. The Rockets, by contrast, agreed to pay the Sharks a mere $350,000—the maximum allowed by the NBA—along with nonbinding promises to help out with clinics, coaching, and the search for foreign players.

In Beijing, the sports authorities backed off from their earlier threats to siphon off 50 percent of Yao's earnings. CBA chief Xin Lancheng realized, perhaps, that there would be no way to hold onto Yao—or gouge him for half his earnings—without suffering a media backlash around the world for treating the athlete as a slave of the state. In the wake of the Wang fiasco, moreover, the CBA leader also seemed reluctant to give Yao any more reasons to follow the rebellious path of his old army rival. By the time Zhang and Huizinga sat down with Xin to haggle over the final details, the CBA had lowered its demands significantly—to between 5 and 8 percent of Yao's after-tax income. Yao would still emerge with more financial and political obligations to his homeland than any other NBA player in history. But after the threats and frustrations earlier in the year, he had come out far better than expected.

Yao's political obligations would be even heavier. If Chinese basketball's summer of discontent had revealed anything, after all, it was that the nation's leaders valued loyalty more highly than money—and, some would say, more highly than victory. Before Yao could retrieve his passport and stand in line for his U.S. visa, the giant felt compelled, once again, to offer CBA chief Xin his pledge of devotion to the national team—and his assurance that he wouldn't follow the errant ways of Wang Zhizhi. "Every step I made, the pressure was bigger," Yao would recall later. "The pressure from the U.S. was in front of me. The pressure from China was behind me. I was squeezed between them."

On October 19, the day before his departure to the United States, Yao took a morning flight from Beijing to Shanghai, wedged uncomplainingly into a middle seat in cattle class until a woman mercifully offered him her aisle seat. The moment Yao landed, his bosses at Shanghai Television whisked him away on an obligatory tour through his own childhood. Dressed in a pair of dark corduroys, a brown sports shirt, and a tan tweed jacket—an outfit he would wear for the next fifty-four hours straight—Yao spent the day dutifully paying homage to nearly everyone who had shaped his life, from his first coach, the gruff Li Zhangming, and the staff at the Shanghai Sports Technology Institute, including researcher Wei Guoping, to his longtime Shanghai coach Li Qiuping, and the man who had tried to sell him off more than three years earlier, Sharks deputy general manager Li Yaomin. The forced march through his own history served as a reminder of the strange and tortuous path Yao had taken, often against his will, to get to the NBA. Few people familiar with China could doubt that it was also meant to reinforce just how much he owed the system that created him.

By Yao's side that day was his best friend, Liu Wei, the fresh-faced 6'4" point guard on the Shanghai team. For the past eight years, ever since they joined the Shanghai junior team together, the two players had been virtually inseparable. As kids, they had washed their uniforms together and pooled their tiny allowances to play video games. They had goofed off together on Nike-sponsored trips abroad. The outgoing Liu Wei had even composed love letters that the shy center sent to woo his girlfriend on the women's team. But now Yao was heading off alone, leaving his buddy behind. For all his dreams of playing in the NBA, he seemed to be half-wishing it were the other way around.

That afternoon, then Shanghai mayor Chen Liangyu reminded Yao once again of his obligations at a banquet in his honor. Smiling beneficently as he stood before the city's assembled political hierarchy, Chen told Yao that, as a product of the Chinese system, he had a duty to bring honor to the city and to the nation. Then, making sure Yao's glass was overflowing with Chinese liquor, the mayor made a final toast. His words sounded less like a wish than a warning.

"May you keep the homeland in your heart," he told Yao, "and never disappoint the good wishes of the Chinese people and the Communist Party."

Yao, his face flushed red, downed his glass in a single gulp.

17

In Da Club

"Yo, Yao, when ya gonna get yo' whip?"

Steve Francis, the Houston Rockets' effervescent point guard, peeled off his drenched practice jersey and smiled across the locker room at Yao Ming. The Chinese rookie was sprawled across three chairs in front of his locker, looking utterly exhausted after one of his first preseason practices in the NBA. Yao wore nothing but a pair of shorts, a red cloth bracelet on his left wrist, and—after hearing Francis's question—a furrow across his massive brow. He had no idea what Francis was talking about.

Yao had arrived in the United States just five days earlier, and he'd already picked up more street slang than he'd learned from the English-language book he'd studied for years back in China. He liked how Francis, the Rockets' twenty-five-year-old Pied Piper, sometimes called him "homes"—as if a straitlaced Chinese kid could be considered one of the boys from the 'hood. Every day with the Rockets, Yao's teammates generously expanded his vocabulary with new words like "gangsta," "holla," and "wassup." The last one especially tickled him—it sounded vaguely like a vulgarity in the Shanghainese dialect—and he used it every time he greeted his new teammates.

But he'd never heard of "whip."

"You know, man, your wheels!" Francis said, whipping his hands back and forth on an imaginary steering wheel as if he were darting through traffic at one hundred miles per hour.

Yao laughed, absorbing the new word. Over the course of his rookie season, he would learn what it meant to live large in the NBA, from the "cribs" (houses) to the "ice" (jewelry) to the "hos" (women). But he already knew that for any NBA player, the wheels came first; they were

262

the most visible symbols of wealth and freedom. From the day he arrived in Houston, Yao had been dazzled by the parade of luxury cars. Whisked away from the airport in a white ultra-stretch Navigator limo, he arrived at the Compaq Center just as Francis pulled his convertible Mercedes into the garage next to the other players' Bentleys, BMWs, and SUVs. The 6'3" point guard jumped out to greet Yao with a bear hug—the beginning of the NBA's embrace of the Chinese giant—and promised to take him for a ride in his biggest vehicle, a forest-green Hummer H2.

Back in Shanghai, Yao had only ridden buses, taxis, or bicycles, but now he, too, longed for a car that would turn people's heads, or as his teammates would put it, "break hella necks." A month earlier, during the World Championships in Indianapolis, Yao had put down a deposit on a custom-made Mercedes S430 sedan whose $80,000 sticker price was more than his yearly salary for the Shanghai Sharks. But there was no sign of the car yet, and in his first months in Houston, Yao rode to practice folded up like an accordion in the passenger seat of the boxy Chrysler rental car driven by his translator, a clean-cut former State Department employee named Colin Pine.

"So when ya gonna stop playin' Miss Daisy and get a whip of your own?" Francis teased.

"Don't know," Yao said, "maybe two, three months."

"Man, you gotta ride around with your chauffeur 'til then? Dat's wack."

Yao shrugged his shoulders. Pine was nowhere to be found, and he didn't want to ask Francis for further explanation. Or maybe he was simply reluctant to admit to his supremely cool new teammate that he didn't have a driver's license—indeed, that he didn't really know how to drive.

Three months later, when Yao finally got his whip—he ended up buying a silver Toyota Sequoia sport-utility vehicle instead of the Mercedes—he was ready to roll, and his teammates worried that he would literally "break hella necks." Yao still didn't have a license to drive, and while he had taken several gentle spins around his subdivision, with Pine serving as his driving instructor, he was still the ultimate novice. After a Rockets practice at the Westside Tennis Club one day, Yao slowly wheeled the SUV around the parking lot, clowning for the crowd of onlookers by lifting both hands off the steering wheel. He pulled in for a perfect stop, but then, responding to a Chinese reporter who chastised him for driving only in circles, Yao made a rookie mistake: He backed the Sequoia right into a parked car, crumpling his left rear bumper and denting the fender of the other vehicle.

Red-faced at the blunder, Yao went back inside to apologize to the owner of the car and engage in the American ritual of exchanging insurance information. When he reemerged, Pine took the wheel, and Yao—chastened and embarrassed—climbed back into the passenger seat.

The education of Yao Ming would come in many forms, and it would always seem like a crash course culminating in an excruciatingly public exam. No NBA rookie had ever had to adapt to such a vastly different culture with so much pressure to succeed—and so little time to prepare. For all the formidable skills Yao had developed, he would struggle to adjust to a brutal NBA game whose speed and physicality made hoops in China seem like a polite suburban league down at the YMCA. Yao's learning curve would perhaps be even steeper off the court, where the sheltered product of the Chinese sports factories suddenly encountered the disorienting reality of fame, fortune, and the NBA way of life.

Yao's first lessons began soon after his arrival in Houston. The jet-lagged giant didn't play in the exhibition game that evening, but even sitting on the bench in his street clothes, he was the center of attention. The massive screens on the Compaq Center's scoreboard displayed live-camera shots of Yao cheering for his new teammates. During one time-out, as Yao hovered above the team huddle straining to understand raspy-voiced coach Rudy Tomjanovich, the Rockets' mascot walked out on stilts wearing a black-and-white panda outfit with the words "Yao Bear" stitched onto the back. The loudspeakers blared a new theme song called "It's a Ming Thing." (The lyrics simply repeated Yao's name over and over to the tune of the popular soccer chant, "Olé, olé, olé, olé!") Later, the mascot pulled fans out of the crowd to stand next to the "Yao Ming Growth Chart," a life-size cardboard cutout of Yao that the Rockets had been trotting out for weeks as they waited for the real thing. The crowd laughed hardest when "Yao Bear" brought out a woman whose head didn't reach far above the waistband on cardboard Yao's massive "shorts." The real Yao gamely pretended not to notice.

But, of course, he noticed. The desire for fame had tugged at Yao since he was a child. He remembers how miffed—and thrilled—he was when, at age fifteen, a Chinese fan asked him to sign his first autograph. Yao, then in his first year with the national junior team, carefully wrote out his name in block characters. Four years later, after he'd been selected for the national senior team, Yao typed his name into an Internet search engine and felt a rush of pride looking at the two hundred hits. He then "Googled" his teammates and found that Wang Zhizhi had thousands more. Three years later, Wang's fame soured into infamy—and Yao's hit count soared into the hundreds of thousands.

Even so, by the time Yao left for America, he was still not universally recognized in China. He had never made the media's annual top-ten list for the country's most popular athletes. (Wang had climbed onto the list briefly after his NBA debut in 2001.) The Chinese media tended to focus their hero-making machine almost exclusively on world champions and Olympic gold medalists. Until Yao proved himself on the international stage, he would continue to be overshadowed, in the Chinese public's eyes, by the nation's diminutive divers and Ping-Pong players.

Remarkably, Yao was more famous in America than in China even before he played his first minute in an NBA game. His likeness had never appeared in any advertisements on Chinese television or along the teeming commercial boulevards of his native Shanghai. But in Houston, the Rockets' "Be Part of Something Big" billboards all over town only had to show the square top of Yao's head and everybody knew exactly who it was. In China, Yao never had a song, a mascot, a fan club, an exclusive Web site, or a special section in the local newspaper. Few NBA players had those things in America, but Yao had all of them even before he arrived in Houston. And thanks to the knot of reporters that surrounded him after every practice, his fame soon extended far beyond the Texas plains—indeed, far beyond the realm of sports. Besides the *Sports Illustrated* cover, Yao soon appeared in feature stories in the nation's biggest publications, from *People* to *USA Today* to the *Wall Street Journal*. In those early days, Houston Rockets owner Les Alexander couldn't resist becoming the hypemaster-in-chief. "This is the biggest individual sports story of all time," he said. "Mark my words: In two or three years, he'll be bigger than Tiger Woods or Michael Jordan."

In the Rockets' locker room, though, Francis and friends treated Yao as just one of the guys, giving the big man the kind of refuge he needed from the madness outside. NBA locker rooms are notorious for being highly charged racial environments, where the black majority often doesn't mingle with the white minority, and the arrival of a much-heralded Chinese rookie who was neither black nor white could have caused friction on all sides. Francis, in particular, could've resented getting nudged out of the limelight. Up until then, he was "the man" in Houston, the star whose lightning-fast first step and acrobatic dunks had inspired fans to dub him "Stevie Franchise." But the Rockets' team leader quickly became one of Yao's best friends and biggest fans. "Franchise" even christened the newcomer with a nickname of his own: "Dynasty."

During stretching exercises at their first practice together, Francis sprawled out on the hardwood floor next to Yao, keeping up a banter that the Chinese center, for all his nods and smiles, only partially understood. At one point during that first practice, Yao spun into the lane, barreling through two players before gently laying the ball off the glass with his left hand.

"Yo, Steve, that's gangsta!" yelled Moochie Norris, a wisecracking backup point guard with a monster Afro. "Yao Ming is MVP!"

Francis looked up, licked his pencil-thin mustache, and smiled. "Homes, I'm stayin' outta there!" he said.

After practice that day, Francis and Yao got dressed in the locker room together before taking the promised spin in the Hummer—the point guard looking like a rapper in his cool shades, purple Minnesota Vikings jersey, and heavy metal necklace; the Chinese import towering over him in the same tan shirt and wrinkled brown, chem-student corduroys he'd been wearing for the previous four days straight. Never before, perhaps, have two teammates struck a more startling contrast, yet Francis gushed about Yao as if he were a long-lost twin separated at birth. "He is just like me," he said, "only 7'6" and Chinese!"

It was in the locker room where Yao's new hoop brothers gave him the lowdown on life in the NBA. Some of the talk touched on basketball, but it often revolved around the "bling-bling" life of cribs, threads, and women. Music often blared from the boom box, and it wasn't the saccharine melodies of the boy-band Westlife—one of Yao's favorites—but the hard-edged rap anthems of Tupac, Jay-Z, and 50 Cent. During the most rapturous moments that season, Rockets players would dance around the locker room rapping along with 50's "In Da Club"—"my flow, my show brought me the dough"—as Yao looked on in bemused contentment.

The Chinese big man might not have known any of the lyrics, but the Rockets veterans made him feel "in da club." They taught Yao how and when to "dapp" (the standard ghetto handshake of bumping fists), gave him plenty of "kwan" (respect and acclaim, the American inner-city version of face), and joked that the straitlaced Chinese giant could have his pick of the female groupies who clustered outside the locker room in every city. (Just one woman, in fact, would hit on Yao the entire season, and she only wanted to convert him to Christianity.) With Francis egging him on, Yao showed his own goofy sense of humor, whether it was with his jeans tucked into unlaced Timberland boots, mimicking one of coach Rudy T's half-time rants, dressing up like a gangsta, or putting Moochie's shoes on the basketball rim where the vertically challenged point guard couldn't reach them.

In those early days, Yao's teammates even tried to get him to join them on their nocturnal excursions to the "gentlemen's establishments" that made Houston's strip malls live up to their name. ("Wine, Women, and Thong" was a local favorite.) On Yao's first road trip with the team to nearby San Antonio, the Rockets' stylish shooting guard Cuttino Mobley invited him out to a local strip club. Yao looked confused, but when Mobley turned to Pine for help, the translator shook his head.

"Don't go shakin' your head!" Mobley said. "You gotta translate everything! That's your job, right?"

One of Pine's many jobs, in fact, was to steer the big man away from trouble. Erik Zhang, after all, had chosen Pine from a pool of three hundred applicants not simply for his linguistic ability and his enthusiasm for basketball. Zhang liked the fact that the bespectacled twenty-eight-year-old came across as earnest, responsible, and studious—more homebody than homeboy, much like Yao himself. Pine had spent the previous two years sequestered in a basement cubicle at the government-run Voice of America translating Chinese texts, and the 5'9" Baltimore native often seemed more shell-shocked by the NBA media circus than Yao himself.

Pine's anxiety came, in part, from his awareness of how much was riding on Yao's every word and action—a lesson that was reinforced just four days into the job, when he and Yao raced in a limo through the rain to meet with Chinese president Jiang Zemin in College Station, Texas. This was Jiang's last official visit to the United States as head of state, and one would be forgiven for thinking he had timed it to coincide with the Chinese rookie's debut.

When Yao strode into the auditorium minutes before Jiang, the collective gasp that shot through the crowd of American CEOs and politicians quickly transformed into a joyous ovation. Later, when Jiang finished making his speech, the Chinese president searched for Yao in the audience and, somehow failing to see him through his bug-eyed glasses, asked him to stand up. When Yao rose to his feet, Jiang reeled backward. "Wah, you're so tall!" he exclaimed, with all the amazement of the gawking crowds on the street. "I'm only 5'8"!" For years, Jiang had been seeking his place in history by force-feeding the nation his ponderous theory of the "Three Represents." But here, rising above him, was somebody who, in the truest sense of the word, "represents."

For all the efforts to make Yao part of the team, China's national treasure would never be quite like Francis and the others, and it wasn't just that meeting China's paramount leader was a normal part of his itinerary. Yao had grown up in a system that put collective values first, and even in his early days in the NBA, he made it clear that one of his top priorities was to bring honor—or, rather, not to bring dishonor—to the Chinese nation. That alone would have been enough to rule out any carousing at Texas's finest strip clubs. But Yao's reluctance to join his teammates on their escapades also reflected his allegiance to the two most influential women in his life—his girlfriend and his mother.

While other players hit the bars and clubs, Yao spent hours at home surfing the Internet, playing video games, and calling his "bona fide" in Beijing: the lissome twenty-one-year-old forward on the women's national team, Ye Li. The couple had begun dating in late 2000, but for a long time, Yao kept the details of their relationship a secret from the media and from his parents—even hushing a friend who mentioned Ye Li's name in front of his father. Once word got out about the courtship of the 7'5" center and the 6'3" forward in 2002, the Chinese media couldn't resist dreaming about the potential implications for the next generation of Chinese basketball players.

Leaving Ye Li behind was a difficult adjustment for Yao. When he arrived in Houston, one of the first things he did was place her framed photograph—a glamour shot in soft focus—on his bedside table and another on his cell phone screensaver. As a reminder of their mutual commitment, Yao wore on his left wrist a red macramé bracelet Ye Li had given him, identical to the one she wore on her right wrist. The bracelet aroused curiosity on the team, especially because Yao fiddled with it obsessively on court. One day at practice, Francis finally asked about the piece of cloth, and Yao, after explaining its significance, teased the guard: "You could wear them, too, but I think maybe you need ten!"

In the locker room that day, as Yao stretched out over three chairs, the Rockets' beefy backup center Kelvin Cato sauntered out of the showers and asked Yao about the house he had bought in a gated community west of Houston.

"So when are you gonna invite us all out to your crib?" Cato asked.

"Sometime," Yao said, vaguely. "No furniture yet."

"But that's the best time to throw a party," Cato said. "You can trash the place and nobody will care!"

Yao didn't respond. He wouldn't be having a party at his house anytime soon, and the reason was more than slightly embarrassing: His mother wouldn't allow it.

Mothers occupy a special niche in the macho world of the NBA. For all the players' bluster about their exploits with women, NBA players find little shame in heaping praise on their mothers, especially because so many were raised by admirably strong single women struggling to survive in the American inner city. But until Yao arrived in the NBA, there were very few, if any, players who actually lived with their mothers—and seemed to obey their every command.

Yao's mother, Fang Fengdi, decided to accompany her son "to help ease everybody's mind," as her confidant Zhang put it. The government officials who granted her a leave of absence (and, eventually, early retirement) from her work unit seemed relieved to know that a strict disciplinarian and loyal Communist Party member would be watching over their national treasure. With Da Fang supervising the situation, the officials believed, there would be less chance for Yao to be swayed by the corrosive Western individualism they blamed for Wang's defiance. (Yao's father, still employed at the Shanghai port, would join the family for part of the season before being allowed to retire.) The arrangement would strike many Chinese and Chinese-Americans as an endearing affirmation of Asian values. But to many other American sports fans, it would seem more confusing than Confucian: How could they begin to understand a 7'5", 296-pound mama's boy?

The arrangement, in truth, was also unusual for Yao. He had not lived with his parents in more than eight years. The family of three had forged a powerful bond when he was young, but ever since Yao left home at age thirteen to begin training full-time, he returned to the family apartment only one day a week, mostly to eat and sleep. Once he began playing for the national junior team two years later, he spent more than half of every year living in Beijing and rarely saw his parents. "It was like 'The mountain is high and the emperor is far away,'" Yao recalled, quoting a famous Chinese proverb. "My parents had no control over me. I got used to it."

Now, at age twenty-two, he was moving back in with his parents, and the reunion—for all the comfort it might provide—would create new challenges for all of them.

If Yao was traveling a long distance to play in the NBA, it couldn't compare to the staggering leap that his fifty-two-year-old mother was making—from Team Mao to Team Yao. The former Red Guard, who had once attacked leaders for displaying even the slightest glimmer of capitalist thinking, was now, in effect, the chief executive officer of a capitalist corporation, guiding every decision that would affect her son's multimillion-dollar career. With little formal education beyond the maxims of Mao's *Little Red Book,* Da Fang didn't pretend to understand the minutiae of endorsement contracts, the NBA's collective-bargaining agreement, or the Houston property market. But she was a practical woman, and the experience of being misled and manipulated back in China had only deepened her desire to protect her only son.

Da Fang had landed in Houston more than a week before her son to clear the way for his arrival. Joined by Zhang on this, her first trip to America, she toured the Rockets' practice facility, met with team executives and players, and—most urgently—searched for a new family home. The Realtor eventually led Da Fang to Windsor Park Lakes, a gated community carved out of old cattle pastures some twenty miles west of Houston. The pristine neighborhood of faux-Mediterranean mansions exudes a sense of self-satisfied peace and theme-park perfection that could have been lifted straight out of *The Truman Show*. Inside the development's front gate, past the uniformed guards with their uniform smiles, stands an artificial lake with a bubbling fountain, a pair of sculpted bronze egrets rising from the shallows, and a decorative yellow gazebo perched on a tiny, man-made island.

Da Fang settled on a $500,000, four-bedroom home that seemed perfect for a family of giants. With so little time to spare before her son's arrival, she asked the Realtor to help furnish the cavernous, 4,000-square-foot home. Perhaps understandably, given the Realtor's usual clientele of professional athletes, she filled the place with a profusion of black leather couches, glass bookshelves, and black patterned bedcovers—making it seem more befitting the lair of a rap impresario than the home of a modest Shanghainese family that had lived until recently in a spartan two-room apartment or, in Yao's case, a simple dorm room. On the eve of Yao's arrival, Da Fang stayed up until well past midnight frantically cleaning the house, stopping only occasionally to ease the chronic pain in her back.

Worrying about her son was Da Fang's full-time job now, and she did it with the same combination of prodding and pampering that the sports system had shown throughout Yao's life. She cleaned his room, did his laundry, gave pep talks, offered basketball advice, and prepared his favorite meals. Yao's father, who did a lot of the grocery shopping, would joke that he and his wife were their son's only unpaid employees. When Yao returned to the house late from road trips—often arriving at 2:00 A.M. or 3:00 A.M.—Da Fang would never fail to be waiting up for him with a pot of his favorite homemade chicken soup or a wok full of stir-fry vegetables. "My son plays so hard," she said. "If he doesn't eat well, how could he have enough energy?"

The most coveted feature in Yao's new home was its vast, open-design kitchen, which stood like a chrome-covered altar a few steps up from the living and dining rooms. Da Fang, however, had no use for it.

To cook her Shanghainese specialties, she converted the small laundry room on the side of the house into an enclosed, Chinese-style kitchen—the better to keep in the billowing smoke created by stir-frying. The open kitchen was almost never used, except to store Yao's cases of Coca-Cola in the double-wide refrigerator.

Adjusting to American life would be far more difficult for Da Fang and Da Yao than it would be for Yao himself. Neither of them spoke English or had any real interest in adapting to Western ways. In Shanghai, Da Fang and Da Yao lived in the pulsating heart of the city, never more than a short bicycle ride away from their favorite markets, shops, and friends. But in America, they were stuck in an isolated community far outside the Houston city limits—and without any means of escape.

Houston boasted a vibrant Chinese community of fifty thousand. But the markets in Chinatown were more than forty minutes away by car, and though Yao's new house boasted an enormous two-car garage, the family of three didn't have a driver's license among them. Colin Pine, the obliging translator they invited to live in the guest room across the hall from Yao, ferried the family around in his rental car and helped them negotiate the basics of living in America—paying bills, opening bank accounts, setting up mortgage payments. But when Pine and Yao headed off to practice or on road trips, the parents were stranded in their perfectly manicured American island. Many months later, all three family members would earn their driver's licenses and Yao would buy two luxury cars to fill the garage. His parents would never feel completely comfortable behind the wheel—Da Yao would get a ticket for driving too *slowly* on the highway, Da Fang a citation for rolling through a stop sign—but at least they would have more freedom than they had in those early days in Houston.

On the night of Yao's highly anticipated home debut, a preseason game against the Philadelphia 76ers, his parents insisted on sitting at home waiting for the cable-company man to come install their television service. When somebody suggested they reschedule the cable guy so they could see their son's home debut, Da Fang demurred: "No, the serviceman told us to wait for him." It was a perfectly Chinese response, rooted in a culture of pliancy, but it revealed just how much she had to learn about being rich and famous in America. Da Fang and Da Yao had traveled several thousand miles to watch their son play in the NBA. But they missed the game entirely. It was only after their son and Colin Pine returned late that night that they heard about the carnival-like atmosphere, Yao's performance (thirteen points), and the wondrous praise he received from the 76ers' star guard Allen Iverson: "He's a gift from God."

After one of Yao's early practices, Da Fang arrived at the Rockets' facility with her son's lunch—a few bags of McDonald's hamburgers and french fries—urging him to eat quickly because they had scheduled a shopping expedition that afternoon. As Yao gobbled down his burgers, Mobley emerged from the locker room in a tailored lavender suit. "That shit's gonna kill ya," he said to Yao, before turning to Da Fang. "Hi, Mrs. Yao," he said, as if it were perfectly normal for a mother to bring her boy lunch at an NBA practice. Flashing a seductive smile, Mobley leaned in and kissed her on the cheek. Da Fang visibly recoiled.

The shopping trip had all the feel of a mother hauling her seventh-grade boy to the mall to get outfitted for the upcoming school year. After stopping off at a furniture store, where the proprietor offered to make Yao a nine-foot, super-king-size bed gratis, they pulled into the Rochester Big & Tall clothing store. Eager to diversify his wardrobe— or at least to alleviate the need to wear his tan shirt and brown cords every day—Yao gravitated to the stylish black V-neck pullovers that many of his teammates wore. Da Fang, however, kept picking out clothes that reflected a stylistic sensibility locked in the 1970s. At one point, she held up a jagged-striped, gold-and-rust-colored sweater that could have been pulled straight off the back of the cartoon character Charlie Brown.

"This is nice, isn't it?" she said brightly, holding up the sweater.

Yao glanced over and grumbled a noncommittal reply.

"Don't you think this is good-looking?" she asked Pine.

This would be a test of whether Pine had absorbed any diplomatic skills during his years as a State Department employee. Apparently, he had.

"Not bad," he said, nodding his head.

One of the Big & Tall tailors—a tiny Cuban-American man who stood, incongruously, no more than 5'3"—stepped forward with a tape to measure Yao's outseam. "Fifty-four inches!" he announced in a tone of awe, perhaps realizing that he stood less than a foot taller than Yao's leg. "We don't even carry anything beyond a 44!"

Yao groaned. "I guess I need a Big-Big-Tall-Tall store," he said.

Yao appreciated his mother's coddling, but sometimes, even a giant could feel suffocated. When Yao's hair got a little shaggy, Da Fang scheduled a hairstylist to come to the house—and got angry when Yao showed up a few minutes late. When Yao, still without his driver's license, offered to pull Pine's rental car into the garage late one night, she rushed out to the front walk to anxiously oversee the maneuver, even though he drove the car, at three miles per hour, little more than the distance of a three-point shot. When Yao suggested inviting some friends over to the house, Da Fang quashed the idea, saying she wanted to protect the family's privacy. Yao might have been an adult now, a twenty-two-year-old professional with an $18-million-dollar contract, but he lived in his mother's thrall, even to the point where he had to ask her for his weekly allowance.

Yao's friends had always warned him that his biggest adjustment in the United States would be dealing with his newfound freedom. But in many ways, Yao enjoyed even less freedom in America than he did in China—and Da Fang's smothering attention only made it seem worse. Back in China, Yao had enjoyed a degree of independence from his mother. But even then, Da Fang's nagging and nit-picking occasionally bothered Yao so much that he avoided going home on his day off, staying out late with friends playing video games or hanging out in the dorms at Meilong. "My mother is like a mosquito constantly buzzing around my ears," he once complained to a friend.

Now the buzzing became louder. After one preseason practice, Yao brought his friend Yang Yi, the Shanghainese journalist, over to the house. Da Fang threw a fit when she saw Yang walk through the door.

"How did you get here?" she demanded.

Yao tried to calm his mother down, but she had made her feelings clear, and Yang quickly left. When the journalist mentioned the name of their gated community in an article, Da Fang was so furious that she forbade Yao from speaking to Yang again. That evening, during a pregame warm-up, Yao came up to Yang and told him gravely, "You're finished."

Up until then, the two had enjoyed an easy friendship, and Yang published admiring accounts of their conversations in the *Beijing Youth Daily* and *Titan Sports Weekly*. But now, Da Fang was putting an end to it. "Listen, it's my mother's fault," Yao explained. "She's way too sensitive. But *meiyou banfa*—nothing can be done." Yang later patched up his relationship with Da Fang and continued writing about his conversations with Yao, but at the time, he felt so discomfited by her blowup that he left Houston two weeks earlier than planned.

In public, Yao never failed to sing his mother's praises. Her chicken soup, he repeated often, was his favorite food in the world; her knowledge of basketball was so great, he said only half-jokingly, that she should be made a Rockets assistant coach; and her judgment was so sound that he left all major decisions up to her, even calling her the "CEO" of Team Yao. In private, however, Yao sometimes chafed at the restrictions she put on his life. He didn't disobey her, but shortly before one of his first road trips, he told a friend that he had finally mustered the courage to give her an oblique warning.

"You just put up walls around me," Yao told her, "but one day you may notice that you put yourself outside the wall. What will you say then?"

Every sight and sound in Indianapolis's Conseco Fieldhouse flew at him in a kaleidoscopic blur: the burst of a thousand camera flashes; the bring-it-on glares from his tattooed opponents; the sound of his name blaring over the stadium loudspeakers; the mock-Chinese taunts from the hecklers behind the Pacers' bench. Yao Ming had dreamed about his NBA debut for years, but now that it had arrived, during the Rockets' October 30 season opener against the Indiana Pacers, he could hardly breathe.

The most intense pressure on Yao, however, came not from inside the arena that night, but from the hopes and expectations of all the people outside. The ringmasters at the NBA had hyped this spectacle so much that it was being televised live across the United States. Millions of fans would soon have a chance to decide on their own whether Yao was a star or a stiff. But far more disconcerting was the fact that the game was being beamed live to 287 million households back in China—nearly three times the number of TV households in the entire U.S.—and Yao's compatriots were depending on him to bring honor to the nation, the culture, the entire Chinese race.

There was little honor in that first game. The Pacers came at Yao in waves, making him look confused and paralyzed—almost as if, were he not the tallest man on court by nearly half a foot, he was willing himself to disappear. Within seconds, Pacer forward Jonathan Bender knocked Yao back on his heels and banked in a short jumper. Score. Yao fumbled his first touch on the left baseline and lost the ball. Turnover. Thirty seconds later, Yao received the ball down low and was again stripped clean. Turnover. Guard Erick Strickland danced around Yao for a reverse layup, making the statuesque Chinese center look as mobile as a Michelangelo. Score. Forty seconds later, the Pacers' all-star center Jermaine O'Neal started to go directly at Yao, making the first of three buckets right in the big man's grill. Score, score, score. Yao took only one shot during his eleven minutes on court, a fadeaway that missed badly. Indiana ended up winning, 91–82, and Yao's stat line—zero points, two rebounds, two turnovers, three fouls—barely began to express how miserable his performance had been.

"It was like a war," Yao told the pack of journalists from all over the world that converged on him after the game, wondering what went wrong. Looking for some solace, he recalled how badly he had bungled his first game in the CBA when, as a cadaverous seventeen-year-old, he got knocked to the floor fifteen times—and then came back to eventually dominate the league. "I am quite sorry for tonight, but everything has to have a beginning," he said. "This is my start."

The next two weeks, however, showed little improvement. Dazed by the blazing pace and bruising physicality of NBA ball, Yao stumbled through the first five games, scoring a total of just thirteen points combined while logging more turnovers than field goals. The critics circled like vultures. They gleefully ripped into the bumbling number one draft pick, comparing him to such infamous flops as Chuck Nevitt and LaRue Martin, a top draft pick who never played a meaningful minute in the NBA. Things got so bad that ESPN's *SportsCenter* started airing, for its viewers' entertainment, nightly "lowlight" reels splicing together Yao's worst gaffes: There he was fumbling the ball, falling to the floor, reeling in confusion as a guard darted around him, and, most shamefully, getting dunked on by a player a foot and a half shorter than him.

Yao's supporters came swiftly to his defense, pointing out that he had less experience—and more pressure—than any other player. "Nobody has gone through what this kid's gone through," said Houston coach Rudy Tomjanovich, a former NBA all-star who knew something about enduring hardship. (His playing career was shortened by a 1977 on-court brawl in which the L.A. Lakers' Kermit Washington crushed nearly every bone in his face in a near-fatal swing that became known simply as "The Punch.") Bill Walton, the outspoken former NBA center and television commentator, cautioned fans against expecting too much too soon. "When I joined the NBA," the former UCLA star recalled, "I came from the greatest program in college basketball, and I still found myself without question, without reservation, absolutely unprepared. And now here is a guy who grew up in a completely different culture than our throw-it-down-in-your-face culture, and we're expecting him to come out and completely change the NBA in two weeks. Those expectations are unfair to Yao Ming and are a sad reflection on us as people and as a culture." Walton added: "Is it a stretch to say that this is as hard a transition as somebody who was put on Earth from Mars?"

Indeed, everything about the NBA felt alien to Yao. Only weeks before, he had been immersed in Chinese-style basketball, easily dominating games that had a languorous pace and minimal physical contact. Now, suddenly, he found himself being outmuscled and outmaneuvered by the chiseled athletes of the NBA. The Houston coaches recognized that the 296-pound center had powerful legs and a sizable rear end, but they desperately wanted to beef up his spindly upper body, which had been virtually neglected in China. The team's trainer, Anthony Falsone, put Yao on a strict program of protein shakes and four-day-a-week weight-training sessions, measuring his body fat and muscle mass every two weeks. But despite all the talk of Yao's need to build upper-body strength, it was the speed of the NBA game, not its power, that would prove his greatest challenge.

Yao's toughest critics refused to believe he had a chance of surviving in the NBA. Charles Barkley, the former all-star forward who got paid to bloviate on TNT's basketball broadcasts, had ridiculed the Rockets, his former team, for drafting Yao. Now, as Yao struggled, Sir Charles couldn't resist piling on. During a broadcast before the Rockets' November 9 game with the Golden State Warriors, Barkley launched into a diatribe about all of Yao's deficiencies, finishing with a flourish. "I tell you what," Barkley told his on-air colleague Kenny Smith, "if Yao Ming can make nineteen points in any game this season, I will kiss your ass."

Word of Barkley's wager quickly filtered down to the Rockets' locker room, and Pine gamely tried to translate. Mandarin has no equivalent phrase, and Yao apparently thought Barkley had proposed to kiss *his* ass. Eager to avoid such a fate, Yao joked: "Then I'll just score eighteen."

That night against the Warriors, Yao scored just three points—and Barkley's bet seemed safe. Less than a week later, Barkley repeated his wager on his television talk show, *Listen Up!,* before the Rockets' game against the Phoenix Suns. "Yao Ming makes Shawn Bradley look like Bill Russell!" Barkley exclaimed when Smith pointed out Yao's potential. "He might be a good player someday, but he is not ready. He's never seen a brother in China. The black guys and white guys, they aren't like those China guys, they're a little bit different over here."

In public, Yao took the taunts in good humor, but privately, he fumed. "This fellow knows nothing except uttering bullshit," he told a reporter friend.

That night, Yao showed some signs of life—making five of six shots to score in double digits (ten points) for the first time—but he also provided some irresistible fodder for Barkley and ESPN. At one point early in the third quarter, Yao found himself at the top of the key all alone guarding the Suns' fleet-footed 6'2" point guard Stephon Marbury. With a wicked combination of crossover dribbles, Marbury whirled past Yao, causing the big man to fall, like a giant redwood, straight onto his rear end. The players on the Suns' bench fell into one another's laps, convulsing with laughter.

Above the din, somebody shouted: "Timber!"

By the time the Rockets rolled into Los Angeles to play the NBA champion Lakers on November 17, few people still believed the preseason hype that Yao might be a worthy rival for Shaquille O'Neal, the Lakers' 7'1" superstar. The man who referred to himself as "MDE" (Most Dominant Ever) made no secret that he resented all the attention being paid to the Chinese rookie. He vowed to welcome Yao with "a 'bow to the nose," and Lakers coach Phil Jackson seemed almost relieved that night when Shaq's injured big toe hadn't healed in time to let him return to the lineup. "He'd break [Yao] in two," Jackson said.

That night, however, with Shaqzilla confined to the sidelines alongside the front-row Hollywood regulars, Yao put on a show of his own. Entering the game in the second quarter, he pounded away at the smaller Los Angeles defenders (none over 6'10") with two dunks, one jumper, and three layups, including a spinning reverse that reminded many fans of the old moves of Hakeem Olajuwon. He returned to the game in the fourth quarter with the Rockets trailing by five and quickly drained a lay-up and a feathery jump hook. Then, with just a minute left to play and the Rockets leading by one, Juaquin Hawkins—the team's other China connection—drove hard to the hole and dished the ball to Yao for a one-handed slam dunk. Fouled on the play, Yao calmly drained the free throw, sealing the Rockets' first victory over the Lakers in three seasons. Lakers guard Kobe Bryant led all scorers with forty-six points, but Yao was the game's true revelation. He not only had a perfect shooting night—9-for-9 from the field, 2-for-2 from the free throw lane—and the game-winner. In just twenty-three minutes, he'd scored twenty points—ensuring that Barkley would have to pucker up.

After the game, O'Neal played the perfect diplomat. When a reporter asked him if he would "break Yao in two," as Jackson had suggested, the hobbled superstar ignored the question and instead gave Yao some props. "Congratulations to Mr. Ming," he said, mistaking Yao's given name for his surname. "He's done a lot for his country . . . He has all the tools. He can shoot. He can dribble. He's no slouch." Half an hour later, when the Rockets emerged to board the team bus, Shaq was there waiting to greet Yao with a homeboy hug.

"You played pretty good, Yao Ming," he said.

"That's because you weren't there," Yao replied with a smile.

"I'll be there next game," O'Neal said.

"I'll be waiting for you."

Yao got on the bus, and waved back at O'Neal. It was a friendly ex-change, and Yao was touched that Shaq—known as "Big Shark" in Chinese—would seek him out for a personal greeting. Both players knew, however, that the first time they faced each other on court—in Houston on January 17—would be more like a war.

Four nights later, Barkley appeared on national television staring warily at a mule named Shorty. His colleague, Kenny Smith, had rented the animal from an Alabama farm for $500 to stand in as his proverbial ass. Powdering up Shorty's left haunch, Smith cajoled Barkley into bending down and making good on his bet. The ass-kissing played out as a fun bit of theater on national television, but it mainly served to in-tensify the interest in Yao. In a matter of days, he had gone from bum-bling rookie to emerging star.

That same night, Yao would prove that his turnaround was no fluke by dominating the league's tallest player, 7'6" Shawn Bradley. The oft-maligned Dallas Mavericks center was, like his undefeated team, off to his best start ever, and he seemed determined to put the Chinese rookie in his place, from the pregame photo shoot of the two giants posing back-to-back (Yao smiled, Bradley glowered) to their first head-to-head sequence on court (Bradley swatted away a Yao jump shot). The rest of the game, however, was all Yao. Though Dallas pulled away to a 103-90 victory, Yao ended up with thirty points (on 10-for-12 shooting) and sixteen rebounds. Bradley didn't score a point. All the media cared about now was Yao, whose shooting percentage over the previous five games—88 percent (thirty of thirty-four shots)—put him just shy of Wilt Chamberlain's decades-old record.

Yao's first appearance in the Rockets' starting lineup came one night later, on November 22, against none other than Michael Jordan and the Washington Wizards. The NBA's past and future were finally facing off against each other, and the future won. In a span of just forty-six sec-onds, Yao showed a full range of skills, sinking a twelve-foot turn-around, blocking a shot, grabbing a rebound, and feeding Hawkins for an assist. Yao steered Houston to victory with eighteen points (on 7-for-11 shooting) and eight rebounds, while a struggling Jordan scored only eight points (on 4-for-15 shooting). After the game, Jordan offered his ultimate compliment: "He's for real."

Despite all the buzz that Yao had generated in the NBA, a few hoop pundits pointed out that he still hadn't proven himself against any legitimate all-star centers. Yao silenced them on December 2, when he outdueled the NBA's toughest inside tandem—7'1" David Robinson and league MVP 6'11" Tim Duncan of the San Antonio Spurs. After pouring in seventeen points in the first half, Yao dominated the fourth quarter with his defense, blocking dunk attempts by both Duncan and Robinson before grabbing an offensive rebound and throwing down a dunk of his own to put the game out of reach. The Rockets won 89–75, and Yao's gaudy stats were notable not just for the points (twenty-seven) but for the rebounds (eighteen), which were as many as Duncan and Robinson had combined.

The performance sent Yao's self-confidence soaring, propelling him on a run of fifteen straight games with double-digit scoring, including nine "double-doubles" (double digits in both points and rebounds). Beating up on perennial all-stars in a nationally televised game also helped win Yao millions of new converts. Even on ESPN's *SportsCenter*, the ridicule had turned into something close to reverence that night, as anchorman Stuart Scott kept repeating:

"Yao Ming has arrived! Yao Ming has arrived!"

18

American Idol

It was billed as a heavyweight title fight, a battle of behemoths in which a mere two syllables augured the collision of two worlds.

Yao versus Shaq.

For months, fans, journalists, and sports executives on both sides of the Pacific had been pumping up the potential rivalry between the Chinese rookie and the American superstar. And on January 17, 2003, the day of reckoning had arrived. The Lakers-Rockets game that night in Houston was just a mid-season matchup, but the hype over Yao's first showdown with Shaquille O'Neal gave it the electricity of an NBA championship finals. More than a hundred reporters showed up to see Yao at the Rockets' shootaround that morning, forcing Colin Pine to stand on a stepladder to translate Yao's responses to the crowd. The nationally televised game would attract more American viewers than any other regular-season broadcast that season. Tens of millions of mainland Chinese fans would tune in, too, dodging work or skipping class to catch the live morning feed. Everybody, it seemed, was hungry for a new hero.

Shaq versus Yao was a culture clash in microcosm—the ultimate confrontation between the force of an American gladiator and the finesse of a Chinese giant. No rivalry in the NBA had featured such a contrast of styles and personas since Larry Bird and Magic Johnson traded championships in the 1980s, and none at the center position since Wilt Chamberlain battled Bill Russell in the 1960s. On court, Shaq was a 7'1", 346-pound hurricane who flattened everything in his path to the bucket, often finishing his assaults with backboard-shaking slam dunks. Yao, four inches taller but nearly fifty pounds lighter, tended to shy away from direct physical challenges, relying more on spin moves and fadeaway jumpers that showed off his soft shooting touch.

Off the court, the two men's styles were radically different, too. Shaq reveled in his larger-than-life persona, while Yao seemed almost embarrassed by his size. The "Little Giant" had spent much of his life trying to undercut his height with humor and humility; he desperately wanted people to like him, to treat him like one of the guys. Yao was the polite, old-school player who wore a macramé love bracelet, lived with his parents, and sent saccharine-sweet Christmas cards to his coaches and opponents, including one to Shaq that read:

> Dear Mr. O'Neal:
> Best wishes for the Holiday. Thanks for the upcoming year. Thanks for the encouragement. You are my #1 player. Be like Shaq.
> Mr. Yao Ming

O'Neal, of course, wasn't known for his extensive Christmas-card list. Flaunting a Superman tattoo on his massive bicep, he preferred to pose as a genial rap-music star, giving himself honorary titles (such as LCS—"Last Center Standing") and making movies in which he played comically overblown superheroes (such as the dismal *Steel*). Shaq was more bluster than gangster, but the thirty-year-old married father of two still seemed like an overgrown adolescent who couldn't accept losing the limelight to anybody. Openly dismissive of Yao since the day of the draft, Shaq showed irritation with reporters who kept asking him about the upstart, responding tartly: "Who's Yao Ming?"

O'Neal's predilection for mouthing off would get him into trouble on the eve of their showdown. More than six months earlier, appearing on a nationally syndicated television broadcast—Fox's *Best Damn Sports Show Period*—Shaq was asked what he thought about the number one draft pick. His reply:

"Tell Yao Ming, 'Ching chong yang wah ah so!'"

The mock Chinese slur aroused no reaction until it was replayed in December on a national sports-radio show on Fox. A thirty-two-year-old Texas resident named Irwin Tang was so infuriated by the comment that he wrote an op-ed column in *AsianWeek* magazine at the beginning of January, charging that Shaq was "aiming a racist barb" at Yao. Bemoaning the kind of casual racism that Asian-Americans suffered, Tang wrote: "If a white player had, for instance, made monkey sounds to taunt a black player, it would have been a national controversy. But Yao is Chinese and Asians are fair game."

The national media picked up on the controversy, and soon the showdown between the two centers had an undercurrent of racial confrontation. Before the game that evening, reporters swarmed around the Lakers' center, trying to elicit a response. "If I offended anybody, I apologize," O'Neal told reporters, sounding contrite until he launched into his self-defense. "To say I'm a racist against Asians is crazy. I'm an idiot prankster. I said a joke. It was a 70–30 joke. Seventy percent of the people thought it was funny. Thirty didn't." He kept backsliding until it hardly sounded like an apology at all. The guy who wrote the article, he said, is "just somebody who doesn't have a sense of humor, like I do."

After he finished, O'Neal walked off to the team lounge, turning around halfway to throw a couple of mock kung-fu moves at the reporters.

Later, the media hordes descended on Yao. Did he think Shaq's comment was racist? All season, Yao had delighted journalists with playful quips and quirky observations—a welcome relief from the wooden jock-speak that afflicted most players. After games and practices, he would lean back in his chair, almost supine, responding to questions with a rub of the chin or a smile that broke up the broad expanse of his square face. After dominating 7'6" beanpole Shawn Bradley, Yao didn't gloat, except to say: "Now I know I'm not the skinniest guy in the league." When a Chinese reporter corrected one of Colin Pine's translations, Yao laughed at his sidekick: "He's a rookie, too. We're all rookies here!" The media mobbed him in every city he visited, eating up his pearls of wisdom—about handling pressure ("sleep"), his first Thanksgiving turkey ("dry"), or the American landscape ("big")—as if he were Confucius or the unintentionally brilliant Chauncey Gardiner in *Being There*.

At times, Yao wanted nothing more than to escape the media onslaught, but his advisors on Team Yao had persuaded him that his commercial success depended on cultivating a positive public persona. It was a marked difference from China, where the shy giant never had to think about his image—and where he often came off as boring, reserved, even glum. "The biggest change," he told a Chinese reporter later, "is that instead of avoiding the media, [I told myself]: 'Why don't you go and face it? Strike an image of yourself for them, and let them make you popular. This is the only way, or else you will be crushed by them.'"

Now, as reporters crowded in to hear his thoughts on Shaq and racism, Yao was wading into dangerous territory. After just three months in the NBA, he could hardly have been aware of the issue's potential explosiveness in America. Racism was something Yao had rarely thought about before. As a member of the Han majority, which constitutes all but 7 percent of the Chinese population and almost its entire eastern seaboard, Yao had virtually no contact with the minorities who have been marginalized in his homeland. Indeed, although many Han hold derogatory views of Chinese minorities—particularly Muslim ethnicities—Chinese schoolchildren are taught that there is no such thing as racial disharmony in their country. Yao's first response reflected that view: "We don't have racism in China." The comment, which didn't fit the message Team Yao had painstakingly advised him to make, was not translated for the American reporters. They would only hear his far more gracious follow-up.

"I don't think there's any animosity," Yao said of Shaq's remarks. "We all live together on this earth. We're all trying to understand each other. . . . I think there are a lot of difficulties in two different cultures understanding each other, especially countries of very large populations [such as] China and the United States."

Then Yao lightened up, poking fun at Shaq's sing-song mock Chinese.

"Chinese is a hard language to learn," he quipped. "Even when I was little, I took a long time to learn Chinese."

The reporters burst into laughter.

The overwhelmingly positive response to Yao's self-effacing charm indicated just how much the NBA needed someone to reinvigorate the league. For all of the NBA's success—its revenues had jumped from $100 million in the mid-1980s to $2.5 billion in 2002—the league was struggling at home. Domestic television ratings, stadium attendance, and ticket receipts had fallen in the years before Yao arrived, as the heroes of the 1980s and 1990s—Magic Johnson, Larry Bird, and Michael Jordan—had all retired. (Well, Jordan was nearing his *third* retirement.) The new crop of NBA stars, such as Kobe Bryant and Tim Duncan, were talented players but hardly transcendent personalities. Although the NBA remained the global arbiter of cool, the games themselves often devolved into low-scoring brickfests with the athleticism of the league's ever-younger players unable to hide the decline of such fundamental skills as passing and shooting. Even more disturbing was the proliferation of players whose rap sheets were as long as their stat sheets, with charges ranging from drug and sexual abuse to domestic violence. Members of the Portland Trail Blazers had so many run-ins with the law that even locals took to disparaging them as the "Jail Blazers."

To many observers, especially white fans watching the game from their suburban living rooms, Yao seemed the perfect antidote to the NBA's ills: a clean-cut, 1950s-style team player who exuded humility rather than hubris. Even his playing style was modest and methodical— a "blue-collar game," he called it—with none of the high-flying flourishes that normally set off the crowds. Yao was, in essence, the anti-superstar, and fans—including top corporate sponsors and NBA executives—couldn't get enough of his retro appeal. The NBA even commissioned a full-length documentary film about Yao's rookie year and produced a television spot in which Yao leads a class of referees, mascots, and players in the graceful movements of tai chi. "*Wo ai zheige bisai,*" says Yao at the end of the commercial. "I love this game."

And the game loved Yao. In Houston, fans started coming back to the stadium as the team, which had ended the previous season with a 28–54 record, fought for a spot in the playoffs, carrying a 22–15 record into the game against the Lakers. With Yao on the roster, the Rockets had also become one of the NBA's most popular road teams, filling stadiums from Miami (where eight thousand fortune cookies were handed out, even though such confections don't exist in China) to Oakland (where public-address announcements in Mandarin advertised "Great Wall" ticket packages to catch Yao's games).

Fueling the excitement were Chinese-American fans who delighted in watching the 7'6" giant (he actually grew another half inch that season) smash the stereotype of the weak and diminutive Asian, offering payback for all the jokes about geekdom and Communism. Here, finally, was a strong, wholly positive image of China, a young man who had nothing to do with trade wars or spy planes, Chairman Mao or massacres at Tiananmen Square. Back in China, people who had ignored Yao now embraced him as a national hero. The numbers were staggering. When Sohu.com hosted a ninety-minute online chat with Yao in December 2002, nine million fans logged on, crashing the system in six of China's largest cities. A regular-season game that drew one million viewers in the U.S. now attracted more than fifteen million in China—and the figure would often double for games featuring Yao. For a country consumed by the desire to become a great nation, the twenty-two-year-old center seemed to prove that China could compete against the world's best in any arena.

More unexpected, however, was the fervor with which American fans who had no connection to Asia embraced the Chinese rookie. Yao somehow managed to make the alien seem familiar, the freakishly tall endearingly small. And that, along with his emergence as the only potential rival for Shaq, helped turn him into such a fan favorite that he blew past the Lakers' center in the All-Star balloting by more than two hundred thousand votes. Shaq grumbled that "two billion Chinese" had skewed the balloting because they could for the first time cast their votes via the NBA's new Chinese-language Web site. NBA officials insisted, however, that Shaq had also lost to Yao on the paper ballots filled out in U.S. arenas.

Yao's popularity wasn't simply a function of his game or his personality. Race was a factor, too—an irony that wasn't lost on many African-Americans who watched the Shaq controversy unfold that day. The NBA is arguably the most progressive league in American sports; it was the first to have an African-American coach, general manager, and owner. But the league also faces a statistical discrepancy: Three-quarters of its players are black, while nearly the same percentage of its fans are white, along with the majority of corporate sponsors. As Charles Barkley said: "The white audience doesn't like to see a bunch of guys with tattoos and cornrows who get in trouble all the time."

Yao, of course, was supposed to transcend black and white. But when he leaped into the spotlight that season, several commentators groused that Yao had won over fans, the media, and corporate sponsors because he was considered "an honorary white." Like Asians in American society as a whole, they said, Yao was liked because he was a model minority, "the good immigrant" praised for his hard work, team-first attitude, and respect for authority. NBA executives scoffed at such critiques. But few could deny that Yao was the antithesis of the "gangsta" baller who might frighten off corporate executives and the wealthy white fans who could afford the NBA's ever-rising ticket prices.

Another part of Yao's appeal, however, had little to do with black or white but with the mysterious allure of the Middle Kingdom. Had Yao hailed from any other place—Chechnya, Chile, even Chicago—his presence in the NBA wouldn't have been invested with so much meaning. But he was from China, and that made all the difference. Thousands of U.S. companies had already plunged into China to get a piece of the fastest-growing market in the world. Even the average American consumer was aware of the rising economic superpower just by seeing the "Made in China" tags attached to nearly every item on sale at Wal-Mart or Home Depot. As China loomed ever larger in the American consciousness, U.S. audiences were also cozying up to Chinese culture. Popular magazines displayed Hollywood stars wearing Mandarin-collar silk jackets and brocaded dresses and dedicated articles to the transforming effects of feng shui and the kung-fu hits *Crouching Tiger, Hidden Dragon* and *Hero*.

But for all the growing interest, China was still a nation without a recognizable face. In the American mind, it was a place of teeming masses, home to 1.3 billion people virtually indistinguishable from one another. For decades, that was exactly how the Communist Party wanted to keep it, as the government exalted the ideal of an egalitarian society. Even by the time Yao arrived in 2002, only a few American aficionados might have recognized the moon-faced actress Gong Li or then-Chinese president Jiang Zemin in his bug-eyed glasses. Ask the average American to name a living person from mainland China and he would likely have drawn a blank. Almost by default, Yao would become the face of China.

In the anxious hours before the Lakers-Rockets game, nobody let Yao forget that a battle was about to begin—least of all his mother. Da Fang had been nagging her son to watch a DVD of Shaquille O'Neal that Bill Duffy had put together to help him prepare. Yao had refused the night before—the very thought of getting bludgeoned by the 346-pound behemoth unsettled him—and that afternoon, he resisted again. He wanted to take a nap instead. Still, his mother kept bugging him, so finally, Yao flipped the DVD into the machine. After a few seconds, he turned it off and buried his head back into the pillow.

Of the many reasons Yao had to be apprehensive, the most discouraging was his recent slump. He had hit the infamous "rookie wall." NBA teams were starting to muscle him, and the Chinese giant—already exhausted by years of nonstop basketball and new commercial commitments—wilted under the assault. His legs felt dead, his energy low. His dazzling December (17.5 points a game) faded into a joyless January (barely eleven), and Yao pinned some of the blame on cultural differences. He had grown up in a system that favored finesse over force. "I used to look down on the use of physical strength," he said. "But now I've discovered that I should use my physical advantages fully." It would take time, though, and the more immediate worry, as he faced the most physically punishing player in the game, was simply keeping his energy up. Yao's family was so concerned about his condition that when his father traveled to Shanghai, he had met with his son's old medical advisor, Wei Guoping. Da Yao returned to Houston before the Lakers game with a stash of cordyceps, the "caterpillar fungus" tonic meant to increase endurance and eliminate fatigue.

No amount of traditional Chinese medicine, however, could have given Yao the jolt of adrenaline he received as he walked onto the court to face Shaq that night. Amid the deafening roar of the sellout crowd, Shaq leaned over and shouted into Yao's ear. "I love you, man," Shaq said. "We're friends." Yao smiled and nodded.

From the opening tip, Shaq dispensed with any sentmentality and tried to run right over Yao. On the Lakers' first possession, he caught the ball on the wing and wheeled immediately toward the middle, lowering his shoulder into Yao as he attempted an up-and-under move. Yao stood his ground and swatted the ball away as Shaq fell awkwardly on his back. The crowd roared. Seconds later, at the other end of the floor, Yao received a pass in the post and calmly dropped in a four-foot hook shot over Shaq. The cameras panned the ecstatic stadium crowd, zooming in on a Houston fan madly waving a sign that read: HEY SSHAQ, WHO'S YAO DADDY?

The stadium was still shaking when, amazingly, the scene repeated itself a minute later. Shaq posted up on the left side of the lane and spun quickly toward the hoop, but again, Yao met him at the rim and blocked the shot. Diesel was dazed, and Yao raced back on offense, catching a pass in the lane and banking in an easy four-footer. Thirty seconds later, Yao spotted up on the left side and made a fadeaway over Shaq's extended hand. Wide-eyed and almost frantic now, the Lakers' star seemed bent on showing the rookie who the real all-star was. Receiving the ball down low, Shaq pivoted toward the baseline and leaped toward the basket—only to have his shot blocked, once again, by Yao.

Less than three minutes had elapsed, but Yao had already scored six points to Shaq's zero. More stunningly, he had blocked three of Shaq's shots in a row. For 173 seconds, at least, it seemed clear that Shaq wasn't the Last Center Standing.

Yao's adrenaline burned off quickly, however, and as Shaq got stronger, the Chinese giant virtually disappeared, missing seven shots in a row before making another late in the fourth quarter. Rockets guard Steve Francis was dazzling, though, and his three-pointer sent the game into overtime. Shaq reeled off ten of the Lakers' final twelve points in the extra period. But with ten seconds left in overtime, and the Rockets still clinging to an improbable two-point lead, 102–100, Francis zipped a pass inside to Yao. The rookie threw down a two-handed dunk to seal the Rockets' victory. The roar of the crowd practically lifted the roof off the stadium.

After the game, Yao was so exhausted he could hardly move. "I am still alive," he said, smiling wearily. The Rockets had just beaten the NBA champions, and Yao had provided a fitting exclamation point. But Shaq clearly won the showdown—he scored thirty-one points and grabbed thirteen rebounds while Yao notched ten points, ten rebounds, and six blocked shots—and the Chinese newcomer couldn't stop marveling at the man he described as "a wall of flesh."

"I have never seen anybody so awesome," Yao said. "I could never imagine that such a human being exists on this earth."

Still, before that night, few people could have imagined that there existed a 7'6" Chinese man capable of challenging the most powerful player in the game. Yao still had a long way to go, but his tantalizing rivalry with Shaq had officially begun.

Mountains tend to form in one of two ways. They either burst into being through a series of volcanic eruptions, or they rise slowly above the seams where the earth's tectonic plates collide. To the casual observer, Yao Ming seemed to explode onto the American scene like a volcano. But his emergence actually owed more to the shifting tectonics of history. It was, after all, the convergence of two of the most powerful forces in the twenty-first century—a rising superpower and global capitalism—that would thrust Yao to heights far beyond his imagination, turning him into the most famous living Chinese person in the world.

When Yao was born, in 1980, this grand convergence was almost impossible to conceive. China was still reeling from the devastation of the Cultural Revolution, its first tentative market reforms barely more than a notion in Deng Xiaoping's mind. The forces of global capitalism, likewise, had yet to fully emerge. Satellite television, the computer revolution, the Internet, even the demise of Communism: In 1980, these were all ideas in embryonic form. In those days, Nike was better known as a Greek goddess than as a shoe company. And the NBA had such a small audience that CBS had to broadcast the 1980 NBA Finals between the Lakers and 76ers after midnight—on tape delay.

By the time Yao arrived in Atlanta for the NBA's 2003 All-Star Game, the world had changed. Riding two decades of nearly double-digit growth, China had become a magnetic force that seemed to bend the global economy to its needs. The Middle Kingdom was no longer just the world's most efficient factory. It had also become one of the planet's most ravenous consumers of natural resources, construction materials, foodstuffs, and electronics. China had more cell phones and television sets than any other country, and it was the fastest-growing market for automobiles. Now the world's sixth-biggest economy, China was quickly approaching the top two, the U.S. and Japan.

Sports, meanwhile, had experienced a similar explosion worldwide. Political historian Walter LaFeber claimed that, after drug trafficking, the sports industry had become the most globalized and lucrative business in the world. The NBA, in that light, just happened to be one of sports' most successful international cartels. The league, which had just four international players in 1980, boasted sixty-six foreigners from thirty-six countries in the 2002–3 season, including five others beside

Yao who would appear in the All-Star Game. (By 2005, the number of foreign players would rise to more than eighty, accounting for 15 percent of all starters.) But the NBA's international broadcasts reflected the most staggering change. The 2003 All-Star extravaganza would be the most widely broadcast event in NBA history, available in 212 countries to an estimated 3.1 billion viewers—nearly half the world's population.

Nobody had to remind David Stern that several hundred million of those potential viewers were Chinese; he'd been thinking about how to reach them for most of his career. For years, the NBA had tread cautiously in China, worried about getting burned like countless other Western companies rushing blindly into the Middle Kingdom. But with Yao's emergence, the NBA opened its first mainland office in Beijing, launched a Chinese-language Web site, and signed new (and, for the first time, modestly profitable) television contracts with twelve different provincial stations. All told, 168 NBA games would be broadcast in China that season, more than double the year before. "Yao is a dream for David Stern and the NBA," says Houston Rockets president George Postolos. "He takes globalization to a new level."

Under the klieg lights of All-Star weekend, Yao shined brighter than any other player. Top executives from America's biggest companies—including rivals Coca-Cola and Pepsi Co.—begged for an audience with Team Yao to discuss potential endorsement contracts. Even Stern seemed awed. Before the Chinese center's first public appearance that weekend, the NBA commissioner walked up and introduced himself. The most powerful man in basketball seemed worried the rookie wouldn't remember him from their first meeting in Sydney nearly three years before. Later, Stern presented Yao to a crowd of businessmen by referring slyly to the All-Star votes he had received from mainland fans: "He's the leading vote-getter in the history of any election in China."

A full two hours before Yao's scheduled appearance at the press center, more than a hundred reporters and cameramen were already jostling for position around his table. When Yao finally loped in, photographers backpedaling madly in his path, the media scrum grew even larger. One reporter asked Yao what he'd most like to do, and he responded half-jokingly: "I'd like to leave this place as soon as possible." A few feet away, Steve Francis—like Yao, a first-time All-Star—sat virtually alone at his table, chatting with a couple of reporters who had given up on getting close enough to hear the Chinese rookie. "The media is entirely too much," Francis said, shaking his head before going back to describing how he and Yao were "going to be Batman and Robin." Francis clearly meant that Yao would play the sidekick, but if that scene proved anything, it was that the boy wonder had already leaped into the leading role.

Amid all the hoopla, it almost didn't matter that Yao was arguably the worst player on court when the All-Star Game finally took place. Aside from an alley-oop dunk off a pass from Francis to open the game, Yao looked overwhelmed by the game's furious pace, bobbing up and down the court like a buoy on a roiling sea. Benched early on, Yao sat out the entire fourth quarter and two overtimes while Shaq scored nineteen points and grabbed thirteen rebounds to lead the Western Conference squad to a rollicking 155–145 victory. Yao ended up with just two points and two rebounds in seventeen minutes, the poorest stats on the team.

Nothing, however, could stop Yao's rise as a cultural icon. His image could be found on bobblehead dolls, celebrity ducks, even a life-size wax figure at Madame Tussaud's in Hong Kong. His name would turn up in the lyrics of a Jay-Z rap song that goofed on his rivalry with O'Neal: "Stand out like Yao Ming, I'm what's sparkin' now. Like, fall back Shaq, I'm startin' now." But what truly propelled Yao into stardom was a string of clever television spots for Visa, Gatorade, and Apple Computer. In the Apple ad, the 7'6" giant smiles down at the tiny man sitting next to him on a plane, the 2'8" actor Verne "Mini-Me" Troyer, who is watching *Crouching Tiger, Hidden Dragon* on a much-larger version of Yao's own laptop. The commercial played shamelessly on Yao's freakish size, but somehow, without uttering a word, the Chinese center was able to convey a sweetness and affability that made him seem utterly human.

Already, Yao was making more as a pitchman than as a player. In his rookie season, he earned an estimated $10 million in endorsements, a figure that would rise sharply by the end of 2003. It no longer seemed unreasonable to believe that Yao could rocket into the endorsement stratosphere previously occupied only by Tiger Woods and Michael Jordan. During All-Star weekend, his advisors on Team Yao sifted carefully through dozens of proposals, looking for ones that would enhance the six qualities they wanted to associate with Yao's name—respectful, heroic, hardworking, talented, light-hearted, self-confident.

They turned down most of the offers.

"Sure, we'll take some of the low-hanging fruit," said Bill Duffy, who oversaw many of the meetings. "But we want to wait for his value to rise even further. Then we'll have everybody by the balls."

Where was Nike?
Midway through Yao's rookie season, that was the question on every

sports marketer's lips. Apple, Visa, Gatorade, Pepsi, China Unicom: All had signed seven-figure deals with the NBA's hottest new property, and now, across China and America, Yao's face could be seen everywhere—on buses, billboards, television—flacking their products with a "light-hearted" smile or a "heroic" gaze. Other corporate giants, such as McDonald's, would soon be making their own multimillion-dollar pitches to Team Yao. Few companies, it seemed, could resist making a run at the athlete who would almost certainly be *the* symbol of the business bonanza known as the 2008 Beijing Olympic Games.

But Nike, strangely, was nowhere to be found. Everyone figured the world's most powerful sports company, which had practically invented the concept of the global icon, would be trumpeting its client's success. Nike, after all, had spent six years nurturing Yao's development, and the time seemed ripe for the company to begin cashing in on its long-term investment. In 2002, Nike's international sales surpassed domestic sales for the first time, and while its $100 million in mainland revenues accounted for a small sliver of the company's $10.7 billion total, China was Nike's fastest-growing market, expanding by more than 30 percent a year. Nike already sold more basketball shoes in Greater China (including Hong Kong and Taiwan) than anywhere in the world outside of the United States. And Phil Knight wanted to boost the company's China sales to $500 million by 2008. Who better to lead the way than Yao, a star with mass appeal on two continents?

And yet, the company was largely ignoring its tallest client. A Nike print ad ran briefly in parts of China in December 2002, but otherwise, there was virtually nothing: no ad congratulating Yao for completing his long journey to the NBA, no sepia-toned spot showing how Nike had taken every step with him since he was sixteen, no commercial playing off his newfound celebrity. By the spring of 2003, Nike simply supplied him with standard-issue, size-18 Shox and paid out the final year of the small contract he had signed as an eighteen-year-old—less than $50,000.

Nike executives came up with plenty of excuses for the company's vanishing act. Big men make bad pitchmen, they said. The company's global ad campaign for the season had already been set before Yao's breakthrough. Nike didn't want to drive up Yao's asking price before they started to negotiate a new contract. The underlying truth, however, was that Beaverton thought Yao might be a flop—and by the time he proved them wrong, it was too late.

"Nothing in my twelve-month plan is more important than getting Yao signed," Nike's director of global basketball, Ralph Greene, said in early 2003, even before signing both Kobe Bryant and high-school phenom LeBron James. But that spring, Nike sent a rep to Houston to begin negotiations, and over the course of several weeks, the man never received an invitation to the family home; nor did he share a single meal with Yao. The chilly reception was, in part, a symptom of Da Fang's lingering resentment over what she saw as the paltry terms of the original Nike contract and the company's excessive influence over her son in China. But it also reflected Erik Zhang's irritation with Nike for showing too little faith in Yao's potential—and too little respect for his own authority.

A year earlier, just as Yao was leading Shanghai into the 2002 CBA finals, Ralph Greene had sent Bill Duffy an offer sheet guaranteeing Yao $300,000 per year for seven years, with incentives that could earn him another million dollars. Duffy, whose clients almost all wore Nike, was tempted by the deal, but Zhang resisted. Why lock Yao up for seven years, he asked, when other shoe companies could bump up the price in a bidding war? Moreover, Greene's gentle threat—that the offer expired in four days—seemed to stem from either arrogance or ignorance. Did he not realize that Yao still had another year left in his current contract? Two days after Greene sent his letter, Yao scored forty-nine points in the first game of the CBA finals, making all twenty-one shots from the field. The astonishing performance confirmed Zhang's belief that Yao could be an NBA star—and that his value would rise as his exposure increased. He let the Nike offer die.

Later that summer, taking over the negotiations from Duffy (whom he felt was too close to Nike to play tough), Zhang traveled to Beaverton with John Huizinga for a meeting with Greene. The chubby Chinese-American and the tweedy professor may have seemed out of place on the hyper-athletic Nike World Campus. But they laid down the bottom line: $1 million a year. Nike's director of basketball was flabbergasted. Everybody knew the big shoe deals were reserved for players who fly above the rim, like Michael or Kobe or LeBron, not hulking 7'6" centers who had yet to prove themselves. "Who the hell *are* these guys?" Greene asked a colleague afterward. "Are they for real?"

Greene hoped that the newcomers would eventually come to their senses. But as the season wore on, and Yao burst into the limelight, Zhang kept raising his asking price: first $2 million a year, then $3 million, then $5 million. The numbers might have seemed like figments of his imagination. But by the summer of 2003, they were very real. Reebok, a firm whose $25 million in annual China sales lagged far behind Adidas ($85 million at the time) and Nike (more than $100 million), offered Yao a six-year deal worth more than $40 million. Suddenly, Zhang's original million-a-year demand didn't seem so outrageous. Nike pulled out the stops and matched Reebok's offer, confident that it could woo Yao back. After all, in its thirty-one-year history, Nike had never lost a head-to-head battle over an athlete.

The shoe wars reached a climax in Harbin, the northeastern Chinese city that played host to the Asian Championships in late September. Yao vowed to sign a shoe contract before the tournament began, and Nike, whose four envoys stayed in the same walled government compound as the national team, quickly gained the inside advantage. The reps dropped by Yao's room every day, talking up ad campaigns and performance incentives and showing the center the sleek, red-and-white prototypes Nike's designers had produced for him. Yao loved the look but coyly hid his intentions. "When the Nike guys come in, I put on Reebok," he told a friend. "When the Reebok guys come by, I put on Nike."

Reebok's emissaries tried to convince Yao that he would shine more brightly at a company where the only other major basketball star was Allen Iverson, and where he could receive something that Nike would be reluctant to offer: a stake in its China business. The setup intrigued Yao, and the negotiations went back and forth until less than forty-eight hours remained before the tournament began. "This is just like a basketball game," said one participant. "The real battle is not getting the offer on the table, but who gets the last shot?"

With the clock running out, Nike seemed to have the deal locked up. But Reebok made one last-gasp effort to woo the sentimental giant, resorting to a plan that came from an unlikely source: Terry Rhoads. The former Nike evangelist had left the company in the summer of 2002 after a dispute with headquarters. With two other ex-Nike hands— Frank Sha and Tor Petersen—he set up a sports-marketing firm in Shanghai called Zou Marketing. Zou means "go" in Mandarin, and Rhoads had been a whirl of movement that year, signing up Chinese athletes, hiring staff, and helping foreign companies that wanted to expand their business in China through sports marketing.

Ever since meeting Reebok executives at the 2003 All-Star Game, Rhoads had been quietly advising them on how to lure Yao away from Nike. Yao felt a little guilty about his sudden wealth, Rhoads told them, but China wasn't a society where athletes handed out cash to their posses. Nevertheless, Yao wanted to take care of his friends, and he valued no one more than his old buddy on the Shanghai team, Liu Wei, the talented 6'4" guard with whom he had played since age thirteen (and who happened to be a Zou client). Rhoads had a suggestion: Why not offer Liu a six-figure contract as well? Yao would surely want to show loyalty to his friend, grateful for the chance to spread the wealth.

In the final twenty-four hours, Nike bumped up its offer one last time. But the lure of an equity stake in Reebok's China business—and the chance to make a friend rich in the process—apparently turned the tide. Just hours before the tournament began, Yao signed a multiyear contract with Reebok worth more than $60 million. If the heavy incentive clauses kicked in, the deal's value could rise to $100 million—potentially the largest shoe contract ever given to an athlete.

Nike's reps in Harbin were shell-shocked. They begged Yao and his advisors to reconsider, but it was too late. Nike had lost its first head-to-head battle over an athlete, and Frank Sha attributed it to the arrogance of power. If his former company had treated Yao with a bit more respect during his rookie NBA season—giving him a bonus, producing an admiring ad—he would still be wearing Nikes. "It's a war and Nike had no real strategy," Sha says. "They think having the most powerful guns, cannons, and weapons is enough. But sometimes guerrillas can win from behind the lines."

It was Nike, of course, that had always prided itself on its rebel image, and the company would survive the loss of Yao in China by emphasizing its role as the edgy arbiter of American youth culture—even if such a strategy carried risks as well. One of the most notorious setbacks would come in late 2004, when Nike aired an ad that featured LeBron James slashing through a series of cartoon dragons, kung-fu masters, and mythical women in traditional Chinese attire on his way to the hoop. The sight of an American icon trampling Chinese culture outraged many Chinese viewers, and after a firestorm broke out on the Internet, Beijing banned the ad for insulting "our national dignity." Nike was forced to scrap the ad campaign. (There was no such outrage, however, when China Unicom released a similar ad featuring Yao spinning through a group of hapless African-American players on his way in for a dunk. The ad still plays today all over China.)

Nike would not relinquish its lead in the China shoe wars, and indeed, Reebok—which didn't have a single full-time employee in China—didn't seem to have a thought-out strategy beyond bagging Yao. But in Harbin, the Nike reps couldn't help but feel humiliated by Yao's defection to the competition. The company sponsored the Chinese national team, but its biggest star wore Reeboks throughout the Asian Championships, pouring in thirty points against South Korea in the finals to secure China's berth in the Athens Olympics. The day after the championship game, Nike held a publicity event for the victorious Chinese team in Harbin. All but one player was there. Yao Ming had already flown back to Beijing.

19

Generation Next

Wang Zhizhi shuffled off the Los Angeles Clippers' team bus into the garage of Houston's Compaq Center two hours before game time, a duffel bag slung across his shoulder, his unkempt hair creeping down toward his eyes. At that moment, on the evening of March 12, 2003, a silver Toyota Sequoia glided into the garage. The SUV's front seat was set so far back that no driver was visible—just a massive hand on the steering wheel guiding the vehicle into a parking space. Wang stopped and watched as a familiar flattop head emerged from the car, followed by the slowly unfolding eighty-nine inches of Yao Ming's famous frame. Yao had driven himself to the arena that evening, and now, looking across the parking lot, he spotted Wang, the man he had chased for most of his childhood and whom he had now eclipsed in every way.

The former rivals greeted each other with a nod of recognition. No homeboy hugs for these guys. Just a simple *hao jiu bujian*—"long time, no see"—and the two Chinese centers started chatting quietly as they walked toward the locker rooms. Nearly eight months had passed since Wang had made his last desperate attempt to rejoin the Chinese national team in Oakland. So much had transpired since that day that the two players hardly knew what to say. In a couple of hours, they would be facing each other in an NBA game, just as they had always dreamed about back in China. But it was hard to imagine two men sharing so much history—and following such divergent paths.

If Yao had become the most visible sports star in Chinese history, Wang was fast becoming the most invisible. Nobody wanted to be associated with a pariah, least of all U.S. or Chinese businesses eager to promote their products on the mainland. Nike let its contract with Wang quietly expire in the summer of 2002, and it seemed that no other enterprise would ever come near him again. In a special directive issued in the fall of 2002, the Chinese government forbade the nation's broadcasters from airing any of Wang's NBA games—even those that also featured Yao. The NBA usually insisted that foreign broadcasters air a full package of games to ensure parity among its twenty-nine teams—but in the case of China, the league was apparently willing to make an exception.

Even if Wang's games had not been blacked out in China, viewers wouldn't have seen much of him. The former Bayi star spent most of his time slouching at the end of the Clippers' bench. He played in less than half of the hapless team's games, and even in those—usually the final minutes of a blowout loss—he logged an average of ten minutes, notching just 4.4 points and 1.9 rebounds a game. It wasn't simply that he wasn't being given a chance; his air of self-assurance had evaporated. His coaches thought the blank-faced center lacked intensity. Wang claimed he was trying his hardest. But his battle with Beijing had rattled his confidence and trapped him in a demoralizing cycle: As his playing time declined, his confidence and conditioning further eroded, giving coaches more reason to keep him glued to the bench.

Wang was an invisible man off the court as well. Shy by nature and paranoid by experience, he retreated into the isolation of his $2.2 million mansion in the bucolic L.A. suburb of Arcadia. The trappings of the American dream offered some solace—the luxury cars, the bank account, the house just around the corner from Chinese movie star Jet Li—but they couldn't hide the fact that Wang was living like a recluse. If Yao was a cultural bridge between China and America, Wang seemed lost in the chasm between both worlds. His ties to China had almost all been severed. The only person back home with whom he spoke regularly was the journalist Su Qun. Wang missed his parents, but on the infrequent occasions he called them he guarded his words. "I never tell them bad news," he says, "because I don't want them to worry."

Even in his adopted country, Wang cut off contact with nearly everybody but his wife, Song Yang, and his translator-advisor, Simon Chan. He made little effort to bond with his teammates, a group of young players struggling through another losing season, and the language gap only made things worse. His English hadn't improved much, and he no longer seemed motivated to learn much more. Why bother? In his Chinese cocoon in Arcadia, he could get all of his dry cleaning and take-out food without speaking a word of English. Wang joined his wife on occasional jaunts to Las Vegas, and sometimes he'd cruise in his BMW through the scrub-covered hills around Arcadia, which made him nostalgic for the arid mountains around Beijing. But most of the time, he hung out in his mansion, popping DVDs into his home theater or heading to the cineplex with the free tickets the Clippers provided their players. Wang saw so many films he had the Hollywood formula down cold.

"It's always the same plot," he says. "Day one, life is normal. Day two, the change. Day three, back to normal."

The plot of Wang's own life, however, would not get back to normal, largely because he wouldn't stick to the script the authorities back home had written for him. Ever since he refused to return to China, the soldier had been propelled into a drama that seemed less like a Hollywood blockbuster than an epic Chinese tragedy made worse by the spectacular rise of his younger rival.

Wang may have been jealous of Yao—indeed, friends remember how, in the days after the 2002 draft, the soldier angrily ignored Americans who mistook him for Yao—but any hard feelings seemed to have dissipated by the time the two giants bumped into each other in the Compaq Center garage. Wang found himself looking forward to seeing Yao, even musing about inviting him out for a tour of L.A.'s Chinatown and to the best Peking duck restaurant in Texas. Even though the two had never been close—their competitive instincts and contrary personalities prevented that—Wang seemed to realize that Yao was one of the few people who could truly understand his predicament, and perhaps the only one, given the rookie's newfound power, who could help him get back into the good graces of the authorities back home.

In the garage that evening, the sight of the two Chinese giants together attracted a local television crew, which raced over to capture the reunion on film. An advisor for Team Yao rushed over in a panic.

"Stop the cameras!" he hissed. "Yao, we gotta go—right now!"

The advisor grabbed Yao's arm and, without looking at Wang, pulled his star away. The television crew, looking dumbfounded, stopped filming, and Wang walked off to the visitors' locker room alone. The intervention only took a few seconds, but it captured in an instant the Chinese giants' divergence of fortunes. "The Chinese government would freak out if it saw Yao and Wang together," the advisor explained later. "Wang already made it much more complicated for Yao to get out of China. So we have to be careful. We can't afford to tarnish Yao's image now."

On court, Wang did his best to remind Yao and the world of who he used to be. Energized by the chance to play his old adversary, he slashed through the middle for layups, outraced Yao for rebounds and loose balls, and frustrated Yao with harassing double-teams. The Rockets pulled out a 108–104 overtime victory, but Wang played well, scoring eight points in nineteen minutes—double his season averages—while Yao struggled, scoring ten points but committing four turnovers.

The most memorable moment, however, came late in the third quarter. Yao had fallen down going after an offensive rebound, and as the rest of the players raced off on a fast break in the other direction, Wang stayed behind to make sure his old rival wasn't hurt—and then helped him up off the floor. It was the kind of sportsmanship that was more common in China than in the United States. The only thing Clippers coach Denis Johnson noticed, however, was that the compassionate gesture meant Wang failed to get back on defense. Johnson threw up his arms in disbelief and yelled:

"Wang, what the hell are you doing?"

In late August 2003, the prodigal son called his parents with the best news they had heard in more than a year: "I am coming home."

Wang had booked a flight to return to Beijing on August 30, his path to redemption almost clear. The new CBA leader, Li Yuanwei, a genial academic eager to field the strongest team for the 2004 Olympics, had given Wang the green light to be reinstated on the Chinese national team. The head of Bayi sports, Chen Zhaodi, also assured Wang that he wouldn't be punished severely if he came home. She only asked him to write the army a formal appeal. In the faxed letter, dated August 27, Wang acknowledged his mistake in not consulting more openly with his army leaders over the previous year. Though Wang reiterated his desire to return directly to the NBA after the Asian Championships, he expressed his willingness to make a thorough *ziwo piping,* or "self-criticism," and to accept any admonishment the army deemed necessary.

But then Wang added a new request: His military-issued passport was expiring, so could the army officials authorize him to receive a new passport—this time, a personal one? It may have been framed as a simple procedural matter, but the twenty-six-year-old soldier was, in effect, asking to be discharged from the army so that he could become a private citizen. Chinese soldiers and athletes traveling abroad are generally not allowed personal passports; they are issued official government "business" or "military" passports, which—even when not locked up safely by the team leaders—restrict their freedom to travel and curtail their ability to seek residency, employment, or citizenship in a foreign land. The personal passport would be Wang's insurance against being trapped in China, his guarantee that he could travel freely back to America.

The army balked at the last-minute demand. "Since you are still a PLA member, our regulations forbid you from having a private passport," read Bayi's curt response two days later. "When you come back to China and finish the formalities of retiring from the army, only then can you apply for a private passport." Clearly irked, Bayi leaders made no guarantees that Wang would be allowed to return to the NBA.

Two days later, Wang made another appeal, this time revealing a more controversial reason for wanting the personal passport: He was applying for a "green card" to live and work in America. The United States Immigration Service, from what he understood, didn't grant green cards to Chinese citizens bearing official government or military passports. Without a personal passport, Wang feared, his very right to remain in America would be endangered—a fear made more poignant by the fact that his wife was two months pregnant. Wang wanted his child to be born in the United States, where he or she would be entitled to all the rights and freedoms that come with owning a U.S. passport.

Wang's letter was met by silence. August 30 came and went, and Wang's homecoming never took place. A few days later, the CBA announced the national team's lineup for the Asian Championships. Wang's name was conspicuously absent.

Nobody was more disappointed by the failed attempt to return than Wang's parents, who hadn't seen their son in nearly two years. At the end of October 2003, however, the couple would have another chance when Wang traveled to Japan with the Clippers for two season-opening games against the Seattle Supersonics. Not wanting to raise suspicions in Beijing, Ren Huanzhen and Wang Weijun quietly arranged to join a Chinese tour group traveling through Japan—sticking to the official itinerary so faithfully that they missed the first game. On the night before the second game, however, the couple split off from the tour group and sped to Tokyo's Four Seasons Hotel to see their son. There, in the lobby of the posh hotel, Wang's family of three stood together and struggled to hold back their tears.

The reunion was fleeting and bittersweet, weighed down by the continuing shame of Da Zhi's predicament. Wang's parents could see that the turmoil of the previous sixteen months had taken a toll on their son. He had put on nearly twenty-five pounds since they had last seen him, and it wasn't all muscle. His face looked bloated, his arms almost flabby. Worst of all, he seemed defeated. The Clippers didn't seem to have much use for Wang, nor did any of the Chinese officials who traveled to Japan for the games. Wang was the only Chinese player there, but the CBA leaders refused to meet with him, and the spurned soldier implored nearly everyone else he met to intervene on his behalf.

The next night, Wang came off the bench briefly during the Clippers' second straight loss, scoring two points in four minutes in a performance that, in any other circumstance, would have been called meaningless. But with their son banished from the national team—and banned from Chinese television—Wang's parents had been waiting nearly two years for those four minutes.

Less than three weeks later, the Clippers dropped Wang from their roster, barely a year into his three-year, $6-million contract. Disappointed in his performance and desperate for point guards, the Clippers' coaches relegated Wang to the injured-reserve list, telling him that he had no real prospects of playing a significant role again. Wang's agent told him other teams might be interested in picking up his option, so he decided to leave rather than be stuck in purgatory. That day, Wang cleared out his locker, mumbled a few good-byes, and left the building. Before shutting off his cell phone and retreating again into isolation, he had to make one last phone call. Yao Ming was visiting Los Angeles for a game against the Clippers, and the Chinese pair had made plans to go out to dinner that night. But Da Zhi was in no mood to show Yao around L.A. now. The reunion would have to wait.

The Chinese giant was so dazzled by the lights of Las Vegas that he didn't notice the furtive glances of the tourists gathering around him. Trying to unwind after a few days of intense training, the basketball sensation had just taken a ride on the roller coaster atop the Stratosphere tower—he was lucky the ride had no maximum height requirement—and now he was gazing out over the gaudiest stretch of urban landscape in America. He marveled at the brightly illuminated replicas of the Eiffel Tower, the Manhattan skyline, the fountains of Rome. "Las Vegas is the most beautiful city in the world," he said. "Especially at night."

A red-faced American tourist broke the reverie.

"Hey, Yao Ming!" the man shouted. "Yao Ming, you da man!"

It was the last thing the Chinese athlete wanted to hear. He gave a tight smile and then, as politely as he could, he recited one of the few English phrases he had committed to memory.

"I am *not* Yao Ming."

Maybe not. But Yi Jianlian has gotten used to the lofty expectations. A lot of people on both sides of the Pacific are hoping that the 6'11" teenager from southern Guangdong Province will be the next Yao Ming. Ever since Yao burst into prominence, hordes of agents, scouts, and shoe-company reps have descended on China looking for a player to follow in Yao's large and lucrative footsteps. Yi wears size 18 shoes, just like Yao. But it is the glimmer of his potential—the explosive slam dunks, the gazelle-like quickness, the boyish good looks—that has catapulted him, at least commercially, beyond where Yao stood at this point in his career. "There is only one Yao Ming," says Yi (pronounced "ee"), his hooded eyes fixed on the floor after a workout at Guangdong's main sports academy. "I don't like being compared to him. I just want to be myself, and hopefully, I can make it [to the NBA] someday, too."

Operation Yao Ming, the sequel, promises to be no less tortured and tumultuous than the original. Any casual observer might assume that Yao's success would open the door for future Chinese players. But nothing follows such a simple linear path in China, especially when it comes to the country's interactions with the outside world. In many ways, Yao's journey, coupled with the experience of his tragic foil, Wang Zhizhi, has dramatically raised the stakes in the struggle over the next generation of Chinese players, who must still negotiate the perils of the country's constrictive sports system.

Nearly everything about Yi Jianlian—even the truth about his age—has been kept under tight control since he was first discovered in 1999 in the southern boomtown of Shenzhen, just across the border from Hong Kong. The son of two former athletes—his 6'5" father and 5'8" mother were both recruited to play team handball—Yi was barely out of grade school, but he already stood 6'4". His parents, both postal workers, wanted more for their son than the hardship of the sports system. And Yi himself was more interested in watching cartoons. But even in Shenzhen, one of the freest, most capitalist cities in China, the authorities made them feel as though they had little choice.

Within two years, Yi had sprouted into a fleet-footed 6'11" leaper who could touch a spot more than 11'6" off the ground. As Yi developed into a credible mid-range jumper—and fell in love with the slam dunk in all its glorious forms—the shoe companies were the first to come calling. In the summer of 2002, Adidas flew Yi to New Jersey to join America's best high-school players at its ABCD all-star camp. He was the only Chinese player there.

By the following spring, the "Yao Ming Effect" had fully taken hold. Scouts, agents, and shoe-company reps flocked to Yi's games with the CBA's Guangdong Tigers. The taciturn teenager was the first to admit he wasn't quite ready for prime time. "I'm too young and skinny," he said after practice one day, the baggy denim shorts and triple-XL Nike shirt hanging off his narrow frame only reinforcing his point. Before the 2004–05 season, in fact, Yi had only played two seasons in the CBA, and he'd never started a single game for the powerful Guangzhou team. Nevertheless, in the Tigers' final regular-season game in 2003, Yi gave his suitors a glimpse of his potential when he came off the bench to score thirteen points in five minutes, sealing an overtime victory. At the team's post-game meal, agents and sneaker reps crowded around Yi in a local restaurant, toasting him with Tsingtao beer until his face turned beet red.

Yi Jianlian is hardly the only emerging prospect in the Middle Kingdom. Several other youngsters have also started setting off the NBA's Geiger counters. A rail-thin 7'0" center named Xue Yuyang, for example, was chosen by the Dallas Mavericks in the second round of the 2003 NBA draft, but Beijing—rankled by his decision to participate without official permission—has so far refused to let the twenty-three-year-old go to America. Another prospect qualified as one of the tallest human beings on the planet: At a staggering 7'8" twenty-one-year-old Sun Mingming was nearly three inches taller (and, sadly, three steps slower) than Yao Ming, and he hoped to be selected in the 2005 NBA draft.

But the only prospect, other than Yi, who has truly entranced the scouts is sixteen-year-old prodigy Chen Jianghua, a 6'1" ball-handler whose gravity-defying 360-degree dunks look like something out of a Jet Li movie. If Yi is next in the procession of big men produced by the old socialist sports system, Chen represents something absolutely new in China: a normal-size player with flair, imagination, and a touch of rebelliousness—qualities that, though not embraced by the authorities, may help him become China's first world-class point guard.

One of the more puzzling conundrums in Chinese sports is that a vast, basketball-mad nation with an average male height of 5'7" has produced three seven-foot giants capable of playing in the NBA—but not a single point guard. The sports system's fifty-year obsession with cultivating big men has shut out talented youngsters who happened to be too short to make the cut. (If a Chinese recruiter had seen some of the NBA's best point guards as kids—think Allen Iverson, Tony Parker, even 5'5" Earl Boykins—he wouldn't have given them a second glance.) As a result, many Chinese point guards land in their position by default, when their bodies fail to reach their predicted heights, and their primary role is simply to bring the ball upcourt and feed it to the big men inside.

The deeper failure, however, is not physical but psychological. Chinese athletes are given little if any freedom to think for themselves, on or off the court. Any sense of spontaneity or creativity, two crucial in-gredients for a point guard, is usually lost at an early age. The NBA's best court generals, such as Parker or Jason Kidd, make tactical deci-sions on the fly, sensing when to speed up or slow down the tempo, when to create off the dribble or dish off to a teammate. But in China, where the only generals are the coaches on the sidelines—and the bu-reaucrats in their VIP seats—point guards are constantly glancing to-ward the bench for direction or approval.

If Chen Jianghua seems free of those psychological shackles, it is largely because he came to the game out of passion, not obligation. Nobody, after all, ever expected the little kid from a coastal village in Guangzhou Province to play basketball. Neither of his parents were athletes, and his father—a fisherman of modest means—only seemed amused when his son, age six, started taking a basketball with him wherever he went, curling his body around it when he slept at night. A supportive uncle delivered Chen, at age ten, to a powerful sports school in Guangdong, several hours from home. The school coach's initial skepticism gave way to delight when he saw that the scrawny fisherman's kid not only ran faster and jumped higher than his other players; he also displayed a fearless intensity inspired by watching NBA games on television. In an unusual move for a Chinese official, the coach loosened the reins, giving Chen a rare measure of freedom to forge his own style.

Chen's big debut came only two years later, not on a sports-school team but, fittingly, in the 2001 national finals of a Nike-sponsored three-on-three tournament in Shanghai. With hip-hop music thumping in the background, the thirteen-year-old—now 5'11"—used his full array of dunks and street-ball moves to take home the trophy and win a trip to the United States. "The kid was so skinny and shy," recalls Terry Rhoads. "But put a ball in his hand and he transformed in front of your eyes. He would dart into the lane and then, when he went air-borne, it was like ballet. There's no way you can teach that. I kept rub-bing my eyes and asking myself: Is he really Chinese?"

The spiky-haired point guard is, in fact, the very image of the new China. Cool, irreverent, and the possessor of a style all his own, Chen is less like the dutiful cogs in the socialist sports machine than the rest of China's urban youth, the first generation in the People's Republic to have some freedom to choose how they live, work, spend, and express themselves. For some, that means studying English, drinking Starbucks coffee, or wearing knockoff Fubu clothes. But for millions of Chinese youth, it has led to the embrace of the ultimate emblem of American hipness: NBA basketball. Fan surveys show that basketball has zoomed past soccer as the most popular sport in China's urban areas, with men under twenty-five preferring hoops by more than two to one. Basketball is so popular in China these days that one can find a game almost everywhere, from a makeshift hoop in a *longtang*, or traditional Shanghai alleyway, to the court just inside the entrance to Beijing's Forbidden City, where guards play two-on-two during their breaks.

But nothing captures China's passion for basketball more than the most famous street-ball venue in Beijing, a cluster of public courts built by Nike just down the road from Tiananmen Square known as Dongdan. Even on one recent winter afternoon, as the mercury plunged toward freezing, the courts were packed with youngsters who had paid fifteen yuan ($1.90) for admission. The quality of play was uneven at best—few of the players have ever had formal training—but the kids trying to bust NBA-style moves in their retro jerseys provided a sharp, almost subversive contrast with the robotic players going through the motions at the sports schools.

The coolest kid on court that day was Jiang Yunjie, a sixteen-year-old ball handler with a sweatband around his newly shaved head and a stutter-stepping style all his own. When asked about NBA role models, the 6'1" Jiang and his friends politely dismissed Yao Ming. They admired the Shanghai center for being the first Chinese to succeed in the NBA, but they had a hard time identifying with him: He was too tall, too square, too *establishment*. Their favorite player was Yao's polar opposite: Allen Iverson. "Iverson is my size, but he plays harder than anybody else and he takes on big men without any fear," said Jiang. His mobile phone rang, blaring a tinny hip-hop beat, and his buddies finished the thought: From the cornrows to the run-ins with authority figures, Iverson was the rebel, the nonconformist who could fly above the crowd and will himself to win. In their world, that was the ultimate liberation.

Chen Jianghua, the 6'1" fisherman's son, has more than a little of the young Iverson about him, and it isn't just the pogo-stick legs that propel his explosive forays to the hoop. He has also shown disregard, even disdain, for Chinese coaching. When Chen returned from his Nike-sponsored trip to the United States in 2002, he loafed through the regimented Chinese training, straying from set plays, lagging on defense, skipping practices with phantom injuries. His disappointed coach on the Guangdong junior team, Zheng Zhenming, steered visitors away from the sixteen-year-old prodigy. "Don't waste your time talking to him," Zheng advised. "He never listens to our coaching, and he's too lazy to ever make anything of himself."

Chen's problem, however, is not necessarily laziness. He's bored, un-challenged, a hoops Picasso trapped in a paint-by-number world. Guangdong has built the best basketball program in China—thanks to its deep pockets and heavy recruiting among northern children—but like most Chinese teams, its one-size-fits-all training pushes every player, centers and guards alike, through the same drills every day. Chen led the Guangdong junior team to an undefeated record in 2004, but all he really wanted was to play in America. "With point guards, it's more art than science," Rhoads told the *New York Times Magazine*. "Right now, the kid is painting his own canvas, using the paint that's available. But he needs more colors, and he can get them from overseas exposure."

Chen's best chance to brighten his palette would come via Bruce O'Neil, the congenial director of the United States Basketball Academy and de facto dean of Sino-American basketball relations. In 2004, after years of hosting Chinese teams and coaches at his woodsy Oregon hide-away, O'Neil approached Beijing with a novel plan: He wanted to en-roll a few young Chinese players in American high schools, providing them with a year or two of top-notch coaching and competition, along with an American education, before returning them safely to China. That kind of early exposure would lift the level of Chinese basketball and make it more competitive internationally, O'Neil argued. Just look at what happened in soccer: In the mid-1990s, Chinese authorities agreed to let a group of teenage players go to the mecca of soccer, Brazil, for five years of intensive training and competition. Those players now form the nucleus of the Chinese national team, and a couple, including defensive midfielder Li Tie, have made a name for themselves in the English Premier League.

The first candidate for O'Neil's experiment was Chen Jianghua. In the summer of 2004, the American coach made all the arrangements for Chen to become the first Chinese player to spend a high-school season in America. But as authorities in Beijing and Guangdong squabbled over who owned Chen's rights and, more importantly, whether he would ever return to China, the plan fizzled. "It remains the biggest fear for Chinese officials," says O'Neil. "They're afraid if they send their top talent to the U.S., [the players] won't come back."

Yi Jianlian's prospects were even murkier, for they hinged, in part, on the biggest mystery of all: his age. The national team roster listed Yi's birthdate as October 27, 1987, a date that Chinese basketball experts said was deliberately falsified to give him more years of eligibility for junior competitions. Insiders say Yi was actually born in 1984. The practice of "age-shaving" had haunted Wang Zhizhi, and now, nearly a decade later, it hovered over Yi, who, like Wang, presumably had no choice in the matter. If the 6'11" forward turned eighteen in October 2005, as the roster claimed, he would be considered one of the more enticing young prospects in the world. If he turned twenty-one, then his development, while impressive, lagged behind Yao and Wang. Even so, he would be automatically eligible to enter the NBA draft in 2006.

Nobody involved in Chinese basketball wanted to talk about Yi's age controversy, least of all Yi himself. His Guangdong coach declined to confirm or deny the age fraud, saying only that the 1987 birthdate appeared on Yi's official *hukou,* or residency permit. His parents both said publicly that he was born in 1987, but when pressed on the issue, his father smiled blankly without responding. Asked the same question in a private dinner in August 2003, Yi himself turned away and gazed at the patterned carpeting on the floor, filling the room with an uncomfortable silence. He snapped back to attention, however, when his out-of-town visitor explained the biggest consequence of the age manipulation: "Did you know that, according to NBA rules, you won't be eligible to enter the NBA draft without official permission until 2009?"

Yi shook his head forlornly.

"That's a long time," he said. He couldn't afford to say any more.

Yi Jianlian may not be the next Yao so much as the next Wang Zhizhi. In early 2005, as the controversy over Yi's age bubbled on Internet chat rooms, China's official Olympic Web site shifted his birth year from 1987 to 1984. There was no explanation for the sudden bout of truthfulness, and many observers took it as a hopeful sign that the CBA's new leader, Li Yuanwei, was putting an end to the practice of age-shaving. Even so, few people believed that Beijing would let its newest basketball giant go to the NBA anytime soon.

Chinese sports officials, in fact, are caught in the same conundrum that grips the nation as a whole. On one hand, they have an aching desire to show that the products of their system can compete with the best in the world, recognizing that this can only be accomplished by opening up to foreign influences and competition. On the other hand, they fear nothing more than losing control over their players and, increasingly, over their own domestic market. That contradiction was apparent in 2004, when the CBA, in a sign of openness, brought in its first foreign coach—Dallas Mavericks assistant coach Del Harris—to lead the national team in the 2004 Olympics. But when Harris suggested that the only way for China to compete for a medal in 2008 would be to expose its best players to world-class coaching and competition in the European leagues or the NBA, he was met with silence. Even Yao Ming, when asked if he agreed with his coach, refused to touch the sensitive issue.

The question of letting athletes leave China, of course, goes far beyond sports to the realms of politics, economics, and national pride. The Middle Kingdom has long been wary of foreign powers coming in to lay claim to its resources, conquer its markets, and influence its people. Whether the commodity was opium or religion, the fear has always been that the encounter with the West would leave the Middle Kingdom weakened, humiliated. Today, even as a newly powerful China emerges, the same suspicions remain about American basketball. "The CBA looks at the NBA as an imperialistic power," says Yao's manager Erik Zhang. "They see these Americans coming in to take away their best players and offering very little in return."

In public, Chinese sports officials embrace the NBA, vowing to learn from the world's slickest marketing operation to turn their domestic league into "an NBA with Chinese characteristics." Under its new director Li Yuanwei, in fact, the CBA is beginning to implement some NBA-style reforms, expanding the number of games, experimenting with trades, and chasing sponsors more aggressively. But some Chinese officials privately worry that the NBA, beyond purloining its best players, is also causing the nation's youth to turn its back on the domestic league and embrace the NBA's individualistic, hip-hop culture. CBA arenas these days are rarely more than half full—the Shanghai Sharks, in a city of sixteen million, are lucky to pull in one thousand spectators a game—and not a single CBA team turns a profit. Who can blame Chinese fans for staying home to watch the NBA on television rather than forking over forty hard-earned yuan (about five dollars) to see the Yaoless Sharks play the Zhejiang Horses?

Desperate to stop the hemorrhaging, Chinese authorities are in no mood to hand over any more top players to the NBA—especially if they ride the bench in the NBA when they could be anchoring the league in China or if, like Wang, they refuse to come home. The irony is that the CBA's reluctance to relinquish its best players has as much to do with capitalist markets as socialist control. The CBA wants to build its brand around future stars like Yi Jianlian.

All the uncertainty over Yi's future, however, has done little to slow the agents of globalization rushing into China to find the next Yao Ming. Back in the 1990s, Nike was so far ahead of the competition that it could cultivate Yao for years without signing him to a formal contract. In early 2003, however, it had to fend off four different rivals, including local brand Li Ning, to sign Yi to a six-figure, multiyear deal worth more than double Yao's original Nike contract.

A few months later, when Nike lost the frenzied negotiations over Yao, shell-shocked Beaverton executives lavished even more attention on Yi. They ordered up a slick television commercial and ad campaign featuring the untested teenager as the future of Chinese basketball—an ironic reversal for a company that neglected to produce any ads with Yao during his breakout season. In a Nike poster that stared out from the windows of sports shops across China in late 2003, Yi stood tall and solemn, with his arms defiantly crossed.

The clear message: *I'm next.*

Perhaps that's true—but next may be a long time coming.

20

The Flag-Bearer

When, as a young boy, Yao Ming traipsed off to the Gao'an Road No. 1 Elementary School—the only regular school he would ever attend—he longed for one thing above all: to raise the five-star Chinese flag in school ceremonies. Nobody in school earned more respect than the "Honored Flag-raisers," whom teachers chose on the basis of exceptional grades and model behavior befitting the ideals of the ostensibly Communist nation. The young Yao, however, had neither qualification. A mediocre student who showed no discernible leadership qualities, Yao sat up expectantly in the back of the classroom every week when his teacher appointed the flag-raiser. "I waited for five whole years, but I was never picked," Yao recalled. "The teacher's decisions were understandable. My academic performance was so-so and I was quite ordinary in every respect."

It would be many years before his wish came true—and by that time, the whole world could see that Yao was anything but ordinary. On the night of August 13, 2004, the Olympic Stadium in Athens, Greece, was bathed in an ethereal white light as the most symbolic moment in all of sports began: the parade of nations, when athletes from 202 countries spiraled around the track to mark the opening of the XXVIII Olympiad. China's 407-member delegation had barely entered the stadium that night when the seventy-five thousand spectators—and the estimated 3.9 billion television viewers around the world—could see the towering athlete hoisting the Chinese flag. With his bright red blazer, freshly cropped hair, and broad smile, Yao looked almost as if he were a schoolboy again, an "Honored Flag-raiser" at last. Even when all 10,500 athletes had formed a mass of sporting humanity in the center of the stadium for the fireworks display, Yao was the one who stood above the rest, the only athlete who could be clearly seen from all the way across the stadium—indeed, from across the world.

Nearly every nation, of course, appreciates the symbolism of the Olympics. But few countries invest the Games with more significance than China, which views its climb up the Olympic medal chart as a reflection of its inevitable emergence as a superpower. There could be no clearer sign of China's desire to stand tall—and its continuing obsession with height—than its choice of flag-bearer for the opening ceremony. China's sports system has produced hundreds of gold medalists in dozens of disciplines, and yet, none of them has ever carried the flag in the Games' opening ceremony. That role has been reserved for athletes who project an image of strength and stature vis-à-vis the rest of the world—athletes who can literally make the five-star flag fly just a little higher than every other nation's. In the six Summer Olympics in which China has participated since 1984, the flag-bearer in the opening ceremonies has always been a basketball player. The shortest was 6'8"; the tallest was Yao Ming.

Yao, of course, brought more to the role than just his height. He was already far and away China's most recognizable athlete and perhaps the most famous living Chinese person on the globe. The Beijing authorities, in selecting Yao, lauded his virtues as a role model who has made the successful leap to the West without losing the humility and team spirit of the East. "Yao is very tall and represents a positive image for Chinese athletes," said Xiao Tian, head of the Chinese delegation. "He is a man of integrity . . . the perfect flag-bearer."

Less than forty-eight hours later, Yao hardly seemed the model Chinese athlete. Near the end of an 83–58 thrashing by Spain in the first game of the tournament, the normally even-keeled center did something no Chinese athlete had ever done in international competition: He acted like an ugly American. During a time-out, Yao stormed off the court screaming at his teammates, waving his arms, and stomping his feet emphatically. Yao himself had played miserably, scoring just twelve points on 4-of-11 shooting while committing seven turnovers. But his teammates, he said, had just given up. They had stopped playing defense, ignored the coach's plays, and jacked up so many off-target threes that Yao, their star, had hardly seen the ball in the post all night.

After the game, Yao was still fuming. "I've lost all my hopes for this team," he told a reporter as he came off the court. "I think some of my teammates don't cherish the honor of playing for their nation." It had only been a few days since Yao was heaping praise on his teammates, especially the young Yi Jianlian. Like an ancient Chinese warrior, he vowed not to shave for six months if the team failed to make the top eight. But now, Yao was so infuriated that he even hinted that he might renounce his national-team obligations. "I am thinking about retiring from the national team," he said. "Maybe not right now, but soon I will."

Yao's outburst took nearly everybody by surprise. Could this be the same sweet-tempered center who had beamed like a schoolkid while carrying the flag in the opening ceremonies? Some Americans watching the game, including coach Del Harris, saw some benefit in Yao's show of assertiveness. It was the first sign of the toughness that NBA coaches had been trying to cultivate in Yao for two seasons. The inexperienced Chinese squad, moreover, needed somebody who could ignite their passion for the game. Yao was providing that spark; in the eyes of the Americans, he had finally become a leader.

Many Chinese, however, had an entirely different view of the new Yao. In a culture built on "saving face," Yao's public eruption broke all the rules of deference and decorum. At the postgame press conference, a Chinese television reporter almost scolded Yao: "Do you think this sort of behavior is appropriate?"

Yao rubbed his chin for a few seconds. Then, paraphrasing the revered Chinese writer Lu Xun, he responded with a sly smile: " 'If you don't explode the silence, you will die in the silence.' "

Within hours, the Chinese delegation to Athens issued a statement reprimanding their celebrated star. Chinese media carried interviews with unnamed sports officials who were apoplectic. "How could he say that?" one official asked. "Any irresponsible speech like his, any action to split the team, is definitely forbidden." Few Chinese readers could have failed to notice the verb "to split"—an old favorite in the Communist vernacular used to smear and eventually sideline enemies within the party.

Almost reflexively, some Chinese officials blamed Yao's disrespectful behavior on the corrupting influences of American culture, warning that they would be disinclined to send any more impressionable young Chinese players to the trash-talking NBA. When Yao first went to the NBA in 2002, one CBA official was quoted as saying he was "an obedient child" with a "very good reputation." "Now he has changed," the official said. "He's more like an American. He dares to say anything."

Yao's character hadn't really changed overnight. He was still, in most ways, the dutiful Chinese son eager to please his elders, earnestly struggling to balance the sometimes contradictory demands of his superiors in China and America. Yet by the summer of 2004, Yao was beginning to stake out his independence in small but significant ways. His increasingly American attitudes, in fact, were not so different from Wang Zhizhi's—except that, unlike Wang, Yao seemed to have the power and the personality to navigate the divide between East and West.

The first sign that Yao would start standing up for his own rights came early in the summer of 2003, when he filed a lawsuit against Coca-Cola for using his image in China—asking for total damages of one yuan, or about twelve cents. The symbolic lawsuit played into the running battle between Pepsi and Coke for supremacy in China. But it also pitted Yao against his bosses at the CBA. The Rockets' center, after all, had just signed an exclusive multimillion-dollar contract with Pepsi, while the national team, through the CBA, had a preexisting deal with Coca-Cola. In early 2003, Coke began to produce bottles and cans bearing the images of three national-team players—with Yao front and center, larger than the others. Yao's lawsuit, in effect, challenged the CBA's right to peddle his image. In this case, the individual prevailed over the state: Coca-Cola eventually issued an apology and stopped emblazoning cans with Yao's image.

Later that summer, Yao's quiet tug-of-war with the Chinese establishment intensified. Taking advantage of the center's newfound celebrity, the CBA hauled Yao and the national team around China on a grueling monthlong tour, in which they played nine games in nine provincial cities. Participating in meaningless games bothered Yao, but not nearly as much as being carted around like a circus elephant to please the tour's sponsors. He endured endless banquets and photo ops with obsequious businessmen, mob encounters with the provincial media, and the constant crush of star-struck fans who didn't let him sleep or eat in peace. At one provincial airport, fans even chased him into the bathroom with video cameras. When a reporter later asked him where he most wanted to go, Yao responded:

"The moon. Nobody is there."

Yao began to resist with his own brand of civil disobedience. One night shortly before the tour ended, he refused to attend a sponsor's banquet, opting instead to eat a lobster dinner in the privacy of his hotel room. On the day of the last game, in Hefei, the team bus took an unexpected detour and pulled up at the company headquarters of one of the sponsors, who wanted to have their photos taken with Yao and the team. The rest of the players trudged off the bus, but the star stayed in his seat, refusing to budge.

"Nobody told me!" Yao said.

"Get off the bus, Yao," his coach told him.

"I'm not getting off," he said.

It wasn't exactly a Rosa Parks moment. But by remaining in his seat, Yao became one of the first Chinese athletes to disobey his team leaders so flagrantly, causing them to lose face in front of important sponsors. When the players filed back onto the bus after the photo session, nobody said a word—but Yao had made his point. "Chinese men's basketball is not a circus," he told his friend, the journalist Yang Yi, "and I am not a clown."

Frazzled and exhausted, Yao was diagnosed with high blood pressure at the end of the summer, and he used what his advisors called his "temporary condition" to send a message to the authorities. "I always thought I could play in the NBA until I was thirty-five," he said, "but if I continue like this, every day of the NBA season, followed by Chinese training and all the off-court social activities, I won't have time to rest at all. Maybe I will have to retire at age thirty." For Yao, whose relentless schedule over the previous five years had contributed to a late-season swoon, this was not simply an idle threat, but a real possibility.

Before returning to Houston, Yao laid down some conditions for the Chinese authorities. He said he would play in no more than three domestic warm-up games with the national team in preparation for major tournaments, and he would not take part in any activity involving CBA sponsors unless he received fifteen days' notice. Modest demands, perhaps, but they marked one of the first times that an individual athlete has dictated the terms of his participation to Chinese sports authorities. "There has been a shift in power," says Yang Yi. "Before, the CBA completely controlled Yao, and he didn't want to do anything to upset them. Now he is testing the limits of their power."

Back in America, Yao tried to establish a modicum of independence as well. He still lived most of the time with his parents in Windsor Park Lakes, where, despite his request that the family hire a housekeeper, his mother insisted on doing his laundry and cooking all of his meals. But Yao also rented an apartment in downtown Houston for game days and nights, so he wouldn't have to battle traffic in his custom-fitted BMW 745—or deal with Da Fang's cloying attention. Yao's sidekick, the translator Colin Pine, rented his own place, too, so the two were no longer attached at the hip. Independence, though, didn't necessarily mean freedom. Both at home and on the road, Yao still spent most of his down time holed up in his room channel-surfing while his teammates hit the town. Reflecting on Yao's loneliness, Terry Rhoads said:

"If anyone in the NBA needs a posse, it's Yao." The pattern wouldn't change until another foreign giant, the exuberant thirty-eight-year-old Congolese center Dikembe Mutombo, joined the team in late 2004 and began coaxing Yao to join him for dinners out.

By the middle of his second NBA season, Yao's command of English improved to the point where he could speak directly with his coaches and teammates without relying excessively on Pine. The Rockets' new head coach Jeff Van Gundy, a dour workaholic with perpetual bags under his eyes, even banned the translator from team practices to accelerate Yao's progress. Soon the center was finding his own voice: yelling out plays, bantering with teammates, even engaging in some mild trash-talking. (The harshest would come when he warned Chicago Bulls center Tyson Chandler: "Watch out or I'll knock your mouthpiece down your throat.") Pine still translated for Yao during his encounters with American reporters, creating a much-needed buffer zone against the media. Yao's penchant for hiding behind his mother tongue even became a punch line on an episode of *The Simpsons*. When Yao's character, a guest on the show, pretended to speak only Mandarin, little Lisa Simpson challenged him: "Hey, I read you speak perfect English!" Yao replied: "Shut up, kid, I've got a good thing going."

On court, Yao had a pretty good thing going, too. Despite some ups and downs in his second season, he boosted his scoring average by four points to 17.5 points per game (including a pair of thirty-point masterpieces against Shaquille O'Neal), earned the starting position in his second straight All-Star Game (this time scoring sixteen points compared to just two in his first outing), and led the Houston Rockets to the first round of the playoffs (where they succumbed meekly to Shaq and the Lakers). Through it all, Yao handled himself with such grace and good humor that even Shaq allowed that Yao, though not yet his equal on court, was the one NBA player he respected enough not to "punk."

But Yao's progress was hardly fast enough to please his fans or critics. Despite his massive size, he still got muscled out of the lane too easily, stripped of the ball too frequently, and leaped over for dunks and rebounds by players more than a foot shorter than he. An unheralded rookie might have been forgiven for such shortcomings, but not a top draft pick who was supposed to revolutionize the game—and who had, moreover, just cashed in on his celebrity by signing a shoe contract worth up to $100 million. Yao was still one of the NBA's most productive centers, but opposing teams' fans jeered his every mistake and even loyal supporters wondered why his progress lagged behind other younger players such as the Phoenix Suns' musclebound center Amare

Stoudemire and the Miami Heat's Dwyane Wade. As Yao seesawed maddeningly between brilliance and mediocrity, he couldn't escape the NBA's most damning epithet: His game, critics said, was "soft." The very gentility that had endeared him to fans and advertisers, earning him tens of millions of dollars in endorsements, was ultimately hurting him on court.

Van Gundy did his best to unleash Yao's inner thug. The Rockets' pugnacious coach, who was notorious for having thrown himself into a couple of on-court melees, pushed Yao to be more aggressive, to throw his elbows around fighting for rebounds and fending off double teams. In team meetings, Van Gundy even chided the giant for crossing his legs like a lady. Yao may have been one of the NBA's most eminently coachable players—a hard worker who arrived at the gym first and left last—but this lesson didn't take. He could become more physical on court, but the mean streak didn't materialize.

Yao's passivity wasn't simply a function of personality, but also of the insulated atmosphere in which he had been raised. Being an athlete in China, Yao explained, was "like being a plant growing in a greenhouse." The Chinese sports system may have helped him to develop his skills, but it shielded him from the kind of harsh, competitive forces that most other athletes around the world face every day. Moving from that protective shell to the brutal NBA environment, Yao was caught, once again, in the contradictory middle ground between China and America. Although he reiterated his patriotic commitment to play for the national team, like Wang before him, he told friends that toughening up his game would require spending more time in the off-season training with his NBA peers in the United States—and less time going through the monotonous and uncompetitive grind of national team workouts. Yao showed a keen appreciation for the values he had learned in China—skill over strength, passivity over aggression, collective honor over individual achievement—but he realized they were no longer enough to help him reach his full potential. "I have to find a way to balance the two sides," he said.

In Athens, Chinese officials thought Yao had completely lost his equilibrium. The day after his outburst, CBA chief Li Yuanwei called Yao in for a private meeting. Whether out of respect for Li or a realization that his commercial success hinged on maintaining good relations with Beijing, Yao backed off his remarks about leaving the team. Li, meanwhile, quieted the government's rhetoric. "There has been a lot of media coverage of Yao Ming's outburst," Li said. "He just lost his cool and delivered his remarks in a fit of temper. I hope the media and the fans do not regard his words as too important. We shouldn't place too much pressure and excessive demands on Yao. After all, he is not a diplomat." Li didn't mention that the government itself had developed Yao to be just that: an ambassador-at-very-large for the glorification of the motherland. But the truth was that China couldn't afford to alienate its most famous international envoy; nor could Yao risk damaging his ties to Beijing. Li's soothing words defused the controversy, and Yao helped salve the wound two days later by scoring thirty-nine points in a 69–62 victory over New Zealand.

Full redemption wouldn't come for another week. On the brink of early elimination after lopsided losses to Argentina and Italy, the Chinese team faced two-time world champion Serbia-Montenegro. A win would put China in the final eight for only the second time in its Olympic history; a loss would send the team home in disgrace. With just seven minutes left, China trailed by seven points—as good as dead against a squad that boasted five NBA players and draft picks. But China chipped away, and Yao knotted the score with less than two minutes to play. A minute later, he calmly drained two free throws—giving him twenty-seven points—to cap a stunning, come-from-behind victory, 67–66. When the buzzer sounded, the Chinese players mobbed each other at center court, jumping up and down in uncharacteristic glee. At the center of it all was Yao, whose happiness seemed as profound as his frustration the week before.

Yao's heroics gave the Chinese men's basketball team its best finish (eighth) since Wang's Olympic debut in 1996. But they were a mere footnote to China's overall performance in Athens, which did not so much portend the rise of a superpower as trumpet its full-blown arrival. Back in 1988, China had won just five gold medals, compared to fifty-five for the Soviet Union and thirty-six for the United States. In Athens, China netted thirty-two golds, five more than the Russians and only three less than the Americans. The gold-medal haul surprised even Beijing authorities, who had sent a youthful delegation to Athens (323 of China's 407 athletes were first-time Olympians) as preparation for 2008, when the hosts truly want to shine. Now flush with confidence, Chinese officials whisper excitedly about surpassing the U.S. in gold medals in 2008—a feat that, coming on home soil, would be the nation's ultimate vindication.

Nevertheless, Beijing officials knew that one obstacle remained: shaking the perception that China competes in a parallel Olympics. U.S. and Chinese athletes rarely square off in gold-medal rounds because the two countries excel at completely different events. Whereas the Americans pile up gold medals in the prestige events—swimming, track and field—the majority of China's gold medals come in seven disciplines that are (except for the final two) considered minor sports in the West: table tennis, badminton, shooting, judo, weight lifting, diving, and gymnastics. In Sydney, twenty-six of China's twenty-eight gold medals came in those seven sports; in Athens, twenty-two of thirty-two. Heartened by its success in a few more mainstream sports—with golds in women's tennis, swimming, and volleyball—China desperately wants to prove that it can compete directly with the West in the Olympics' limelight events.

It was no accident, then, that China's biggest hero in Athens was 110-meter hurdler Liu Xiang, who raced to the gold (and tied the world record of 12.91 seconds) in a prime-time track event long dominated by black athletes. The Chinese media, who peddle the widely held belief that genetic shortcomings leave Asians at a disadvantage in short-distance events, dubbed Liu "The Yellow Bullet." The playful 6'2" Shanghai native himself called his gold medal a victory for "all people who share the same yellow skin color." Later, he told reporters: "I think we Chinese can unleash a yellow tornado on the world."

No moment will symbolize China's stunning rise more potently than the 2008 Olympics. The Games' long-awaited arrival in Beijing, coming a full century after YMCA missionaries first issued their challenge, will mark China's return as a global superpower, a nation that has leaped from the darkness of the Cultural Revolution to the bright lights of the world's center stage in a single generation. The Olympics have always been freighted with political meaning, and national pride naturally surges in host countries. But predictably, given the size of its population and historical ambitions, China has taken it to another level. Beijing is throwing the full power of the central government into Olympic preparations, clearing away huge swaths of the city's historic neighborhoods with an authoritarian flick of the hand to make way for billions of dollars in fanciful new stadiums and highways. The prestige of the nation—one-fifth of the world's population—seems to hinge on that single fortnight in August 2008. By staging a successful Olympics that showcases the country's "peaceful rise" (and erases a darker history), the leaders hope to prove to the world—and to their own people—that this truly is China's century.

The star of this global coming-out party will, almost inevitably, be Yao Ming. Other athletes such as hurdler Liu Xiang are immensely popular in China, but Yao alone is a global icon, famous both at home and abroad, an instantly recognizable embodiment of China's emergence in the world. Moreover, as Beijing prepares to dazzle the world with its development, the nation's sports authorities seem eager to excel in basketball, a "big ball" sport with not only deep roots in the Middle Kingdom but also future import as the quintessential global game. Eighth place will not be good enough this time around. Chinese authorities are already promising the country's first-ever men's basketball medal in 2008—and the pressure will be on their 7'6" center to lead the way.

The mandarins in Beijing will not be the only ones counting on Yao in 2008. So, too, will the moguls of corporate America. The Beijing Olympics will arrive just as Yao, at age twenty-seven, reaches his prime both as a player and as a pitchman, a moment when his endorsement income alone could rise to more than $100 million. His day job shouldn't be paying him badly either. In 2006, the Houston Rockets—or another NBA club with deeper pockets—are expected to sign him to a multiyear deal that NBA insiders say could be worth close to $100 million. The figure—staggering for anyone, much less a family that earned barely $1,000 a year a decade ago—will reflect not only Yao's steadily growing value as a player, but the pipeline into China he gives teams and their sponsors. Team Yao, however, is already looking ahead to 2008. "Beijing is the big day, the pinnacle of Yao's earning power," says Bill Sanders, who handles marketing for Team Yao. "The world will be watching."

The multinationals responsible for turning Yao into a global brand are pursuing their own kind of gold in 2008. PepsiCo Inc. hopes Yao can give the company enough fizz in China to surpass archrival Coca-Cola. McDonald's, which dropped Kobe Bryant during his 2004 rape trial in favor of the clean-cut Yao, is depending on its "first-ever worldwide ambassador" to inspire Chinese youth to wolf down more Big Macs, or *juwuba*, as they are known in Mandarin. With the local hero on board—and its designation as the "Official Restaurant" of the Olympic Games—McDonald's hopes to close the gap with market leader KFC, nearly doubling its number of outlets (to about one thousand nationwide) before the Games' opening ceremonies.

Perhaps no company is banking more heavily on Yao than Reebok. After wresting him away from Nike in late 2003, Reebok CEO Paul B. Fireman said the company planned to ride the popularity of both Yao and the NBA (with whom it has a worldwide apparel agreement) to a 20 percent share of the Chinese athletic shoe and apparel market by 2008. The prediction was wildly optimistic, given that Reebok's meager

$25 million in annual sales in China constituted less than three percent of the $1 billion market, lagging far behind the big three in China—Nike, Adidas, and local firm Li Ning. So far, Yao has hardly been a silver bullet. Reebok's sales in China have climbed to about $40 million in the two years since signing him (and becoming the NBA's official apparel partner), but the company's share of the China market has actually declined. "The truth is," says one marketing consultant in Shanghai, "that few kids really want to 'Be like Yao.' They love him like a brother and follow his progress obsessively, but Yao is so big that nobody can imagine being like him."

There are times, of course, when even Yao can't fathom how he's gotten so big. Just as when he was a child growing up in Shanghai, shy and sensitive about his height, at times he now appears overwhelmed by the expectations placed on him from both sides of the Pacific. Even inside China, Yao can't escape the pressure as he navigates a country that is caught between two poles—one that is still closed, controlling, and fiercely nationalistic, and another that is increasingly open, competitive, and commercial. No realm is more affected than sports, which despite the economic experiment unleashed in other parts of Chinese society, has changed very little in the past fifty years. Even as tens of millions of Chinese shed the socialist work unit, the sports machine remains one of the last "womb to tomb" social structures, a relic of the past that continues only because it has been so successful. "It's sad, really," says Xu Jicheng, the Xinhua journalist. "Sports were the first area in which China could compete with the world, but they will be the last area to reform—more than twenty years after the rest of the country."

As a newly confident China flexes its muscles around the globe in more tangible ways—in business, politics, and diplomacy—sporting prowess is bound to lose a measure of importance as a barometer of national worth. But that almost assuredly won't happen before 2008. The prospect of hosting the Beijing Olympics has only intensified China's hunger for athletic glory—a hunger that will lock the system in place until at least 2009. "Winning the 2008 Olympics was the best news China could ever have received," says Big Xu. "But it was the worst news for the sports system, because it keeps it from reforming." Who wants to tinker with a proven gold-medal formula?

Yet sports cannot completely avoid the reality of a changing China. Even as they toil in unair-conditioned gyms and learn Communist slogans in ideology class, athletes in the new, commercially minded China have become marketable icons. China's state-run television, pressured in part by the rise of competitive provincial stations, no longer shy away from peddling sport as entertainment, even if patriotic paeans to Olympic champions are still a CCTV staple. Foreign and domestic companies are also descending on local sports heroes, signing them up for lucrative ad campaigns. Yao is hardly the only product of the cloistered system to encounter sudden wealth. There are dozens of others, in every sport from table tennis to soccer. Liu Xiang, for example, has signed several million dollars worth of new contracts with Nike and Coca-Cola. And Tian Liang, an Olympic gold-medal diver with movie-star looks, wasted no time after Athens to nab dozens of different endorsement contracts, including a seven-figure deal with a Hong Kong entertainment company.

The commercial embrace of top athletes has flummoxed China's control-obsessed sports leaders. An editorial in one state-run paper warned that excessive commercialization must be stopped because it was breeding avaricious athletes. But that's easier said than done. "These star athletes get a taste of freedom and wealth and they become a challenge to the state," says Terry Rhoads. "But it's hard to put the genie back into the bottle."

Not that the sports authorities aren't trying. Even with his newfound power as a global icon, Yao still hands over a healthy portion of his after-tax earnings to the Shanghai Sharks and the CBA—and he'll likely be doing so for the rest of his career. Track-and-field authorities, meanwhile, take about 40 percent of Liu Xiang's endorsement income. Tian Liang suffered far worse. The twenty-eight-year-old champion, nearing retirement, was kicked off the national team for letting commercial interests come before his commitment to the motherland. Team leaders apparently wanted to make an example of Tian because he had signed contracts without informing—or paying—the sports authorities. Tian's fellow diver, Athens gold-medalist Guo Jingjing, received a similar reprimand, but she saved her spot on the team by humbling herself in a tearful "self-criticism" in which she professed: "I belong to the nation."

Tian, like Wang Zhizhi before him, made no such show of obeisance.

A few minutes before game time on the evening of October 14, 2004, Yao Ming walked alone to center court in Shanghai's jam-packed sports stadium. The crowd went silent, and Yao's voice trembled into the microphone: "Welcome to the NBA China Games." So began the grand convergence that the sports world had been anticipating, the night Yao returned home to headline the first NBA games ever played on Chinese soil. The preseason contests between Yao's Houston Rockets and the Sacramento Kings would not count in the official standings. But a pair of meaningless games never meant so much. For a basketball-mad nation (China) and a China-obsessed league (the NBA), this was a seminal event—not simply a chance to enhance their prestige and profits, but the moment when the world's fastest-growing sports enterprise finally made landfall in the world's fastest-growing market.

And Yao alone united the two worlds.

Standing at center court in his red Rockets' warm-up suit, the crew-cut giant bowed his head as he made his brief welcoming speech, as if he were suddenly aware of the magnitude of the moment or the size of the audience (tens of millions of television viewers in 176 countries). But as the twenty-four-year-old glanced around that night, he may simply have been overtaken by a simple realization: The stadium was filled with nearly everyone who had ever played a significant role in Operation Yao Ming, both in China and the United States.

Directly in front of Yao, sitting in the stadium's most prominent courtside seat, was Yao's mother, Fang Fengdi, a simple woman whose life, even more than her son's, embodied China's metamorphosis. Dressed in a stylish gray pantsuit, Da Fang was flanked on one side by her gently smiling husband, Yao Zhiyuan, and on the other by Erik Zhang, the pudgy business-school graduate who was trying to parlay Team Yao's success into a marketing business on the mainland. The public-address announcer for the game that night was none other than Xia Song, the former Nike pit bull who was now one of China's most ambitious sports entrepreneurs. Further up in the stands, Bill Duffy—now one of the NBA's hottest agents—watched the proceedings in wonder with his eldest son and the rest of Team Yao, while across the stadium sat his former adversary: Li Yaomin, the Shanghai Sharks' manager who had once held Yao's fate in his hands but was now struggling, once again, to fill the half-empty Sharks' stadium. Terry Rhoads, the former Nike evangelist whose new company, Zou Marketing, was angling to get a piece of Yao's business in China mingled before the game with Madame Liu Yumin, the CBA official who had first opened the Chinese game to foreign influences—and whose lifelong friendships with Da Fang and Wang Zhizhi's mother had endured every twist and turn.

At the center of it all, perched on the seat of honor in the red-carpeted VIP section, was David Stern. The globally minded NBA commissioner had been working toward this day for more than two decades, ever since he first invited the Chinese national team to tour America in 1985. "That trip and this trip," Stern said, "are the perfect bookends to my career." The outcome of the game that night—an 88–86 Rockets victory in which

Yao scored fourteen points—wouldn't matter to Stern nearly as much as the fact that the game took place at all. This, after all, was the event he had been awaiting for twenty years, the game that would finally break open the China market for the NBA.

One pivotal figure in Yao's life, though, wasn't present: Wang Zhizhi. Four nights earlier, the two old rivals had exchanged greetings before the Rockets' preseason game against the Miami Heat. For all the emotional turmoil Wang had been through, he seemed reconciled at last to his life in America. After failing to get reinstated on the Chinese Olympic team the previous summer, the 7'1" center worked harder than he ever had in his life to earn a spot on the Heat roster as a backup for Shaquille O'Neal, who had been traded to Miami in the off-season. Hindered by his weak defense, Wang would rarely get off the bench, and he would not make the Heat's playoff roster. Even when an injury to Shaq gave him a couple of chances to shine, Wang still had no assurance that his stint in Miami would last beyond the season. Even so, the erstwhile soldier exuded a rare serenity, perhaps borne of something more meaningful than the nation he felt had deserted him.

In April 2004, Wang's wife, Song Yang, had given birth to a baby boy. The child, not unlike two infants born in China more than two decades before, was far bigger than the other newborns in the hospital. But the proud father quickly laughed off any suggestion that his son would be an athlete. "I won't force him to play basketball," he said, smiling. "Whatever he does, he will surely achieve more than I have achieved—but it will all depend on his own interests."

Wang may have sounded like any new father, dreaming of all the possibilities open to his son. But for a man with his family history, the statement was extraordinary. Both of Wang's parents—and Wang himself—had been recruited into the Chinese sports system because of a quirk in their genetic makeup. Perhaps their selection was an honor, and it could be argued that it ultimately improved the quality of their lives. But being an athlete wasn't their choice. Since then, hundreds of millions of Wang's countrymen have started to follow paths of their own choosing, enjoying more freedom than they've had at almost any time in Chinese history. But that independence does not extend to the sports system, where the most genetically gifted young girls and boys still sacrifice their own dreams for the aspirations of the motherland.

In Wang's family, at least, that cycle would now be broken. In a statement that angered many Chinese back home, Da Zhi proudly announced that his son, Wang Xilin, was American and hastened to give him an American name: Jerry. When Jerry grows up, with the U.S. passport that is his birthright, his life will be his own. No matter how tall he grows, he won't be forced to dribble a basketball nor will he struggle with the torturous dilemma his father still faces, where the desire to prove himself against the best in the world—the very desire that drives his nation—can be considered an act of betrayal.

From the beginning, it was always supposed to be the two of them—two children of destiny, one from Beijing, the other from Shanghai—who would make the leap to America and build a bridge between two cultures. Yao Ming and Wang Zhizhi had both made the journey, but only one had found his way back home. In the end, it was Yao, not Wang, who was the loyal soldier, the obedient son, the towering icon who made Chinese feel good about themselves and their nation's place in the world. Wang, on the other hand, was an historical footnote, a far more complicated symbol of what can happen even in contemporary China when an individual's wishes are at odds with the state.

Yao Ming's future, unlike Wang's, will almost assuredly be lived between two worlds. With the power he has gained and the diplomatic skills he has developed, it's unlikely he will be forced to choose between China and America. To some extent, Yao owes this freedom to his old rival, who, in frightening the sports authorities, also pushed Beijing to show more flexibility toward Yao—if only so they wouldn't be put in a position to lose another national treasure. ("I have paved a bloody path, haven't I?" Wang said ruefully when asked about his role.) Yao knows that Wang's tragic slide into invisibility—his rival's name has nearly been erased from the nation's collective memory—has only intensified his own rise. Had Wang returned to China, the blessings and burdens of stardom might have been shared more equitably. But now, even as Yao's ambivalence about bearing the hopes of his nation grows, he will be asked to shoulder a load that is heavier with each passing year. And he will be carrying it all alone.

In many ways, Yao's life revolves around a search for the golden mean. He says he doesn't want to become an American citizen, but he now has a green card, and he can't help becoming more Americanized with every season he spends in the NBA. He respects China's aspiration to stand tall as a nation, but he feels free enough to suggest that children shouldn't be forced to play sports just to feed that desire—and that sports themselves should be seen as more than just a symbol of national pride. "We shouldn't entirely get rid of the nationalism, but I do think that the meaning of sport needs to change," Yao told the *New Yorker* in 2003. "I want people in China to know that part of why I play basketball is simply personal." With his expanding sense of personal power, many Chinese wonder what will happen if he and his longtime girlfriend, 6'3" Ye Li, decide to get married and have children, as most suspect they will. Will they have more than one child? And will Yao want them to be Chinese or American—or both?

For now, the only certainty is that Yao will continue to be an oversize symbol on both sides of the Pacific. Already he's the most famous living Chinese person in the United States. And as China's first NBA star, he is a conduit for American business and sports coming to the Middle Kingdom. On Nanjing Road, where the Red Guards—including Yao's mother—used to march their humiliated prisoners, loudly denouncing their "capitalist crimes" and "foreign connections," there was no more ubiquitous capitalist brand during the NBA's October 2004 visit than Yao Ming himself. His somber, lantern-jawed face stared out from a succession of China Unicom posters pushing mobile phones. His broad, American-style grin beamed from a McDonald's outlet, giving new meaning to the phrase "Supersize me!"

Nothing could compare, however, to the display outside the Portman Ritz-Carlton Hotel at No. 1376 Nanjing Road—just a mile down from Da Fang's old training grounds—where a gigantic Reebok advertisement featuring Yao in action rose nearly seven stories above the crowded street. The photograph curved around the luxury hotel's entire facade, giving every passerby a view of China's biggest export grabbing a muscular rebound above the trees.

There was one more telling detail. Yao's colossal image on the Ritz-Carlton literally dwarfed the grandly pillared building directly across the street, the former Sino-Soviet Friendship Building that stood as a monument to China's early Communist benefactors in Moscow, the very people who gave the People's Republic the sports system that has endured half a century. Here, across a street resonant with history, was the ultimate encounter of Communism and capitalism, of past and future, of East and West—with Yao himself presiding over the scene.

END NOTES

This book originated in a series of stories that I wrote for *Newsweek* magazine between 2000 and 2003. Although the narrative is based on years of personal interviews and research, several external sources have proven invaluable in fleshing out the full story. The following notes are meant to serve as a brief guide to supplementary material not self-evident in the book.

PART I

1. Birth of a Giant

For insights into China's sports history, I benefited greatly from conversations with Andrew Morris, whose excellent book, *Marrow of the Nation: A History of Sport and Physical Culture in Republican China* (Berkeley: University of California Press, 2004), traces China's quest to become a modern state through athletics. Judy Polumbaum's article, "From Evangelism to Entertainment: The YMCA, the NBA, and the Evolution of Chinese Basketball" (*Modern Chinese Literature and Culture,* Spring 2002), provided the quote from Max J. Exner, along with useful background about basketball during the late Qing dynasty and the Communist Army's Long March. M. V. Ambros's letter to James Naismith and basketball sage Bai Jinshen's comments were cited in Alexander Wolff's delightful book, *Big Game, Small World* (New York: Warner Books, 2002). Also helpful was Chip LeGrand's August 19, 2000, piece in the *Weekend Australian*, "China: Socialism and Sport, Children of the Revolution." Some details of Yao's early family history came from Xiao Chunfei's *Yao Ming Zhilu [Yao Ming's Journey]* (Beijing: China Intercontinental Press, 2003).

2. Red Guard Rising

Stella Dong's *Shanghai: The Rise and Fall of a Decadent City* (New York: Perennial, 2000) offers the best account of the city's rip-roaring, prerevolutionary history. Robert Urquhart's famously shortsighted speech appeared on the "Tales of Old China" Web site. Especially helpful in providing background on the Cultural Revolution in Shanghai were Elizabeth J. Perry and Li Xun's *Proletarian Power: Shanghai in the Cultural Revolution* (Boulder, Colorado; Westview Press, 1997) and Nien Chang's *Life and Death in Shanghai* (New York: Penguin, 1988).

3. Mao's Fallen Star

For background on the debate over eugenics and China's one-child policy, I found helpful Steven Mufson's "China Plans to Restrict 'Inferior' Births," the *Washington Post*, Dec. 22, 1993; Kathy Wilhelm's "China Defends Law for 'Better Births,'" *Associated Press*, Dec. 29, 1993; and Graham Hutchings's *Modern China* (Cambridge, Mass.: Harvard University Press, 2000).

4. Childhood Denied

Orville Schell's *Mandate of Heaven* (New York: Simon & Schuster, 1994), offers fine insights on Deng Xiaoping and his ambitious reforms. The editorial citing the importance of gold medals came from *Sports Daily* and was quoted by R. Wilkinson in the *International Herald Tribune*, Dec. 5, 1980. The "Ten Rules for Athletes" appeared in *People's Daily* in April 1981. Jean Loup Chappelet's "The Emergence of a Sports Giant" (*Olympic Review*, #174, April 1982) gave insights into China's gold-medal strategy. Hannah Beech's Dec. 17, 2001 article in *Time*, "High Hopes," offered details about leg-lengthening operations and China's continuing obsession with height. Some material on the early history of Yao Ming and Wang Zhizhi appeared in my *Newsweek* story, "Dreams Deferred," April 10, 2000. The article about Yao's fourth birthday appeared on Sept. 14, 1984 in *Xinmin Evening Post*, "A Little Pearl of a Basketball Family," by Jiang Jiafeng and Zhang Jingsheng. The journalist Yang Yi told me the milkman story, which he also included in his book, *Huojian Cuansheng de Yao Ming [Yao Ming, the Rising Rocket]* (China Unicom, 2004). Further details about Yao's first shot in elementary school came from Xiao Chunfei's *Yao Ming Zhilu*.

5. Cogs in the Machine

Several books and articles supplemented my firsthand research on China's sports system, including Zhao Yu's unusually frank critique, *Qiangguo Meng [Superpower Dream]* (Dangdai, 1988); Susan Brownell's *Training the Body for China: Sports in the Moral Order of the People's Republic* (Chicago: University of Chicago Press, 1988); and *Sport and Physical Education in China*, edited by James Riordan and Robin Jones (New York: Routledge, 1999). Other helpful early pieces include Trip Gabriel's April 24, 1988, article in the the *New York Times Magazine*, "China Strains for Olympic Glory"; two *Sports Illustrated* special reports, one on August 15, 1988 ("An Old Dragon Limbers Up"), another on October 16, 1995 ("The China Syndrome"); and a series in the *Atlanta Journal-Constitution* in April 1994 entitled "China's Olympic Obsession."

6. The Experiment

China's doping crisis in the mid-1990s yielded a flood of articles; among the most illuminating was Elliott Almond and Rone Tempest's Feb. 12, 1995, piece in the *Los Angeles Times*, "The Crooked Shadow." For details on the exploits of Ma Junren's Family Army, I relied on several sources, including Zhao Yu's investigative book on the controversial track coach and Jeff Hollobaugh's Dec. 4, 1993, piece in *Track & Field News*, "A Giant Awakens." Also helpful in understanding the role of science and medicine in China's sporting culture were Randy Starkman's Jan. 16, 1998, article in the *Toronto Star*, "China drug syndrome"; Jeremy Page's dispatches for *Reuters,* including "China Asks What's in the Turtle's Blood?" (Sept. 4, 2004); and two articles by Hannah Beech in *Time*—"Ma's Army" (Sept. 27, 1999) and "Rocky Road" (Sept. 18, 2000).

PART II

7. NBA Dreams

David Stern related details of his first bewildering visit to China during an interview in his Manhattan office on Feb. 25, 2003. His comment about modeling the NBA on Disney appeared in E. M. Swift's *Sports Illustrated* profile, "From Corned Beef to Caviar" (June 3, 1991). Stern's oft-told "red oxen" anecdote appeared in, among other places, Tim Povtak's Nov. 7, 1996 piece in the *Orlando Sentinel*, "NBA Seeks to

Cover the World." Walter LaFeber's fascinating book, *Michael Jordan and the New Global Capitalism* (New York: Norton, 1999) offers insights into how the NBA, Nike, and the sports industry went global. Ma Jian's bittersweet story is based on a series of personal interviews, although several articles—including a short Nov. 29, 1993 *Sports Illustrated* piece and Peter Hessler's Aug. 20, 2000 *Boston Globe* story, "China Blocks Hoopsters Eyeing the NBA"—provided useful background.

8. The New Evangelists

For background on Nike Inc., I found two books especially helpful. J. B. Strasser and Laurie Becklund's book, *Swoosh: The Unauthorized Story of Nike and the Men who Played There* (New York: Harper-Collins, 1991), recounted Phil Knight's first trip to Beijing. Donald Katz's equally useful, even if officially sanctioned, book, *Just Do It: The Nike Spirit in the Corporate World* (Holbrook, Mass.: Adams Media Corporation, 1994), gave a colorful glimpse of life "behind the berm." Katz's earlier profile of Nike in *Sports Illustrated*, "Triumph of the Swoosh" (August 16, 1993), mentioned the poll of Chinese schoolchildren that ranked Jordan ahead of Mao. Some details on foreign investments in China come from Joe Studwell's deliciously contrarian book, *The China Dream: The Quest for the Last Great Untapped Market on Earth* (New York: Grove Atlantic, 2002). The story of Yao's first game against Wang Zhizhi in 1997—including his bragging afterwards—were recounted to me by Yang Yi, who also included the anecdote in his book *Yao Ming, the Rising Rocket.*

9. Strangers in a Strange Land

Yao's comment about his aversion to dunking was cited in *ESPN The Magazine*, "Next Athlete: Yao Ming" (Dec. 25, 2000). One article that foresaw the East-West dilemma inherent in Yao's situation was Indira A.R. Lakshmanan's Jan. 16, 1999, piece in the *Boston Globe*, "China's Center of Attention."

10. The Gathering Storm

Michael Coyne's description of his efforts to bring North Korean center Ri Myong-hun to the NBA was supplemented by several articles, including Alexandra A. Seno's May 16, 1997, piece in *Asiaweek*, "The Giant from Pyongyang." The one contemporaneous story about the Evergreen deal was Jackie MacMullan's short piece in *Sports Illustrated*,

"Really Big Country: Ming Travesty" (May 11, 1999). Coyne recalled his dealings with Li Yaomin and Yao's family in several interviews and email exchanges with me, but other reports were also helpful, including Chris Tomasson's story in the *Akron Beacon Journal*, "Team Drafting Yao Might Miss the Boat" (May 19, 2002); Susan Vinella's article in the *Cleveland Plain Dealer*, "Bouncing Overseas for 'Big Men'" (July 29, 2001); and Dave D'Alessandro's piece in the *Newark Star-Ledger*, "As the Yao Affair Shows, Greed has no Boundaries" (April 15, 2001).

11. Mavericks and Mandarins

For background information on H. Ross Perot, Jr., I relied on several articles written at the time, including Allan Meyerson's July 11, 1999, *New York Times* profile, "A Son Rises In Texas." Perot's quote about not rebelling comes from Andrew Park's Feb. 18, 2002, story in *Business Week*, "Another Time, Another Ross Perot." Perot's first encounter with Wang was related by Steve McLinden in his Sept. 11, 2001, *Fort Worth Star-Telegram* piece, "Ross Perot Discusses Rationale behind Purchase, Sale of Dallas Basketball Team."

12. Hoop Diplomacy

The rivalry between Yao and Wang Zhizhi—and the East-West struggle over their fate—formed the basis of my April 30, 2001, report in *Newsweek*, "Basketball Diplomacy." Yao debuted as a hot international prospect in Alexander Wolff's *Sports Illustrated* cover story on China's three big men, "The Great Wall" (Sept. 10, 2000), and on the *ESPN The Magazine* cover, "Next Athlete: Yao Ming" (Dec. 25, 2000). Yao's comment about people eyeing him hungrily after the Olympics was cited in Yang Yi's book, *Yao Ming, the Rising Rocket*. The drama around China's Olympic bid also appeared in my Feb. 26, 2001, story in *Newsweek*, "Beijing's Olympic Moment." The detail about Donnie Nelson drooling over Yao Ming came from Randy Galloway's Jan. 21, 2003 article in the *Fort Worth Star-Telegram*, "Yao Wowed Little Nellie Early On."

13. The Battle for Yao Ming

Bill Duffy provided me with a copy of Yao Ming's blistering March 25, 2001 letter to the NBA Players Association. Details of the agents' turf war also appeared in Ron Thomas's series of articles in the *San Francisco Examiner* in March 2001. Ric Bucher's story in *ESPN The Magazine*, "Yeow!" (May 27, 2002), artfully described Yao's NBA audition in Chicago.

PART III

14. Soldier Gone AWOL

The *Dallas Morning News* article that frightened Wang appeared on June 6, 2002, "Mavs' Wang AWOL," by Jodie Valade. The message on Wang's answering machine was cited in the *Contra Costa Times* (California), "Missing: 7-foot-1 Maverick" (June 8, 2002). Wang's fears about the end of his NBA career appeared in *Titan Sports Weekly* on July 1, 2002, while his comments about his inability to think and decide for himself in China came in an interview with *All Sports Magazine* on Oct. 1, 2003. Journalist Su Qun offered the most thorough account of Wang's saga, both in interviews with me and in his articles in *Titan Sports Weekly*, including his Sept. 2003 piece, "Saving Private Wang."

15. Houston, We Have a Problem

Erik Zhang related the story of his confrontation with Bai Li over the Evergreen contract in an interview in Washington, D.C., February 27, 2003. Stern's ironic quote about Arvydas Sabonis was cited in Jonathan Feigen's June 7, 2002, *Houston Chronicle* piece, "Rockets Await Invite for Yao Discussions." Additional details from the June 22, 2002, Team Yao press conference came from *Oriental Sports Daily*, "Green Light from the Shanghai Sharks" (June 23, 2002).

16. Summer of Discontent

The CBA's July 26, 2002, letter to Wang was published in the Aug. 22, 2002 edition of *China Sports Daily*. The CBA's angry August 26, 2002, memo, "A Fact on Wang Zhizhi's Not Returning," was released that same day to various Chinese media, including *Life Daily*. Yang Yi's story on Wang's last desperate attempt to rejoin the team in Oakland, published in *Titan Sports Weekly*, prompted national sports authorities to threaten shutting down the newspaper. The editor managed to avoid that, but he did fine one editor 4,000 RMB—about a month's salary—for disobeying the state-ordered blackout on Wang stories. Mark Cuban's dismissive quote about Wang was cited in Dwain Price's Oct. 17, 2002 piece in the *Fort Worth Star-Telegram*, "Mavs, Wang Say 'Bye." Yao's comment about being squeezed by pressure from China and the United States came during an August 5, 2003, interview on China Central Television (CCTV).

17. In Da Club

A portion of my firsthand account of Yao's first weeks in Houston appeared in *Newsweek*, "High Hopes" (Issues 2003 special edition, Dec. 2002). During the season, I came to appreciate Jonathan Feigen's perceptive beat coverage in the *Houston Chronicle*, as well as Su Qun and Yang Yi's coverage in *Titan Sports Weekly*. The Web site, Yaomania.com, also provided wonderfully detailed descriptions of Yao's every move, which were especially helpful when I was back in China. Further details about Yao's first fender-bender in a Houston parking lot appeared in Ric Bucher's piece for *ESPN The Magazine*, "Yao Ming: American Idol." Bill Walton's comments on Yao Ming's cultural leap were cited in David Barron's *Houston Chronicle* column, "Walton: Rockets Must Handle Yao with TLC, but Let Him Learn," Nov. 15, 2002. Yao's angry reaction to Charles Barkley's wager was reported by *Titan Sports Weekly*, as was his friendly exchange with Shaq after the first game in Los Angeles.

18. American Idol

Shaquille O'Neal's stepfather Philip "Sarge" Harrison recited Yao Ming's Christmas card to Shaq live on ESPN during its Jan. 18, 2003, broadcast. Irwin Tang's piece criticizing Shaq for his apparent ethnic slur appeared in the Jan. 3–9 issue of *AsianWeek*. Yao's comment about looking down on physical strength came during an August 5, 2003, interview on China Central Television (CCTV), while his thoughts about crafting his media image—and seeking refuge on the moon—came from an interview with Wu Xiaoli that aired on Hong Kong's Phoenix Television on August 11, 2003. Charles Barkley's quote about the NBA's discomfort with black players appeared in Dan McGraw's article, "The Foreign Invasion of the American Game," in the May 28–June 2, 2003 edition of *Rolling Stone*. Ralph Frammolino's April 21, 2003, *Los Angeles Times* piece, "Nike Keeps Yao in Backcourt as Clock Runs Out on Its Deal," offered helpful background on Nike's reluctance to promote Yao during his rookie season. Yang Yi recounted details of the Nike-Reebok shoe wars, as did Peter Hessler's Dec. 1, 2003, article in the *New Yorker*, "Home and Away."

19. Generation Next

Wang's wry comment about the predictable plots of Hollywood movies appeared in a July 6, 2003, article in the *Pasadena Star-News*.

Su Qun helpfully recounted—both in interviews and in his *Titan Sports Weekly* stories—the details of Wang's last formal communication with his army superiors. Jeff Coplon's evocative Nov. 23, 2003, piece in the *New York Times Magazine*, "The People's Game," detailed Chen Jianghua's rise. For more on how basketball captures Chinese youth culture, see Andrew Morris, " 'I Believe You Can Fly': Basketball Culture in Postsocialist China," in *Popular China: Unofficial Culture in a Globalizing Society* (Lanham, Maryland: Rowman & Littlefield Publishers, Inc., 2002).

20. The Flag-Bearer

Yao's outburst in Athens was recounted in several different Chinese media. Geoffrey York's August 18, 2004, article in the *Toronto Globe and Mail*, "Chinese Officials Jump on Yao Over Remarks," was the most thorough Western account of the controversy. Yao's recollections about never getting picked to raise the flag in primary school came from an August 13, 2004, *Xinhua News Agency* story, "Yao Ming Realizes Olympic Dream."

ACKNOWLEDGMENTS

Where to start? So many people have been indispensable to the creation of this book that it's hard to know whom to thank first. Perhaps it's only fitting, then, to begin with the tallest. This project certainly would not have been possible if Yao Ming and Wang Zhizhi hadn't been generous enough to let me take extended glimpses into their complicated lives. The two were already big—over seven feet tall—when I first met them in 1999, but as I followed them from China to America, they both seemed to grow in stature, not just as players but as individuals trying to find their balance in a disorienting new world. I am grateful to both of them, especially for letting me hang around like a fly on the wall at the most critical junctures of their journeys to the NBA.

One of the unexpected joys of delving into this project came from making contact with older generations of Chinese coaches, athletes, and leaders, each of whom filled in a fascinating piece of the puzzle. I am humbled in particular by the generosity and lucid memories of Mou Zuoyun, Wang Yongfang, Wang Chongguang, and Madame Liu Yumin. Sadly, I cannot mention everyone who helped me in China, for even in the realm of sports, some topics are still too sensitive to address openly in the People's Republic. Sources who provided sensitive information must remain nameless, but they know who they are—and they have my deepest gratitude.

A number of guides have helped me navigate the Chinese sports system, never failing to steer me in the right direction or to stoke my enthusiasm along the way. I owe deep debts of gratitude to hoop impresario Xu Jicheng, for showing such warmth and generosity in welcoming a curious *laowai* into his world (and his weekly basketball games); Terry Rhoads, for sustaining a lively five-year conversation about Chinese sports; and Xia Song, for offering insights and introductions along with generous helpings of home-style Guizhou food. A heartfelt *xiexie*, as well, to several others who helped me understand the Chinese system: Ma Jian, Frank Sha, Tor Petersen, Wang Fei, Jimmy Qin, Sun Baosheng, Zhang Weiping, Richard Avory, Tom McCarthy, Cheong Sau Ching, and two sharp young journalists, Su Qun and Yang Yi.

During my reporting trips to the United States, I relied on the warmth and generosity of Bruce O'Neil, the dean of Sino-American basketball relations; Donnie Nelson, Dallas's true maverick; and Bill Duffy, the NBA agent who helped set the "operation" in motion. Special thanks, also, to others who helped along the way: Simon Chan, Daniel Chiang, Juaquin Hawkins, Andrew Morris, Colin Pine, Tony Ronzone, Christie Zhu, and my old colleague Bill Ide, who unwittingly helped initiate this project with an innocent call back in 1999.

Speaking of beginnings, I want to thank the editors at *Newsweek*, where I was privileged to work for eleven years and in whose pages the glimmers of this project found their first expression. I am especially grateful to Mark Whitaker, Michael Glennon, Steven Strasser, Fareed Zakaria, and Nisid Hajari, all of whom, at one point or another, let me indulge my passion for sports. Perhaps they were just humoring me. But I like to believe they shared my conviction that a compelling sports narrative, as much as any other story, can illuminate deep truths about societies and cultures—while also being hugely entertaining. Dinda Elliott, then of *Newsweek*, now of *Time*, was the first editor to encourage me to pursue the story of the two Chinese basketball giants. Years later, her husband, *Time* executive editor Adi Ignatius, kindly commissioned a piece that advanced my reporting on the next generation of Chinese athletes. Michael Elliott, my former boss at *Newsweek* and now the editor of *Time*'s Asian and European editions (ah, what an incestuous bunch, and I've only revealed the half of it!), has been an encouraging presence from the start.

Many thanks to my agent, Rafe Sagalyn, who immediately understood the deeper story I was hoping to tell and helped guide my proposal into the sure hands of Bill Shinker and Gotham Books. Brendan Cahill, my editor, offered keen suggestions and cheerful support every step of the way—even when my research extended not only the book's scope, but its deadlines, too. Thanks also to Gotham's Patrick Mulligan, who ably shepherded the manuscript through its final stages, and to production editor Joseph Mills.

Throughout this project, I've had the good fortune to count on the assistance of several top-notch interpreters, translators, and fact-checkers whose contributions can be felt on every page. My deepest thanks to Tao Yu, translator extraordinaire, as well as to He Zili, Bu Hua, Kim Wu, and Zhou Xingping.

Several friends were kind enough to read early drafts of the manuscript, often saving me both from myself and from China. I owe a special debt of gratitude to my good friends and neighbors in Shanghai, Peter Goodman of the the *Washington Post* and Nina Train Choa, who, aside from their sharp pencils and wits, showed (along with Nina's husband, Christopher) an especially high tolerance for basketball references during our many wonderful dinners in Shanghai. In Beijing, fellow scribbler Oliver August and dear friend James Baer not only gave helpful suggestions on early drafts, but along with the *Los Angeles Times*'s Henry Chu, they generously provided me with places to stay during my research trips to Beijing. I've also benefited immensely from conversations over the years with the *Financial Times*'s Richard McGregor and old Shanghai hand Patrick Cranley, whether they were aware of it or not! My old pal David Marcus, though in the throes of finishing up his own fine first book, offered constant support, encouragement, and (more often than not) commiseration. This book would have been far worse without the support of these friends; that it is not better is my fault alone.

Few things gave me more satisfaction than sending chapters off to the wordsmiths in my family, including my brother, Paul Larmer, and my parents, Dawn and Peter Larmer. My mother, a fine and indefatigable editor, sprinkled her comments with words of gentle encouragement. My brother, Eric, and his wife, Jennifer Thomas-Larmer (another editor!), provided steady support and, on one reporting trip, a much-needed place to stay, and my parents even let their prodigal son return home for a few weeks near the end to write in their lakeside idyll. My heartfelt thanks to all of them, and especially to my parents, who long ago inspired in me a passion for both words and sports.

Finally, I would like to express my love and gratitude for my wife, Hannah Beech. Despite her demanding job as a foreign correspondent, Hannah has lived, talked, and breathed this project from the beginning, when she presented me with a Japanese *daruma* doll. As per tradition, we made our wish that day by painting one eye of the *daruma*, saving the second for the wish's fulfillment. Since then, Hannah has nourished every aspect of the book with a constant flow of wisdom and grace—without complaint and, too often, without a dinner companion. For her love and patience, I will be forever thankful. With Hannah by my side—and our good and faithful pooch, Cassius, by our feet—I consider myself truly blessed. And now, finally, I can tell her: It's time to paint the second eye of the *daruma*. Wish fulfilled.

Index

Abdul-Jabbar, Kareem, 116
Adidas, 129, 134, 292, 301, 319
Adi Jiang, 80, 136, 244–49
"age-shaving," 82–83, 168–71,
    305–306
Alexander, Les, 240, 265
Ambros, M. V., 7
Apple Computer, 290, 291
Artists Management Group, 248
Asian Championships, 293, 294,
    299
Asian financial crisis, 137
Asian Games, 36, 37–38, 52, 70,
    93, 131, 248, 251, 252, 258
Athletes in Action, 142, 167
Atlanta Hawks, 137, 191

Bai Jinshen, 14, 232
Bai Li, 210, 231–32, 234
Baker, James A., III, 236
BALCO scandal, 95
Barkley, Charles, 241, 276, 277,
    278, 285
Basketball Hall of Fame, 111
Baumann, David, 203
Bayi basketball team, 74, 77,
    147, 179–80, 182–83,
    209–10, 219, 220
    drafting of Wang Zhizhi by
        Dallas Mavericks and, 173
    permission for Wang Zhizhi to
        play for the Mavericks and,
        184–88
    seeks Wang Zhizhi's return,
        244–49, 252–53, 254, 256
    training methods, 80–81
    Wang Zhizhi as member of,
        123, 139–40, 186
    Wang Zhizhi joins, 61–65
Beijing basketball team, 62
    Wang Zhizhi and, 61–62, 64
Beijing Evening News, 144
Beijing Sports University, 167,
    168
Beijing Steel, 62
Beijing Workers' Stadium Spare-
    Time Sports School, 53–54,
    55
Beijing Youth Daily, 273
Bender, Jonathan, 274
Best Damn Sports Show Period,
    The, 281
Bird, Larry, 107, 280, 283

Bol, Manute, 86
"bone age," 87, 115
Boston Celtics, 107
Boxer Rebellion, 6
boxing, 50
Boykins, Earl, 302
Bradley, Shawn, 278, 282
Brown, Dale, 180
Brown, Hubie, 173
Brown, Larry, 181
Brown, Sandy, 110
Brown, Willie, 149, 218
Bryant, Kobe, 212, 277, 283,
    291, 318
Bunn, John, 9
Bush, George H. W., 236
Bush, George W., 166, 190

Carlesimo, P. J., 212–13, 214
Carter, Jimmy, 48
Carter, Vince, 181
Cato, Kelvin, 268
Chamberlain, Wilt, 280
Chan, Simon, 221, 224, 225,
    245, 246, 249, 254, 296
Chandler, Tyson, 148, 314
Chen Jianghua, 302–305
Chen Liangyu, 260–61
Chen Zhaodi, 176, 177, 178, 298
Cheong Sau Ching, 175
Chicago Bulls, xiii, 109, 111,
    113, 149, 212, 213
China:
    Communist Revolution, 10–11,
        20
    Cultural Revolution in, see
        Cultural Revolution
    economic reform under Deng
        Xiaoping, xiii, 49, 57, 70,
        74–75, 128–29, 135, 285, 288

eugenics and, 40–41
foreign rule of, 19–20
future NBA prospects from,
    301–308
Great Leap Forward, 15, 36
history of basketball in, 5–9,
    10–11, 109, 132, 317
isolationism, 12–13, 36
Long March, 10–11
National Games in, 6, 10, 91,
    95, 100, 103, 139–40, 219
one-child policy, 40, 42–43
People's Liberation Army
    (PLA), see People's
    Liberation Army (PLA)
personal passports in, 298–99
racism and, 197, 282–83
Taiwan and, see Taiwan
-U.S. relations, 36, 190,
    191–92, 207
China Basketball Association
    (CBA), 161, 179, 306–307
African-American players par-
    ticipating in, 145–47
central government's continued
    control over, 144, 155
championship games, 209–10,
    219, 220
individual statistics and, 135,
    145
Nike and, 132–33, 144–45,
    155–56
1997 All-Star game, 147–48,
    151
power shift between Yao and,
    312–13
reforms, experimentation with,
    307
release of Yao to play for NBA
    and, 229–43, 255–56,
    259–60, 320

China Basketball Association (*cont.*)
  Wang Zhizhi's absence and,
    224–25, 226, 250–51, 255
  Wang Zhizhi's dismissal from
    Chinese national team,
    257–58
  "Yao Ming Rules," 210–11,
    220, 229
  see also individual teams
China Central Television (CCTV),
  14, 132, 173, 319–20
  NBA basketball and, xiv,
    107–14, 204
  Nike ads on, 130, 135, 136
China's state-run sports system,
  4, 13–16, 33–34, 49–51,
  130–33, 144, 319
  ambition of individual players
    and, 114–20, 120–24,
    203–204, 267–68
  during Cultural Revolution, 27,
    33, 49
  doping and, *see* doping of
    Chinese athletes
  entertainment factor and, xiv,
    132, 179, 320
  fate of failed athletes, 72–74
  "Friendship First," 33, 49
  "Gold-Medal Strategy," 49–50,
    51, 70, 95
  ideological indoctrination and,
    21, 22
  Mao's politicization of sports
    and, 4, 9–12, 36–37, 50
  measurements to predict future
    growth, xi–xii, 84–88, 115
  physical examinations, xi–xii,
    84–88, 98–101
  point guards and, 302–303,
    305
  prestige of China and, 49–50,
    52–53, 114, 132, 179,
    267–68, 319
  romantic relationships and, 39
  Soviet system as model for, 4,
    12, 22, 324
  "team first" culture of, 135,
    136, 142, 143, 267–68
  training methods of, 21, 22–23,
    50, 51, 66–67, 68–69,
    114–15, 144, 146–47, 305,
    315, 324
  *see also individual athletes and
    sports*
China Unicom, 291, 294, 324
Chinese medicine, 96, 101–2, 286
  doping of athletes and, 88–96
Chinese national basketball team,
  xiii, 62, 63, 181, 253–54,
  299, 312–13, 315
  junior team, 170, 171, 173
  Ma Jian and, 116–18, 120
  Nike and, 131
  at Olympics in Athens, 2004,
    310–11, 315–16
  Wang Zhizhi's attempts to
    rejoin, 249–53, 254, 255
  Wang Zhizhi's dismissal from,
    257–58
Chinese Olympic Committee, 93,
  158
  Anti-Doping Commission, 94
Christofferson, Chris, 213, 214
Ci Xi, Empress Dowager, 5–6
Cleveland Cavaliers, 111
Clinton, Bill, 192
CNN, Beijing bureau of, 240–41
Coca-Cola, 289, 312, 318, 320
Coyne, Michael, 157–62, 201,
  232
Crouching Tiger, Hidden Dragon,
  285

Cuban, Mark, 185, 190, 191, 217, 257
Cultural Revolution, 24–32, 36, 44, 60, 242, 288
    Red Guards, 5, 24–27, 29–33, 44, 45, 231
    revival of sports during, 33–35

Daimatsu, Hirofumi, 22
Dallas Mavericks, 151, 188, 278, 302
    drafting of Wang Zhizhi, 166–78
    permission for Wang Zhizhi to play for, 183–88
    Wang Zhizhi with, *see* Wang Zhizhi (Big Zhi, or Da Zhi), as Dallas Maverick
Dallas Morning News, 225
Dawson, Carroll, 214, 235
defection, 53, 207
    fears of Wang Zhizhi's, 218, 225
    fears of Yao's, 229
    of Hu Na, 52, 124
    measures to prevent, 150
    Wang Zhizhi and, 124
Deng Xiaoping, 34, 44, 200
    economic reform under, xiii, 49, 57, 70, 74–75, 128–29, 135, 285, 288
    height of, xii, 48–49
    power struggle with Mao, 26
    sports and China's prestige, 49–51, 70
Denver Nuggets, 209, 253
Dongdan, 304
doping of Chinese athletes, 88–96, 101–2, 103
drug testing, 90–91, 93, 94, 95

Duffy, Bill, 170, 173, 194–203, 253, 286
    background of, 195
    Evergreen contract and, 161–62, 197, 200
    Wang Zhizhi and, 197–98, 221
    Yao Ming and, 194–203, 213, 229, 290, 292, 321
Duncan, Tim, 279, 283

East Asian Championships, 219
East Germany, doping of athletes by, 94
Empower China Games, 55
Esherick, Craig, 121, 122, 123
ESPN, 173, 254, 275, 279
ESPN: The Magazine, 183
eugenics, 40–41
Evergreen Sports Management, 157–62, 163, 197, 200, 201, 206, 231
    terms of contract with Yao Ming, 159, 161–62, 232
Ewing, Patrick, 114, 121, 123, 205
Exner, Max, 6

Falk, David, 198–203, 206
Falsone, Anthony, 276
Fan Bin, 80
Fang Fengdi (Da Fang) (Yao Ming's mother):
    appearance of, 3
    arranged marriage, 39–42
    as basketball player, 33–39, 44, 52, 57, 138, 232
    described, 34–35
    drafting into sports system, 4, 18–19

Fang Fengdi (*cont.*)
  Evergreen contract and,
    158–61, 162, 200, 201, 231,
    232
  guiding of Yao Ming's career,
    139, 151–52, 154, 158–60,
    162–64, 195–96, 199–200,
    202, 203, 206, 231–34,
    240–42, 269–70, 286, 292,
    321
  indoctrination of, 21, 22
  job in sports system, 45–47,
    57–58
  life in America, 268–74, 313
  Nike contract, Yao Ming's,
    162–64
  political rise of, 34, 44
  poverty of, 47, 56–59
  raising Yao Ming, 56–61,
    70–72, 74–77
  with Red Guards, 5, 24–26,
    44, 46, 231, 269
  Frank Sha and, 139, 200
  training as basketball player,
    18–19, 20–21, 22, 23
  Erik Zhang and, 199–200, 213,
    269, 270
Female Basketball Player No. 5,
  11
Finley, Michael, 189
Fireman, Paul B., 318
Fitch, Bill, 119
FlorCruz, Jaime, 115, 241–42
Follett, Ken, 174
Ford, Gerald, 121–22
Forrest Gump, 193
Fortune, 192
Francis, Steve, 262, 263, 265–66,
  268, 287, 289
Friedman, Thomas, 192
Fujian province, 57

Gang of Four, 27, 37, 44
Garnett, Kevin, 181
Gatorade, 290, 291
Georgetown University, 120, 121,
  123, 149
gigantism, 74, 100
Goldberg, Michael, 235–40, 255,
  256
Golden State Warriors, 108, 244
Gold Star Pen Factory, 16–17
Gong Li, 286
Goodwill Games, 167
Granik, Russ, 162
Greene, Ralph, 149, 291–92
Guangdong province, 57, 135
Guangdong Tigers, 301–302, 305
Guangzhou, China, 128–29
guanxi (connections), xiv, 130,
  137, 138, 139, 167–68, 196,
  200, 223
Guo Jingjing, 320

Harlem Globetrotters, 71, 145
Harrick, Jim, 115–16, 118
Harris, Del, 306–307, 311
Hawkins, Juaquin, 145–46, 147,
  277
Hayes, Elvin, 108
He Long, Marshal, 11, 14, 27
Hero, 285
Hill, Martha, 128
Hitler, Adolf, 8
Hodges, James, 147
Hong Kong, 19
Hooters, 188, 189
Houston, Allan, 212
Houston Chronicle, 242
Houston Rockets, 114, 145, 188
  drafting of Yao Ming and
    negotiations with China for

his release, 214, 220,
  228–43, 252, 255–56, 259
NBA China Games of 2004,
  320–22
scouting of Yao Ming, 150,
  214
Yao Ming as player with, 145,
  262–301, 314–15, 318,
  320–22
Yao Ming's contract with, 259,
  318
Howard, Juwan, 189, 191
Huang Xiafei, 45
Huili Rubber, 9
Huizinga, John, 213, 229–30,
  233, 255–56, 259, 292
  see also Team Yao
human rights, 92, 229
Hu Na, 52, 124
Hunter, Billy, 162, 202, 211
Hu Weidong, 136, 137

Indiana Paces, 274
Indianapolis Star, 149
infanticide, female, 42
International Basketball
  Federation (FIBA), 8
International Management Group
  (IMG), 132, 155
International Olympic
  Committee, 49, 186
International Olympic Federation,
  13
International Table Tennis
  Federation, 14
Iverson, Allen, 271, 293, 302, 304

Jackson, Phil, 277
James, LeBron, 292, 294

Japan, 7–8
Jay-Z, 290
Jerry Maguire, 212
Jiang Qing, 28, 37
Jiang Xingquan, 116, 117, 118
Jiang Yunjie, 304
Jiang Zemin, 21, 267, 286
Johnson, Denis, 298
Johnson, Earvin "Magic," 107,
  280, 283
Johnson, Teyo, 148, 150
Jordan, Michael, xiii, 109, 111,
  113–14, 283, 290
  agent of, 198, 200, 202
  Nike and, 127, 130
  Yao Ming and, 149, 201, 278

KFC, 318
Khrushchev, Nikita, 22
Kidd, Jason, 303
King, Martin Luther, Jr., 195
Kissinger, Henry, 48
Knight, Phil, xiii, 125, 127, 128,
  291
Krause, Jerry, 149, 212–13
Kuang Lubin, 244, 245–46, 251,
  252–53, 254, 256
Kung Fu, 195

LaFeber, Walter, xiii, 288
Layden, Scott, 212
Life and Death in Shanghai (Nien
  Chang), 28
Li Jun, 72–74
Lindsey, Dennis, 150
Li Ning, 307, 319
Lin Li, 91
Lin Meizheng, 23, 27–28
Lin Zhiwei, 90

Li Qiuping, 97, 173, 260
Listen Up!, 276
Li Tie, 305
Liu Changchun, 7–8
Liu Shiyu (Fat Liu), 41–42
Liu Wei, 98, 150, 260, 293–94
Liu Xiang, 317, 320
Liu Yudong, 81
Liu Yumin (Madame Liu), 45, 64,
    65, 321
  as director of Chinese basket-
    ball, 45, 121–23, 131, 136,
    137, 147, 321
  Nike and, 131–33, 136, 147
  Wang Zhizhi's mother and, 45,
    64, 65, 121, 227, 321
Li Yaomin, 260
  background of, 153, 154
  Evergreen Sports Management
    contract and, 157–60, 161,
    162, 197, 200, 206
  Shanghai Sharks, and Yao
    Ming, 149, 153–60, 197,
    198, 201, 205–207, 210,
    211–12, 229, 230, 231, 321
Li Yuanwei, 298, 306, 315–16
Li Zhangming, 66–67, 68–69, 71,
    72, 73, 74, 84, 97, 260
Loeb, Dan, 131
Los Angeles Clippers, 119, 257,
    259, 295–98, 299–300
Los Angeles Lakers, 107, 145,
    154, 212, 213, 277, 280,
    286–88, 314
Los Angeles Sparks, 137
Louisiana State University, 121
Lu Bin: 23, 31, 35, 37, 38, 45, 60
Lu Hao, 230, 233
Luis, Nelson, 235
Luo Xuelian, 34–35
Lu Xun, 311

McCarthy, Tom, 122, 206
McCormack, Mark, 132
McDonald's, 114, 129, 291, 318,
    324
McHale, Kevin, 195
McKillop, Harry, 174, 176, 177,
    186–87
Majerus, Rick, 118
Ma Jian, 114–20, 123, 137
Mao Zedong, xiv
  Cultural Revolution, *see*
    Cultural Revolution
  death of, xiii, 37, 44
  Khrushchev and, 22
  Little Red Book, The, 24, 25
  Long March and, 10–11
  politicization of sports and, 4,
    9–12, 36–37, 50
  "Study of Physical Culture, A,"
    10
Marbury, Stephon, 276
Marciulionis, Sarunas, 108, 151,
    167
Marquette University, 121
marriage, arranged, 39–42
Martin, LaRue, 275
"Ma's (Ma Junren's) Family
    Army," 91–92, 94, 102
Ma Yuehan, 8
Memphis Grizzlies, 231
Mengke Bateer, 51, 62, 81, 181,
    198, 209, 253
Messick, Andrew, 204
Miami Heat, 212–13, 315, 322
Mobley, Cuttino, 267, 272
Mourning, Alonzo, 121, 134, 205
Mou Zuoyun, 7–9, 13, 14, 49,
    111
Muresan, Gheorghe, 86
Mu Tiezhu, 81, 108
Mutombo, Dikembe, 121, 314

Naismith, Dr. James, 5, 7, 8, 9
Nash, Steve, 189, 217
Nationalist Chinese, 10–11
  see also Taiwan
NATO bombing of the Chinese
  embassy in Belgrade, 171
NBA (National Basketball
  Association), xiii, xiv, 202,
  288
  All-Star Games, 109, 288,
    289–90, 314
  China Central Television and,
    xiv, 107–14
  China Games of 2004, 320–22
  draft rules, 169
  future Chinese prospects,
    301–308
  international success of,
    288–89
  limit on agent commissions,
    161–62
  Ma Jian and, 114–20, 137
  NBA/China Friendship Tour of
    1985, 111
  Stern and, see Stern, David
  Yao's importance to reinvigo-
    rating, 283–85, 289
  see also individual teams and
    players
NBA Players Association, 202
NCAA basketball, 116
  Ma Jian and, 118, 120, 122
  Wang Zhizhi and, 120–24
Nelson, Don "Nellie," 167, 172,
  173, 175–78, 185, 191, 219,
  220
Nelson, Donn "Donnie," 175–78,
  187–88
  Wang Zhizhi and, 166–72,
    175–78, 185, 186, 187, 193,
    220, 222

Yao Ming and, 151, 187–88
Nevitt, Chuck, 275
Newsweek, xvi, 56, 192
New Yorker, The, 324
New York Knicks, 114, 212
New York Times, The, 192
New York Times Magazine, The,
  305
Nichols, Rle, 141–42, 181
Nien Chang, 28
Nike Euro Camp, 139
Nike Hoop Summit, 120–21, 181
Nike Inc., xiii, 125–33, 141, 150,
  288, 307–308, 319, 320
  basketball in China and,
    129–40, 147–48, 151,
    155–56, 303, 304
  "Local Heroes" campaign, 136
  production in China, xiv, 127,
    129
  Wang Zhizhi and, 136–37, 140,
    163, 168, 180, 250, 295
  World Campus in Beaverton,
    126, 292
  Yao Ming and, see Yao Ming,
    Nike and
Nixon, Richard M., 36
Norris, Moochie, 266
North Korea, 157–58
Nowitzki, Dirk, 151, 189, 217

Olajuwon, Hakeem, 114, 122,
  205
Olympic Games, 7–8, 10, 13, 49,
  52, 90, 91, 92, 120, 123,
  167, 181, 317
  1984, in Los Angeles, 51,
    52–53, 90
  2004, in Athens, 309–11,
    315–16, 317

Olympic Games (*cont.*)
  2008, in Beijing, 291, 316–18, 319
  China awarded right to host
    2008 Games, 208, 209
  China's campaigns to host, 91,
    92, 94, 176, 185–86, 187
O'Neal, Jermaine, 274
O'Neal, Shaquille, 121, 122, 180,
  277–78, 280–83, 284–85,
  286–88, 290, 314, 322
O'Neil, Bruce, 145, 305
On Wings of Eagles (Follett), 174
Opium Wars, 19
Orlando Magic, 137

Parker, Tony, 302, 303
Payton, Gary, 181
People magazine, 192, 265
People's Daily, 39
People's Liberation Army (PLA),
  xiii, 33
  Bayi basketball team, *see* Bayi
    basketball team
  drafting of Wang Zhizhi by
    Dallas Mavericks and,
    173–78, 180
  50th anniversary celebration,
    34, 44
  permission for Wang Zhizhi to
    play for the Mavericks,
    183–88
  Wang Zhizhi as soldier in, 63,
    77–83, 123
  Wang Zhizhi goes AWOL,
    217–27, 233, 236, 244–54,
    255, 256
Pepsi Co., 289, 291, 312, 318
Perot, Ross, Jr., 165–66, 173–76
Perot, Ross, Sr., 174
Petersen, Tor, 293

Philadelphia 76ers, 271
Philadelphia Inquirer, 121
Phoenix Suns, 108, 314–15
  Ma Jian and, 119
physiological inferiority, Chinese
  sense of, 15, 89
Pine, Colin, 263, 264, 267, 271,
  272, 276, 280, 282, 313,
  314
Ping-Pong, *see* table tennis
Polumbaum, Judy, 6
Portland Trailblazers, 150, 283
Postolos, George, 289

Qian Limin, 176, 177, 184
Qin, Jimmy, 134

Rambis, Kurt, 195
Raveling, George, 149
Red Army, 10–11
  see also People's Liberation
    Army (PLA)
Reebok, 292–94, 318–19, 324
Ren Huanzhen (Wang Zhizhi's
  mother), 15–16, 77, 321
  as basketball player, 34, 55, 77
  Bayi basketball team recruits
    son of, 61–65
  job of, 64
  Liu Yumin and, 45, 64, 65,
    121
  reunion with Wang Zhizhi,
    299–300
  Wang Zhizhi's disappearance
    and, 226–27, 249
Rhoads, Terry, 125–33, 147,
  206–207, 305, 320, 321
  Duffy and, 195, 201–202
  Li Yaomin and, 156–57

as Nike's sports marketing direc-
tor in China, 119, 125–26,
127–40, 150, 151–52, 156,
167, 169, 170, 173
Wang Zhizhi and, 124,
136–37, 173
Yao Ming and, 133–40, 141,
149, 150, 151–52, 161–62,
163, 200, 201–202, 293,
313–14
Riley, Pat, 212–13
Ri Myong-hun, 157–58
Robinson, David, 122, 279
Rockefeller, Nicholas, 212
Rong Guotuan, 14, 27
Rong Yiren, 200
Ronzone, Tony, 151, 167, 168
Rupp, Adolph, 9
Russell, Bill, 149, 280

Sacramento Kings, 320–22
Salmon, Matt, 197
Sanders, Bill, 318
Schwartz, Jeff, 248
September 11th, 2001, 208–209
sexual development, monitoring
of athletes', 87–88
SFX Entertainment, 198
Sha, Frank, 27, 293, 294
childhood relationship with
Yao Ming, 43, 137–38
leaves Nike, 228
NBA draft, and Yao Ming,
228, 233, 241
Nike, and Yao Ming, 137–39,
151, 160–61, 162–64, 200,
202
Sha Feng'ao, 41, 43, 138, 164
Shang Congyue, 30
Shanghai, China, 197

The Country Club in, 19–20
economic depression of 1980s,
57
economic revival of, 57, 74–75,
129, 135
Western control of, 19–20
Shanghai Morning Post, 210–11
Shanghai Oriental Television,
155, 233, 260
Shanghai Sharks, 176, 179–80,
182–83, 186, 201, 219, 307
Bai Li negotiates for, 231–33,
234
deal to buy out Yao Ming's
contract with, 258, 320
Li Yaomin and, see Li Yaomin
ownership in perpetuity of their
players, 155, 205
Yao Ming plays for, xv,
133–34, 147, 185, 204–205,
275
Shanghai Sports and Athletic
Competitions Direction
Section, 18–23, 44–45
Cultural Revolution and,
28–32
Democratic Life Meetings at,
21
history of, 19–20
training at, 20–21, 22–23
Shanghai Sports Commission, 28
birth of Yao Ming and, 4
Evergreen contract and, 162
"Operation Yao Ming," 4,
41–42, 58
ownership of Shanghai Sharks,
155
Yao Ming's ability to play outside China and, 139
Zhu Yong as deputy director
of, 45, 58, 60

Shanghai Sports Science Research Institute, 46, 84–88
Shanghai Sports Technology Institute, 96–103, 161, 260
Shan Tao, 62
Shi Kangcheng, 94
Simpsons, The, 314
slam dunk, 147, 280
  CBA and, 145
  traditional Chinese view of, 132, 142–43
  in U.S. basketball, 143
  Yao Ming and, 141–42, 148, 149
  Yi Jianlian and, 301
Smith, Kevin, 278
Sohu.com, 284
Song Tao, 137
Song Xiaobo, 38
Song Yang (Wang Zhizhi's wife), 192, 193, 217, 220–21, 223, 246, 247, 296, 299, 322
South Korea, Asian Games and, 37–38, 258
Soviet Union:
  modeling of China's sports system after Soviet system, 4, 12, 22, 324
  Olympic games of 1984 and, 52
Spencer, John Anthony, 147
Sporting News, The, 127
Sports Illustrated, 181, 254, 265
Springfield College, 9
Steel, 281
Steinberg, Lee, 212
Stern, David, xiii, 107–14, 127, 203, 233, 238, 241, 289, 321–22
steroids and doping of athletes, 88–96, 101–2, 103

Stoudemire, Amare, 314–15
Strickland, Erick, 274
Sun Baosheng, 144
Sun Mingming, 302
Sun Yat-sen, 6
Su Qun, 225, 251, 296

table tennis, 13–14, 15, 27, 36, 93, 317
  introduction to China, 10
tai chi, 12
Taiwan, 13, 49, 52
Tang, Irwin, 281
Team Yao, 213–14, 254
  release of Yao Ming to play for NBA and, 228–43, 255–56, 259
  2008 Olympic Games and, 318
  Yao Ming in America and, 282, 283, 289, 290–94, 321
Texas Rangers, 166
Thompson, John, 149
three-point shot, 147
  in Chinese basketball, 143
  Yao Ming and, *see* Yao Ming, three-pointer and
Tiananmen Square, massacre of protesters at, 63, 70
Tian Fuhai, 17
Tian Liang, 320
Time, 192
Titan Sports Weekly, 211, 245, 251, 273
TNT, 241, 276
Tomjanovich, Rudy, 114, 235, 253, 264, 275
track and field, performance-enhancing drugs and, 91–92, 93
"trophyism," 27, 28, 31

Troyer, Verne "Mini-Me," 290
Tsinghua University, 8

Ueberroth, Peter, 52
United Nations, 36
United States Basketball
    Academy, 305
U.S. Immigration Service, 299
U.S. Olympic basketball team
    (Dream Team), 122, 123,
    181
University of California at Los
    Angeles, 116, 117, 224
University of Minnesota, 195
University of San Francisco, 149
Urquhart, Robert, 19
USA Today, 265
Utah Jazz, 108
Utah Valley State Junior College,
    118

Vancouver Grizzles, 170, 173
Van Gundy, Jeff, 314, 315
Van Horn, Keith, 118
Visa, 290, 291
volleyball, 15
    at Olympic games, 53
    World Championships, 51–52

Wade, Dwayne, 315
Wallace, Ben, 253
Wall Street Journal, 265
Walton, Bill, 116, 183, 275
Wang Chongguang, 4, 97
Wang Fei, 111, 183, 245, 251,
    253, 258
Wang Junxia, 91
Wang Qimin, 72, 76, 87

Wang Wei, 190, 192
Wang Weijun (Wang Zhizhi's
    father), 15, 16, 77
    as basketball player, 53, 55
    Bayi basketball team recruits
        Wang Zhizhi, 61–65
    coaching job, 53–54
    reunion with Wang Zhizhi,
        299–300
    Wang Zhizhi's success and, 56,
        188
    Wang Zhizhi's vilification and,
        54–55, 226–27
Wang Xiaopeng, 233
Wang Yongfang, 9, 28, 29, 32,
    39–40
Wang Yun, 87
Wang Zhizhi (Big Zhi, or Da
    Zhi), xiv–xv, 151, 264–65
    astronomy, interest in, 55
    goes AWOL, 217–27, 233,
        236, 244–54, 255, 256
    basketball training, 55, 80–81
    birth of, 4, 16, 55
    birth year, government's alter-
        ation of his, 82–83, 168–71,
        305–306
    childhood of, xi, 55–56
    Chinese national basketball
        team, attempts to rejoin,
        249–53, 254, 255
    competition with Yao Ming,
        xv–xvi, 34, 77, 139–40,
        147–48, 180–81, 182–83, 220
    contract terms with Dallas
        Mavericks, 190
    as Dallas Maverick, 188–93,
        208, 218–19, 220, 257
    defection and, 124
    drafted by the Dallas
        Mavericks, 166–78

Wang Zhizhi (*cont.*)
  Duffy and, 197–98
  as father, 322–23
  height of, xv, 55, 56, 61, 63,
    77, 103
  life in America, 188–93,
    220–21, 224, 296–97,
    322–23
  with Los Angeles Clippers,
    257, 258, 293, 295–98,
    299–30
  measurements to predict future
    growth, xi–xii
  NBA Finals of 1994, viewing
    of, 113–14, 122
  NCAA basketball and, 120–24
  Nike and, 136–37, 140, 163,
    168, 180, 295
  personal passport, attempt to
    receive, 298–99
  as PLA soldier, *see* People's
    Liberation Army (PLA),
    Wang Zhizhi as soldier in
  recruited to Bayi basketball
    team, 61–65
  sneakers for, 63–64
  Yao Ming plays against in NBA
    game, 295–98
Washington, Kermit, 275
Washington Bullets, 108
Washington Wizards, 201, 278
Wei Guoping, 96, 98–101, 102,
    140, 260, 286
Wei Jingsheng, 92
West, Jerry, 212–13
Whitsitt, Bob, 150
Williams, Jay, 252, 254
Wilson, Brock, 156, 157
Wolff, Alexander, 14
Women's National Basketball
  Association (WNBA), 137

Wooden, John, 116
Woods, Tiger, 290
"work units," China's socialist,
    75, 144, 319
World Basketball Championships,
    250, 251, 252, 254, 255
World Swimming
  Championships, 92–93, 94
World University Games, 219
Wu Yanyan, 94

Xiao Tian, 310
Xia Song, 63, 137, 161, 165,
    192, 193, 226, 230–31, 321
  Duffy and, 198–99, 221
  leaves Nike, 173, 184
  permission for Wang Zhizhi to
    play for the Mavericks and,
    183–88
  Wang Zhizhi as draft pick of
    Dallas Mavericks and,
    167–72, 175, 176, 177
Xinhua News Agency, 173
Xin Lancheng, 176, 223, 225, 229,
    230, 235, 236, 237–39, 245,
    250–51, 255–56, 259, 260
Xinmin Evening Post, 59
Xu, Dr., 101–2
Xue Yuyang, 302
Xu Haifeng, 53
Xuhui District Spare-Time Sports
  School, 60, 66–67, 68–69,
    71–77
  physical exam at, 84–88
Xu Jicheng, 35, 63, 113, 132,
    146–47, 180, 183, 319
Xu Kuangdi, 197
Xu Minfeng, 218
Xu Weili, 28, 45, 60, 71, 72, 74,
    75, 76

Yang Buyong, 76–77
Yang Yi, 251, 256, 273, 313
Yao Ming, xiv–xv, 168, 175,
   187–88, 193, 262–73,
   262–301, 300
  aptitude for basketball, 59, 74,
    97, 148
  audition for NBA draft,
    210–14
  basketball training, 60–61, 67,
    68–69, 97–98
  birth of, 3–4, 42
  childhood of, xi, 56–61, 67–72,
    74–77, 309
  commercials featuring, 290
  competition with Wang Zhizhi,
    xv–xvi, 34, 77, 139–40,
    147–48, 180–81, 182–83,
    220
  departure for the U.S., 260–61
  endorsements, 290–94, 312,
    314, 318, 319, 324
  Evergreen Sports Management
    and, see Evergreen Sports
    Management
  fame and media attention,
    264–65, 267, 274, 283–86,
    288, 289–90, 309–11,
    317–18, 324
  height of, xv, 59, 60, 74, 85,
    97, 98, 99, 102–3, 181, 284
  Houston Rockets and, see
    Houston Rockets
  life in America, 262–73,
    313–14, 323–24
  "loyalty pledge," 239, 260
  NBA China Games of 2004
    and, 320–22
  NBA draft, release by China
    and, 228–43, 252, 255–56
  NBA Finals of 1994, viewing
    of, 113–14
  NBA scouts and, 150, 210–14
  Nike and, 133–40, 141, 150,
    151–52, 162–64, 181, 199,
    201–202, 290–94, 307
  nutritional supplements and,
    96, 101–2, 103, 286
  Olympic Games in Athens,
    2004, 309–11, 315–16
  patriotic education, 70
  personality of, 59–60, 68, 266,
    310–12, 319
  physical examinations to pre-
    dict future growth, xi–xii,
    84–85, 87–88, 98–101
  rookie year, 145, 271, 274–90
  Shanghai Sharks and, see
    Shanghai Sharks
  slam dunk and, 141–42, 148, 149
  summer of 1998 in America,
    141–42, 148–51, 156
  Wang Zhizhi plays against in
    NBA game, 295–98
  Wang Zhizhi's disappearance
    and, 252, 253, 255, 259
  World Championships of 2002
    and, 254–55
Yao Songpin, 139, 162
Yao Xueming (grandfather of Yao
   Ming), 16–17
Yao Zhiyuan (Da Yao) (father of
   Yao Ming), 3, 151–52, 321
  arranged marriage of, 41–42
  as basketball player, 34
  birth of, 16
  drafting into sports system, 4, 17
  guiding of Yao Ming's career,
    154, 158–60, 195, 196, 231,
    240–42, 286
  job at Shanghai port, 46–47,
    57, 269

Yao Zhiyuan (*cont.*)
　life in America, 269, 270, 271
　poverty of, 47, 57–58
　raising Yao Ming, 59–61,
　　70–71
　Sha and, 139
Ye Li (Yao Ming's girlfriend),
　208, 209–10, 268, 324
Yi Jianlian, 300–302, 305–306,
　307, 308, 311
YMCA International Training
　School, 9
Young Men's Christian
　Association (YMCA), history
　of basketball in China and,
　5–6, 7, 10, 125, 317
Yuan Yuan, 94

Zhang, Erik, 226, 269, 270, 307
　as advisor and manager of Yao
　　Ming, 199–201, 203, 210,
　　213–14, 229–34, 236, 237,
　　238, 240, 254, 256, 259,
　　267, 292, 321
　background of, 199, 200
　see also Team Yao
Zhang Weiping, 36–37
Zhao Yu, 39, 69
Zheng Haixia, 40, 134, 137
Zheng Zhenming, 304
Zhou Enlai, 14, 34, 113
Zhu De, 10–11
Zhu Rongji, 200
Zhu Yong, 21–22
　Da Fang and, 5, 21–22, 24–26,
　　31–32, 43, 44, 45, 46
　as deputy director of Shanghai
　　Sports Commission, 45, 58,
　　60
　rehabilitation of, 44–45
Zou Marketing, 293, 321